D1796718

The Political Philosophy of Zionism
Trading Jewish Words for a Hebraic Land

Zionism emerged at the end of the nineteenth century in response to a rise in anti-Semitism in Europe, to a deteriorating economic predicament for Jews in Eastern Europe, and to the crisis of modern Jewish identity. This novel, national revolution aimed to unite a scattered community defined mainly by shared texts and literary tradition into a vibrant political entity destined for the Holy Land. As this remarkable book demonstrates, however, Zionism was about much more than a national political ideology and practice. This movement pictured time as wholly open and aesthetic in nature, attempted to humanize space through collective action, and enlivened the Hebrew language but stripped it of its privileged ontological status in Judaism. By tracing the origins of Zionism in the context of a European history of ideas, and by considering the writings of key Jewish and Hebrew writers and thinkers from the nineteenth and twentieth centuries, this book offers an entirely new philosophical perspective on Zionism as a unique movement based on intellectual boldness and belief in human action. In counterdistinction to the studies of history and ideology that dominate the field, this book also offers a new way of reflecting on contemporary Israeli politics.

Eyal Chowers is a Senior Lecturer of Political Science at Tel Aviv University in Israel, where he also serves as the co-head of the graduate program in political leadership. He is the author of *The Modern Self in the Labyrinth: Politics and the Entrapment Imagination* (2004).

A poster by the Histadrut, The General Federation of Labor in Israel, calling upon new immigrants that came to Israel in the 1950s to take part in the mass campaign "hanchalat halashon" (fostering the language) and register for Hebrew classes provided by the Histadrut and other organizations all over the country. The poster was created by Eliyahu Vardimon (the exact year is unknown). Courtesy of The Central Zionist Archives, Jerusalem.

The Political Philosophy of Zionism

Trading Jewish Words for a Hebraic Land

EYAL CHOWERS

Tel Aviv University

CAMBRIDGE
UNIVERSITY PRESS

CAMBRIDGE UNIVERSITY PRESS
Cambridge, New York, Melbourne, Madrid, Cape Town,
Singapore, São Paulo, Delhi, Tokyo, Mexico City

Cambridge University Press
32 Avenue of the Americas, New York, NY 10013-2473, USA

www.cambridge.org
Information on this title: www.cambridge.org/9781107005945

First published 2012

Printed in the United States of America

A catalog record for this publication is available from the British Library.

Library of Congress Cataloging in Publication data
Chowers, Eyal.
The political philosophy of Zionism : trading Jewish words for a Hebraic
land / by Eyal Chowers.
p. cm.
Includes bibliographical references and index.
ISBN 978-1-107-00594-5 (hardback)
1. Zionism. 2. Zionism – Philosophy. 3. Hebrew
language – Political aspects. 4. Hebrew language – Social
aspects. I. Title.
DS149.C446 2011
320.54095694–dc22   2011006214

ISBN 978-1-107-00594-5 Hardback

Contents

List of Illustrations

Acknowledgments

I started working on this project a long time ago, erroneously believing it would take me just a few years to complete. But the more I delved into the subject of Zionism and its relation to modernity, the more subtle and fascinating this subject became, in my opinion at least.

There are certainly many downsides to writing a book over an extended period of time, but one of the advantages is that one can consult with and benefit from many friends, colleagues, and students.

I would like to thank Janet Benton, Leora Bilsky, Eppie Kreitner, David Myers, Natalie Oman, Yoav Peled, Nancy Schwartz, Idith Zertal, and Yael Zerubavel for reading parts of this manuscript and helping me to improve it substantially. Thanks, especially, to Charles Blattberg and Aharon Klieman for their many useful comments and for being generous with their time. I also benefited from illuminating discussions with Revital Amiran, Seyla Benhabib, Eva Illouz Yaron Ezrahi, Azar Gat, Ariel Hirschfeld, Steven Smith, Bernard Yack, and Ronald Zweig. Thanks also to Lior Erez, Dimitry Kortukov, and Yonatan Preminger from Tel Aviv University for their help at different stages, as well as to Anat Banin and Nechma Kanner from the Zionist Archives.

I would also like to thank the Shalem Center in Jerusalem for supporting the early parts of my research and for its hospitality, and the Van Leer Jerusalem Institute for allowing me to use its splendid library for many years.

My students at Tel Aviv University (and, during one semester, at Yale University) have been extremely helpful in the formation of this book. They have tolerated my half-baked ideas during many classes, challenged me, and enriched my thought immensely; I am very grateful to them.

I am beholden to Eliyahu Vardimon (1912–81), the creator of the beautiful poster reprinted on the cover of this book. Mr. Vardimon, a chalutz, artist, designer, and author of archaeology books, came to Mandatory Palestine from Dresden, Germany, in 1934. He created many posters for various Zionist organizations such as the Jewish National Fund and Keren Hayesod, and he was a chief designer of numerous international exhibitions representing the government of Israel and others. Vardimon's poster conveys the attempt of Zionists to displace foreign languages with Hebrew, not to trade Jewish words for a Hebraic land – but as we shall see, these ideas are akin.

Many thanks also to my editor, Marigold Acland, for her trust, insightful guidance, and very substantial help along the way. I have also benefited much from the comments of the anonymous readers for Cambridge University Press.

In the production of this book, I was very fortunate to receive excellent professional assistance and a friendly attitude from Phyllis Berk, Mark Fox, and Regina Paleski. Thanks also to Joy Mizan for her patience and for facilitating the communication among all those involved.

I am especially grateful to Yael Agam, who encouraged me along the way.

I would like to dedicate this book to two young and extraordinary persons I loved who died during their military service: Michal Amit (1961–80) and my cousin Ephraim Chowers (1960–82).

Earlier versions of some parts of this book have been published elsewhere. I would like to thank the following publishers for kindly allowing me to make use of the following materials: "The End of Building: Zionism and the Politics of the Concrete," by Eyal Chowers, *The Review of Politics*, Vol. 64 (no. 4), Sept. 2002, pp. 599–626, © 2002 University of Notre Dame. Reprinted with the permission of Cambridge University Press; Eyal Chowers, "Language and Democracy in the Thought of Hannah Arendt," in *Hannah Arendt: A Half-Century of Polemics*, Idith Zertal and Moshe Zuckermann (eds.), pp. 33–48 (Tel Aviv: Hakibbutz Hameuchad, 2005), © 2005 Hakibbutz Hameuchad. Reprinted with the permission of Hakibbutz Hameuchad; Eyal Chowers, "The Marriage of Time and Identity: Kant, Benjamin, and the Nation-State," *Philosophy and Social Criticism*, May 1999, Vol. 25 (no. 3), pp. 55–80, © 1999, Sage Publications. Reprinted with the permission of Sage Publications; Eyal Chowers, "Gushing Time: Modernity and the Multiplicity of Temporal Homes," *Time and Society*, Sept. 2002, Vol. 11 (nos. 2 & 3), pp. 235–249, © 2002, Sage Publications. Reprinted with the permission of Sage

Publications; Eyal Chowers, "Time in Zionism: The Life and Afterlife of a Temporal Revolution," *Political Theory*, Vol. 26 (no. 5), Oct. 1998, pp. 652–85, © 1998, Sage Publications. Reprinted with the permission of Sage Publications; Eyal Chowers, "Ahad Ha'am and the Jewish Volkgeist," in *Global Politics: Essays in the Honour of David Vital*, A. Ben-Zvi and A. Kleiman (eds.), pp. 267–82 (London: Frank Cass Publishers, 2001), © 2001, Taylor & Francis. Reprinted with the permission of the Taylor & Francis Group.

Introduction

There are rare moments in one's life when radical change becomes inescapable. We do not seek these moments; they most often occur when all other options have been pushed to the ground, and collapsed. We have a number of tactics to cope with challenging times, tactics we cling to more tightly when we are desperate to escape radical change. Some of us flee into the present: We immerse ourselves in the little pleasures of life, in intimacy and bonding, in the objects we possess and the achievements we have marshaled; the rest, the dreadful memories and cloudy prospects – the events that are too certain and those that are wholly uncertain – we tend to deliberately ignore. Not to think too much is the credo of the present seeker. Or some of us try to trust in the future, hoping to gradually reform ourselves and the world, believing, like Hegel and Marx did, that the contradictions in human life must be resolved through progress in history, that the promise of harmony, fulfillment, and happiness eludes us just because we are limited by our location in the narrative. We may be devoured by opposing forces, commitments, relations – but on a higher plane, to which we shall be carried by the wings of time, these forces are not incompatible. Still others among us flee to the past: We believe that tradition possesses the ultimate authority, that it contains truth and wisdom, that if we cling to the old ways of dwelling in the world we will not only maintain dignity and identity, but will also be able to cope well with the contingencies of circumstances.

When these and other strategies of escape have been exhausted, however – when the present becomes too harsh, the notion of the future as progressive betterment is revealed as an illusion, and tradition is experienced as totally at odds with actual circumstances – the moment arrives

when we accept that we must face a decision: to make a radical transformation in the ways we act and think or to relinquish the hope of
becoming a whole, or at least capable, individual. This is a moment of
both sadness and excitement, of letting go of one mode of existence that
shaped us and exploring the unknown.

Something similar happens to communities. They also, at rare times
to be sure, reach points at which they must make decisions: change or
disappear, create themselves anew or perish in their old ways. These
are times for beginning from scratch, for destroying and inventing,
for forgetting and imagining. When individuals transform their lives,
they seclude themselves or change their vocation, or alter relations, or
exhume their inner voice; when communities seek transformation, they
give birth to or breathe new life into politics.

This book is about the crisis of the Jewish people in modernity, and
especially about the radical politics some of them have embraced in the
form of Zionism. Zionism is the creation of politics: of new institutions
and resources, of zealous leaders and committed movements, of lofty
ideologies and practical strategies and planning, of a public sphere (even
prior to the existence of a territory) and a language enlivened mainly for
the sake of that sphere – and ultimately, of course, of collective action
and mass mobilization. As a phenomenon embodying radical politics,
Zionism is inherently intertwined with a temporal crisis faced by some
Jews at the end of the nineteenth century: a dire present in which they
found themselves due to increasing anti-Semitism across Europe and to
economic deterioration in the East; a disbelief that the future promised
genuine integration into European nation-states or into a cosmopolitan
community; and a disenchantment with faith in an almighty God and
the enduring relevance of tradition. Underlying the rise of Zionism is
a transformation in the way a number of Jews viewed the meaning of
history, perceived its direction or lack thereof, conceived of its dangers
and potentials, and interpreted the times in which they were living: "In
the life of nations, as in the life of the private individual, there are rare,
weighty moments, and the way these moments are being handled would
determine that fate of the people or person in the future, for good or for
bad. We are currently undergoing such a moment."[1]

---

[1] Leo Pinsker, *Auto-Emancipation* [Selbstemanzipation, 1882], at http://www.benye-
huda.org/ginzberg/pinsker_autoemancipation.html. I have been assisted in the translations from this text by the English translation of the original German by Dr. D. S.
Blondheim, Federation of American Zionists, 1916, at http://www.jewishvirtuallibrary.
org/jsource/Zionism/pinsker.html. (Unless I indicate otherwise, all translations in this
book are mine. EC)

Yet this study also seeks to go beyond Zionism, or rather to reflect on certain aspects of modernity by virtue of understanding Zionism. Specifically, the predicament of Jews in general and of Zionists in particular serves as a springboard for reflection on the temporal imaginations of modernity, since in the European scene the modern Jews are *the prime temporal agents*. They are considered by others (and sometimes by themselves) to be the ultimate strangers, an uprooted people, and therefore they have often become the most ardent believers in visions of a future cosmopolitan society, for in such a future they will finally be at home with others and enjoy equal rights and respect regardless of primordial, territorial, cultural, national, religious, or other particularistic attachments. The Jews are also steadfast believers in their tradition: They epitomize the power of human memory in their insistence on certain practices and customs, rituals and holidays, legal codes and learning. Their identity seems to depend on their capacity for remembrance and on their ability to reinterpret and reproduce the past. Yet the Jews are also the people most identified with industrialization, commerce, and market capitalism generally. Therefore, they are often identified with the present-centeredness of this economic system, with its promotion of immediate gains, its cultivation of self-interest without regard to prior or succeeding generations, its constantly looming materialism and hedonism. In short, the Jews are the people most immersed in time, as they lack a space or a polity of their own as alternative anchors of identity. It is not an exaggeration to say, in fact, that the story of Jewish temporality since the late eighteenth century reflects the story of modern temporality at large.

I have used the term *temporal imagination*. By this I mean (to put it briefly at this stage) the ways that people represent the nature of time, as when they ponder such things as whether it is quantitative or qualitative, what connection (or lack of connection) exists among proximate and distant events, and what the overarching structure and direction of time is (ranging from a tight, progressing totality to complete arbitrariness). But before I say more about the temporal imaginations of modernity – and about their critical effects on Zionism – let us bear in mind the familiar and important accounts of the crisis of modern Jewry and the reasons for the emergence of Zionism.

This emergence is often described as the upshot of the deteriorating status of citizenship experienced by Jews in the late nineteenth century. In France, observes David Vital, "the question Jews had … increasingly to face was less whether they would be allowed to become citizens of the state than whether they would be granted membership in the nation."² What was true in France was even more acutely felt in Central and Eastern European countries, where organic nationalism, *Volkish* ideologies, racism, and traditional stereotypes led many to view Jews with suspicion because of their distinct religion, culture, language, and origins. Indeed, toward the end of the nineteenth century, the universalism and equality of citizenship that had characterized the emancipation of the Jews since the French Revolution and the rise of bourgeois liberalism were gradually evaporating, and they felt increasingly discriminated against socially and humiliated.³ Although formally Jews gained equal rights, this did not mean that they became part of the nation; the attempt of state institutions (especially in Germany and France) to integrate them into the general population ebbed with the emergence of new, populist forces that made use of the emerging public sphere and transformed the political discourse and practice by presenting Jews as interlopers. If in France this phenomenon was epitomized in the Dreyfus affair, in Tsarist Russia – where Jews were never considered equal citizens – matters were much worse: The hundreds of pogroms that occurred in southern Russia during the early 1880s demonstrated to them that their (limited) bond with the state was finished, that because of its need to boost its shaky legitimacy, the state withdrew its hold over the population and let Jews be the prey of the city mob, the frustrated peasants, or the various national minorities within its bounds.

In fact, Jews had begun to understand that even the equality of rights that started to elude them everywhere would not have promised *respect* in the eyes of nations, since such respect can only be given to members of a cohesive nation with a place and political institutions of its own, not to dispersed individuals that are alien everywhere and are always dependent on the goodwill of others.⁴ It is not only the respect of others that was missing, to be precise, but also self-respect, the profound other-dependency of Jews affecting their perception of themselves and

---

² David Vital, *A People Apart: The Jews in Europe, 1789–1939* (Oxford: Oxford University Press, 2000), p. 248.

³ For a history of the Jews in nineteenth-century Europe, see J. Frankel and S. Zipperstein, eds., *Assimilation and Community: The Jews in Nineteenth-Century Europe* (Cambridge: Cambridge University Press, 1992).

⁴ As Leo Strauss notes, political Zionists, in particular, argued that the goal must be "the restoration of their [Jews'] honor through the acquisition of statehood and therefore of a country – any country." Strauss seems to concur that Jewish honor and self-respect are at the core of Zionism. See Leo Strauss, *Spinoza's Critique of Religion* (Chicago: University of Chicago Press, 1997), p. 5. On Strauss and Zionism, see Steven B. Smith, *Reading Leo Strauss* (Chicago: University of Chicago Press, 2006), Chap. 2.

diminishing them internally. Because the Jews refuse to disappear as a distinct people, on the one hand, but do not exist as an independent and cohesive nation, on the other, noted Leo Pinsker, the world considers them as an "uncanny form of one of the dead walking among the living," as a kind of "ghostlike apparition of a living corpse." At times, the antipathy toward them is manifested through actual discrimination and violence, and at other times through being "tolerated" with effort and designated as a group needing special protection by the authorities. But, according to Pinsker, "to be robbed as a Jew or to be protected as a Jew is equally humiliating, equally destructive to the self-respect of the Jews." Only the restoration of the Jewish nation as an independent political body in a land of its own would restore Jewish honor and sense of self-worth.[5]

Economics and demographics also played their part in generating the Jewish quandary of modern times. In the Pale of Settlement, at least a third of the Jews were destitute and dependent on charity. They were forced to leave the villages and move to the towns; there, the artisans earned meager wages, the workers toiled in small businesses and mostly as unskilled laborers, and the traders were often confined in their business to the local level. As the fastest-growing population in Russia (as well as in more prosperous Germany, incidentally), Jews lived in terrible sanitary conditions, with entire families most often crowded into one room, and with poor health services. In other words, many Jews of Eastern Europe experienced some of the typical developments of modernization (they became more urban people and underwent a vast change in their communal life and sheer demographics), yet they could not enjoy the benefits offered by this modernization (e.g., promising vocations, better quality of life, access to higher education). Their distinctiveness prevented them from becoming members of the proletarian class that was emerging in the heavy and more established industries, nor could they become an integral part of the middle class due to severe restrictions on their movements, education, and mobility.

The economic and political crisis of modern Jewry was intermingled with a more basic, existential one of individual and collective identity. In order to become a part of the German nation, for example, Jews had to master the German language and relinquish (at least in public) their beloved Yiddish, to change their long-established commercial occupations into "productive" ones, and to embrace bourgeois mores

---

[5] Pinsker, *Auto-Emancipation*.

(e.g., an emphasis on hygiene, propriety, external appearance, emotional restraint, and the small family unit),[6] rather than maintain their more expressive and communal way of life. Jewish identity devolved into a state of confusion, veering between waning tradition – whose fixed practices and values offered less and less relevant answers – and secularization, whose openness posed multiple and conflicting options. Primary among these options were choosing Jewishness as a culture (rather than as a religious faith) or embracing the general culture of the relevant nation (which nevertheless remained foreign); eating kosher, not working on the Sabbath, covering one's head, teaching the children Hebrew, and so forth or ignoring all of these customs and traditions by surrendering oneself to the demands of the external world. Should a Jew choose communal life, which some experienced as suffocating, or a lonely existence with a much-shrunken family structure in the city? Should he or she choose loyalty to the collective and to Jews wherever they are (*arvut hadadit*) or give in to the nagging voice of self-interest characteristic of the modern era? The Jews, in other words, were troubled by irresolvable dilemmas in the most basic realms of their existence.

Although this generalized account of the emergence of Zionism is enlightening, it is insufficient: The political, economic, and existential crisis of modern Jewry does not lead naturally or necessarily to Zionism, as some scholars suggest. The fact that a community experiences a breakdown in its old ways of life and that external circumstances become dire does not mean that it will inevitably find a solution to that crisis, and certainly not a radical new path; history is the graveyard of countless communities that did not muster the power and inventiveness to overcome the troubles that beset them. Moreover, the history of Jews in the Diaspora is saturated with disasters that did not lead to radical solutions. In Western Europe alone, Jews were occasionally massacred (commencing with the massacres in the Rhineland during the First Crusade in 1096), expelled abruptly (from England [1290], France [1306], Spain [1492], and Portugal [1497]), ghettoized (first by Pope Paul IV in 1555), harassed by accusations of ritual murder, discriminated against economically and degraded to utter impoverishment, and so forth. None of this, however, led them to collective action aimed at returning to their ancient land, and Jews optimized strategies of adaptation, not of revolution. Indeed, it is not crisis alone that propels people to great deeds: They also

---

[6] Shlomit Volkov, *Bama'agal hamechushaf: yehudim, anti-shemim, vegermanim acherim* [The magic circle: Germans, Jews and Antisemites] (Tel Aviv: Am Oved, 2002), p. 172.

need to feel that action is possible, that the *world is malleable and can be crafted by humans*; no less crucial, they need to perceive themselves as potent beings, effective actors on the stage of history. Not even the rise of nationalism in modernity explains how (some) Jews found the boldness to define themselves as a viable nation – and succeed. How is it, then, that around the turn of the twentieth century, a small but decisive number of Jews began to see human affairs as hospitable to deliberate intervention and willful rupture?

Before answering this question, it is worth bearing in mind the scope of the Zionist revolution. Zionism emerged during the last decade of the nineteenth century, mainly in Eastern and Central Europe. While originally a movement of a small minority of Jews that was considered outlandish by their peers, its institutional ingenuity, combined with pressing external circumstances, gradually turned it into a viable option for the Jewish masses. At the most basic level, Zionism aimed to restore to the Jews a political body they could claim as their own; national independence was seen as the way to guard the individual against physical threats and economic want, and the collective against the menace of assimilation and disintegration. Most Zionists – seeking to legitimize their claim for nationhood and to echo the glorious Hebraic past of self-government – thought that this modern project of renewal could succeed only in *Eretz Israel* (Palestine). But Zionism meant more than political independence in Palestine. It promised both material and spiritual transformation: a modernized economy of and for the Jews, which would eliminate their threatened, fleeting patterns of survival as well as their dependent occupational structure (which often left them socially backward), and the revival of the Hebrew language, which would launch a secular, fresh cultural experiment and introduce new substance into the Jewish collective identity. Some even hoped to form a new Jew: natural, assertive, self-reliant, productive, and so on. Once we consider the radical and unprecedented nature of these goals, the question arises even more forcefully: Where did the Zionists find the *audacity* to take on such an all-engulfing experiment?

The answer has two components. The first concerns the nature of modern men and women as historical, and the second, the specific temporal quality of the late nineteenth century and of the Zionist perception of time in that era. Beginning with the French Revolution, asserts Reinhart Koselleck, time "colored the entire political and social vocabulary." Since that period, he adds, "there has hardly been a central concept of political theory or social program which does not contain a coefficient of temporal change."[7] This new centrality of time in social and political thought is familiar. Thinkers of the seventeenth century tended to view time as neutral and could therefore envision a great degree of permanence in the world order and humans' place in that order. Locke, for example, believed that the obligations of the Law of Nature "cease not in Society." Thus, he added, "the Law of Nature stands as an Eternal Rule to all Men, legislators as well as others."[8] For Locke, then, the Law of Nature, which defines our individual rights and commitments to one another, was inscribed everlastingly in the world by the Divine.[9] This Law, and the overall order of which this Law forms a part, are wholly transparent to human reason and are judged as inherently sensible by that reason. Since neither the order and Law of God nor human reason and judgment ever change, history is characterized by continuity and coherence, rather than by constant transformation and difference.[10]

From the middle of the eighteenth century onward, however, this view was no longer tenable. In Rousseau's *Second Discourse*, for instance, time itself became a factor in human life and was conceived as shaping human consciousness, needs, motivations, character, options, and more; in short, the individual, and the species as a whole, became historical. This creed was formulated later by such diverse writers as Kant, Arndt, Comte, Hegel, Marx, Spencer, and countless others. Since the late eighteenth century, then, "time is no longer simply the medium in which all histories take place; it gains a historical quality. Consequently, history no longer occurs in, but through, time. Time becomes a dynamic and historical force in its own right."[11] In the new vista, each epoch in history (especially each century) possesses a distinct quality evident in all spheres of human existence: political institutions and economic modes of production, fashion and arts, practices and habits, moral codes and overall visions of life. To understand individuals and societies, we must be attuned to all of these spheres and how they are shaped by history.

---

[7] Reinhart Koselleck, "*Neuzeit*: Remarks on the Semantics of the Modern Concepts of Movement," in his *Futures Past* (Cambridge, MA: MIT Press, 1985), p. 259.

[8] John Locke, *Second Treatise of Government* (Indianapolis: Hackett, 1980), p. 71.

[9] Locke professes that if we examine the reason imbued in Nature, we shall discover that we have a right to life, health, freedom, and property – and that we must respect the right of others to the same. Moreover, Locke's Law of Nature is essentially oriented toward the preservation of humankind and the enhancement of human sociability.

[10] Locke, *Second Treatise of Government*, p. 104. For a general discussion of natural law in the seventeenth century in authors such as Grotius, Pufendorf, Cumberland, and Locke, see Knud Haakonssen, *Natural Law and Moral Philosophy* (Cambridge: Cambridge University Press, 1996), esp. Chap. 1.

[11] Koselleck, "*Neuzeit*: Remarks," p. 246.

There is no belief in human nature as such and no model of a "best regime" that is transhistorical. Indeed, there are considered to be no predetermined, tradition-laden confines to what humans can will and do; it is our specific location in time that opens some options of existence and closes others. In order to understand this location correctly, we must fathom the ontology and course of time by transcending its particular manifestations. Historical time should be contemplated abstractly – as a system with certain categories, rules, structure, rationale; in fact, some even believe that we should see it as a totality, as a coherent phenomenon that embraces all epochs as well as all places – as a world history. This overarching vision is necessary not only to understand the quality of a distant era but even more importantly to understand ourselves and the paths receptive to our actions.

More specifically, history is essential for us as we seek to fathom the answers to two clusters of critical questions. Firstly, what is the meaning of our lives in this particular time and place, and of which emerging order do we form a part? Are we the moral agents promoting in our daily moral actions a universal community of justice and Right? Are we the small cells cultivating the ancient spirit and body of the nation? Are we the proletarian threshold from which a classless society will be formed and solidarity reign? History answers these questions for us, for meaning is not merely an individual project but is dependent on our accurate comprehension of history and the truth that emerges from its unfolding.

The second cluster of questions that history answers concerns whether a certain action or policy is legitimate. For example, if history leads us by its underlying narrative toward a mosaic of nation-states, then it would be a senseless policy to weaken these institutions by strengthening transnational bodies or by forming fluid boundaries around the nation's distinct culture. When we debate with each other about what is proper to think and do, we must base our arguments on the nature of history, since if our actions are counter to its essence they would be morally wrong and politically pointless, even dangerous. The emergence of Zionism should be explained in this context: If modern men and women are indeed historical, and if Jews are prime temporal agents, then *it is the Zionist conception of time we should first probe* – even prior to the political, economic-demographic, or existential reasons for the emergence of this movement. The Zionist revolution presupposed a *temporal revolution*, a shift in the way Jews began to experience time, understand its ontology, and thereby understand their political responsibility and potential. To be perfectly clear, without this temporal revolution, the Zionism revolution would not have been possible.

The significance of this study should be understood in the context of the existing scholarship on Zionism, which includes – surprisingly enough – little substantial political-philosophical dimension. A society formed to a large extent by the ingenuity of political institutions and actors – and a society in which philosophy blossomed through founding figures such as Martin Buber, Nathan Rotenstreich, Shmuel Hugo Bergman, and Yeshayahu Leibowitz (all of whom wrote about modern Jewish nationalism)[12] – nevertheless has failed to develop a significant tradition of political philosophy with which to reflect upon itself: No key problems have been identified, relevant concepts invented, pathbreaking and founding texts accepted. To be sure, there are plenty of studies of Zionist ideology[13] and a vast number of historical writings on Zionism (as well as studies of its sociology, language, culture, and more); these resources stand, however, in odd contrast to the relatively few political-philosophical writings that emerged from within Israel.[14]

Gershom Scholem believed that this predicament (he referred to philosophy generally) stemmed from the chaotic character of the young Hebrew language. "I think," he noted, "that what is evolving here and is alive cannot be articulated by a system or an enduring thought. I think that the lack of language and concepts are objective not subjective matters, and do not derive from the weakness of philosophers but from actual

[12] Martin Buber, *On Zion: The History of an Idea* (New York: Schocken Books, 1973); Buber, *A Land of Two Peoples: Martin Buber on Jews and Arabs* (New York: Oxford University Press, 1983); Nathan Rotenstreich, *Jewish Philosophy in Modern Times: From Mendelssohn to Rosenzweig* (New York: Holt, Rinehart and Winston, 1968); Shmuel Hugo Bergman, *Bamish'ol* (Tel Aviv: Am Oved, 1976); Y. Leibovitch, *Yahadut, am yehudi umedinat yisrael* [Judaism, the Jewish People, and the State of Israel] (Tel Aviv: Schocken, 1975).

[13] See, in particular, Zeev Sternhell, *The Founding Myths of Israel: Nationalism, Socialism, and the Making of the Jewish State*, trans. David Maisel (Princeton, NJ: Princeton University Press, 1998); Shlomo Avineri, *The Making of Modern Zionism: Intellectual Origins of the Jewish State* (New York: Basic Books, 1981); and Gideon Shimoni, *The Zionist Ideology* (Boston: Brandeis University Press, 1995).

[14] Among the notable exceptions to the general picture painted here are Rotenstreich's *Jewish Philosophy in Modern Time*; Yael Tamir, *Liberal Nationalism* (Princeton, NJ: Princeton University Press, 1993); Yaron Ezrahi, *Rubber Bullets: Power and Conscience in Modern Israel* (Berkeley: University of California Press, 1997); Adi Ophir, *Lashon hara'a* [*The order of evils: Toward an ontology of morals*] (Tel Aviv: Am Oved, 2000); Yoram Hazony, *The Jewish State: The Struggle for Israel's Soul* (New York: Basic Books, 2000); and Chaim Gans, *A Just Zionism: On the Morality of the Jewish State* (New York: Oxford University Press, 2008).

circumstances."[15] Scholem's insight is compelling: In fact, the Hebrew language is still chaotic and rapidly evolving, with books written 40 years ago often looking anachronistic, their vocabulary seemingly odd and dated. Moreover, the revived Hebrew does not lend itself easily to abstractions, so that philosophical concepts seem highly artificial (e.g., *sochen* [agent] *musari* [moral], which stands for "moral agent") or lack the dimension of abstraction altogether (e.g., the word *diyyon* means "deliberation," but does not have the connotation of thoughtfulness and reflection associated with the English word).

Perhaps, however, it was not only the chaotic nature of language that was (and maybe still is) at fault but also its powerlessness in a polity in which actions (such as armed conflicts that lead to conquest and defeat, settlement and evacuation) prevail over words. This hierarchy is ingrained in the very foundations of Zionism and is essential for understanding this movement's history as well as the Israeli state's present: The Jewish Agency, for example, decided to celebrate the centenary of the First Zionist Congress (1997) with the slogan "Zionism is about *doing* – yesterday, today, and tomorrow" (my emphasis; I will return to this slogan and its broader meaning later in the book). While this may at first seem counterintuitive, my choosing to write this book first in the English language stems in part from the need to cope with the intense changeability and matter-of-fact orientation of contemporary Hebrew, as well as with its relative futility in shaping reality. As for the relation between action and words in Zionism, this problem is one of my central concerns here.

While this work offers a different order of reflection on Zionism, it also calls for a departure from the prevalent theories and vocabularies typically used to examine this movement. Contemporary scholarship on Zionism is based on the dramatic rise of two political ideologies and practices – nationalism and colonialism – during the last decades of the nineteenth century. Scholars debate over which of these phenomena was most decisive in shaping Zionism.

Critics of Zionism (who include some of the scholars known in Israel as the "New Historians") point to the colonial and imperialist elements in Zionism, such as its economic exploitation of the native Arab population, its fixation on land acquisition through dubious methods, its attempt to accumulate weapons and organize itself militarily, and its perception of itself as the messenger of progress and high culture in a

---

[15] Gershom Scholem, *Devarim bego* (Tel Aviv: Am Oved, 1975), p. 48 (in Hebrew).

backward environment. This approach argues that (most) early Zionists were not interested in forming significant economic, political, or indeed social relations with the Arabs and remained a self-enclosed community; nor did these Zionists acknowledge the depth of the Arabs' historical-cultural and religious attachment to the land. The critics also point to the partial expulsion of the Palestinian population by Israeli forces in 1948, the reluctance of Israeli leaders to accept responsibility for the fate of these refugees, and the lukewarm reactions of Israel to various Arab peace initiatives.[16]

In contrast, those who sympathize with the movement's aims underscore its affinity with other national liberation movements that evolved during the nineteenth century, arguing that Zionism was a legitimate reaction to anti-Semitism and the exclusion of Jews from European nation-states. Not only is Jewish nationalism as legitimate as any other, but Jews were actually pushed by their neighbors to embrace this political ideology. From this perspective, Zionism sought to solve a crisis – one of physical security, economic existence, and collective identity – not to exploit and control others.[17] The sympathizers note that, beginning with Herzl's *Altneuland* (1902), Zionism always contained strong liberal principles despite its national goals, and that it aspired to act toward Arabs as equals and partners. The friendly scholars suggest, however,

---

[16] Revisionist works on Zionist historiography include Gershon Shafir, *Land, Labor, and the Origins of the Israeli-Palestinian Conflict, 1882–1914* (Cambridge: Cambridge University Press, 1989); Gershon Shafir and Yoav Peled, *Being Israeli: The Dynamics of Multiple Citizenship* (Cambridge: Cambridge University Press, 2002); Ilan Pappe, *The Making of the Arab-Israeli Conflict, 1947–1951* (London: I. B. Tauris, 1994); and Benny Morris, *1948 and After: Israel and the Palestinians* (Oxford: Clarendon, 1990), as well as *1948: A History of the First Arab-Israeli War* (New Haven, CT: Yale University Press, 2008). Despite the troubling history he helped to uncover, however, Morris is a Zionist.

[17] This line of interpretation has been formed in Israel by historians such as Ben Zion Dinaburg and Yitzhak Baer. The latter, for example, writes that "the Galut [Diaspora] has returned to its starting point. It remains what it always was: political servitude, which must be abolished completely." See Yitzhak Baer, *Galut* (New York: Schocken Books, 1988), p. 118. See also Baer, *Mehkarim umasot betoldot am yisrael*, 2 vols. (Jerusalem: Hahevra Hahistorit Hayisraelit, 1985); Ben Zion Dinaburg, *Bema'avak hadorot shel am yisrael al artzo mihurban betar ad tekumat yisrael* (Jerusalem, Mossad Bialik,1975); and Dinaburg, *Bemifne hadorot* (Jerusalem, Mossad Bialik, 1971–72). Nonrevisionist, contemporary historians in Israel are less driven by Zionist ideology, but they are nevertheless inclined to highlight the just cause of this movement rather than its colonial elements. See, e.g., David Vital, *The Origins of Zionism* (Oxford: Clarendon, 1975); Vital, *A People Apart*; Walter Laqueur, *A History of Zionism* (New York: Holt, Rinehart and Winston, 1972); and Anita Shapira, *Land and Power, The Zionist Resort to Force, 1881–1948* (New York: Oxford University Press, 1992).

that the benign intensions of Zionists were answered with continuous acts of terror by Palestinians toward Jews since at least the 1920s and with propaganda against them, which began even earlier. These scholars also point to the Jewish leadership's acceptance of the principle of partition since 1937 and their approval of the United Nations partition plan in 1947, while the Palestinians rejected this plan as well as others, and to the invasion of Palestine in 1948 by the armies of the Arab League and their responsibility for the deteriorating relations with the Jewish state.

Although these interpretations differ in their normative presuppositions and theoretical frameworks, as well as in the facts they highlight, they are nevertheless similar in their attempts to see Zionism through comparative lenses that de-emphasize its singularity.

My purpose is to depart from these debates and to help move the discussion on Zionism to a different level of inquiry. The current approaches tend to impose a theoretical grid for the sake of ideological battles; they resemble one another in that their underlying concern is the legitimacy or illegitimacy of the Zionist movement and the Israeli state. As Benny Morris notes, "If Israel, the refuge of a people who have been continuously harassed, was born in a pure-hearted and honest way, then she deserves grace, material assistance and political support.... If, on the other hand, Israel was born tainted and disparaged because of a primal sin [the partial expulsion of Palestinians in 1948], then she is not worthy of this assistance more than its neighbors."[18] Yet this debate, important as it was and is, can also limit our understanding of Zionism: When it dominates the scene, it becomes difficult to explore the deeper political-philosophical dimension of Zionism, and to highlight its distinctiveness.

Zionism, this study suggests, is a unique national movement: It departed from its milieu in its intellectual boldness and belief in the unqualified efficacy of human action, carrying then-novel notions of time (such as the formlessness of history, the possibility of introducing intentional breaks in time, and the spiritual marriage of distant periods) to their logical conclusions and translating them into a revolutionary practice. The study of time, I would argue, offers a broader and perhaps more important perspective for understanding Zionism than the current theories that have examined it primarily in the context of nationalism and colonialism (or imperialism).

---

[18] Benny Morris, *Tikun ta'ut* [Correcting a mistake] (Tel Aviv: Am Oved, 2000), p. 28 (in Hebrew).

Zionism is also a movement that combined two contradictory aspects of modernity: a project-like logic involving rational planning and premeditated shaping of the future, as well as valorization of ancient images and aesthetic existence. It is a movement, moreover, that revived a language but downplayed its ontological significance, displaying skepticism toward any language-based construction of the world (as exemplified by its distrustful attitude toward international law and agreements, a distrust reinforced ever since the mutual violations of the 1949 armistice agreements). These aspects of early Zionist political philosophy profoundly shaped the movement's enduring notions òf collective action, territory, and nation building, language, and democratic ethos. If the past *and present* of Zionism are to be better understood, in short, the current disciplines and theories that dominate the field must be surmounted.

The first chapter of this study attempts to set the temporal stage in which Zionism burgeoned. In order to explicate this context, it develops a theory of time in modernity that makes two fundamental claims: firstly, that since the late eighteenth century we can distinguish among three incompatible temporal imaginations, and, secondly, that these all gained weight in modern culture (rather than superseding one another). The three imaginations that this chapter examines are a) the present-centered, b) the teleological-progressive, and c) the semicyclical; in the late nineteenth century, these imaginations achieved a kind of balance of power in the modern's consciousness. Of particular interest are the teleological and semicyclical imaginations, since Zionism emerged with the decline of the former and the rise of the latter. I examine the teleological imagination of the Enlightenment (which underlies the project of Jewish emancipation in Europe and of the *Haskala*) through the writings of Kant, for whom linear and uniform time legitimizes expectations that the individual would heighten his or her universal attributes and play a part in the constant expansion of a moral community. The desired end of Kantian philosophy is the establishment of an integrated, homogeneous human space, a cosmopolitan stage upon which history is finally redeemed.

This vision of time began to ebb toward the end of the nineteenth century and the *fin de siècle*; instead, writers such as Freud, Proust, and later Benjamin underscored the semicyclical nature of time (all of these writers, perhaps not incidentally, were of Jewish origin). This temporal imagination suggests that the progressive notion of time is dangerous, since it generates forgetfulness and the inner impoverishment of the individual and the community. Instead, these writers advance a fragmented conception of time, one that allows conversation between distant moments and the grounding of identity in concrete images or events. This rather poetic recovery of memory involves the openness of historical actors to the past; it leads them to exhume and relive the distinct and exclusive memory of their community – rather than to promote a universal and cosmopolitan identity. Such a vision of time was a prerequisite for making the idea of return to the Holy Land feasible, even necessary. On the one hand, then, this chapter suggests that Zionism is comprehensible only within the context of these two temporal imaginations; on the other hand, it contends that because the movement demonstrates these imaginations' changing standing in European consciousness, Zionism may help us to reflect on modernity at a critical juncture. Indeed, my effort here and elsewhere is both to anchor Zionism more fully in modern thought *and* to make manifest this movement's temporal boldness and singularity. (This chapter could appeal, in particular, to readers interested in the intellectual background of Zionism, the main focus being the European notions of time.)

While the semicyclical temporal imagination played a critical role in the formation of Zionism during the twentieth century, the role of this imagination in Zionist politics remained unclear, at least until the end of the Uganda debate (1906). Was Zionism a movement aimed at Jews' *survival* – indifferent to the historic nature of the territory it settled – or was it committed to a genuine national revival, to a restoration of the triangle of people, ancient land, and the Hebrew language? The choice was made, and with this choice a particular temporal imagination was embraced. But prior to that choice, things were more ambiguous: The end of the nineteenth century is characterized by the existence of numerous temporal imaginations, a temporal predicament which allowed a unique sense of formlessness and openness. This offered individuals a chance to take history into their own hands, to choose their own vision of time and history, so to speak.

The second chapter, therefore, examines the emergence of Zionism in the context of a particular temporal ontology that could be termed *sundered history*. By this I mean a picture of history as shapeless, devoid of binding meta-narratives or underlying structure. Such a historical moment is most often short: Communities often seek to ground collective action in a certain temporal order, and the belief in formless history is hard to bear. But while the hiatus lasts, there is a sense of both concern and excitement in the air, concern that human reality is intrinsically chaotic and uncertain, and excitement because precisely in these circumstances everything is seen as possible and malleable. This experience of temporal fluidity is epitomized by early Zionism and helps to explain both its belligerent attitude toward existing reality and its sense of urgency and insecurity. These themes (evident in otherwise very diverse strands of Zionism) were not only essential for the emergence of the movement but also became *constitutive* of its political praxis.

The third chapter explores how the Zionist, revolutionary notion of time was translated into practice and how it molded the spatial vista of this movement. Space was vigorously formed because shapeless time also carried a sense of potency and of a narrow opportunity to act in finding solutions to the increasingly dire predicament of European Jews. Early Zionists often felt, for good reason, desperate and powerless. Yet in Zionism, the experience of sundered history was also turned into a radical conception of collective action that (in terms of the imagination at work) is nearly unfettered by external circumstances and that pictures participants as constructing their own edifice in toto, from the foundation up.

It is no accident that the Zionist project in Palestine was very often conceptualized as the production of a concrete and massive object, as the making of a national building (*binyan leumi*): More than any other artifact, buildings convey not only the power of human beings but also their ability to inaugurate (and complete) complex projects in time according to their own design. The celebration of building as the Zionists' prime metaphor also conveys, of course, their desire to escape the rootless diasporic predicament by generating tangible anchors of identity. Yet by conceptualizing their collective project as a building and envisioning themselves as builders, Zionists espoused a problematic understanding of democratic politics, since the practical skills required by builders are different from those required by citizens, and the nonverbal solidarity among builders is essentially different from the solidarity required by a plurality of citizens. In other words, the ethos of capable builders that was essential for establishing a commonwealth from scratch is fundamentally at odds with the ethos required for an ongoing, democratic polity. As Aristotelian republicanism suggests, a polity requires the valorization of language as the main sphere that forms and sustains the community – and territory, army, or other tangible achievements cannot generate a lasting bond. From a temporal perspective, moreover, thinking of the nation as a building is highly problematic, since buildings are merely objects and project-like, involving a type of completion that is alien to political life, which is ongoing and constantly reinvented through language.

The fourth chapter further probes the relation between time and language in Zionism. It begins by looking into the status of the Hebrew language in Judaism and explores the transformations this language underwent with its revival in modernity. In general, one could argue (as Scholem did) that the Hebrew language became caught between its religious status as the bearer of divine truth and revelation, on the one hand, and its possible interpretation as an utterly secular, somewhat concocted new language that essentially lacks or hides its historical-religious depth, on the other. Both understandings of Hebrew rendered it problematic from a democratic-political point of view, since for the political sphere a trusted, culturally rooted yet man-made notion of truth is essential. The chapter then examines two main attempts to cope with the status and nature of modern Hebrew by exploring the notions of language of Ahad Ha'am and Chaim Nachman Bialik. These two Jewish nationalist writers posed powerful visions of the Hebrew language as an alternative anchor for the Zionist endeavor (instead of the building-oriented notion, that is). Yet I argue that their visions are problematic from a democratic point of view, partly because they belittle the standing of the individual as an independent, critical, and creative public persona, and partly because, in the case of Bialik, language performs a dangerous function of concealing fundamental aspects of existence, rather than being committed to continuously revealing them.

The difficulties that emerge in theorizing a proper relation between Hebrew and democracy in the writings of Ahad Ha'am and Bialik require us to look for a better understanding of democratic language. The fifth chapter thus begins with an exploration of Hannah Arendt's writings on democratic language, especially its role in revealing the world and articulating truth claims about it, and in substantiating the role of the individual as citizen and public speaker. On the basis of this discussion and that of the previous chapter, I then examine the role of tradition in democratic language, and suggest that the challenges facing contemporary Hebrew include avoiding both alienation from its linguistic tradition *and* an uncritical submission to the contents of religious tradition.

PHOTO 1. Israel and Rivka Pollack upon their arrival at the moshav Ein Ayala, Israel (1951). Photo by Zoltan Kluger, courtesy of The Central Zionist Archives, Jerusalem.

Developing one aspect of Bialik's view of language, I espouse a playful and poetic notion of language that is attuned to (a secularized) tradition as a source of inspiration and meaning but not of binding authority, a notion that aims at the cultivation of the individual as a creative yet judicious public speaker. Perhaps this type of citizen may arise now that the embedded builder is no more.

I

Jews and the Temporal Imaginations of Modernity

Men's curiosity searches past and future
And clings to that dimension. But to apprehend the point of intersection of the timeless
With time, is an occupation for the saint –
For most of us, there is only the unattended Moment, the moment in and out of time

T. S. Eliot, Four Quartets

Well before modernity, understanding the nature of time was considered essential for uncovering the meaning and nature of human existence. Yet two fundamental changes occurred at the dawn of the modern era, changes that helped set the temporal context in which Zionism later burgeoned. One was the evaporation of eternity as the divine measure against which human time is understood; the other: the disappearance of our certainty that the past, present, and future join harmoniously in the self's experience and in the human world as a whole. In order to explore these changes, however, we must begin with ideas that might initially seem rather removed from Zionism.

Let us compare, then, the modern understanding of time with older religious conceptions, such as Saint Augustine's. "Time [and] times are words forever on our lips,"[1] he famously observes while placing the concern with temporality and redemption at the heart of the Judeo-Christian tradition. Augustine grounds his well-known reflections on time by

---

[1] Saint Augustine, *Confessions*, trans. R. S. Pine-Coffin (New York: Penguin Books, 1961), p. 270.

distinguishing between God's eternity and human time: In eternity, he suggests, all is present, without growth and decay, before and after, being and nonbeing. "Your years are completely present to you all at once," writes Augustine of God, "because they are at a permanent standstill.... They do not move on, forced to give way before the advance of others."[2] From the viewpoint of eternity, what for us is ordered chronologically is all alive contemporaneously. This is true even of God's Word, which created the world and even time itself. The Divine Word is not one in which words give way to those that follow, nor a speech that requires sequential order to be intelligible. Rather, "in your Word all is uttered at one and the same time, yet eternally. If it were not so, your Word would be subject to time and change, and therefore would be neither truly eternal nor truly immortal."[3]

Human time (and language), in contrast, is subject to the "havoc of change,"[4] he writes – to inevitable mutability and unpredictability. Both our surroundings and our internal life are constantly transformed; the things we perceive and know, the thoughts and feelings that spring inside us, and the words we use to articulate our experiences are all shifting without necessarily evolving. The world as it is revealed to us does not house the past and the future at a standstill, but rather gradually converts the latter into the former. Augustine thus advances a view of time that hinges on the mind's state in the present: Humans have a past and future to the extent that they are able to hold those times in the present of their mind. "It might be correct to say that there are three times," he writes. "A present of past things is the memory; the present of present things is direct perception; and the present of future things is expectation."[5] Guided by divine light from within, human beings attempt to emulate God and to distend the mind so that it would integrate and gather as much of the past (memory) and future (expectation) as possible and thus approximate eternity. To be sure, our prospects of reaching eternity are very limited: Ours is a subjective experience of the imagination and not one of contemporaneous objective being; ultimately, time slips away because its abundance and constant change are stronger than human attention and ability to gather experience. Yet the positioning of God's eternity as an ideal provides the self with the sense of a possible

---

2 Ibid., p. 263.
3 Ibid., p. 259.
4 Ibid., p. 279.
5 Ibid., p. 269.

continuity of time, with a sense that there are meaning and measure to the human temporal experience.

From the late eighteenth century onward, in contrast, the past, present, and future increasingly parted, losing their continuity to a great extent because they lost their transcendental measure – the sphere of eternity that promised their harmonized coexistence. They were now understood and imagined separately, so that each pulled in a different direction and posed conflicting claims upon men and women. In some nations, members were called to ignore chronology and reach into the distant past, to salvage distinct moments in the life of the group, and thus to think of time as the bond between qualitatively like situations or even periods that connect across time. In the booming civil-commercial society, the individual was called to zoom in on the present in an essentially quantitative, clock-dominated time, to cultivate temporal horizons that befit an agent operating in market capitalism and in a synchronized society; this individual must be attuned to shifting economic circumstances and simultaneous information while acting within the temporal bounds of self-interest. Yet as a moral being with an increasingly universal consciousness, the modern individual was also called to extend his or her temporal perspective by putting faith in the continuous progress of humanity, in the growing potential of reason and science to shape a better life socially and politically (as well as materially). These and other competing, uniquely modern, temporal imaginations have coexisted in Western societies since the late eighteenth century, and their concomitant appeal is the paramount source of the constant strife in our personal deliberations, public conversation, and political praxis.

Moreover, in modernity, the *weight*, so to speak, of temporal imaginations increased dramatically. This occurred for at least two reasons: a) the intense search for new sources of meaning and b) the quest for new ways of legitimizing social-political orders (both of which are associated with secularism). According to Max Weber, Western notions of selfhood were formed through religious experience, typically shaped by a prophet for whom "both life and world, both social and cosmic events, have a certain systematic and coherent meaning, to which man's conduct must be oriented if it is to bring salvation, and after which it must be patterned in an integrally meaningful manner."[6] Weber believes it was this desire for meaning that led to the association of redemption in the afterlife with

---

[6] Max Weber, *Economy and Society*, ed. G. Roth and C. Wittich (Berkeley: University of California Press, 1978), p. 450.

the totality of human behavior, action, and thought in mundane earthly life (as was epitomized by Protestantism and the religious significance allotted to work). Secularization, however, meant that the hunger for meaning in all departments of life was left hanging; the vibrant search of the self for import – the upshot of centuries of cultivating this search in the sphere of religion – remained, but was now (with the death of God) met by silence.

New notions of how to find redemption through time thus emerged: through promoting the good of humanity in this world, fulfilling the destiny of the nation and salvaging its memories and golden age, celebrating one's individual existence by attending to and extracting from each moment as much as possible, and so on. Time, however, was also harnessed to advance theories of a social-political order that allegedly develops throughout history. With the decline of natural law theories (and deism), moderns were facing an unbounded world in which their own Promethean powers were among the forces threatening to induce a menacing chaos (e.g., Mary Shelley's *Frankenstein*).[7] To counter this prospect, historical time was often used to interpret human events in such a way that a rational, reassuring arrangement was shown to be gradually mushrooming; Kant, Condorcet, Hegel, Comte, Marx, and Spencer all advanced a notion of an emerging order that hinged on an ontology of historical time and its progression.

In sum, then, modern men and women are often seen as historical beings who understand themselves in light of their position in a particular epoch; self-consciously and reflectively, it has been suggested, they should shape their identity and responsibility toward others based on this understanding. Grasping the nature of historical time accurately had become a precondition for living a fully meaningful life and for choosing a conduct that is met by a receptive human order. Time ceased to be an important element in a large corpus of theological thought and often became the foundation that defines individual existence and political order. The evaporation of eternity as the counterpoint to human time did not reduce the importance of the latter; on the contrary, it made historical-human time the foundation of our understanding of the world.

Modernity presents us, then, with a distinctive marriage: Radically conflicting temporal imaginations, each pulling the self in a different direction, nevertheless *gained increasing weight* in this epoch because

---

[7] See Eyal Chowers, *The Modern Self in the Labyrinth: Politics and the Entrapment Imagination* (Cambridge, MA: Harvard University Press, 2004), Chap. 1.

they shaped the way people understand themselves and the social order in which they are enmeshed. This marriage is naturally central for understanding the Jewish national revival as well, not only because this revival occurred in modernity and was shaped to a large extent by the dynamic among the temporal imaginations in this epoch, but also because Jews were probably more attentive to these imaginations than others. As I have suggested, the Jews were perhaps Europe's prime temporal agents, since they lacked alternative anchors of identity to claim with certainty as their own (such as land or state). In what follows, I will discuss the three primary temporal imaginations I sketched previously and mention their relationship to European Jews and Judaism. (While surely there are other temporal imaginations in modernity, these three are the most essential for the present study.)

Before discussing these imaginations, however, a few words about the term *temporal imagination* are in order.[8] Often, we use the word imagination to refer to the human ability to reproduce in the mind an object or event that was accessible to the senses prior to that reproduction; the imagination can also be creative, an original picture composed of elements of reality that have been experienced, stored – and rearranged in the mind. Time, however, cannot be sensed in this way; it is not palpable in the strictest sense. Temporal imagination means, rather, the ways in which people represent the nature of time: It could be conceived of as fragmented and chaotic, or as a purposeful totality in which each event finds its meaning in relation to the whole. It could be conceived of as composed of qualitative moments, each distinct and irreplaceable, or as composed of essentially identical segments that acquire their significance as a mass, as a sum. It could be conceived of as cyclical as Nature itself, or as telos driven, containing an end that is gradually being materialized, and so forth.

To be represented, temporal imaginations necessitate mental pictures, images, and symbols. Hence, Saturn (Kronos), who devours his children, is a symbol of the constant and unbeatable movement of time, the arrow is a symbol of linearity. The clock is a symbol of regularity and cyclicality, the hourglass is a symbol for time running out. In addition to visual representations, temporal imaginations are also associated with certain vocabularies, ones that – in contrast to God's Word – are concerned with change and mutability. The language of progress, for example, thus

---

[8] In developing the notion of "temporal imaginations," I am indebted to Charles Taylor, *A Secular Age* (Cambridge, MA: Harvard University Press, 2007), esp. Chap. 4.

advances notions such as the distant future, amelioration and better-ment, the malleability of human nature, humanity as an ultimate goal, destiny, inevitability, linearity.

By using the term, however, I do not mean to suggest that temporal imagination is merely a subjective experience, or the product of indi-vidual authors; rather, the term refers primarily to a *public mode* of thinking, talking, and picturing time. Temporal imaginations are social and cultural creations.[9] While I will explore these imaginations through the interpretations of texts, I have chosen those that articulate (and that helped to shape) widely shared understandings of time, rather than being merely the idiosyncratic creations of their authors.

I. KANT AND THE FUTURE INTEGRATION OF HUMAN SPACE

Zionism promised European Jews a way to improve their predicament and to create a modern society, polity, and economy in Palestine. "Every valuable invention which exists now, or lies in the future, must be used," writes Herzl. "By these means a country can be occupied and a State founded in a manner as yet unknown to History, and with possibilities of success such as never occurred before."[10] Relatively free from pre-existing fetters – ossified economic structure, class divisions, confining bureaucracy, and so forth – Zionism embraced the notions of progress and enlightenment that were integral to modern thought and practice. The Jewish State, its visionary professed, would be the ultimate embodi-ment of moderns' achievements in the sciences, culture, and government. The fact is, however, that Zionism emerged only once the promise of progress – as a notion pertaining to all spheres of human life – *had collapsed.*

---

[9] Temporal imaginations are also linked to certain practices, actions, events, insti-tutions, and technologies. Thus present-centeredness, for instance, is perhaps epitomized by the homogeneity of clock time, by new means of instantaneous com-munication, by practices such as the trading of stocks and goods, and by public insti-tutions that regulate the market and its constant changeability. While my discussion here focuses on temporal imaginations as they are expressed in texts and words, it is also important to remember that they also exist in everyday social life; in this sense they can "impose" themselves upon the individual, generating demands on and com-mitments within the self.

[10] Herzl, *The Jewish State* [Medinat hayehudim] ([1896] 1946), trans. Sylvie D'Avigdor, published by the American Zionist Emergency Council, at http://www.jewishvirtuallibrary.org/jsource/Zionism/herzl2e.html.

Numerous pictures of progress and/or teleology evolved during the late eighteenth and nineteenth centuries.[11] Yet Jews in Western and Central Europe found the liberal notion of progress especially appealing: It promised their incorporation – as a rapidly rising middle class – into the political, social-cultural, and economic life of the various states. Many Jews of the Haskala (the Jewish Enlightenment) were profoundly influenced by the visions of progress suggested by the Revolutionists and the Encyclopedists in France or by Lessing and Kant in Germany. They were attached to the notion of a state in which citizens are not distinguished by and discriminated against because of their religion or ethnic background, language, or appearance; their membership in the political community would be defined by law (or at least not defined by blood) and their broader acceptance granted by an ongoing *Bildung* of the individual. The idea of progress as future incorporation into the *Rechtsstaat* – and into the nation not defined by shared descent – propelled some of these Jews to see their distinctive religion as separate from their national identities, and often as secondary to the latter. Even proud Jewish thinkers such as Mendelssohn – who did not accept the notion of moral progress[12] – anticipated the privatization of religion and the increasing incorporation of Jews into the social and political life of Europe;[13] the Napoleonic Code and the German Constitution of 1871 later confirmed some of these aspirations. The Jewish hopes for a new time (especially until the ambiguous outcomes of the 1848 revolutions) were expressed by such diverse writers as Naftali Wessely, Lazarus Bendavid, Josef Wolf, Gotthold Salomon, Leopold Zunz, and Heinrich Graetz. Contemplating the status of German Jews, Isaac Marcus Jost even wrote that "all of us, who were still in our childhood thirty years ago, are witnesses to

[11] These include Comet's positivism, social Darwinism, biologically inspired nationalism and racism, Hegelian idealism, and historical materialism.

[12] "As far as the human race is concerned," writes Mendelssohn, "you will find no steady progress in its development that brings it ever closer to perfection." See M. Mendelssohn, *Jerusalem, or on Religious Power and Judaism*, trans. Allan Arkush (Hanover, NH: University Press of New England, 1983), p. 96.

[13] As Amos Elon notes, the young Mendelssohn, the future "German Socrates," entered Berlin in 1743 through the gate reserved only for Jews and cattle. He lived in the city without the right of citizenship and was constantly in fear of deportation; certainly he could not even dream of a university position. Yet about 150 years later, Cohen and other German Jews suggested that there is an affinity between Judaism and German idealism; they argued that Jews made a critical contribution to the history and culture of Germany and to the telos of humanity as a whole. See Amos Elon, *Requiem Germani* [The pity of it all: A history of the Jews in Germany 1743–1933] (Tel Aviv: Kinneret, Zmora-Bitan, Dvir, 2004), Chap. 2 (Hebrew version).

unbelievable transformations.... We have wandered, or better, flown through a thousand-year history."[14]

Moreover, not only were Jews attached to liberalism in the confines of the state, but they also embraced its meaning at the transnational level (this was perhaps most evident in the case of the Russian Jewish *maskilim*, the adherents of the Haskala). They often championed the idea of humanity's moral progress – of respect for individuals, of the expansion of political and social rights, of mutual responsibility and brotherhood, of rationalism in moral deliberations – for they saw these liberal ideas as fully in accord with the nature of Judaism and *its* own telos in history. Rather than accentuating the divergent origins of nations on earth, they believed that a shared, universalist home was possible. "The classical concept of our religion," wrote Herman Cohen, "points toward the future of mankind, and not toward the past of an ethnic community whose holiness, rather than being tied down to a geographical location, is bound up with its world historical idea. We ... see *the entire historical world as the future abode of our religion. And it is this future alone which we acknowledge as our true home*"[15] (my emphasis).

Now the thinker who had the most profound influence upon German Jews (and thus on Central European Jewry generally)[16] was Immanuel Kant. His Jewish followers included such diverse writers as Solomon Maimon, Salomon Ludwig Steinheim, Immanuel Yoel, Moritz Lazarus, Kurt Eisner, and Herman Cohen[17] (the latter even claimed that there was "an innermost accord between the systematic dispositions of Kant and the basic orientation of prophetic Judaism").[18] Although Kant's views about Judaism are debatable,[19] Jews saw his moral theory – which

---

[14] I. M. Jost, *Offenes Sendschreiben an Herrn Geh. Ober-Regierungs-Rath K. Streckfuss zur Verständigung über einige Punkte in den Verhältnissen der Juden* (Berlin, 1833), p. 65. Quoted here from Nils Roemer, "Between Hope and Despair: Conceptions of Time and the German-Jewish Experience in the Nineteenth Century," *Jewish History* 14 (2000): 350. I am helped here by Roemer's illuminating discussion on German Jews' response to modernity.

[15] Herman Cohen, *Reason and Hope: Selection from the Jewish Writings of Herman Cohen*, trans. Eva Jospe (New York: Norton, 1971), p. 170.

[16] The elite among young Eastern European Jews also tended to study in German universities, since their options in Poland and Russia were very limited.

[17] On the centrality of Kant to German Jews, see, e.g., Paul Mendes-Flohr, *German Jews: A Dual Identity* (New Haven, CT: Yale University Press, 1999), Chap. 2; and Zeev Levi, "Kant and Jewish Ethics in Modernity," *Daat*, no. 23 (Summer 1989): 89–97.

[18] Cohen, *Reason and Hope*, p. 88.

[19] Kant held anti-Semitic views and criticized Jews for their monetary conduct (as moneylenders) and their alleged attachment to worldly material concerns. Moreover, he saw Jews as epitomizing heteronomy, since the source of their morality was not

underscores the notion of the law and of obedience to it – as akin to the main tenets of Jewish morality as celebrated by the rationalist school in that faith. More generally, many German Jews viewed the moral, political, and historical facets of Kant's thought as the most solid foundation supporting their struggle to be incorporated into a liberal German state and into a shared human community. As George Mosse observed, "the attraction of Kant for so many Jewish thinkers was in large part based on his cosmopolitan humanism."[20] Given the enormous influence of Kant's temporal-moral vision on moderns in general and on Central European Jews in particular, we should look at it more closely.

History, for Kant, is a narrative with a purpose: to reach the highest good (*summum bonum*). This anticipated ideal provides an architectonic and totalizing structure for human striving and conduct in history, establishing a unity among the moral actions of each person and weaving the deeds of different persons into a meaningful whole. According to Kant, the highest good has two facets: It "is formed by the union of the greatest welfare of the rational beings in the world with the supreme condition of their good, or, in other words, by the union of universal happiness with the strictest morality."[21]

Externally (phenomenologically), the highest good optimizes our chances for happiness as natural beings, since it involves (utility-motivated) peace among nations, well-ordered political communities regulated by positive laws, and material well-being that is the outcome of civil and international peace. Internally (noumenologically), the highest good entails the establishment of an ethical, cosmopolitan community or kingdom of ends where all abide by the formal laws of practical reason.[22] As such, this condition epitomizes human virtue, the disposition of individuals to act continuously out of duty and keep in mind the good of mankind as a whole. For Kant, then, history is the theater where

autonomous reason and free will but uncritical obedience to God. For recent discussions on these matters, see Michael Mack, *German Idealism and the Jew* (Chicago: Chicago University Press, 2003), esp. Chap. 1; and Yirmiyahu Yovel, *Dark Riddle, Hegel, Nietzsche, and the Jews* (University Park: Pennsylvania State University Press, 1998), pp. 15–20.

[20] George Mosse, *German Jews Beyond Judaism* (New York: Hebrew Union College Press, 1997), p. 64.

[21] Immanuel Kant, *The Critique of Judgment*, trans. J. C. Meredith (Oxford: Oxford University Press, 1973), p. 122. For a discussion of the Enlightenment idea of happiness, see Darrin M. McMahon, *Happiness: A History* (New York: Atlantic Monthly Press, 2006).

[22] See Kant's discussion of the "Highest Good" in *Critique of Practical Reason*, trans. Mary J. Gregor (Cambridge: Cambridge University Press, 1996), pp. 227–46.

we establish the legal and political circumstances that will allow us both to realize ourselves as noumenal, moral beings and to be content as desiring creatures – without the threat of heteronomy and a structural contradiction between the two realms of our existence.[23] From this perspective of an impending harmony within the self *and* in relation to empirical reality, conceptions of history as chaos (e.g., Voltaire's *Candide*), decline (e.g., Rousseau's First Discourse), or lack of progress (Mendelssohn's *Jerusalem*) are deemed by Kant to be existentially and morally destructive. His critique of historical time is meant to refute them.

Kant famously posited two tracks of historical progress. The first, the external one, is a plan of Nature: In his philosophy of history,[24] he suggests a unidirectional conception of time[25] and progress that is

[23] Kant's vision concerning the interdependence of history, on the one hand, and of practical reason, on the other, has been elucidated in Yirmiyahu Yovel's *Kant and the Philosophy of History* (Princeton, NJ: Princeton University Press, 1980). See also Paul Stern, "The Problem of History and Temporality in Kantian Ethics," *Review of Metaphysics* 39 (March 1986): 505–45.

[24] As expressed in essays such as "Perpetual Peace," "Theory and Practice," and "Idea for a Universal History."

[25] Kant's view of historical, teleological time is presented independently from his epistemology. Nevertheless, there seems to be an elective affinity between time as introduced in Kant's philosophy of history and time as understood in Kant's inaugural dissertation and the transcendental aesthetics of the *First Critique*. In his dissertation, Kant argues that time is a necessary form of cognition, an a priori representation: "But pure intuition (human) is not a universal or logical concept *under which*, but a singular concept *in which*, all sensible things whatever are thought, and thus it contains the concepts of space and time. These concepts, since they determine nothing as to the quality of sensible things, are not objects of science, except in respect of quantity." See Immanuel Kant, "Inaugural Dissertation," in *Theoretical Philosophy, 1755–1770* (Cambridge: Cambridge University Press, 1992), p. 390. Time is the infinite container in which all experience transpires; it is the constantly moving, identical, and singular form that houses fleeting external phenomena and inner experiences. Time is quantifiable: Kant argues that we should think of time as we think of numbers; that is, time is composed of uniform units that are added to one another but are not inherently connected. Time is simply an accumulation of the identical. Kant also argues that this accumulation has a certain direction. We cannot represent time, he contends, "save in so far as we attend in the drawing of a straight line (which has to serve as the outer figurative representation of time)." See Immanuel Kant, *The Critique of Pure Reason* (New York: Macmillan, 1968), B 154; see also A 163 and B 203. If we were attuned to the workings of our consciousness, we would feel the accretion of moments as going from here to eternity – in an orderly and continuous fashion. There is a considerable literature on Kant's concept of time. See, Wayne Waxman, "What Are Kant's Analogies About?" *Review of Metaphysics* 47 (September 1993): 63–113; Lorne Falkenstein, "Kant's Account of Intuition," *Canadian Journal of Philosophy* 21 (June 1991): 164–93; William Barrett, *Heidegger, Kant, and Time* (Bloomington: Indiana University Press, 1971); and Sadik J. Al-Azm, *Kant's Theory of Time* (New York: Philosophical Library, 1967).

not dependent on human will and intentions. Rather, he transports Adam Smith's argument from the economic sphere to the historical and phenomenal one, depicting a historical, invisible-hand-like mechanism ("unsocial sociability") whereby men and women "unconsciously proceed toward an unknown natural end."[26] Human beings, who are driven solely by self-interest and a desire to preserve their possessions and status, gradually learn that their own personal good necessitates several things: republican-constitutional regimes that protect equal individual rights and promote human dignity, as well as demand public consent before engaging in wars; a league of nations that promotes and enforces peace, making citizens receptive to a cosmopolitan consciousness; and global trade and economic cooperation that enhance well-being, develop human abilities and technology, and ingrain civility into human intercourse. The unconscious historical mechanism grants a step-by-step improvement of the human condition, almost presupposing that the mere piling up of indistinguishable time units equals progress. While Kant is willing to concede that certain periods in history may be plateaus where the betterment of the human predicament is temporarily halted, his conception of time precludes ideas of decline or cyclicality: "Since the human race's natural end is to make steady cultural progress, its moral end is to be conceived as progressing toward the better. And this progress may well be occasionally *interrupted*, but it will never be *broken off*."[27]

The second track, the internal path of progress toward the highest good, depends on man and woman alone – on their ability to be the unconditional source of moral action and on their conscious decision and temporal awareness. As is well known, Kantian morality argues that individuals are able to be autonomous legislators of moral laws – unchained by natural causality – and that they express their freedom precisely by this act of legislation and by their capacity to act according to it. Here, the human will and practical reason spontaneously lead to action according to duty, severing the bonds of the moral mind

---

[26] Immanuel Kant, "Idea for a Universal History with a Cosmopolitan Intent," *Perpetual Peace and Other Essays* (Indianapolis: Hackett, 1983), p. 29.

[27] Kant, "Theory and Practice," in *Perpetual Peace and Other Essays*, p. 86. Kant does not suggest that the plan of Nature has an ontological status, only that this narrative is not contradicted by historical developments as we see them; it is an imaginary exercise of "as if," which may help us systematize history, assign it a telos, and remain hopeful about the future. Most importantly, this view of history would boost us in promoting our task as noumenal beings and advance the second narrative of progress.

from anticipated consequences or rewards; each time we enact the right universal law, propelled by the right inner motivations, we manifest our capacity to disengage from our phenomenal, body-dominated nature. Yet Kant suggests that acting in this way demands something in addition to duty: Since human beings are creatures hungry for meaning – and since they demand "Ends" and can generate them – their separate, atomistic actions require some totalizing End. The Kantian category of an "Idea" is germane here,[28] since by this he means a picture in the mind that is a priori and whole; it does not depend on external circumstances and knowledge of the world (although it may be inspired by them).[29]

The Enlightenment is an important stage in history, since now individuals are aware of the telos of history and their moral abilities and obligation to promote it. *The two paths of progress – of Nature and human deliberate action – have finally joined hands*, granting the acceleration of progress. As Habermas observes in a different context, in modernity the future has "already begun," and it is an "epoch that lives for the future, that opens itself up to the novelty of the future."[30] Kantianism exemplifies this openness and expectation; its conception of history legitimizes future fixation and human action that consciously propels history toward its architectonic goal. With Kant, humanity's redemption is no longer dependent on transcendental forces and is not a gift bestowed upon us; we are the agents responsible for bringing it about. The most basic imperative, he claims, is that individuals valorize the distant future as their chief concern and free themselves from their confined temporal horizons. The self who fathoms the inevitable flow of time and

---

[28] In the discussion of Kant's notion of "Idea" that follows, I am indebted to Golan Lahat, "Rethinking Progress: The Political Implications of Kant's Epistemology," Ph.D. diss., Tel Aviv University, 2007.

[29] The Idea provides ultimate ground for beliefs or actions, so that no further justification is called for. The Idea, moreover, is the fruit of "reflective judgment" (*reflectierende Urteilskraft*); in contrast to "determinate judgment" (*bestimmende Urteilskraft*), which "determines under universal transcendental laws furnished by understanding" and is intertwined with sense-data, reflective judgment is not constitutive of reality. Rather, reflective judgment can "only give as a law from and to itself" (Kant, *The Critique of Judgment*, pp. 18, 19; it generates regulative ideas that allow us to search for unity in events, systematize our experience and make it meaningful, and guide our future actions according to rules. The Idea points to what *should* exist in the world, the picture we must constantly assay to materialize – without necessarily accomplishing its outlines in practice. The progress toward an Idea – especially the Idea of the highest good – is very gradual, uncertain, and open to tactical changes according to circumstances: It is not dogmatic.

[30] Jürgen Habermas, *The Philosophical Discourse of Modernity* (Cambridge, MA: MIT Press, 1987), p. 5.

the possibility of shaping it cultivates faith in futurity. Kant emphasizes that the ability to be *future oriented* is "the distinguishing characteristic of man's superiority,"[31] and that this anthropological attribute should be celebrated and acquire moral import.

While Kant's concept of happiness remains mostly caught within the mechanistic and causal vista, he also presents the self as in need of a self-determined ultimate purpose that synthesizes its autonomous yet disconnected actions, rendering its evanescent existence an element within an enduring story. The ideal future is therefore not only something that we have a "duty to strive towards with all [our] abilities"[32] to realize but also a spiritual necessity. "[T]he need for an ultimate end that is set out by pure reason and that includes the totality of all ends within a single principle," writes Kant, "is a need felt by an unselfish will that extends beyond the observation of formal laws in bringing its object (the highest good) into existence."[33] Acting only according to the moral imperatives is virtuous, to be sure, but may render life aimless, without enduring achievement. Particularly with the emerging materialistic mind-set and secularization of modernity – when the present becomes overwhelmingly alluring – the self must expand its temporal frontiers, becoming interested in history not as the annals of actual, contingent and singular events but as containing a universal and overarching path. The self then becomes guided by a constant expectation and hope in regard to the ecumenical destiny of the human race; the rational comprehension of history's end is not a neutral, empty exercise of the mind, but molds the most basic ways we approach the world, supporting our audacious belief that we can shape reality.

The teleological concept of time, then, deepens our embeddedness in the human family. The individual, claims Kant, must be motivated by intergenerational commitment, having "the duty so to affect posterity that it will become continually better." Indeed, he writes, "this duty can rightfully be passed on from one generation to another."[34] Thus, he reintroduces the notion that successive generations bear obligations to one

[31] Kant argues that the "ability not merely to enjoy life's present moment but to make present to himself future, often very distant time, is the distinguishing characteristic of man's superiority, for in conformity with his vocation he can prepare himself in advance for distant ends." See Immanuel Kant, "Speculative Beginning of Human History," in *Perpetual Peace*, p. 52.

[32] Immanuel Kant, "Theory and Practice," in *Perpetual Peace*, p. 64n.

[33] Ibid.

[34] Ibid., p. 86.

another, arguing that once moderns cultivate horizons that encompass the necessary development of history, they must thereby view themselves as an integral part of that progressive movement. In this way, the future of civilization holds sway over the present. To deny our responsibility toward posterity and slight our location in time is not only to act selfishly and erroneously but also to display a lack of self-esteem. In fact, Kant presents a novel belief: Replacing aristocratic or republican notions of honor, history becomes the new proving ground for human character, where men and women confront their natural cowardice and display their "personal worth."[35]

To be worthy, however, the Kantian self must embrace temporal distancing as a way of life. "Nothing so much arrests the progress of things, nothing so much limits minds, as excessive admiration for the ancients," wrote Fontenelle in the early eighteenth century.[36] The Kantian, enlightened self is summoned to espouse a similar creed. It views knowledge of the world as well as self-knowledge as an open-ended project: It develops uneasiness with the given, cultivating a critical skepticism toward itself and the past it bears.[37] The rules human beings live by must have the authority of autonomous reason, not of transmitted tradition. *Selbstdenken* is imperative, since history is imbued with false beliefs and errors of thought, models of brutality and exploitation. Kant not only rejects the binding authority of inherited customs and practices but also demands a free public sphere in which old dogmas and conventions can be continuously exposed and criticized according to the contemporaneous level of enlightenment. In contrast to the customary Jewish view, Kant suggests that human progress hinges upon a *disenchantment with tradition* and the questioning of its present and future pertinence; he is undeterred by the threat of meaninglessness that this disenchantment

---

[35] Kant writes that "personal worth, which man can only give to himself, is presupposed by reason, as the sole condition upon which he and his existence can be a final end [of Creation]." We acquire a sense of personal worth by consistent moral action, aimed at realizing the highest good. See Kant, *The Critique of Judgment*, p. 153.

[36] Fontenelle, "Digression sur les anciens et les modernes," *Oeuvre*, 4 (Paris, 1767), quoted here from Paul De Man, "Literary History and Literary Modernity," *Daedalus* 99, no. 2 (1970): 404.

[37] "One age," writes Kant, "cannot bind itself, and thus conspire, to place a succeeding one in a condition whereby it would be impossible for the later age to expand its knowledge, to rid itself of errors, and generally to increase its enlightenment. That would be a crime against human nature, whose essential destiny lies precisely in such progress.... The criterion of everything that can be agreed upon as a law by a people lies in this question: Can a people impose such a law on itself?" See Immanuel Kant, "What Is Enlightenment," in *Perpetual Peace*, pp. 43–4.

may introduce, since man – as the End of Creation[38] – no longer needs the past as a source of import and direction.

Instead of highlighting the uniqueness and authority of tradition, the Kantian self is urged to foster the sameness within it, as defined by the formal laws of reason and the conception of human agency underlying them. The end of historical time is a kingdom of ends, where complete agreement reigns in the motivations, conduct, and ends of human beings. This sameness promises transparency – the confidence that the world is familiar and hospitable to us, that no deviant or inexplicable behavior will be encountered. Kant, however, urges that this transparency of the ethical community be buttressed in praxis by the following: first, a "universal civil society" where constitutions heed liberal notions, protecting the rights of individuals for privacy, equality, autonomy of choice and action, and more; and second, the existence of a great "body politic" (*Staatskorper*), by which he presumably means that political bodies would share some transnational organization or league.[39] This two-layered synchronization in the political world ensures a "universal cosmopolitan condition" (*ein allgemeiner weltburgerlicher Zustand*)[40] – and an all-engulfing harmony between human beings as moral agents and their political and legal institutions. We may say, then, that progressive, teleological time is needed in order to promise a homogeneous, predictable human space, and this space could expand, in principle at least, ad infinitum, to include the entire human race: "[A]ny assignable number of men ... cannot be regarded as the ethical state itself, but only as a branch of it; each partial and more limited society endeavoring to come to a complete uniformity and concordance with every other, in order to arrive at that absolute ethical whole."[41]

There are numerous elements in this Kantian conception of history, time, and self that were appealing to Jews, including the emphasis on duty

---

[38] Kant argues that man is the final purpose of Creation, since only he (as moral agent) is able to act freely, unconditioned by a chain of causality. See Kant, *Critique of Judgment*, pp. 100–8. See also Peter Fenves, *A Peculiar Fate: Metaphysics and World-History in Kant* (Ithaca, NY: Cornell University Press, 1991). For a discussion on the relation between freedom and teleological time in Kant, see Amihud Gilead, "Teleological Time: A Variation on a Kantian Theme," *Review of Metaphysics* 38 (March 1985): 529–62.

[39] Kant, "Idea for a Universal History," in *Perpetual Peace*, pp. 33, 38. Kant clarifies his conception of transnational political bodies in his later essay "Perpetual Peace."

[40] Kant, "Idea for a Universal History," in *Perpetual Peace*, p. 38 (translation altered).

[41] Immanuel Kant, *Religion Within the Boundary of Pure Reason*, trans. J. W. Semple (Edinburgh: Thomas Clark, 1838), p. 121.

and a heightened, universal demand for moral existence; the depiction of humans' yearning to overcome nature, including their own nature, and emulate God's transcendence; and the vision of an idealized, distant future that the individual has the obligation to promote. More specifically, Kant's philosophy helped pave the way for the Reform Movement in Germany, which saw Judaism as having a unique role in modernity: This faith no longer had narrow national aspirations and became the forerunner in celebrating the cosmopolitan vision. According to the reformer Abraham Geiger, a rabbi and leading figure in the emerging *Wissenschaft des Judentums*, the Jew is the consummate *Aufklärer*; history finally vindicates this believer since its true telos and import now shine in conformity with the spirit of the Jewish faith. The dispersion of the Jews all over the world served a universal purpose because Judaism promoted the idea that humans are equal, spiritual beings with divine-like moral capabilities.[42] "I believe," Geiger declares, "that Judaism is above any national body, since its mission is to unite and affirm all peoples and languages. Therefore, it is the primary obligation of all believers of Israel to free Judaism from any national boundaries, which do not belong to its essence and only restrict its development. Instead, Judaism should be transformed from a religion of one nation to a religion of the world."[43]

This vision was later articulated even more forcefully by Herman Cohen. He saw himself as a fully German citizen and patriot, and expressed allegiance to the *Rechtsstaat* as a great achievement of civilization. Attacking Zionists such as Martin Buber for their inability to separate religion from nationality, he claimed that "Jews have an ethical obligation to the modern state,"[44] for it has granted them equal civil and political rights and invited them to take part in the cultural and intellectual life of the country. To him, Jews should maintain their heritage and distinctiveness, yet they are a part of the German state and do not need a Jewish political body in the Holy Land in order to feel rooted. But Cohen goes beyond politics, averring that there is "an innermost accord"

---

[42] Abraham Geiger, *Judaism and Its History* (London: University Press of America, 1985), p. 211.

[43] Abraham Geiger, *Nachgelassene Schriften* (Berlin, 1875–8), letter written on April 9, 1841. Quoted here from Micha Josef Berdyczewski, *Kol ma'amarei Micha Josef Berdyczewski* [The collected essays of Micha Josef Berdyczewski] (Tel Aviv: Am Oved, 1954), p. 95. For a contemporary discussion of the Reform movement, see Michael Mayer, *Response to Modernity: A History of the Reform Movement in Judaism* (Oxford: Oxford University Press, 1988).

[44] Cohen, *Reason and Hope*, p. 166.

between "the German spirit and our Messianic religiosity," a profound affinity epitomized in the writings of Kant. Cohen, who devoted a well-known essay to elucidating these affinities, notes that in both Kant and Judaism God is abstract, wholly transcendental, an Idea that does not have tangible manifestations. More generally, Judaism is a rational religion (especially as it was interpreted by Maimonides), one that of course does not deny Revelation but suggests that the divine "Law" also has justifications that are explicable to human reason; this moral, sensible Law is based on notions of human duty rather than on a eudaemonic principle, and on freedom of choice rather than blind obedience.

Judaism, observes Cohen, is a religion that takes history as its plane of development and the sphere in which human perfection must be cultivated; it takes, moreover, the entire human race as the "End" of its messianic mission. Judaism is not merely a religion of an ethnic group, concerned with its own redemption, attached to a particular piece of land. For Cohen, the essence of this "world religion" (beyond its monotheism) is its faith in the holiness of man and woman. Humans, for both Kant and Judaism (as intimated in the Book of Genesis), are the final purpose of Creation. Kant also continues the insights of the prophets by suggesting that humans' will epitomize their moral-historical mission in conditions of peace and brotherhood among nations – without abolishing the existence of separate nations (*Goyim*). Cohen even asserts that Judaism and Kant share the same orientation toward time: The former is a religion centered on hope and faith in the future, on "turning away from the actually given," and on "the liberation of man's mind from the overpowering grip of reality,"[45] it assumes a philosophical grasp of possibilities and ideals to be materialized in history, rather than an imprisonment within empirical conditions.[46] (And in fact, as Y. C. Yerushalmi has observed, there was very little historiography by Jews until modern times.)[47] The prophets were the first to free themselves from narrow political ambitions for their own people, from the chains of space and place, from the confining present or the longing for the lost past – and

---

[45] Ibid., p. 184.

[46] Cohen was among those neo-Kantians who criticized the dominance of historicism in German intellectual life and argued that philosophy should provide the foundation for interpreting history and directing its future course. On this point, see David Myers, *Resisting History: Historicism and Its Discontents in German-Jewish Thought* (Princeton, NJ: Princeton University Press, 2003), Chap. 2.

[47] Yosef Hayim Yerushalmi, *Zakhor: Jewish History and Jewish Memory*, The Samuel and Althea Stroum Lectures in Jewish Studies (Seattle: University of Washington Press, 2005).

to think of a shared future of humanity built through mutual ethical conduct. "As a historical concept of time, this notion [of the future] constitutes the true significance and real discovery of their messianic thinking,"[48] concludes Cohen. In this sense, modernity is the vindication of the prophets' conception of time and history.

II. SEMICYCLICALITY AND THE POETIC REDEMPTION OF TIME

As Cohen was writing these pronouncements about the essential affinity between modernity, Enlightenment, and future-oriented Judaism, many other Jews and Europeans generally were already viewing the notion of progress with growing skepticism. This doubt and disillusionment fed the emergence of the second temporal imagination of modernity, which could be termed semicyclical: A profound qualitative affinity is supposed to exist between the present and a distinct moment from the past, an affinity that transforms the meaning of both moments.

Visions suggesting that cyclicality rules political life are nothing new, of course. Polybius's anacyclosis, according to which different

PHOTO 2. A mosaic floor with Hebrew-Aramaic inscription in a fifth-century synagogue in Jericho. Photo by Milner Moshe, May 19, 1968. Courtesy of the Government Press Office, Israel.

[48] Cohen, *Reason and Hope*, p. 120.

constitutions logically follow one another is a well-known example.[49] Polybius suggests that "such is the cycle of political revolution, the course appointed by nature in which constitutions change, disappear, and finally return to the point from which they started."[50] The modern semicyclical vision is, however, distinct. Firstly, the cyclicality it discovers in the world of politics and in other realms of human existence is not based on *physis*, cosmological patterns, Nature, or any other necessity that inheres in things; in modernity, cyclicality is most often an option – not an underlying ontological structure. The affinity between the present and a particular moment of the past is not simply objectively given, but rather depends also on contemporary agents' ability to see and follow this affinity. Moreover, previous cyclical visions sprang from a sense of decline and decay and from a longing for a bygone golden era; the modern semicyclical temporal imagination, in contrast, often submits a critique of contemporary ideas of narrativity, teleology, and especially incessant betterment and progress in history – and shapes itself in light of this critique. It is the unwelcome upshots of the ideology and practice of progress (even when this progress is successful according to its own measures) that opened the way for the emergence of the semicyclical temporal imagination.

Yet this imagination is also distinct since it involves new notions of the self, which evolved during the nineteenth century. The self is seen now as lacking a coherent and stable experience, as constantly on the move and flooded with unrelated pieces of information. Tradition and the social structure of memory (e.g., a community with its holidays and rituals) have been almost demolished, and thus memory has fewer anchors and triggers than in former generations; memory has thus become more a matter of chance, of unpredictable opportunities one must learn to grab. The past is not lost, yet it is less accessible; much more effort is needed for resurrecting it. In order to create an affinity between the remembered past and the present, one cannot rely on the unchangeability of the landscape and location or on the stability of collective practices; no, such affinity demands creativity, flights of the imagination, and generally an aesthetic-poetic existence.

Now, many writers can be seen as contributors to the evolution of this imagination (Henri Bergson, William James, H. G. Wells, and more), but perhaps the most important ones were Freud, Proust, and (later) Walter

---

[49] According to Polybius, the order is as follows: monarchy, kingship, tyranny, aristocracy, oligarchy, democracy, and ochlocracy.

[50] Polybius, *Histories*, trans. W. R. Paton (New York: G. P. Putnam's, 1923), VI. 9.

Benjamin (who, while not yet writing in the first years in which Zionism began to form, perhaps best articulates a temporal dimension central to this movement). Presumably, the three writers' Jewish roots had something to do with their valorization of memory; for lack of space, however, I will not explore this particular influence here.

Before examining the semicyclical imagination, a few words on Zionism and progress are called for. The significant critique of progress and of the Enlightenment's optimism about the future began with Rousseau and Hamann, if not before, but it gained increasing momentum toward the middle of the nineteenth century. Some writers at that time predicated – on the basis of the second law of thermodynamics, the dissipation of mechanical energy, and the rise of entropy – that the earth would be unfit for habitation in the future (William Thomson Kelvin and later Oswald Spengler). Speed and technological inventions were blamed for increasing the tension and pressure of modern life, for creating endless new sensory shocks on the brain, for causing diseases of the nervous system and the functioning of the mind – in short, for causing degeneration (George Beard, James Crichton Browne, and especially Max Nordau).[51] Nietzsche believed that in modernity all the values, ideas, and purposes cultivated in Western tradition had been broken, that nihilism was becoming pervasive; Weber later feared the "iron cage" and the loss of meaning in a world dominated by instrumental rationality and bureaucratic mass organization. The growing urbanization and density of human population led to concerns about cities: their pollution and lack of hygiene, as well as the anonymity and the breakdown of solidarity they fostered. Cities were also considered to be the locus of booming social problems, such as prostitution and venereal disease, suicide, and crime (Morel, Lombroso, Maudsley). Still others were alarmed by the rise of the mob or crowd in these cities – a new entity that was irrational, uncontrollable, and unpredictable and that increasingly threatened the social and political order of Western societies (Taine, Le Bon).[52] This list could be expanded.

The decline, degeneration, or even breakdown were presented as either those of humanity at large, of Western civilization, of certain races, or of distinct nations and states. While the Jews could probably not be

---

[51] See Stephen Kern, *The Culture of Time and Space, 1880–1918* (Cambridge, MA: Harvard University Press, 1983), p. 125.

[52] See Daniel Pick, *Faces of Degeneration: A European Disorder, c. 1848–c. 1918* (Cambridge: Cambridge University Press, 1989).

blamed for the threat of increased entropy, they were often blamed for many other sources of supposed threats to organic societies: the weakening of patriotism and the rise of cosmopolitanism, the atomization brought about by the capitalist social order, the ascent of self-interest and of calculating commercial spirit, the "genetic weakening" of other races, the too-slow realization of the promised human progress because of their lack of *Bildung* (in Germany) or *régénération* (in France) – and so on. Thus, the Jews were among the first not only to embrace the creed of progress and especially the political principles of liberalism but also to experience the failures of this worldview, the shadows of modernity, if you will.

Jews had specific reasons for being leery about the notion of progress. More than others, they had grounds to believe that progress is not an all-embracing phenomenon, that the different spheres of human life do not march forward hand in hand as many believed just a few generations before. For example, during the same year that Herzl published *The Jewish State* (1896) – and after reporting in his newspaper from Paris about the Dreyfus trial – he wrote a short story about a guided flying machine. There, Herzl expresses faith in and admiration for the technological inventions of the modern age, but he is also unsure about the way these inventions will be used. He notes that the harbingers of change still experience shame and ridicule: It is evident that not much improvement was made in humans' prejudices, tolerance, and overall moral fabric despite the unfolding scientific revolution. The flying machine, for instance, might be used for beneficial and benign purposes by the good people of the future, but, he observes, it is also possible that this invention would be used for the purposes of war and would "raise new forms of misery."[53]

Herzl's spirit of skepticism toward human nature generally, and the possibility of peaceful cooperation among nations particularly, is in fact evident in his very understanding of the nation. A national consciousness, he argued, does not emerge because of a common language, religion, or even laws and mores; some of these, at least, might also be the effects of national life, not necessarily its causes. Rather, according to Herzl, this consciousness emerges out of shared memories and current

---

[53] Theodor Herzl, *Siporim*, [Stories] (Jerusalem: Zionist Library, 1971), p. 91 (in Hebrew). Herzl sometimes compared this machine to the Jewish State and himself to its inventor, since both this machine and the state demand departure from existing reality, faith in the imagination, and an ability to steer in the air, as it were. See ibid., p. 86n.

needs, and thus he concludes that "the nation is an historical group of people, whose bonds with each other are evident, and *who are united by a common enemy*" (my emphasis).⁵⁴ Herzl's grim view of national politics as involving constant strife between the nation and its foe(s) is greatly removed from the universalist, liberal visions of the nineteenth century. Anti-Semitism was for him a manifestation of a more general phenomenon concerning the relations among peoples with collective self-awareness. This vision, needless to say, also raises questions as to how the Jewish state will be able to overcome national diversity within its bounds. (To be fair with Herzl, in his utopian society – as described in his novel *Altneuland* – the Jews and Arabs cooperate with each other fully,⁵⁵ have equal citizenship status and rights, and experience no discrimination on an individual or group basis.)

Other Zionists expressed similar doubts regarding moral-political progress. Herzl's greatest critic, Ahad Ha'am, argued that the Dreyfus affair exposed the slogan "freedom, equality, and fraternity" as empty in the case of the Jews; a century of progress since the Revolution and Napoleonic Code had led nowhere, in their case. Perhaps moral progress is not a chimera for other French people and is relevant for them, he wrote; it does not apply, however, to the predicament of Jews in their midst, for Jews are denied the fruits of humanism and even simple generosity and fairness. "The weight of general progress should be recognized, as long as one acknowledges the exception to this progress," he notes. "This exception is the Jews." It is as if people say, "when we are concerned with humanity, we will forget the Jews, and when we deal with the Jews we will forget humanity."⁵⁶

---

⁵⁴ Theodor Herzl, "Hayahdot haleumit shel Dr. Gidman" [The national Judaism of Dr. Gidman] (1897), at http://www.benyehuda.org/herzl/herzl_009.html.

⁵⁵ In Herzl's novel, the native Arab of Palestine explains to visitors who come to examine the Jewish state that Jews brought many advantages for the locals: "places to work, food, success." "You cannot imagine," he tells the foreign visitor, "a more extreme squalor than the one that existed in an Arab village in Palestine at the end of the last [nineteenth] century. The peasants used to reside in small clay huts that were not even fit for cattle. The children used to sit naked and neglected ... and grow up like animals. All this has changed now." Theodor Herzl, *Altneuland* (1902), http://www. benyehuda.org/herzl/tel_aviv.html. Throughout this work, in my translations from the Hebrew version of this book I have consulted the English translation from the original German. See Theodor Herzl, *Old New Land*, trans. Lotta Levensohn (New York: M. Wiener, 1987).

⁵⁶ Ahad Ha'am, "Haprogress vsina'at Israel [Progress and the hatred of Israel]" (1898), p. 1 at http://www.benyehuda.org/ginzburg/Gnz_048.html.

Herzl's and Ahad Ha'am's disenchantment with the ideology of progress and liberalism is nothing compared to Jabotinsky's, however. In
1910, the future leader of the Revisionist Party wrote an essay titled
"Homo Homini Lupus" (after a familiar Roman proverb). Although
Jabotinsky's picture of a Jewish state contained significant liberal principles (and multicultural ones; he thought there should be collective,
political-cultural rights for Arab citizens), he disavows them on the international level. Reflecting on the predicament of Jews and other minorities in Russia, he notes that liberalism is "a universal dream woven out
of sympathy, tolerance, a belief in the basic goodness and righteousness
of man." Yet this is a dangerous dream, avers Jabotinsky:

> It was a wise philosopher who said "man is a wolf to man"; worse than the wolf
> is man to man, and will not change for many days to come. Stupid is the person
> who believes in his neighbor, good and loving as the neighbor may be; stupid
> is the person who relies on Justice. Justice exists only for those whose fists and
> stubbornness make it possible to realize it.... Do not believe anyone, be always
> on guard.[57]

This dark picture of human relations and politics lead Jabotinsky to
embrace the well-known policy of the "Iron Wall," according to which
it is expected that the settlement in Palestine will be fiercely opposed by
the Arab native population (a legitimate opposition from their point of
view) and the only way to succeed in the Zionist project is thus by relying
on an uncompromising, united, and resolute front of the Jewish nation –
and on the barrel of the gun.

Zionists disagreed among themselves on many issues, but the need to
distinguish sharply between the moral-political and the technological-
functional spheres of progress seems to be a conviction most of them
shared (see also my discussion of Borochov in the next chapter). While
various strands of Zionism continued to embrace and express faith in
modernity as promising tangible advancement and betterment in the
material spheres of life, the Kantian, cosmopolitan moral vision (as
well as other competing visions of moral improvement) was increasingly
rejected by disenchanted and disappointed Jews in France, Germany,
and Eastern Europe. Due to the personal experiences of Jews since
the late nineteenth century, the growing conflict with the Palestinians,
and surely after the Holocaust, their overwhelming belief was that it is

---

[57] Vladimir Jabotinsky, "Homo Homini Lupus," in *Ktavim*, vol. 9 (Jerusalem: Ari
Jabotinsky Print, 1947), p. 265 (in Hebrew).

wishful thinking to conflate evident scientific, technological, and economic progress with the manner in which people perceive and deal with
one another as political and moral beings.

Zionists did not relinquish the hope of creating a just society in
Palestine, and at times evoked the vision of the Jews as a "chosen people" or a "people with a special destiny" (*am segula*); in fact, it was
essential for their self-understanding that they could introduce novel
notions of social equality, could sustain a corruption-free society, could
uphold the principle of "doing the right thing," morally speaking. But
most of them (with the exception of the more radical socialists) lost their
faith in "humanity" and its moral progress, and the longing for peace
with one's neighbors was joined with profound suspicion concerning the
possibility of such peace. The circumstances in Palestine seem to have
reaffirmed their own historical consciousness and the cognitive lenses
through which they examined reality. Writing after the fall of Tel-Hai
(1920) and the murder of the settlers there, including Yosef Trumpeldor,
Y. H. Brenner (who would also be killed by Arabs in Jaffa about a year
later) wrote that the "assurances of the Arab, rebelling leaders, according to which their sword will not hover over the Jewish settlements,
were revealed as worthless, *and one should never believe in the Arab's
words* ... but the heart, the faithful heart, it believed in miracles"[58] (my
emphasis). The hopes that sprang from the hearts of Jews (and of many
moderns generally) – of mutual support and tolerance among neighbors,
of trust among nations and peoples – had been nurtured in Europe and
had been badly crushed there; now these hopes failed to find a last refuge in Palestine and were being gradually banished from the hearts of
Zionists.

To be sure, the local Arabs were at times brutal and violent in their
response to the newcomers, yet it would also be fair to say that the
Zionists' policies and conduct in Palestine were partly shaped by their
prior, disenchanted conceptions, and the latter limited their ability to
picture, and their interest in picturing, significant cooperation among
Jews and Arabs (a cooperation that would have been perhaps impossible anyway). Regrettably, the periods in which European Jews had
alternative memories and experiences were too short or too distant to
offer a different tradition and inspire a less grim political vision (and
Jews from Arab countries, who had more multifaceted experiences in
relation to their neighbors, arrived for the most part only after 1948).

[58] Y. H. Brenner, "Tel-Hai" (1920), at http://www.benyehuda.org/brenner/brenner207.html.

The tragic consequences of this lack are still evident today. Jabotinsky's "Homo Homini Lupus" seems to be more relevant than ever to the political frame of mind of the Israeli Right, and for a long time this mind-set fostered the impasse and immobility in the region.

The disenchantment with certain aspects of so-called progress thus left many Jews skeptical about future fixation. But this skepticism regarding the mooring of identity to a distant time also stems from their concern about the breakdown of tradition and of a formerly intimate relation to the past. Jewish identity in the Diaspora was essentially dependent upon a cultivated temporal existence – Jews' ability to reproduce elements of the past in the collective and individual present. Jews in exile had no landscape they could claim as their own, certainly not one they could claim by virtue of their Jewishness; for the most part, they had no monuments, buildings, or sacred and symbolic sites that embodied and could reactivate their memories as a people. Their identity was dependent upon the comprehension of and familiarity with texts, and on a determination to practice the precepts and laws dictated by these texts in their lives; it was an identity that celebrated the power of memory. The rituals and the calendar, the cycle of reading the Torah and the holidays – these allowed collective memory and individual memory to come together and foster each other. The past was not understood through historiography and as a series of distant and detached events, but was something with which one engaged through ongoing dialogue. Future-fixation (as well as present-centeredness) *challenged the role of memory and disrupted this dialogue with tradition*, and the Jews were more vulnerable to such losses than other people. In short, Jews were not only disenchanted with some aspects of the idea of progress – which failed to incorporate them into their respective states as equal citizens and worthy human beings – but also fearful of the loss of their distinct collective past. Modernity threatened to rob them of the latter without granting them the former, to impoverish their particularity without securing them universality.

The modern attempt to develop a semicyclical temporal imagination presupposes the celebration of memory as critical to human identity. This memory, however, is distinctively modern, since it underscores discontinuity and complexity, unpredictability and lack of self-transparency – and the *indestructibility* of the past against all odds. Thus, for example, Theodule Ribot wrote (1875) that "the phenomena of memory, considered in their *ultima ratio*, are explained by the law of indestructibility of force, of the conservation of energy, which is one of the most important laws of the universe. Nothing is lost; nothing that exists can ever cease to be." Then he added these remarkable claims:

We daily experience thousands of perceptions, but none of these, however vague and insignificant, can perish utterly. After thirty years some effort – some chance occurrence, some malady – may bring them back ... the human soul is like a deep and somber lake, of which light reveals only the surface; beneath, there lies a whole world of animals and plants, which [a] storm or an earthquake may suddenly bring to light before the astonished consciousness.[59]

These insights about memory in general and unconscious memory in particular are also shared by psychoanalysis and form a critical part of it. The distant and potent past of the individual and the collective is always lurking nearby, able to assert itself: "[T]he primitive stages [of the mind] can always be reestablished; the primitive mind is, in the fullest meaning of the word, imperishable."[60] In psychoanalysis, selfhood and memory become inexorably linked, and time loses its linear nature. "There is nothing in the Id that corresponds to the idea of time ... no alteration in its mental processes is produced by the passage of time,"[61] writes Freud. Memory traces are contained chaotically and nonchronologically in the mind; they do not form a meaningful story, an order of one kind or another – each stands as a fragment by itself. Time is composed of qualitative moments: In the Freudian view, repressed and potent memories may have critical effects on the self, creating cycles of behavior, feelings, experiences that shape the self and repeat themselves again and again. The present is a theater in which dramas from early childhood play themselves out, without resolution, and engender ongoing emotional suffering. On the basis of these insights, Freud thus advances a new path for healing the self, suggesting that it should uncover, reexperience, and integrate its past (especially its early past). "What we desire," he writes, "is that the ego, emboldened by the certainty of our help, shall dare to take the offensive in order to conquer what has been lost."[62]

59 Théodule Ribot, *Heredity: A Psychological Study of Its Phenomena, Laws, Causes, and Consequences* (New York: Appleton, 1891), pp. 46, 48. Quoted in Daniel Pick, *Faces of Degeneration*, p. 71.

60 Sigmund Freud, "The Disillusionment of the War," in *The Standard Edition of the Complete Psychological Works of Sigmund Freud*, ed. J. Strachey and A. Freud (London: Hogarth Press, 1953–74), vol. 14, p. 286 (hereafter cited as *SE*). My discussion of Freud here is based on the discussion in my book, *The Modern Self in the Labyrinth*, Chap. 3.

61 Sigmund Freud, "New Introductory Lectures," *SE*, vol. 22, p. 74.

62 Sigmund Freud, "An Outline of Psychoanalysis," *SE*, vol. 23, p. 178.

This path of recovering the distant past (and of skipping what Freud considers the psychologically dead time of the in-between), presupposes both that a) memories cannot vanish and are stored in the unconsciousness (individual and collective) and that b) psychic illness is profoundly associated with deliberate forgetfulness, with repression. "Gaps appear in the patient's memory even while he narrates his case: actual occurrences are forgotten, the chronological order is confused or causal connections are broken, with unintelligible results," Freud notes. "*No neurotic case history is without amnesia of some kind or other.*"[63] (In his view, this amnesia is most often linked to the self's psycho-sexual history and its interactions with the environment in this arena.) To surmount neurosis (compulsive behavior, melancholia, phobias, guilt, bodily symptoms, etc.), the resistance to memory must be overcome through a method based on dialogue between therapist and patient; language is the venue for healing, for regaining what has been lost and what actively conceals itself. "The patient brings out of the armory of the past the weapons with which he defends himself against the progress of the treatment – weapons that we must wrest from him one by one," explains Freud.[64] The past is regained and freedom from its dysfunctional effects established by working through formidable obstacles: To Freud, these obstacles stem from the fact that too much of the present psychic order is invested in leaving things as they are, in living unaware of the forces actually at work in the mind. The patient does not recover the past as a distant observer, however, but must to an extent *relive it*, own it, and incorporate the memory into his or her consciousness and self-narration.

Now it is debatable to what degree Freud was able to successfully apply his understanding of the self to the level of the group (he made a number of attempts). Be that as it may, many of the Freudian themes discussed here – the past as traumatic and as demanding healing, the nonlinear notion of time and the persistence of distant memories, the difficulty of shaking up the present even if it is a sick present, and the need to relive the past, not just to know it – all these and more were relevant to Zionism and were developed in the writings and practice of that national movement around the same time that Freud was conceptualizing his psychoanalytic theory.

[63] Sigmund Freud, "Psycho-analytic Procedure," *SE*, vol. 12, p. 251 (my emphasis). On the place of memory in Freud, see R. Terdiman, *Present Past: Modernity and the Memory Crisis* (Ithaca, NY: Cornell University Press, 1993).

[64] Sigmund Freud, "Remembering, Repeating, and Working-Through," *SE*, vol. 12, p. 151.

Another, somewhat similar celebration of memory is offered by Freud's contemporary, Proust. In the final book of *À la recherche du temps perdu* [Remembrance of Things Past], Proust suggests that most of our lives – especially in modernity – are devoted to our immersion in the present: to constant communication with others, to the absorption in an environment filled with excitations, information, diversions. We approach this contemporaneous world by trying to control it rationally and in a utilitarian fashion, trusting that our conscious intentions and will can guide us from first to last. This reason-based, temporal orientation is flat and shallow, suggests Proust, a distraction from the true meaning of life and from authentic existence. The latter, rather, involves cessation from being wholly engrossed in the present and future and, instead, attention paid to our inner selves by resurrecting distant memories, which are always distinct to each individual and are bound to specific places. "These resurrections of the past," writes Proust, "are so complete that they not only force our eyes to cease seeing the room which is before them ... they force our nostrils to breathe the air of those places which are, nevertheless, so far away."[65]

Memories depend on a *qualitative* experience of time. They are stimulated by the smell of bread coming from a bakery, by the color of an old bicycle, or by certain words (for instance, when we open an old, shabby book. As Proust writes, "a name read in a book of former days contains within its syllables the swift wind and the brilliant sun of the moment when we read it").[66] Memory surely involves a mental activity, that of the imagination being able to put forward an image that no longer actually exists; nevertheless, this activity both depends on the senses, which trigger remembrance in the first place, and retrieves a rich sensual reality from the past, a fullness that contains concrete features and texture. To relish memory means to celebrate humans' ability to imprint within themselves distinct events and experiences – as well as landscapes, smells, sounds, tastes. It is precisely the *fusion* of these events, on the one hand, together with the sensual context, on the other, that is vital to humans' being and identity. When this fusion occurs, a lost time as well as a lost self are regained.

Proust finds books particularly interesting in terms of the aforementioned fusion, since through them a sensual experience of place,

---

[65] Marcel Proust, *Time Regained: In Search of Lost Time* (London: Chatto & Windus, 1957), p. 220.
[66] Ibid., p. 233.

language, and selfhood is intertwined (as Zionists would later suggest in regard to the Bible). He explains:

A book we read does not remain forever united only with what was then around us; it remains just as faithfully one with us as we then were and can only be recovered by the sensibility restoring the individual as he then was.[67]

Images from the past, however, are not retrieved through a commanding will, logical procedures, or general rules; they are revived, rather, by "an act of creation in which no one can take our place and in which no one can collaborate."[68] These images impress themselves upon us unpredictably, and we must summon the courage and curiosity to follow the opportunity they offer, guided only by our instincts and intuitions. Proust feels that remembrance is a good in itself, that it brings the self pleasure and happiness, even when the events recalled are not necessary cheerful ones; here, of course, he seems to submit a mirror image of Freud. Proust suggests further that when one image leads to another and one mode of former existence and fragment of life leads to the next, then the individual who is willing to let the past speak is able to regain that past, to form a narrative, to own his or her life. Remembrance is a venue for self-knowledge and hence for authentic existence, for life according to facets of the self we have not been aware of.

What is most important for Proust, it seems, is the sense that by joining the past and the present we are able to transcend the ongoing flow of time and establish a new sense of temporal existence:

The noise of the spoon upon the plate, the unevenness of the paving-stones, the taste of the Madeleine, imposed the past upon the present and made me hesitate as to which time I was existing in.... [T]he being within me which sensed this impression sensed what ... it had in common in former days and now, sensed its extra-temporal character, a being which only appeared when, through the medium of the identity of present and past, it found itself in the only setting in which it could exist and enjoy the essence of things, that is, outside Time.

Let a sound, a scent already heard and breathed in the past be heard and breathed anew, simultaneously in the present and in the past, real without being actual, ideal without being abstract, then instantly the permanent and characteristic essence hidden in things is freed and our true being which has for long seemed dead but was not so in other ways awakes and revives, thanks to this celestial nourishment. An instant liberated from the order of time has recreated in us man liberated from the same order ... so that he should be conscious of

[67] Ibid., p. 234.
[68] Ibid., p. 226.

it.... [W]e understand that the name of death is meaningless to him, for, placed beyond Time, how can he fear the future?[69]

The unity of past and present involves a kind of bliss that comes from transcending the flow of Time, overcoming the chain of causality and linear history that we are imprisoned in; biological death is doomed to happen, of course, but those who experience the temporal bond of distant moments know that (at certain instances at least) the deep structure of human existence is cyclical and thus immutable. To be precise, the present is never the same as the past, and cyclicality does not mean their full identity. Rather, the two moments contain an essential quality that is akin – one that needs to be unearthed.

Our senses and memories point to this likeness, yet cyclicality and temporal transcendence are not simply given to us or effortlessly "there." This cyclicality also requires our creativity and aesthetic-stylistic capabilities, our ability to establish the bond between distant moments through language, especially metaphors. The latter, Proust suggests, establish a "verbal alliance," articulating a singular experience that is vague and uncertain – and initially expressed merely in images – and turn it through the individual's linguistic interpretation into an experience that is explicit and solid. Poetic experience and writing leave behind us a remnant of our sense of overcoming linear time. Temporal cyclicality, transcendence of death, and language are utterly interwoven. The affinity of this view with certain aspects of Zionism does need articulation.

Both Proust and Freud seem to have established the foundation for Walter Benjamin's view of historical time, including his skepticism toward the notion of social and moral betterment. Yet Benjamin is a far harsher critic of progress than both. "The concept of progress should be grounded in the idea of catastrophe," writes Benjamin. "That things 'just keep on going' *is* the catastrophe."[70] Progress in general, and the modern acceleration toward its realization in particular, presuppose constant renewal and the nonidentity of one moment with the next. With each passing minute, the difference between the present and the past is established, the distance from yesterday affirmed by the constantly renewed

---

[69] Ibid., pp. 216, 218.

[70] Walter Benjamin, *Benjamin: Philosophy, History, Aesthetics*, ed. Gary Smith (Chicago: University of Chicago Press, 1989), p. 64 [N 9a, 1]. It must also be noted, however, that in some of Benjamin's essays, especially in the early 1930s, the critique of progress and technology is less clear-cut. See Michael Lowy, *Redemption and Utopia: Jewish Libertarian Thought in Central Europe, A Study in Elective Affinity*, trans. Hope Heaney (London: Athlone Press, 1992), p. 108.

novelty of the now. In other words, progress and future-fixation generate forgetfulness, and for Benjamin this oblivion is the *gist* of the modern catastrophe. Life without integrated memory is doomed to repeat the same cycle of violence, exploitation, and injustice that is conspicuous in human history, a cycle he designates as "mythic." Our "remembered world (*Merkwelt*) breaks up more quickly, the mythic in it surfaces more quickly and crudely." Hence, he adds, "a completely remembered world must be set up even faster to oppose it."[71] Human history, in Benjamin's view, is a collection of catastrophes that accumulates most rapidly when there is uncritical faith in the amelioration brought about by omnipotent human action. The modern – typified by a future-oriented gaze and a creed of hope – is especially prone to forgetting that the march of civilization is based on subjection and domination[72] – and that this barbarism is a constitutive, not a contingent, characteristic of history.[73]

For Benjamin, the attempt to resurrect a remembered world to combat the mythic character of human history will have to begin by introducing a novel concept of time, one that is not captivated by the hunger for the new but is, rather, open to what has long passed by:

The "Then" has always been interpreted as "fixed" and the present's efforts were to gropingly lead knowledge up to this fortress. The time has come to invert that relationship, and the Then should become a dialectical turning-over [*Umschlag*]; it should become the sudden thought in an awakened consciousness.... Facts turn into something that just happened to us, to establish them is the task of memory.[74]

The potent, vibrant "Then" combines with the dreamy or unaware present in a constellation that Benjamin terms "nowtime" (*Jetztzeit*). In this constellation (or monad, as he calls it), the significance and truth of both are dialectically transformed: The meaning of the past event

[71] Benjamin, *Benjamin*, p. 49 [N 2a, 2].

[72] Walter Benjamin, "Theses on the Philosophy of History," in *Illuminations*, ed. with an introduction by Hannah Arendt (New York: Schocken Books, 1976), sec. vii.

[73] This perspective on the nature of history could be lost with the collapse of tradition and the stories it houses, since for Benjamin these stories are concerned less with legendary leaders or the glorious days of the nation, and more with human imperfection and inadequacies. Benjaminian "tradition" gives center stage to hopes that have been dashed, benevolent plans that have turned into horror, and the suffering involved in any human victory. Tradition is vital not for preserving collective identity as such but for creating ethical beings who remember past misfortunes and are therefore less sure of themselves, less prone to implement their grand political projects.

[74] Walter Benjamin, "Passagen-Werk," quoted here from R. Tiedemann, "Dialectics at a Standstill," in Gary Smith, ed., *On Walter Benjamin* (Cambridge, MA: MIT Press, 1991). In my discussion of this passage, I am indebted to Tiedemann's essay.

only now fully shines through, and it does so precisely by illuminating the present's understanding of itself. Without this fusion of distant moments and of enlivening and reliving remote events, both the past and present will be unredeemed: The past will be doomed to irrelevance and disappearance, and the present will continue to dwell in a dream, without self-knowledge of its possibilities and limitations, significance and responsibilities. To admit the distant moment is to recognize ourselves fully for the first time, since the present cannot be taken as its own measure, its own source of interpretation (Freud demonstrated this in his theory of neurosis, and Robespierre in his celebration of revolutionary France as "Rome incarnated"). If ontological truth emerges out of unity of subject and object, historical truth emerges out of unity of the now and then: Things are constituted in "the now of knowability" (*das Jetzt der Erkennbarkeit*).[75] Benjaminian time is thus somewhat erotic: History is fractured, composed of singular periods and events, and these may lie dormant and passive – even for thousands of years – until they find a receptive and longing present. In this vision, truth and meaning in history are the offspring of a temporal marriage, the fruits of attraction between qualitatively different moments.

The conjoining of and conversation between different moments is not, however, simply a natural, spontaneous occurrence. Benjamin believes that we cannot be indifferent spectators of reality but must, rather, open ourselves to a concealed truth beyond the surface of phenomena: "[T]he intensive observer finds that something leaps out at him from the object, enters into him, takes possession of him, and something different – namely, the non-intentional truth – speaks out of the philosopher."[76] Any present is an *opportunity* for two moments to interact and effect mutual knowledge; the realization of this opportunity, however, depends upon individuals. This relational dependency of the past upon the present means that the human experience of time has no fixed patterns, no transcendental conditions or predestined direction: It has only a *potential for cyclicality*. The now, each and every moment, cannot be grasped separately from those who live it, since it is their awareness and openness that give this now its depth and import. Nor can the past itself be taken as given, since its authority and

[75] Walter Benjamin, "Theory of Knowledge," in *Selected Writings*, vol. 1 (Cambridge, MA: Harvard University Press, 1996), p. 276.

[76] Walter Benjamin, "On the Topic of Individual Disciplines and Philosophy," in *Selected Writings*, vol. 1, p. 404.

meaning are time dependent; there is no universal, ahistorical truth of an event: "Authority [of an event or object] stands in opposition to the conventional concept of objectivity because its validity, that of the non-intentional truth, is historical – that is to say, anything but timeless; it is bound to a particular historical base and changes with history."[77] Humans can experience the immense richness of perspectives and truths that are potentially open for them, but moderns tend to flee from this experience, locking themselves within false, socially constructed certainties. Philosophically, this flight is epitomized by Kant's theory of knowledge, with its list of universal categories of cognition and human faculties; for Benjamin, indeed, this theory is concerned with (perhaps) "the lowest order of reality."[78] God (and a redeemed humanity) may possess truth as absolute and whole, but for mortals the notion of objective history induces aloofness from the past and its lessons. "Timelessness [*Zeitlosigkeit*]," writes Benjamin, "must be unmasked as an exponent of the bourgeois concept of truth."[79]

The weaving of memory allows us to overcome the fragmentation and "shock" of modern life and to see ourselves as authoring an intelligible narrative with its own internal coherence.[80] "The true measure of life is remembrance," writes Benjamin. "He whose life has turned into writing, like old people's, likes to read this writing only backward. Only so does he meet himself, and only so – in flight from the present – can his life be understood."[81] The places we have been, the people we have encountered, the pains and joys we have felt – these shape our characters and determine who we are. The separate and accidental events that seem to dominate our existence are, from the vantage point of the end (i.e., of old people), interconnected, even necessary; and the choices we have made in specific contexts reveal their true meaning only when examined against the background of our life as a whole. Every life contains a "story," and every story is the site of wisdom – of lessons to be learned, of things to be emulated and avoided. Thus, it is only by

[77] Ibid., pp. 404–5.
[78] See Walter Benjamin, "On the Program of the Coming Philosophy," in *Selected Writings*, vol. 1, p. 100. On Benjamin's critique of Kant, see Richard Wolin, *Walter Benjamin: An Aesthetic of Redemption* (New York: Columbia University Press, 1982), Chap. 2.
[79] Benjamin, "On the Topic of Individual Disciplines and Philosophy," pp. 404–5.
[80] See Walter Benjamin, "On Some Motifs in Baudelaire," in *Illuminations*, pp. 158–9.
[81] Walter Benjamin, "Conversations with Brecht," in *Reflections: Essays, Aphorisms, Autobiographical Writings*, trans. Edmund Jephcott, ed. with an introduction by Peter Demetz (New York: Schocken Books, 1986), pp. 209–10.

looking backwards that the meaning of one's existence is revealed to oneself as well as to others.

This fullness of memory and, hence, of self-knowledge cannot be achieved by willful reflection (*mémoire volontaire*), only by a chain of associations brought about by an accidental object or event that raises a distant image within us (*mémoire involontaire*). This finite experience becomes a "key to everything that happened before it and after it,"[82] since memory is like an infinite, interrelated web. In modernity, those who are able to weave this web, to consummate the fullness of their being, are those who live *poetically*.[83] The modern self must set at bay its rational, control-oriented, and predictable modes of thought, fostering instead a hunger for unexpected images and for their free dance in its mind.

The poetic quality of memory is complemented by its *moral intent*. Memory is a corrective act; it brings *Tikkun* (in the Kabbalistic sense of "healing") by allowing us to come to terms with our failures, with the joys and experiences that have narrowly escaped us. We may feel happiness only by confronting what did and did not happen to us – by facing our fate. "Happiness," suggests Benjamin, is "what releases the fortunate man from the embroilment of the Fates and from the net of his own fate."[84] The full moral import of this commitment to recall the "could have been" is evident on the collective level. "The past," he famously wrote, "carries with it a temporal index by which it refers to redemption. There is a secret agreement between past generations and the present one.... Like every generation that preceded us, we have been endowed with a weak Messianic power, a power to which the past has a claim."[85] With Kant, Benjamin points to the moral, intergenerational responsibility that the present has with respect to the history of the community and of humanity in general; he transforms, however, both the temporal direction of this responsibility and its contents, displacing the idealized future with the tortured past, those who are not yet living with those who lived without leaving a trace. Hence, Benjamin calls for the

---

[82] Walter Benjamin, "The Image of Proust," in *Illuminations*, p. 202.

[83] Benjamin, "On Some Motifs in Baudelaire," p. 157. In this respect there is a striking resemblance between Benjamin and Heidegger. See Howard Caygill, "Benjamin, Heidegger and the Destruction of Tradition," in *Walter Benjamin's Philosophy*, ed. A. Benjamin and P. Osborne (London: Routledge, 1994), pp. 1–31.

[84] Walter Benjamin, "Fate and Character," in *Selected Writings*, p. 203.

[85] Benjamin, "Theses on the Philosophy of History," in *Illuminations*, sec. ii.

redemption of those *who have been* exploited, marginalized, oppressed, exiled – arguing that their sufferings and misery possess an almost corporeal existence; their fate must be corrected by the present. This redemption is both possible and necessary, since he tacitly espouses the Freudian teaching according to which forgotten traumas remain powerful and active despite the passage of time, as they have an urge to overcome repressive forces and resurface into consciousness. Not only does the rescuing of past sufferings fulfill a moral obligation to those who perished, but in being recovered, the past also ipso facto fosters the correction of the present. The critical reading of history manifests to the hopeful present the true import of historical, non-Messianic time.

Benjamin seems to believe that a self able to hear the murmurs and sighs of the dead – of those who have engaged in the building of civilization or who have been destroyed by its march – is bound to become skeptical of profane notions of progress. Perhaps the ultimate redemption of the dead is achieved only when we recognize that their misfortunes and pains *have not been for nothing*: The redemption of traumatic memories and their being painted with a moral brush are essential for amending contemporary social and political action; only an audible past, a past that speaks, can shape humbled selves. (Benjamin did not pay enough attention to the danger of misusing collective memories; the past often serves to promote both inflated self-esteem and self-pity, and distant events are often employed to justify hate and violence toward others.)[86]

---

[86] Efforts at bridging the distant moments in new and changing constellations have a redemptive quality. But while Benjamin believes that human efforts are essential to redemption, he is cautious not to allow humans a sense of omnipotence and ultimate control over their destinies: He expresses complete disillusionment with the Enlightenment's legacy. In agreement with the prophetic and mystic Jewish tradition (and in contrast to the Kantian vista), Benjamin poses a sharp distinction between historical time and the redemptive moment, between the inescapably flawed moral universe established by humans and the higher reality that is the fruition of external intervention. "Only the Messiah himself," writes Benjamin, "consummates all history, in the sense that he alone redeems, completes, creates its relation to the Messianic. For this reason nothing historical can relate itself on its own account to anything Messianic. Therefore the Kingdom of God is not the telos of the historical dynamic; it cannot be set as a goal." Walter Benjamin, "Theologico-Political Fragment," in *Reflections*, p. 314. Whether Benjamin believed in the actual realization of the Messianic age is unclear, but he maintained it as a critical idea. In light of the Messianic, history appears not only as inherently unjust but as unfulfilled, as waiting for the miraculous, whose coming is a constant possibility. The notion of Messianic time is essential in Benjaminian thought, for it highlights the redemptive potential of the profane – and demands the sacredness of the now.

In sum, Benjamin believes (with Karl Kraus and Lurianic Kabbala)[87] that "origin is the goal." Origin is the goal of the individual who seeks the fullness of his or her life, the goal of the community that seeks both to retain and correct its tradition, and the goal of humanity that seeks its redemption by approaching the first moment of revelation.[88] Thus, the fundamental Benjaminian quest is the integration of different layers and fragments of time into a complete, living whole ("only for a redeemed mankind has its past become citable in all its moments"). Rather than striving to gradually rid ourselves of our particularity, we should embrace and explore this particularity as individuals and communities; it is only the recovery of specific and endlessly differentiated memory that promises the composing of an inclusive temporal totality. The semicyclical imagination thus suggests that the world we inhabit is imbued, saturated with pasts that cannot be ignored, and this imagination continues to echo strongly in contemporary culture and politics. In *Beloved*, for example, Toni Morrison writes: "[I]t's so hard for me to believe in it [time].... Places are still there. If a house burns down, it's gone, but the place – the picture of it – stays, and not just in my memory, but out there, in the world. What I remembered is a picture floating around out there outside my head. I mean ... even if I die, the picture of what I did, or knew, or saw is still out there. Right in the place where it happened."[89] Whether it is African slavery or the genocide of Native Americans, the exile of ancient Jews or the more recent Palestinian *Nakba*, we have become the "shepherds" of the living images of these happenings by allowing them to shape our commitments and self-understanding. Memory has its own natural, expansive flow; instead of aspiring to the transcendence of difference, however, memory is attracted to the tangible, to what has been especially silenced, and to what holds the most potent images.

Now the temporal imagination explored here is quite characteristic of nationalism. As Aviel Roshwald has argued, one may find that

---

[87] On the influence of Lurianic Kabbala on Benjamin, see Robert Alter, *Necessary Angels* (Cambridge, MA: Harvard University Press, 1991). For a comprehensive study of the notion of revelation in Judaism, see Gershom Scholem, *The Messianic Idea in Judaism* (New York: Schocken Books, 1971).

[88] These projects of recovery are interdependent, since the memories of the individual are intertwined with those of the community, and since the events and stories of the community are partly shaped by its interactions with other communities. For Benjamin, the individual who recollects private memories could ultimately find that his or her experience leads to an infinite ocean of memories, an ocean shared by humanity.

[89] Toni Morrison, *Beloved* (New York: Alfred A. Knopf, 1987), p. 38.

nationalism often oscillates between a desire, on the one hand, to think of the nation as continuous and as progressing in a linear fashion, and on the other, as embodying some form of cyclical and mythic notion of time.[90] (As I suggested here, the term *semicyclical temporal imagination* seems to me more apt, since what is involved is not a naive return to the past.) Because of the dispersion of Jews around the world and their separation from their land, Zionism had to reject concepts of teleology and especially of biologically inspired nationalism (see next chapter), and could claim continuity based mainly on a notion of shared origins, common memory, and a literary tradition. In other words, it could submit only a weak form of continuity in terms of the organic philosophies of nationalism, and its cause was therefore much more dependent on the semicyclical temporal imagination of modernity.

Scholars of nationalism often point to the importance of myths, symbols, shared memories, rituals, and practices – in short, for lack of a better word, tradition – in forming a common identity. On many occasions, these traditions are imbibed from religion and from the related literary corpus of the nation. Ethno-symbolists, such as Adrian Hastings, Anthony Smith, John Armstrong, and Aviel Roshwald, suggest that these features of collective identity have deep and enduring roots, that they represent genuine, if latent, identities, and that they have always played a significant role in shaping the self-understanding of collectivities. Others, such as Eric Hobsbawm, have emphasized the creative aspect of the formation of national identities (either by the state's educational system and bureaucracy or by various movements in civil society), and the fact that neither the groups that will eventually form one nation nor the latter's particular tradition can be predicted in advance. But even Hobsbawm admits that "conscious intervention succeeded mainly in proportion to its success in broadcasting on a wavelength to which the public was ready to tune in."[91] Despite the disagreements about the authenticity of traditions and whether they have an enduring essence, it seems that there is a general agreement that nations (and especially nation-states) need traditions and are hungry for them, that they celebrate shared memories as a key part of their identity (while forgetting and suppressing other

---

[90] See Aviel Roshwald, *The Endurance of Nationalism: Ancients Roots and Modern Dilemmas* (Cambridge: Cambridge University Press, 2006), Chap. 2.

[91] Eric Hobsbawm, "Mass-Producing Traditions: Europe, 1870–1914," in *The Invention of Tradition*, ed. E. Hobsbawm and T. Ranger (Cambridge: Cambridge University Press, 1983), p. 263.

periods and events that challenge the notion of unity, blemish the sense of honor and strength of the nation, or mention its past sins).

Now, as Hobsbawm demonstrated, these traditions and memories are celebrated through various means: Past heroes are honored, monuments commemorating such heroes or past events are constructed, memorial days marked, symbols from the past resurrected and printed on stamps and flags, and so on. Sometimes the events and heroes are distant; at other times they are nearer (in Germany, for example, Herman the Cheruscan as opposed to Wilhelm I). The invention or shaping of tradition is always complicated since it must include contents that are not too controversial among the members of the nation, and that can appeal to minorities and peripheral groups who do not necessarily see themselves as part of the nation and whose hearts must be won. Often, there are battles over which historic figures to celebrate, and over the significance of their actions. (As Roshwald suggests regarding Joan of Arc, "while the free French played on her resistance to foreign occupiers as an inspiration to the anti-German struggle, Vichy emphasized the English identity of the fifteenth-century occupiers, a message better suited to the collaborationist regime's effective alignment with Nazi Germany.")[92] Moreover, there is the added complication that the weight of tradition in forming national identity is inexorably linked to the revival or cultivation of distinct languages (which, at times, are controversial among the members of the supposed nation), since it is the names and stories in one's national language that are most likely to revive memories and steer the imagination. National languages facilitate access to the past, but the need to access this past also leads to the revival of the language (as the Zionist case demonstrates).

Not every part of tradition alludes to the semicyclical imagination in the strong sense that has been used here; more often, events and past figures, places and symbols become part of tradition just to remind us who we are, how we came to be this particular nation. But at other times, such as in the Zionist case, the distant past plays a completely different role: There is a call for a genuine meeting of two different eras, a highlighting of their similar qualities and attraction to each other, a celebration of the specificity and the sensual dimension of human existence – and an understanding of the correction and happiness, fulfillment and direction, courage and meaning that the temporal marriage could establish. When there are no "people" among whom to inaugurate

---

[92] Roshwald, *The Endurance of Nationalism*, p. 54.

a legal bond (as in the French and especially American cases) through a spectacular revolutionary event, and when the teleology of a united national body progressing through time can hardly be evoked, it is the semicyclical temporal imagination that can become the main anchor for the project of national revival.

Zionism is a paradigmatic case as far as the power of the modern, semicyclical imagination is concerned. Here, the faith that "origin is the goal" led exiled people – who otherwise had little communication among or identification with each other – to leave their entire lives behind and take a bold, giant step to their spatial root and to the new way of life this spot promised. The dangerous present demanded action; the far-away past demanded correction. The present offered only confusion and bafflement; the past, inspiration and direction. Many Zionists saw themselves as creating a new nowtime, a new constellation in which the ancient Hebraic times and their own epoch become profoundly attached and transformed each other. The longing for the Holy Land was depicted as almost erotic, as a craving for the flesh of the soil, the singularity of the landscape, the distinct vegetations and fragments; images and sensual imprints from collective memory – as they were inscribed in a holy book – suddenly became alive. As A. D. Gordon imagined in his dream (1909), the land was speaking to him:

And a voice came out of the ruins and said: man, look at these ruins ... and know ... that it is your own soul that has been ruined. And the destructive force is the destructive force in your own life, since you have lived in foreign countries.... And if you will continue to look attentively, you shall see that beneath these ruins there is still a glowing, orphaned ember – whispering about those lives, which others once created – and that were left hidden and survived from the old days. And the wind of this land is blowing and reviving this ember ... and when you will arrive here to create for yourself a new life, a life of your own – it will live again and generate great flames.[93]

Alongside the opportunity to revive an entire ocean of memories and sensual experiences (and thus a more rounded human existence), the return to the Holy Land was also an attempt to redeem exile and the subsequent national humiliation by going back to the place where the catastrophe of national subjection had begun.

Zionism, we see, had a Janus face: a Proustian sense that reliving distinct memories is a source of energy that infuses actors with profound

---

[93] A. D. Gordon, "Hachalom vepiterono" [The dream and its solution], 1909 at http://www.benyehuda.org/gordon_ad/haavoda_02.html.

joy, and a Freudian belief that it is possible to heal a national trauma only by going back in time to the childhood of the nation, to the moment when and the place where this trauma had commenced.

For Zionists, then, the present became a unique and urgent opportunity to meet the distant past without the mediation of extensive parts of the tradition, a moment that also offered a break with the overbearing continuum of Jewish existence in the Diaspora. In a sense, they exemplified Nietzsche's notion of "monumental history" in which historical consciousness becomes very selective and has a one-dimensional aim: to highlight great people, as well as inspiring events and eras from the past, and thereby induce daring action and effort. "The ancient Jewish past suddenly becomes near, intimate, real, perfect, as it is described in the Holy Bible; and the recent Jewish past becomes distant, strange, repulsive," states Ben-Gurion.[94] As a part of this leap backward, heroic images from the past of political independence (or the quest for it) were exhumed and celebrated. Thus, for example, according to Ben-Gurion, the Jewish national revival requires that we examine, in a fresh manner, factual truths and the meaning of historical events as these have been asserted and interpreted by the tradition. This reexamination, Ben-Gurion suggests, is called for "since the events of our day shed new light on ancient ones." "I know," he continues,

that each historical event is also clearly unique. But I think the majority of our people could not comprehend the basic concepts of [our] ancient history, since they have been severed from their land and lost their independence. Our tradition has thus been distorted. Conquest, settlement, tribe, a people – I wonder if a nation that has been dispersed and disjointed, and that did not have soil of its own or independence could fathom what these words genuinely mean and their full weight. They did not deal with conquest and did not know what it involves; the same applies to settlement. *Only with the revival of Israel in our time these abstract notions became flesh and bone....* Since we now grasp them, however, we must freshly reexamine biblical stories and try to understand what happened then in a naturalistic [not miraculous] manner.[95]

Another key Zionist leader, Berl Katznelson, suggests that "with the loss of political freedom, Jewish historiography lost its freedom as well.... [T]he power of forgetfulness and omission in Jewish history is

---

94 David Ben-Gurion, *Netzah Israel* [The eternity of Israel] (Tel Aviv: Ayanot: 1957), p. 222. Quoted here from Naomi Mandel-Levy, *Ancient Language in a New Reality*, Ph.D. diss., The Hebrew University, 2009, p. 76.

95 David Ben-Gurion, *'Iyunim batanach* [Biblical reflections] (Tel Aviv: Am Oved, 1969), p. 74.

great.... That which escaped from external censorship was caught by internal censorship.... Those expressions of Hebrew heroism that did not result in victory were doomed to oblivion." Now, however, the past could be recovered: "With the rise of Zionism, a new light was shed on the defeated and neglected Jewish heroism. The forgotten people of Masada were saved from a foreign language; Rabbi Akiva now appears to us not only as the old man who sat in the yeshiva, but also as the prophet of the revolt; and Bar Koziba has been transformed back to Bar Kochba[96] in people's minds."[97]

The Benjaminian ethical connotations of the semicyclical temporal imagination – the notion of the present as the shepherd of the memories of past catastrophes and their *universal* moral lessons – have been too often selectively embraced by Zionists[98] (for instance, most Israelis still find it difficult to identify with Palestinian refugees, despite their own experience in the Diaspora). This phenomenon, I have suggested, stems in part from the Jews' skepticism toward the vista of modernity as promising moral-political progress; the longing for the ancient past was unleashed without what some may consider the gist of Judaism, *its moral import* as understood by Cohen and other interpreters of the tradition, especially those writing in the nineteenth century. Instead, the semicyclical imagination has been used mainly for these several aims: for salvaging a forgotten political tradition of independence and the heroes that fought for it (a path that was inaugurated by the writer M. Y. Berdyczewski), for recovering a bond to the ancient land with the biblical stories associated with it and the sensual fabric unique to it, and for reviving the Hebrew language as a mediator between distinct territory and ancient history and a people seeking redemption. Perhaps it is fair to say that while the semicyclical imagination could boost and expand our moral consciousness, it is equally prone to self-absorption and a shortsightedness toward the other: It points inward and is concerned with the memories, past experiences, and identity of a person or a group, a concern that does not exclude others but could view them

---

[96] Bar Kochba (star, in Hebrew), the great hero who lead the last revolt of ancient Israel against the Romans (132–136 C.E.), was called by later generations Bar Koziba (deception) because the revolt failed in disastrous ways.

[97] Berl Katznelson, "Introduction," in *Sefer hagvura* [The book of heroism], ed. Israel Heilperin (Tel Aviv: Am Oved, 1941) (in Hebrew).

[98] A notable exception in this regard is Martin Buber, who called for a revival of the biblical, utopian themes of the prophets in the emerging national movement. Scholem, Benjamin's close friend, rejected such cyclicality, and believed it to be a dangerous chimera. See his *Od davar* (Tel Aviv: Am Oved, 1989), p. 371. See also note 23, Chapter 4 this volume.

mainly in terms of their role within one's own narrative, rather than as claiming a place of their own. Perhaps national movements are naturally inclined to interpret semicyclicality in this manner; Zionism has not escaped this disposition either.

Finally, and as noted, according to the semicyclical imagination, memory is something that depends on the fullness of our senses and is attached to specific and singular people, objects, and places. Reason aspires to universality, memory to singularity; reason for abstracting from specific circumstances, memory for the richness and specificity of sense-based experience. Memory could be based on language alone, of course, but it gains more weight when attached (also) to a tangible place: to landscape and the texture of the soil, to the quality of the air and light, to certain roads and buildings. Hence, the conflict in Palestine/ Eretz Israel is not just about territory and resources, or even about security, as it is often presented today. It is also between two communities, Jews and Palestinians, for whom land as a *meaningful* place is critical precisely because political institutions (to a different degree in each case) are having a hard time being such a source of import and cohesiveness. Each community developed a rich sense of place and celebrated it in its writings, mythologies, ideologies, and practices (see Chapter 3). This sense of place was and is fiercely preserved because it allows the cultivation of identity across time, cultivation through the reactivation and preservation of a memory in which the past and the present enliven each other. And while a heightened sensual experience is the venue for possessing such place-bound memory, this experience is also a good in itself, promising a fuller human existence (that Jews, at least, lacked in the Diaspora) and a certain mode of being that is grounded in the world.

III. SPATIAL MOBILITY, SELF-INTEREST, AND THE ASCENT OF PRESENT-CENTEREDNESS

The third temporal imagination of modernity identifies this epoch as essentially present-centered, and it was significant for the rise of Zionism: It involved a view of human life as less bound by tradition and authority and saw the concerns of the concrete, living Jew as the paramount consideration for how individual and collective action should be shaped. As did other Europeans, Jews began to see time as a limited resource that could be crafted by human endeavor and be used in beneficial ways; moreover, the present was in a sense the realm of freedom – unfettered by the past, not chained to a meta-narrative and a binding future. In daily life, Jews (especially in Western and Central Europe) were increasingly inclined to limit the time devoted to prayers and the study of ancients texts, to communal events, ceremonies, and practices (such as the *mikve*); instead, modern Jews tended to utilize time carefully, devoting more of it to the economic sphere and the cultural one (e.g., in the spirit of *Bildung*).[99] This activist and matter-of-fact attitude toward time was conducive to the determination of Zionists to take history into their own hands; for the Zionist individual, time became a religiously neutral resource open to an ethos of initiative and shaped by the modern's cultivated imagination.

Toward the end of the nineteenth century, Jews were increasingly propelled to embrace present-centeredness, since the sense of danger – physical, economic, identity-related, and more – boosted the imperative to act: "[C]an we in fact not focus on the present even for one minute?" asks the writer Brenner,[100] and Borochov, the Socialist-Zionist leader, states that "[w]e must not wait."[101] Furthermore, present-centeredness was enhanced in Zionism since, like other national movements, the development of a national consciousness and identity among widely dispersed Jewish people hinged in part on the establishment of a contemporaneous consciousness and a shared public sphere. In this, the Jewish press, which had been emerging since around the middle of the nineteenth century and included some publications in the revived Hebrew language (such as *Hatzefira, Hakarmel, Hamelitz, Hashahar, Hashiloah,* and *Hazman*), played a major role.

We should begin exploring the present-centered temporal imagination by noting the emergence in modernity of new modes of living and working, of institutions and social interactions that fostered or called for it (the need to coordinate a complex railway system within and across countries being a prime example). The importance of the present or now, and the necessity to determine an absolute, agreed-upon one, were epitomized by a moment in 1884, when the International Prime Meridian Conference in Washington, D.C., established Greenwich as the zero meridian, divided the earth into 24 equal-sized time zones, and defined a universal day that "is to begin for all the world at the moment

---

[99] See Israel Bartal, "Secularization of Time and the Culture of Recreation," in *New Jewish Time*, ed. Y. Yovel et al. (Tel Aviv: Keter, 2007), vol. 1, p. 272.

[100] Quoted here from Anita Shapira, *Brenner* (Tel Aviv: Am Oved, 2008), p. 36.

[101] Dov Ber Borochov, "She'elot beteoria tzionit" ("Regarding Questions in Zionist Theory"), in *Ketavim nivharim* (Selected writings), vol. 1 (Tel Aviv: Am Oved, 1944), p. 41 (in Hebrew).

of mean midnight of the initial meridian." At the close of the nineteenth century, then, the universal clock achieved its victory, turning time into an accumulation of identical, repetitive, empty, and unrelated units; as a result, time was wholly neutralized, depoliticized, and freed from religious import – and thus it became a uniform and universal domain devoid of hope or longing.[102] The establishment of an abstract, universal time also turned the absolute present into a worldwide consensus; people everywhere began to sense that their lives unfolded according to the same ticking. The uniformity of time could be associated with the uniformity of work, discipline, and routine in modern life; it is just one more domain where plurality receded for the sake of greater functionality. (In the United States alone, 300 different local times existed before 1883.)[103] The invention of the wireless telegraph, of the telephone, and of improved means of interaction in general further enhanced the sense of simultaneity of people around the globe (especially toward the end of the nineteenth century). In the age of imperialism, many believed that the distances of space were overcome by technologies related to time and by the latter's universal stretch; it was now possible to see the world as evolving concurrently and interconnectedly. Hence, being attuned and responsive to the present became a prerequisite for successful action.

We should distinguish, however, between present-centeredness in its narrow sense – the act of focusing on the immediate (needs, desires, actions, etc.) – and present-centeredness that takes the *extended* present, or the present as measured by the life span of the individual, as its main concern. The materialist understanding of the body that has emerged in the West since the seventeenth century espouses the first type of present-centeredness; the liberal individualism that emerged from the same era – and that takes the individual as a rational sovereign capable of setting long-term projects of his or her own – exemplifies the second type. My comments refer mainly to this second understanding of present-centeredness.

Broadly speaking, there are numerous reasons for present-centeredness in modernity, including the rise of representative democracy, of secularization, of formal equality, and even of new visions of the human body; Alexis de Tocqueville's analysis of the rise of this temporal imagination in

[102] Chowers, *The Modern Self in the Labyrinth*, p. 193.
[103] See Kern, *The Culture of Time and Space*, Chap. 3; and David Harvey, *The Condition of Postmodernity* (Cambridge, MA: Blackwell, 1990), Part III.

modernity is especially illuminating.[104] For our purposes, however, two other dimensions of modernity associated with present-centeredness are critical: the new contingent relation to place and the dominance of self-interest (especially in shaping human relations in the economic sphere). In both of these important dimensions of modernity, the role of Jews was considered (by their antagonists) to be central: They were often seen as

[104] As noted, one reason for present-centeredness in modernity is the nature of modern democracy, where elected representatives and executives are evaluated mostly according to their tangible achievements for the sake of contemporary voters, rather than by their contribution to future generations and their well-being, and where current public opinion often shapes decisions and policy. But perhaps a far more profound reason for present-centeredness is secularization: Religion provided not only a notion of order in and a rationale for human affairs but also a spiritual motivation for transcending the present; when faith ebbed, argues Tocqueville, moderns developed a "brutish indifference about the future." Alexis de Tocqueville, *Democracy in America*, trans. G. Lawrence (New York: HarperPerennial, 1969), p. 548.

Religion was able to tame human brutishness by inculcating the notion of an afterlife, a distant and fixed picture of the future: "Religions instill a general habit of behaving with the future in view." But, continues Tocqueville, "as the light of faith grows dim, man's range of vision grows more circumscribed, and it would seem as if the object of human endeavors came daily closer" (pp. 547–8). For believers, this picture was so powerful that it shaped their present conduct and inspired them by "imperceptible degrees to repress a crowd of petty passing desires"; for them, the moment does not stand by itself, but is evaluated according to a much more precious time – the time of salvation. But the "this-worldliness" of an increasing number of secular moderns induces these individuals to view every day as a potential end, a temporal segment all by itself. "As soon as they despair of living forever," writes Tocqueville, they are "inclined to act as if they could not live for more than a day" (p. 548). Once time loses its meaning as an overarching narrative of redemption and immortality, a new way of viewing time and life develops: The extraction of as much pleasure as possible from each and every day becomes a fundamental maxim. Most often, observes Tocqueville, this extraction means materialistic and consumerist enjoyment, which relies on the new possibilities offered by capitalism and modern technology. But the venue through which individuals explore the present is less important than their conviction that such an exploration is a kind of existential obligation toward life itself, that there is no other way really to do justice to life.

Moreover, in democracy, contends Tocqueville, individuals accept the principle of equal opportunity and vie for social and economic positions according to strict rules and procedures. Therefore, in such a democracy, all "see a multitude of little intermediate obstacles, all of which have to be negotiated slowly, between them and the great object of their ultimate desires. The very anticipation of this prospect tires ambition and discourages it. They therefore discard such distant and doubtful hopes, preferring to seek delights less lofty but easier to reach. No law limits their horizons, but they do so for themselves" (p. 631). Present-centeredness emerged also because of the new vision of the human body and its physiology, especially the valorization of the rapidly pacing heart and of the blood cycle as central to human life and health, a vision that replaced the classical vista of bodily constitutions as shaped by a distinct and durable balance of bile. See Eyal Chowers, "The Physiology of the Citizen: The Present-Centered Body and Its Political Exile," *Political Theory* 30 (2002): 649–76.

epitomizing a noncommittal relation to place and the soil of their host nation, as well as embodying the notion of self-interest that propels market capitalism. These aspects of present-centeredness and the ways they were associated with Jews posed a great challenge to Zionism. I begin a discussion of both aspects of modernity with Agnes Heller's argument concerning the present as the new "home" of the self.

The nineteenth century featured a peculiar tension. On the one hand, European countries such as England, France, Germany, Italy, and Belgium attempted to dominate the globe, equating the augmentation of territory, natural resources, markets, and people with power and prestige; on the other hand, the relation of moderns to place and to a spatial continuity among generations became significantly more contingent. At least since the Industrial Revolution, the move from the country to the cities, and the mass movement from Europe to the New World and the colonies, there had been a radical shift in the way that moderns perceived their homes, a shift that may be schematically described as a move away from a spatial notion of home and toward a temporal one.[105] Until the nineteenth century, Heller claims, most people still felt that their place of residence was the ground (so to speak) of their identity; location was fate, and one conducted one's life with the expectation that a fixed place would house the particular contingencies of one's life (such as a spouse, offspring, health, wealth, and occupation). But during the nineteenth century, individuals increasingly left their homes, and more than once; locations began to play only secondary and even marginal roles in constituting human activities and aspirations, memories and attachments, predispositions and judgments. The growing devaluation of place since then, she writes, is intertwined with a growing allegiance to a global culture, to social and humanitarian concerns in places distant from one's own, and to fashions and cross-national practices; a specific "now" is shared by individuals through the latest political and stock-exchange news, sports events and heroes, best-selling novels, popular TV programs, and so forth. In the course of the nineteenth century, then, the "Present" began to embrace ever more regions of the earth; this Present, by its very nature, does not tolerate other, coexisting presents.

A space-based home, avers Heller, is a familiar place (even if not always an enjoyable one) that allows the self to become reacquainted

---

[105] Agnes Heller, "Where Are We at Home?" *Thesis Eleven* 41 (1995): 1–18; see also Agnes Heller, *A Theory of Modernity* (Oxford: London, 1999), Chaps. 1 and 12. On the loss of place in contemporary culture and architecture, see Karsten Harries, *The Ethical Function of Architecture* (Cambridge, MA: MIT Press, 1998), esp. Part III.

with itself by evoking certain recollections, emotions, and evaluations. Self-recognition in all of these layers of existence (which is central to the semicyclical imagination, as we saw) emerges by situating oneself in the spatial context that molded one's identity and by evoking primary, sensual experiences. A place reminds us of who we are not so much by rational reflection but because we hear the resounding voice of the neighbor next door, smell the sweet scents of another neighbor's cooking, see the bare trees in the yard during winter. A part of the human soul is drawn to the sensual, and this part is mostly space specific; it presupposes access to and conversation with a particular location (see preceding section). Yet this space-centered, sensually dominated, detail-oriented notion of identity has been shattered in the West. "There is a general tendency," Heller claims, "to move away from spatial home-experience toward temporal home-experience."[106] She demonstrates this point by discussing the sense of home of persons whose vocation and lifestyle involve constant mobility and what she terms "geographic promiscuity." In modernity, we have seen the gradual evolution of nomads, such as businessmen and women, academics and corporate executives, journalists and software experts, who are at home everywhere and nowhere.[107] Because of their frequent dislocations, these individuals are disposed to think of space abstractly and to detach themselves from its sensual dimension; they conduct themselves in a world in which they can feel oriented without profound familiarity with the landscape or cultural background.[108] A place that is foreign can create an uncanny experience, demanding deciphering, translation, adaptation; but today there is an evaporation of genuine belonging as well as of strangeness, and "in the absence of alien places, we know that there is no home."[109]

For moderns who are inspired by notions of self-realization and success through a vocation and by authenticity defined in individual terms

---

[106] Heller, "Where Are We at Home?" p. 7.

[107] In this context, Heller argues that "to be a member of the club of the united tourists is not linked to high professionalism or substantial income. Moving from the countryside to the city, from the city to the suburbs, or from the suburbs to another city, transforms a person into a tourist in his or her home country." See Heller, *A Theory of Modernity*, p. 190.

[108] The architecture of an increasing number of buildings (hotels, airports, hospitals, corporate offices, public transportation, etc.) answers the dispositions of such persons. These "non-places" are indistinguishable, receptive of transition, inclusive of a variety of cultural backgrounds, and wholly functional in nature. See Mark Augé, *Non-Places: An Introduction to the Anthropology of Supermodernity* (London: Verso, 1995).

[109] Heller, "Where Are We at Home?" p. 192.

alone, space has become a manacle: The place of birth begets claustrophobia and is perceived as fencing selves' capacity to bring their potentials to fruition and fulfill their needs. Their perfection as human beings is no longer anchored in a place but necessitates an avulsion from place – especially from any provincial, confining, or demanding place. Contingency, which was once limited to the narrative of life but absent from its theater, is now inseparable from the experience of space itself; the spirit of the times, concurrently, has become ever more peremptory. Heller calls this present "absolute" because "the future which is beyond our horizons is unknown"[110] and because tradition is no longer considered relevant for the current age; only the present really matters, and we are responsible only for our contemporaries (not our offspring and predecessors, who are outside the sphere we see ourselves as able to effectively shape). As Zygmunt Bauman notes, "the long term, though still referred to by habit, is a hollow shell carrying no meaning; ... infinity, like time, is instantaneous, meant to be used on the spot and disposed of immediately."[111]

Finally it should be noted that Heller's argument concerning present-centeredness echoes those made by Benedict Anderson and Reinhart Koselleck, both of whom associate modernity with the institution of contemporaneous consciousness (national or otherwise) that creates a temporal bond among people who live in distant places and may inhabit different social milieus.[112] Both writers believe that this consciousness of simultaneity appeared in the late eighteenth century and is intertwined with the creation of new public spheres.

The unmooring from place in modernity is associated with another critical notion that has contributed to present-centeredness: self-interest. This mode of thinking and acting – which should not be confused with other types of love of self and egoism – is distinctively modern and has a strong affiliation with the rise of market capitalism and the concept of the individual as a free economic agent. In feudal society, people were defined in terms of the estates, corporations, guilds, and so on to which they belonged, as well as the privileges, distinct status, traditional obligations, and social commitments characteristic of each of these segments of civil society. The gradual destruction of this feudal society, and later of an ossified class structure generally, gave rise to the atomized individual. This development was most evident in America, where Tocqueville

---

[110] Heller, *A Theory of Modernity*, p. 10.
[111] Zygmunt Bauman, *Liquid Modernity* (Cambridge: Polity Press, 2000), p. 125.
[112] Benedict Anderson, *Imagined Communities: Reflections on the Origin and Spread of Nationalism* (London: Verso, 1983); Koselleck, "*Neuzeit*: Remarks."

observed that "man is brought home to himself by an irresistible force"[113] that leads him to examine all of his actions in light of his own utility. The self that is shaped by the emerging commercial and business-dominated spirit does not simply act out of spontaneous selfishness. Rather, it consciously embraces self-interest as a constant, calm, internal, as well as public, principle of action.

Self-interest severs individuals from those who preceded them and from those who will follow, yet it does not mean a minute segmentation of time and ongoing changeability. The modern self is present-centered in the sense that it shuns intergenerational commitment, but it also sees the promotion of its interest as a long-term project, a project that demands the suppression of passing desires and the formation of self-discipline. Thus self-interest involves the exercise of rationality: choosing among possible goals, determining the best means for achieving them, methodically and systematically following the preferred course of action, and so on. Especially in the economy (as Weber noted), this necessitates a considerable ability to calculate and plan ahead, and a proficiency at evaluating life in terms of what is tangible and measurable. In other words, self-interest effortlessly speaks the public language of utility, prudence, profit, money. This language is commensurable, easy to understand by all, and open to criticism and evaluation by others; while it does not "aim at mighty objects ... it attains without exertion all those at which it aims."[114]

In pursuing self-interest, furthermore, one is called to shun commitments to the nation and even to the extended family. Notions of shared collective fate, of obligations imposed by tradition, or of emotional ties to others are thrown aside. The aloof individual regards others equally and formally, without sentimental inhibitions and moral considerations: Self-interest allows one to view the other universally but also instrumentally. This ascension of self-interest further legitimizes the separation from place discussed previously, since one is called to move from location to location according to considerations that underscore work and career, opportunities and material gain. Self-interest propels the contingent relation to place, and helps turn the present into an anchor of the modern's identity.

It was common among many Europeans to describe both self-interest and rootlessness *as characteristically Jewish traits*. Marx made perhaps the most famous identification of self-interest – and the modern capitalist

---

[113] Tocqueville, *Democracy in America*, p. 415.
[114] Ibid., p. 416.

spirit generally – with Judaism. In the modern economic sphere (or the Hegelian civil society), the material, practical needs of the individual reign uninhibited. Marx writes that "the god of practical need and self-interest is money," and that money "is the jealous god of Israel, in face of which no other god may exist."[115] To him, the secularized, everyday Jews not only mastered and dominated the financial and commercial facets of capitalism but also turned self-interest, huckstering, and the worship of money into the organizing principles of our time. This line of analysis continued well after Marx. Sombart, for one, suggests that in the evolution of the "modern economic outlook," the Jew had "great if not decisive influence,"[116] partly because "in all relations between sellers and buyers, and between employers and employed, he reduces everything to the legal and purely business basis."[117] Sombart continues to offer an additional long list of qualities that allowed the Jews to play a pivotal role in the ascent of capitalism. These include rationalism, self-discipline and strong will, adaptability and resourcefulness, lack of moral inhibitions, energy, and social mobility.

Of special interest for us, though, is the emphasis Sombart puts on the role of Jews in weaving the different countries of the world into one economic system, thus boosting the notion of simultaneity and present-centeredness, as well as their role in introducing a contingent relation to place. As early as 1712, he notes, it was written in the *Spectator* that the Jews "are so disseminated through all the trading parts of the world that they became the instruments by which the most distant nations converse with one another and by which mankind are knit together in a general correspondence."[118] Jews were multilingual, with family and communal ties that crossed national boundaries and with a keen awareness of changing circumstances from an almost global perspective. This awareness, moreover, often led them to relocate and to regard their place of residence without sentimentality, suggests Sombart. *"Some special characteristic will have to be associated with this people to account for their traveling so easily from land to land*, no less than for their settlement in large cities, a proclivity shown by the Jews already in very early times," he writes (my emphasis). The ongoing migration of Jews

---

[115] See Karl Marx, "On the Jewish Question," in *Karl Marx: Early Writings*, trans. Rodney Livingstone and Gregor Benton (London: Penguin, 1975), p. 239.

[116] Werner Sombart, *The Jew and Modern Capitalism*, trans. M. Epstein (London: Fisher Unwin, 1913), p. 153.

[117] Ibid., p. 277.

[118] *Spectator*, September 27, 1712, quoted from ibid., p. 172.

and their predicament as a diaspora are not due to external circumstances, in his view; rather, this diaspora is "the result of these [Jewish] characteristics"[119] (an inner urge to relocate and a lack of emotional attachment to place). Georg Simmel, in contrast, did not believe in such essentialism and claimed that "restriction to intermediary trade and often ... to pure finance gives the stranger the specific character of *mobility*,"[120] a mobility and strangeness that characterized the Jew. But for Simmel, as for Sombart, geographic mobility (or aloofness from place) and commercial spirit (dominated by self-interest) go hand in hand and are all personified by the Jew. One could conclude from their views, then, that the Jew embodies at least two of the central forces propelling the modern toward present-centeredness.

I have noted that the urgency of the present – the dire state of Jews and Judaism – was a major incentive for the emergence of Zionism; the modern sense that the present could be shaped and must be utilized is essential for understanding this movement. But present-centeredness could have led elsewhere. Indeed, present-centeredness, if I have characterized it correctly, does not goad one to establish an entrenched relation to a meaningful place, to think in a time frame that encompasses both now and ancient times, to value collective identity above all, or to be willing to make great sacrifices for the sake of that identity. As a type of temporality associated with self-interested nomads, present-centeredness does not sit well with a vibrant nationalism and a revolutionary mind-set. Take as evidence of this that most Jews at the beginning of the twentieth century preferred to emigrate to the United States than to Palestine, which was viewed only as a distant possibility. While it highlighted the urgent need to solve the crisis of European Jewry, Zionism was also a rebellion against the temporal imagination of present-centeredness when understood as individually oriented and as generating aloofness from specific locations and community. Contemporary Israeli society, well integrated into the web of globalization, has to struggle with present-centeredness and liberal-economic individualism generally – and with its roots in the Jewish experience in the Diaspora.

To summarize, then, since the early nineteenth century, Jews – with their growing integration into bourgeois society and the modern capitalist

---

[119] Sombart, *The Jew and Modern Capitalism*, pp. 298, 299.
[120] Georg Simmel, "The Stranger" in *Georg Simmel: On Individuality and Social Forms* (Chicago: University of Chicago Press, 1971), p. 145.

system, especially in Central and Western Europe – gradually adopted the European calendar and the notion of secular time prevalent in their surroundings. Thus, religious Jewish time, with its unique rituals and holidays, was relegated to the home and the synagogue. In their contents, Jewish newspapers came to embody the existence of the two worlds, marking both the Jewish and European dates on their front pages[121] (as it became customary to do on tombstones). In becoming increasingly integrated into the social, economic, and political worlds of modernity, however, Jews met the three temporal imaginations that I have described – and even came to exemplify certain aspects of each of these imaginations. They were among the most ardent believers in progress and in the growing similarity among humans as moral beings; they were the people honoring the power of collective memory, the incorruptibility of ancient times, and their legitimate weight in shaping current communal life; and they were the agile players in a present that is characterized by self-interest and spatial mobility.

Jews were also among the first to notice the changes in the interrelations and the status of the three temporal imaginations; they grasped that the end of the nineteenth century, in particular, was a unique point in time at which the teleological imagination of progress in the spirit of liberalism *was losing* its dominance and that these temporal imaginations were available more or less *as equally viable options*. The past, future, and present each offered the self a different horizon of meaning, different options of existence, different paths of political action. Each of the temporal imaginations that emerged also gained increasing independence and weight of its own, and the identification with any of them became a critical, decisive choice now that eternity was losing its status as the ultimate, harmonizing temporal horizon. This also meant, however, that modern actors had the freedom and responsibility to choose which imagination to follow and to decide how to shape individual life and collective history; time was increasingly seen as a domain inviting human creativity and intentionality. In a sense, men and women were no longer caught in the flow of time, but were able to take a step back and behold time as another sphere subject to choice and responsive to human crafting. This sense that history is open was also essential for the emergence of the Zionist revolution and for transforming Jewish life in modernity.

---

[121] See Bartal, "Secularization of Time and the Culture of Recreation," in *New Jewish Time*, vol. 1, p. 272.

PHOTO 3. Defense Minister Moshe Dayan. Photo by Moshe Milner, July 24, 1969. Courtesy of the Government Press Office, Israel.

2

The Zionist Temporal Revolution

"This hour we are facing is not like yesterday, not like what came before," observed the writer Micha Josef Berdyczewski at the end of the nineteenth century. "All the grounds and conditions at home and outside that we lived by have collapsed. Those long nights have ended, and instead new days and conditions have emerged. And the fear in our hearts is not for nothing, since we are no longer standing on the main road. We have arrived at a point where two worlds collide: To be or to vanish! To be the last Jews or the first Hebrews."[1] From this crisis, from this sense of existential void, Zionism was born.

The end of the nineteenth century was a baffling moment for European Jews. Their hopes of integrating into the various nation-states, of having the same equal rights and respect as other citizens, were ebbing. The temporal imagination of progress and betterment, which Central and Western European Jews had been happy to embrace, gave way to the Dreyfus Affair in France, which demonstrated that Jews would always be suspected of being unfaithful citizens; to the rise of the virulent anti-Semite Karl Lugar in Vienna, one of the most important cities in Europe at the time and where Jews had experienced remarkable success; to the highly critical writings of Heinrich von Treitschke, who explained to his fellow Germans that the Jews coming from the East "are alien to the European and, especially, the German essence" and are "our misfortune." These ominous developments were occurring while secularization and cultural assimilation were rising and the Jewish communities

---

[1] Micha Josef Berdyczewski, *Kol ma'amarei Micha Josef Berdyczewski* (Tel Aviv: Am Oved, 1954), p. 29.

were becoming more dispersed and fragmented. For many, neither the tradition's teachings nor its authority seemed to fit modern life. Most Jews still attempted to find solutions in Europe, engaging in either a more thorough assimilation or in Jewish self-assertion within their current locations (e.g., the Bund). Others, such as Berdyczewski, perhaps better grasped the full meaning of the moment – its dangers as well as its groundbreaking potential. They believed that the crisis of Jews and Judaism was profound, that no middle ground was possible any longer, and that the challenges of the moment could be answered only through a *total revolution* in the life of the individual and the collective.

The Zionist revolution was all-engulfing: As noted, it demanded the ingathering of people dispersed for many generations with limited communication among themselves, political independence in a faraway country, and the molding of citizens capable of taking responsibility for their own political life and fate. For socialist Zionists, this revolution also demanded the creation of a new socialist economy and occupational structure, secularization and the creation of a new culture in a revived language, and the formation of a new type of individual who worked with his or her own hands and felt at home in Nature. To achieve these and other radical ends, the Zionist movement needed not only a novel acknowledgment of the power inherent in human deeds but also a recognition that these deeds could give birth to the historically unanticipated, to political phenomena that did not obey any inevitable pattern of evolution but depended on humans alone. *This movement could not have evolved in the context of the teleological visions that governed social and political thought during the nineteenth century*, since these visions did not allow collective action outside the contours of their predicted historical narratives. How is it, then, that around the turn of the twentieth century a small number of individuals began to see history as a sphere to be shaped by sweeping action – one that would allow them to become "the first Hebrews" – and came to see politics as the medium through which to marshal this transformation?

A sudden metamorphosis in the temporal consciousness of Jews and other Europeans made the Zionists' bold faith possible, one stemming from a new constellation among the three temporal imaginations discussed in the first chapter. To begin with, European thinkers at that time were less inclined to speak about history in terms of knowledge and truth – terms that supported the teleological and future-oriented visions of the nineteenth century – and instead advanced notions of human action unhindered by history and existing circumstances. "Overproud

European of the nineteenth century," writes Nietzsche, "you are raving! Your knowledge [of history] does not perfect nature, it only destroys your own nature. Compare ... the heights of your capacity for knowledge with the depths of your incapacity for action."[2] The emergence of Zionism at the onset of the twentieth century was feasible only after such vistas as Kant's "Idea of the Highest Good," the Hegelian interpretations of history as a "world process" that unfolds a "Spirit," or Marx's historical materialism and promise of expected communist brotherhood began to lose their allure and after their claim for knowledge and epistemological ground were shaken. Time thus became a field open to manifold interpretations and, hence, for previously unimagined actions. *Zionism was an augury*, crystallizing and articulating politically this openness and uncertainty that were silently working on the level of ideas.

Zionism presupposes a temporal ontology that could be termed *sundered history*: It posits the existence of a precarious, in-between stage in which various historical narratives have disintegrated and new ones are not yet entrenched. The interrupted historical narratives may be religious or secular, linear or cyclical, eschatological or catastrophic; what matters is the undefined space established within or among them. Sundered history is an interlude during which human existence in time is seen as open and without a clear course, a time devoid of any guidance, whether from divinity, a natural order, an invisible-hand-like mechanism, or the unfolding of reason. The events taking place in this interlude cannot be explained causally; the period is a rupture made possible only by the recognition that history is empty – or at least that a choice is involved in interpreting it and subsequently in crafting it. This singularly modern consciousness of emptiness and unbounded freedom may induce confusion and paralysis, a "fear" in the heart, as Berdyczewski puts it, especially since it is not just the fleeting life of the individual that is at stake but the fate of an entire people, which seems to hinge on the right judgment regarding the options opened by sundered time. Yet the perception of emptiness can also generate grand, radical human action by people who have the daring to shape collective fates with their own hands, to use the formlessness of reality in order to mold it anew according to an overarching aim of their choosing. (The imagination plays a critical role at this moment, since one has to picture a wholly new reality

---

[2] Friedrich Nietzsche, "On the Uses and Disadvantages of History for Life," in *Untimely Meditations*, trans. R. J. Hollingdale (Cambridge: Cambridge University Press, 1985), p. 109.

that cannot be extrapolated from experience, yet must be convincing enough nevertheless.) When such an urge to act and excitement emerge, an accompanying uneasiness may also appear, since the length of the hiatus in history is uncertain: The separated poles of time may meet again; the narrative space left ajar may be slammed shut by overpowering circumstances that also give birth to new visions of order, meaning, or necessity. Sundered history may thus inspire a mode of urgency, an impatient need for action before history again becomes impenetrable, locked within a given course.

Zionism accepts this ontology of sundered history. It exemplifies the collapse of the teleology that permeated the Enlightenment's narrative of progress and the expanding of a universal community, and it is even at odds (as we shall see) with the narrative of the nation as an organic, continuously growing body. Instead, Zionism was a bold revolution with one foot leaping backwards. It was bold because Zionists celebrated the human capacity to begin something absolutely new, with only an idea as a motivating force, eventually constructing a Jewish demographic, political, and cultural actuality where none had existed. "Not the power of an individual, nor his fortune, would be able to move an entire people from place to place; only an idea would be able to do that," suggests Herzl. And the idea of returning to the Holy Land, he argues, demands that "we eradicate from our hearts any foreign and erratic notion, any old and shabby opinion from the long-gone days."[3] As Herzl noticed, the Jewish national revival was conceivable only because history was seen as up for grabs, creating an interval in which innovative narratives could be consciously imagined, formed, and chosen. The ethos that evolved after the founding of the State of Israel in 1948 preserves this spirit; it is inclined to profess that human affairs succumb to the will and imagination, to the longings of the heart. Born in urgent times, though, this ethos also predisposes its bearers to approach social reality urgently, since there is a mistrust of tomorrow. A certain territory might no longer be obtainable, Zionist policies might be rebuffed by unexpected political circumstances, or enemies could suddenly become overbearing. Even for today's Israeli state, the time to act – especially in relation to territory – is now. As we shall see, both the Nietzschean and the socialist strands

---

[3] Theodor Herzl, *The Jewish State* [Medinat hayehudim] (1896), at http://benyehuda. org/herzl/herzl_003.html (in Hebrew). In translating this source, here and elsewhere, I have also consulted the English translation from German by Sylvie D'Avigdor. See note 10, Chapter 1.

of Zionism hold these foundational beliefs in the human potential for metamorphosis and the scarcity of time.

Zionism also points to the past, however. It contains ancient elements, such as the revival of an ancient language and a return to the land of origin. In many ways, this movement epitomizes the potency of the semicyclical temporal imagination we have already seen:[4] It involves a renewed meeting of the present with the ancient era (often disregarding and disparaging the entire era of the intervening Diaspora), a meeting that is seen both as a correction and healing of a past trauma in the place of origin (the expulsion of the people of Israel from their land by the Romans, after they have been humiliated and destroyed as a community), as well as a source for immense joy and a sense of personal and collective fulfillment. To be sure, Zionism was also future oriented, embracing, for example, visions of progressive social justice and of a semiutopian communal life in the kibbutzim. Yet without the notion of cyclicality and the redemption associated with it, Zionism would not have been conceivable as a viable ideology, nor would it have been successful as a mass movement. Needless to say, from a theological point of view, the return to the Holy Land renewed the saga of the Jewish people, a renewal that would not have happened if a Jewish polity had emerged elsewhere (Uganda, Argentina, etc.).

My purpose, however, is to focus on the moment of void in which Zionism was born, the formative moment of sundered history, and to demonstrate how a revolutionary temporal consciousness was necessary for the swift and radical changes this movement demanded. Before we examine this temporal moment further, however, let us explore the traditional Jewish conception of history and the European temporal context.

I. JUDAISM AND REVOLUTION

The novelty and boldness of the Zionist revolution are surprising given that, traditionally, Judaism declined to embrace a view of time and history as allowing rapid, human-based change. "In Judaism," writes

---

4 For studies of the Zionists' attempt to recover the prerabbinic, Hebraic past and to reconstruct this past according to ideological needs in heroic mythologies, see Yael Zerubavel, *Recovered Roots: Collective Memory and the Making of Israeli National Tradition* (Chicago: University of Chicago Press, 1995); and Charles S. Liebman and Eliezer Don-Yehiya, *Civil Religion in Israel: Traditional Judaism and Political Culture in Israel* (Berkeley: University of California Press, 1983).

Gershom Scholem, "the Messianic idea has compelled a life lived in deferment, in which nothing can be done definitively, nothing can be irrevocably accomplished."[5] The mode of lingering and hesitation that characterized Jewish existence in the Diaspora prior to secularization originated from the division of time into two distinct categories. On the one hand, the individual existed empirically in history and had to confront the collective hardships of exile in addition to the inescapable lot of humans on earth, which is often colored by illness, injustice, and want. On the other hand, Judaism anticipates the coming of a Messianic Age, a time that is seen in a radical utopian light. When that age comes, it is believed, the Jews will be gathered from all corners of the world, restored to the Land of Israel, and given an honored position among the nations; the dead will be awakened and will join the community; peace and justice will permeate human relations and humans' interaction with nature; scarcity will cease to exist; and the Lord will reveal Himself fully to humans, becoming transparent and knowable.

In Jewish thought (with notable exceptions, such as Maimonides), an unbridgeable gap separates this world from the coming Messianic one. Redemption, claims Scholem, "is in no causal sense a result of previous history. It is precisely the lack of transition between history and the redemption which is always stressed by the prophets and apocalyptists."[6] Moreover, human actions and intentions have no bearing upon the coming of the Messiah. "Precisely in the biblical texts which serve as the basis for the crystallization of the Messianic idea, it is nowhere made dependent upon human activity," notes Scholem.[7] The Messiah will come unexpectedly, as a total surprise and a miracle, the offspring of a logic that is impenetrable to earthly creatures. Hence, any radical attempt of humans to improve their lives by collective action is condemned as futile; it is considered dangerous and sacrilegious to rebel against the nations of the world, to trust in one's own defiant power, and especially to "press the end" (*lidhok et haketz*), to impatiently seek to effect what solely God can determine. This dependency on the Messiah and the utopian quality of redemption devalued political action. Jewish existence in the Diaspora was not characterized by political passivity and fatalism, though many Zionists unfairly argued that this was the case. In fact,

[5] Gershom Scholem, *The Messianic Idea in Judaism* (New York: Schocken Books, 1971), p. 35.
[6] Ibid., p. 10.
[7] Ibid., p. 14.

Jews have often been very successful at acquiring special or equal rights and privileges and at gaining access to centers of power. It is nevertheless true that they did not believe in politics as a means for restoring their unity and communal life or enabling their return to the Holy Land.[8] Politics is an art of this world, and in Judaism, differences among modes of earthly existence were flattened by contrast with the flawlessness of the Messianic Age.

Such theological impediments to human efforts to end the diasporic existence were reinforced by other factors. For one, rabbinical leaders manifested deep ambivalence toward the return to the ancient land and the overall fulfillment of the utopia. These cautious leaders realized that, in a holy time, the *Halacha* (Jewish law) would become obsolete, rendering their communal and religious authority without foundation. Others, such as Mendelssohn, believed that life in the Diaspora simply exhausted the energies of the Jewish people and oriented them toward prayer and tolerance of suffering, not toward action that could bring about the renewal of their independent political life.[9] For practical and especially theological reasons, then, until the end of the nineteenth century, most Jews did not believe that they could or should shape their history through collective action and human means.

This does not mean that Judaism does not care for history: It is often considered the religion that first promoted the idea of history as a narrative with divine meaning and celebrated the temporal dimension of

---

[8] Throughout the Diaspora, Jews have manifested considerable political adeptness, both in the internal organization of their communities and in their external relations with the relevant centers of power. Without their ability to establish vibrant and cohesive communities, and to ensure external recognition of their special status as both a part of the larger society and a distinct element within it, it is doubtful that Jews could have sustained their identity for so many centuries. While Jews were not politically independent in the Diaspora and mostly remained second-class citizens, they were often able to forge alliances and take part in the exercise of power. For example, during the Middle Ages Jews sometimes achieved a considerable degree of integration into the larger community, chiefly by relying on their economic power and by utilizing the maneuvering space opened by conflicts between the church and local rulers. As urban dwellers, they obtained the rights of burghers, sometimes taking "full part in the life of their city, sometimes occupying municipal offices and contributing to the town's armed defense. In many medieval towns in Germany, France, Spain, and Italy, they were able to obtain full and equal citizenship." See David Biale, *Power and Powerlessness in Jewish History* (New York: Schocken Books, 1986), p. 63. A somewhat different account of the Jewish position in that period is given by H. Ben-Sasson. See H. Ben-Sasson, ed., *A History of the Jewish People* (Cambridge, MA: Harvard University Press, 1976), Part V.

[9] See Aviezer Ravitzky, *Haketz hameguleh umedinat hayehudim* [Messianism, Zionism, and Jewish religious radicalism] (Tel Aviv: Am Oved, 1977), p. 24 (in Hebrew).

human existence. While the Jewish religion includes holidays that mark the cyclicality of Nature, such as Shavuot (Pentecost), the gist of this faith points elsewhere. The Holy Book is composed of stories and unique events; taken together, these form the Jewish experience and identity. Among these singular events a few stand out, such as the pledge of God to Abraham, the miraculous delivery from Egypt, the revelation of God to Moses and the covenant between God and the Hebrew people in the desert, the conquest of the Holy Land, and the building and destruction of the temples. It is impossible to understand the Jewish faith without knowing these and other distinctive biblical events. They explain such things as the bond of the people to the land, the commitment of the people to God and vice versa, and the evolution of the monotheistic idea; *it is the way significant events have shaped people's memory and consciousness that matters.*[10]

God, then, is believed to have helped steer the Jewish people from one meaningful occurrence to another, and the narrative of history is seen as the story of God's relation to his people – replete with lessons and challenges. Yet the destruction of the Second Temple and the subsequent expulsion from the Land of Israel created a sweeping shift in this historical mode of thinking, because in the Jewish mind nothing of significance regarding the collective fate had happened afterward. The historical saga of the Jewish people demanded a dialogue between God and a *united* Jewish people; this saga was also more likely to develop further if the people were in the Holy Land, and if their language was Hebrew (although in the Bible these are not always necessary preconditions). Since these circumstances ceased to exist, the unfolding narrative of the Jewish people was put *on hold.* Moreover, as Amos Funkenstein observes, Jews in the Diaspora saw their status and their "present humiliation in dispersion" as "a definite divine intention to purge Israel of its sins." Details (e.g., new historical events) mattered now only little; they but added more of the same, leaving the predicament of humiliations, suffering, and scattering intact. Given this sense of well-deserved punishment (and the collective existence of the people outside their original geographical theater), Funkenstein adds, "the traditional Jewish attitude toward time and history [in the Diaspora] was neither affirmative nor negative, but indifferent."[11]

---

[10] Thorleif Boman, *Hebrew Thought Compared with Greek*, trans. Jules L. Moreau (Philadelphia: Westminster, 1960), p. 139.

[11] Amos Funkenstein, *Perceptions of Jewish History* (Berkeley: University of California Press, 1993), pp. 16, 254. Yerushalmi, in his seminal work *Zakhor*, suggests that this

The diasporic Jews' notion of history as being "suspended" because of past collective sins, a predicament that only God could determine to alleviate, meant that no Jewish revival movement could have been successful before secularization, and that the attempts at returning to the Holy Land that did arise were associated with the crowning of a Messiah – as in the case of Sabbatai Zevi (1626–76). During the nineteenth century, however, a shift in the understanding of redemption began to occur in traditional Jewish thought. The radical dichotomy between utopian redemption and earthly history was questioned, primarily by two rabbis, Yehuda Hai Alkalai (1798–1878) and Zvi Hirsch Kalischer (1795–1874), who thought that the old orthodoxy calling for Jewish passivity in relation to redemption was mistaken, and had to be set aside. These harbingers of Zionism were both influenced by the national movements in Europe (e.g., those of the Italians, Hungarians, Serbs, and Poles) and emboldened by the emancipation of Jews in Europe. Given these events throughout Europe, the rabbis believed that the nations of the world would also support their ideas of Jewish collective revival.[12] They took note, too, of the new wealth that some European Jews had acquired and were impressed by their growing influence. Seeing these changes, they conceived of their age as an unprecedented one: "[I]t is God's generous wish" wrote Kalischer, "that the holy people will thrive in this generation to a degree unknown since we were exiled from our land."[13]

For Kalischer, then, the success of Jewish emancipation in Europe did not mean abandoning collective identity and succumbing to the individuation of liberalism; in contrast to the prevailing thought among German Jews, he began to speak of redemption in national rather than individual terms. Most important, both Alkalai and Kalischer recognized the importance of natural, pragmatic (and political) means in advancing Messianic time, and they creatively used familiar religious sources and authorities, concepts and vocabulary to advance significant changes. They advocated, among other things, a concerted Jewish effort toward the collection of funds, the purchase of land in Palestine and gradual

---

indifference to temporality lies behind the striking absence of substantive historiography of the Diaspora in Jewish culture, a situation that changed only during the nineteenth century. See Yosef Hayim Yerushalmi, *Zakhor: Jewish History and Jewish Memory*.

[12] According to tradition, this was a necessary precondition for the return to Eretz Israel.

[13] See Zvi Hirsch Kalischer, *Drishat Zion* [Seeking Zion] (1862; reprint, Jerusalem: Rabbi Kook Institute 2002), p. 35.

Jewish migration there, and the establishment of agricultural settlements. Alkalai (who immigrated to Eretz Israel) also called for reviving the Hebrew language so that Jews, men and women alike, would have a shared language once they returned to the Holy Land.[14]

Yet, as Gideon Shimoni notes, "it remains evident that the core problem Alkalai and Kalischer set out to resolve was the cosmic unredeemed state of Jewish existence, not the immediate problems of Jewish distress and assimilation. The conceptual matrix of their intentions was still primarily messianic."[15] While aware of the growing nationalism and social revolutions of their era, the two rabbis and activists did not see the nation as an ultimate value, as an organizing political principle unfettered by religion. They did not propose the search for an independent, modern state (and political power) as a central end in itself but only as an element in an overarching Messianic vision. Moreover, they were not concerned, for the most part, with the physical and economic predicament of Jews in the Diaspora and saw no urgency on these levels. Alkalai and Kalischer mainly pondered the relation between a) human, limited, and measured endeavors toward redemption (immigration, settlement, and some form of political independence in the Holy Land) and b) God's grand deeds – and their metaphysical implications – in bringing about complete and swift redemption. For them, divine salvation remained the ultimate goal and the observant Jewish way of life necessary for its realization. (Kalischer even attempted to reintroduce the practice of animal sacrifice in Jerusalem.)

Moreover, despite their importance to future religious strands of Zionism that still shape Israel today (those springing from Rabbi Kook), during their lives Kalischer and Alkalai were not very influential, and it was not their writings that propelled the decisive forces of Zionism. This national revival movement was the offspring of people who were modern and essentially secular in orientation: They were far more radical and worldly in their aspirations and in their perception of themselves as having a great potential for action, and far more impatient and concerned with the urgency of the times. These people thought that the ingathering of Israel, the settlement of the land, and the Jews' refusal to be subjected to others – while being traditional aims of religious Jews[16] – demanded

---

[14] See Yehuda Alkalai, *Kitvei harav Yehuda Alkalai* [The writings of Rabbi Yehuda Alkalai], ed. Y. Raphael (Jerusalem: Mosad Harav Kook, 1974), pp. 246–47.

[15] Gideon Shimoni, *The Zionist Ideology* (Boston: Brandeis University Press, 1995), p. 75.

[16] See Ravitzky, *Haketz hameguleh umedinat hayehudim*, Chap. 1.

rebellion against religion, not action within its confining theological and institutional frameworks.

Zionism – as an all-embracing revolution – required the profaniza-tion of history and a generalized secularization in order to truly free the human sense of potency in the world. Yet the decline of the Messianic ideal and of religious thought generally also posed a grave danger to the idea of a return. The depiction of history since the late eighteenth century as being directed by some intrinsic mechanism that could be grasped consciously, even scientifically, fostered skepticism toward inno-vative human action that was not in line with predictably unfolding events. So it would be a mistake to assume that any divinity-free notion of time would have been congenial to Zionism; the teleological mind-set of the nineteenth century was just as stifling as the traditional anticipa-tion for, and total dependency on, the Messiah.

II. THE SKELETON OF HISTORY

Before we approach Zionism, then, it is worth taking another look at the modern transformations in the perceptions of time, transformations that made its emergence possible. In the first chapter, we saw that the temporal imagination of teleology and future-fixation, as exemplified by Kantian liberalism, posed a serious obstacle to the emergence of Zionism, since this vista (which was popular among Central European Jews) anticipated the integration of Jews as equal and free citizens into secular, neutral states and the transformation of their faith into a pri-vate matter. But two other forms of teleology also posed a challenge to Zionism because of their underlying temporal perspectives: Marxism and organic nationalism.

The first appealed to a growing number of young Jews who had become disenchanted with liberalism because it failed to promise them cultural and political integration (and positions in institutions such as the army and the bureaucracy) even if they prospered economically and became part of the bourgeoisie, as in Germany. Marx's political philosophy was appealing to them because it expands the notion of universalism beyond the moral sphere as it was conceptualized by Kant. This philosophy calls for the destruction of the liberal state and its private-property, contract-based civil society and for the emergence of new societies where men and women recognize the meaning of their common fellowship – which begins with shared human needs and the production necessary for their fulfillment. Marx's vision proclaimed that history has a clear, ineluctable though dialectical path and that human action advances, consciously or unconsciously, along this path. From the perspective of historical materialism, time is the sphere of certainty and assurance, providing us with a purposeful and rational narrative and with predefined rules for what can be done and expected. Marx thus anticipates the expansion of human bonds and solidarity regardless of contingent nationality, gender, or religion. To promote this end, he demands that moderns who recognize themselves as "other"-oriented and dependent – as "species-being" (*Gattungswesen*) – make the future their center of gravity, crafting their present actions so as to accelerate the progression of history toward a transnational proletarian revolution and the emergence of communism, the true "solution of the riddle of history."[17]

As noted, Marx rejects the accentuation and expansion of shared humanity as envisioned by Kant, considering it abstract and deceptive – and not ambitious enough. For Marx, the universalism of the Enlightenment is merely a necessary step in the march of historical materialism toward the establishment of a *true* unity among humans. The bourgeois state generates fellowship and partnership only at the level of public institutions and the law, while in practice its citizens are divided, estranged, and ruled by contingency. This neutral, "political state" – unencumbered by the need to promote specific religions and thus enjoying the allegiance of all its citizens – fosters the atomization and enslavement of its members. "Where the political state has attained its full degree of development, man leads a double life, a life in heaven and a life on earth," writes Marx. "He lives in the political community where he regards himself as a communal being, and in civil society, where he is active as a private individual, regards other men as means, debases himself to a mean, and becomes a plaything of alien powers."[18] Since the Reformation and especially the French Revolution, citizens consider themselves to be living in a rational (noncapricious) and free political order of their own making, but this does not change their actual predicament. In the economic sphere they remain enslaved, the victims of arbitrary circumstances and fierce egoistic competitiveness.

In this shameful condition, men and women find themselves clinging to religion – the "halo" beyond their "vale of tears"[19] – that helps

---

[17] Karl Marx, "Economic and Philosophical Manuscripts" in *Early Writings* (London: Penguin, 1974), p. 348.
[18] Karl Marx, "On the Jewish Question," in *Early Writings*, p. 220.
[19] Karl Marx, "Critique of Hegel's Philosophy of Right, Introduction," in *Early Writings*, p. 244.

them cope with their misery in civil society but also diverts them from its true causes. But in discussing Judaism, Marx goes beyond depicting it as a halo. This religion, he argues, was not merely an escape from reality, but in fact helped shape social-economic reality in critical ways. Judaism shaped the liberal understanding of the division between private and public, and legitimized the coexistence of egoism and universalism; it advanced, in particular, the now hegemonic role of money and self-interest. In fact, the entire bourgeois order is the ultimate victory of Judaism, contends Marx.

Following a familiar argument of anti-Semites,[20] Marx views the Jewish religion harshly (not the theology but the everyday way of life, the cluster of practices and a mind-set associated with that religion). He assigns it a critical role in generating and sustaining the dualistic, capitalist-liberal system: "[T]he Jews have emancipated themselves insofar as the Christians have become Jews." Jews, he maintains, had an important role to play in human history: They sustained investments of capital, fostered a borderless market and furthered trade, championed abstract human relations through the use of money, and especially promoted a spirit of self-interest in relations among groups.[21] But, he argues, the emancipation of mankind and the establishment of true brotherhood anchored in material life depend upon deliverance from Jewish tenets and practices; Jews have fulfilled their historical role, and their faith is doomed to crumble. "We recognize in Judaism the presence of a universal and contemporary antisocial element whose historical evolution ... has arrived at its present peak, a peak at which it will inevitably disintegrate," he opines. The Jew is about to be released from Judaism, by which Marx means from the general fate of the atomized individual in civil society, as well as from his particular fate as a detested person identified with dehumanizing socioeconomic conditions. Any attempt to cling to the Jewish identity is both anachronistic and impossible; with

[20] Liah Greenfeld, in *Nationalism: Five Roads to Modernity* (Cambridge, MA: Harvard University Press, 1992), shows that Marx's identification of the Jew with the capitalist system in general, and with money in particular, was expressed by many other influential Germans (e.g., Fries of Heidelberg and Wagner). This insight is significant because it implies that embracing socialism, the early Zionists not only were confronting questions of social justice, but were also attempting to cast off traditional stereotypes of the Jew. For a comprehensive study of the intellectual context in which Marx formulated his views, see also Julius Carlebach, *Karl Marx and the Radical Critique of Judaism* (London: Routledge, 1978).

[21] See the discussion of present-centeredness in Section III, Chapter 1.

the impending collapse of the present order, Judaism will "vanish like an insipid haze in the vital air of society."[22]

While this Marxian prediction of the future of Judaism was rejected by Moses Hess, many socialist theorists of the next generation embraced it. Even social-democratic writers such as Karl Kautsky, Eduard Bernstein, and especially Otto Bauer believed that – though national identity and the rights of minorities were real problems to reckon with – the Jews were no longer a nation (in Western and Central Europe) or on their way toward disintegration (in the East). "Their culture has atrophied, their language degenerated, and they have no national literature," wrote Bauer.[23]

According to Bauer, it is fair to say that during the Middle Ages the Jews constituted a distinct nation like any other, to a large extent because they had a singular function in the economy: that of traders and moneylenders – the people facilitating the circulation of commodities and capital. With the development of market capitalism, however, all segments of society are drawn into the same system and all produce commodities for the shared market. They all depend on capital and on the free movement of people, money, and things; they all become, in Marx's and Bauer's words, "Jews." Meanwhile, according to Bauer, the Jews themselves lost their distinct economic position and are being incorporated into all classes of society: workers, bourgeoisie and petite bourgeoisie, intelligentsia, big financiers; "everywhere," in fact, "capitalism and the modern state are working to destroy ancient Judaism."[24] This economic integration, they write, will necessarily lead to a cultural (and political) one, especially among the higher classes, who are driven by their actual circumstances to assimilate into the host nations – adopting their language, education, literature, habits, dress, food, and leisure practices. It is true, writes Bauer, that there are attempts, especially in the East, to revive the Jewish nation, just as others are trying to revive old nations. But in the case of the Jews, he observes, these attempts (e.g., the Bund) will not succeed; lacking a territory of their own and

[22] All three quotations are from Marx, "On the Jewish Question," p. 237. For a theoretical study of socialist Jews in Germany and their attitudes toward assimilation, see Robert Wistrich, *Socialism and the Jews: The Dilemmas of Assimilation in Germany and Austria-Hungary* (Rutherford, NJ: Fairleigh Dickinson University Press, 1982).

[23] Otto Bauer, *The Question of Nationalities and Social Democracy*, trans. Joseph O'Donnell (Minneapolis: University of Minnesota Press, 2000), p. 297.

[24] Ibid., p. 296.

driven by opportunities and material needs to become increasingly dispersed, they are totally exposed to the incorporating forces of market capitalism and the cultural transformations they demand. Hence, "from a historical point of view, the awakening of the Eastern Jews to a new cultural life is nothing but a precursor to ultimate assimilation."[25] Bauer and other social democrats were perhaps less inclined than Marx to celebrate the universal aspect of humans (their species-being) or to speak about history in ontological and certain terms, yet even they employed a complex economic analysis that included a seemingly irrefutable logic elucidating why *assimilation* was the inescapable fate of the Jews.

Another, important teleological narrative of the nineteenth century is founded on the idea of the nation and is typically seen as having been a critical inspiration to Zionism, not an impediment to its development. I would like to suggest, however, that this view is too oversimplifying, since Zionism had to reject some of the basic principles of organic nationalism (with which it is most often associated), and instead it had to depend heavily on the semicyclical notion of time in developing its own version of nationalism.

At the end of the eighteenth century and well into the nineteenth, nationalism was not seen as necessarily contradicting the ideology of progress and the emergence of a universal vision concerning the rights of man; the liberation of a people from external yoke and the liberation of subjects within states developed hand in hand. By the time Zionism emerged, however, things were different: In many countries, nationalism meant not so much merely an attempt to free oneself from external rule and overcome collective humiliation, but more an aggressive assertion of one's uniqueness and needs; less an open definition of membership in the nation and a demand for equal citizenship to all, and more an intolerance toward those considered strangers.[26] Jews, who suffered in particular from the populist and chauvinist directions some national movements were taking, were compelled to think in ethnic-national terms, too. Interpreters thus rightly point out that the aims, ideology, and strategies of Zionism took shape in the light of the European nationalism that became widespread during the last third of the nineteenth century; one could argue that the Jewish national revival represents the

---

[25] Ibid, p. 303.
[26] E. J. Hobsbawm, *Nations and Nationalism since 1780: Program, Myth, Reality* (Cambridge: Cambridge University Press, 1990), Chap. 4.

ultimate proof of the immense appeal of nationalism against all odds. Like other national movements at the time (e.g., those of Ireland, Finland, Catalonia, Serbia, Bulgaria, and many more), Zionism was based on common origins, language, and an immensely rich literary tradition.

Yet nationalism, especially in some of its ethnic versions that were prevalent in Germany (the country that most influenced Jewish political thought at the time) has its own form of teleology, one that makes it somewhat *incompatible* with Zionism. This nationalism often employs biological concepts such as "organism" and "organic growth," postulating a united, complete social body whose parts develop synchronistically and according to one distinctive internal principle that continuously evolves through historical time. These ideas are inscribed in nineteenth-century nationalism and implied that Jews, who for many centuries had been politically dead and geographically dispersed, who had made only limited use of their original language (most Jews used Yiddish, Ladino, or Arabic as a vernacular and did not speak Hebrew), who lacked fresh political symbols and heroes, and (one could argue) did not even share a single ethnicity, could hardly hope to inject new life into their decomposed national body. Let me elaborate on this point.

The idea of "nation" demands legitimacy that is not based on heredity rule or divine authority; in Central and Eastern Europe, this legitimacy was not rooted in law or contract either. For the nation – an essentially horizontal body to which its own members must relate profoundly in order for it to exist and be effective (as Ernest Renan observed) – legitimacy rests on the idea that a distinct, collective heritage, identity, and destiny indeed exist, and that these deserve to be expressed politically in an authentic manner. The lives of nations, however, rarely display clear and unproblematic continuity.[27] Hence, in seeking an enduring identity, nationalists often argue that the nation may, in certain periods, have been politically divided, detached from its language, and forgetful of its customs, but that beneath it all, its identity and wholeness remained intact throughout its trying history, waiting for the right moment to reassert itself. In Germany of the early nineteenth century – politically fragmented, militarily humiliated by the French, its boundaries unclear – nationalists pointed to shared ethnic origins, to ongoing attachment to

---

[27] National holidays are a good indicator as to whether continuity in national identity actually exists. But as Eviatar Zerubavel notes, "around the entire globe, only nine countries actually commemorate on their national holidays anything specifically related to the period from 680 to 1492." See, Zerubavel, *Time Maps: Collective Memory and the Social Shape of the Past* (Chicago: University of Chicago Press, 2003), p. 33.

the soil, and to a common culture and language in an attempt to demonstrate continuity of identity and justify the call for a unifying and assertive German nation. The emphasis on these aspects of identity enabled Germany to offer a model of nationhood that was less dependent on shared political institutions and public sphere (as in France and England) and more on the unique combination of the body and spirit (as expressed in language) of the *Volk*.

Fichte, in his *Addresses to the German Nation* (1808), avers that "those who speak the same language are joined to each other by a multitude of invisible bonds by nature herself, long before any human art begins; they understand each other and have the power of continuing to make themselves understood more and more clearly; they belong together and are by nature one and an inseparable whole."[28] The relative unity of Germans in the Holy Roman Empire[29] gradually receded, avers Fichte, due to the influences of outside forces, especially after the discovery of America and with the competition among the emerging European states for territories overseas. The Germans are victims of others (a common theme among nationalists everywhere), of greedy nations that, on the one hand, saw a united Germany as a threat, and on the other, sought to establish coalitions with its parts (i.e., its many principalities). But as long as the unity of common origins and language remained (to a large extent based on Luther's translation of the Bible into German), it was just a matter of time and circumstance, until the unfolding saga of a united German people would be resumed.

For Fichte, this mission is not only German but also universal, since the particular features of the German spirit (e.g., spirituality, seriousness, abhorrence of brutality such as that of the French) make this nation, at the present stage of history, the greatest embodiment of the human spirit in general. To fulfill this historic, global task, then, Fichte calls upon his fellow Germans to see the unbroken chain linking the ancient German tribes to the yet unborn generations. The latter say to the present generation: "Take care that the chain does not break off

---

[28] Johann Gottlieb Fichte, "Thirteenth Address," in *Addresses to the German Nation*, trans. R. F. Jones and G. H. Turnbull (Chicago and London: The Open Court Publishing Company, [1808] 1922), at http://www.archive.org/stream/addressestothegeoofichuoft/addressestothegeoofichuoft_djvu.txt.

[29] Some contemporary scholars of nationalism concur with this observation, according to which a German national identity already existed in the Middle Ages. See Adrian Hastings, *The Construction of Nationhood: Ethnicity, Religion, and Nationalism* (Cambridge: Cambridge University Press, 1997), p. 106.

with you; see to it that we, too, may boast of you and use you as an unsullied link to connect ourselves with the same illustrious line. Do not force us to be ashamed of our descent from you as from base and slavish barbarians; do not compel us to conceal our origin, or to fabricate a strange one and to take a strange name."[30] In Fichte's imagination, the continuity of the German nation, its march through time, is not spoiled by its lack of political unity and other external, accidental conditions because it is based on more enduring foundations: linguistic and ethnic. But these foundations of German nationalism were laid before Fichte, and not as a mere reaction to the French "mechanistic" and "soulless" model.

Johann Gottfried Herder, one of the leaders of *Sturm und Drang* who wrote a generation before Fichte, had already expressed – forcefully and philosophically – the pivotal ideas in thinking about a nation. He compares the nation to a living being or a plant, a coherent unit (*genetisches Individuum*) influenced by its environment (*Klima*) but essentially driven by its own inner forces. For Herder, each nation is a whole, both horizontally (i.e., in its present existence) and vertically (i.e., in respect to its history). Firstly, he holds that each nation has a singular *Geist* expressed in and formed through the national language. This distinctive spirit pervades the nation's laws, social institutions, customs, religion, and culture; each realm echoes the others, creating a living and coherent totality. Secondly, the *Volk* unfolds like any living creature, whereby each stage follows naturally from the previous one and brings to fruition what was present in an undeveloped form from the start. There are no leaps or radical transformations in this process, and each moment can be explained in terms of the pregiven content (material and spiritual elements) of the social body.

Herder believes that the spiritual element is particularly important in shaping the substance and duration of nations. The laws of mechanics, economics, or statistics are of little help in elucidating change, and historical rules are to him futile efforts of the mind to impose uniform order on a unique spiritual enigma – the distinctiveness of a nation's spirit, the true force that advances its historical journey. For Herder, this spirit gives rise to a specific temporality. "In actuality, every changing thing has the measure of its own time within itself," he explains. "No two worldly things have the same measure of time.... There are therefore (one can state it properly and boldly) at any one time in the

---

[30] Fichte, "Conclusion," *Addresses to the German Nation*.

universe innumerably many times."[31] As Reinhart Koselleck argues, for Herder, time is not a universal and uniform phenomenon; rather, it is conceived of in the plural form, as the expressions of singular social bodies that have their own tempos, their own paces of development and decay. Each temporal unit is secluded, unaffected by the experiences and formation of other units. This biological conceptualization of national time not only insulates the community from without but also gives a certain finality to its inner process.[32] Herder's depiction of the community as a harmonious body implies that decomposition is all-engulfing; once decay gets a foothold in one limb, no part of collective life can escape it. Decay and death are natural, inescapable phenomena that elude the human will.

So, while cosmopolitan and universalist teleology, which we have discussed earlier, presented Jewish identity as a cloak about to be cast off, biologically inspired teleology suggested that the Jews' time had passed, that the Diaspora served as proof that their cycle had long ended and could not be resumed.

What can be extrapolated from Herder about the fate of the Jewish nation becomes more explicit with Hegel. According to the latter, nations not only exhibit a rich heterogeneity (as Herder would have it) but are also interconnected in advancing a shared scheme – world history. The end of this history (as part of the "Objective Spirit") is the materialization and self-realization of the "Absolute Spirit" in time. Thus, for Hegel, world history is not a meaningless assortment of chaotic and tragic events but a totality through which humans progress toward full self-consciousness and, therefore, freedom. Each nation has a particular

[31] J. G. Herder, *Metakritik zur Kritik der Reinen Vernunft* (Berlin: Aufbau-Verlag, 1955), p. 68. Quoted here from Reinhart Koselleck, *Futures Past*, p. 247.

[32] Herder draws inconsistent conclusions from this position in discussing the fate of the modern Jews; in general, however, he did not foresee a Jewish national revival, suggesting that "all that was intended to be wrought [by the Jews] has probably been accomplished." Instead, the Jews should be integrated into existing European states: "A time will come when no person in Europe will inquire whether a man be a Jew or a Christian; as the Jews will equally live according to European laws, and contribute to the welfare of the state" (translation altered). See J. G. Herder, *Outlines of a Philosophy of the History of Man* (New York: Bergman Publishers, 1800), pp. 335, 486. Herder's views of Judaism and the Jews are discussed by Paul L. Rose in *Revolutionary Anti-Semitism in Germany, from Kant to Wagner* (Princeton, NJ: Princeton University Press, 1990), Chap. 7. My own discussion of Herder has benefited from the work of F. M. Barnard. See Barnard, *Herder's Social and Political Thought: From Enlightenment to Nationalism* (Oxford: Clarendon, 1965); and Barnard, *Self-Direction and Political Legitimacy: Rousseau and Herder* (New York: Oxford University Press, 1988).

gradation and unique role in this march, adding a necessary element to the formation of the whole. "The forms which these grades of progress assume," writes Hegel, "are characteristic national spirits of history; the peculiar tenor of their moral life, of their Government, their Art, Religion, and Science. To realize these grades is the boundless impulse of the World-Spirit, the goal of its irresistible urging; for this division into organic members, and the full development of each, is its Idea."[33]

According to Hegel, each nation undergoes three stages in its life: growth, height of power, and decline. Once a nation has successfully brought a distinct idea into the world and objectified it, this nation then becomes dispensable from the point of view of world history and is consumed by the same distinct features that produced its achievements. "The life of a people ripens a certain fruit; its activity aims at the complete manifestation of the principle which it embodies. But this fruit does not fall back into the bosom of the people that produced and nurtured it; on the contrary, it becomes a poison-draught to it. That poison-draught it cannot let alone, for it has an insatiable thirst for it: the taste of the draught is its annihilation."[34] The destruction of nations, though a tragic event, is nevertheless inevitable and irresistible. Throughout history, people may have deluded themselves into believing that their glorious days could return and that the world would once more view them with awe. But this self-delusion is extinguished in modernity, for, according to Hegel, the modern must recognize that everything that occurs in history is necessary, rational, and unidirectional. Genuine freedom comes with this realization, from acting in light of what is actually given; *attempts to intervene in the social and political reality and to go against the course of the Spirit are futile.*

It is easy to see that the Hegelian view of history would have posed – and did pose – a serious challenge to the project of Jewish national revival. The Jews, according to this view, had fulfilled their role by advancing the monotheistic and abstract notion of the divine; their revival as a modern nation with independent political institutions would be an anomaly that contributed nothing to world history. Objective conditions seemed to concur with this verdict. The Jews were scattered all over Europe and the world and could hardly form an organic "body." They barely had any shared concerns or civic culture, and the daily experience of the general public where they resided was much more familiar to them than the

---

[33] G. W. F. Hegel, *The Philosophy of History* (New York: Dover Publications, 1956), p. 53.
[34] Ibid., p. 79.

experience of distant Jews. The Jewish "people" as an undifferentiated mass, a homogeneous whole, simply did not and could not exist.[35] Jews also lacked a territory to claim as their own; their life as a community could not be associated with an existing homeland or a folklore that evolves from such rootedness. The neglect of the Hebrew language was a token of this predicament, and this neglect in turn furthered the decline of the "nation."

Given this background, nineteenth-century narratives of national revival, as far as they were based on organic wholeness and teleology, were *irrelevant* in the Jewish case: Here, after all, the *essential precondi-tions* necessary for the (re)evolution of a nation were missing; the substratum imperative for any organism to flourish (a unity of people and land) was nonexistent. (To be sure, social Darwinism could provide additional explanations as to the inevitability of this predicament.) Furthermore, in order to become a nation, the Jews had a distinctively excruciating task: They had to rebel and discard their *Volksgeist* rather than embrace it as the foundation for their collective identity. For in contrast to other peoples, the Jews had cultivated a tradition that was especially incompatible with a national-political project: Rather than valorizing self-assertion, this tradition valued Messianic expectation; rather than preaching the glories of national power, it aspired (particularly in the nineteenth century) to a strengthening of moral consciousness and cosmopolitanism; and rather than mooring identity to a particular space, it grounded identity on the study of the movable Book. In short, theories such as Fichte's, Herder's, and Hegel's propelled Jews to recognize that their historical experience contradicted a realistic expectation of "nationhood." It is easy to miss this point, as most explanations of Jewish nationalism in fact do, since Zionism, similarly to German nationalism, celebrated national language and defined membership on the basis of ethnic origins. Yet its conception of time (with a few notable exceptions, such as that of Ahad Ha'am, as we shall see later) was wholly different from the German's of the nineteenth century (leaving Nietzsche aside, of course) and presented a combination of voluntaristic and semicyclical approaches to history that eventually shaped its politics to a great extent.

The challenges to Jewish national identity posed by Herderian and Hegelian notions of teleology are evident in the work of Nachman

---

[35] According to Liah Greenfeld, only when the category of the "people" begins to have a meaning and a referent, nationalism has made a decisive inroad. See Greenfeld, *Nationalism: Five Roads to Modernity*, pp. 1–27.

Krochmal (1785–1840), one of the leading Jewish philosophers of the nineteenth century. Krochmal agrees with Herder that organic patterns rule the fate of a nation and its *Volksgeist*, that history obeys essentially biological categories. Human events are seen as a part of Nature, progressing in the same gradual, immanent patterns of development. In a strictly continuous fashion, latent inner forces come to fruition and, after blooming and spending their creativity, inevitably fade away.[36] In addition, Krochmal echoes Hegelian idealism by positing an absolute, spiritual, and divine element (*haruhani hamuhlat*), the full comprehension of which requires an elongated historical process.

Yet it is interesting to note that Krochmal joins themes from these two philosophers to combat the implications of their own teleological views for the prospect of Jewish national awakening. Other nations, Krochmal claims, have advanced limited and particularistic notions of the divine; they therefore remained chained within Herderian organicism, which allows only one appearance on the world stage. But the Jews, by virtue of their abstract monotheistic faith – which is not dependent upon a place, civic life, or any other earthly precondition – have a unique bond with the purely spiritual and are therefore blessed with recurring cycles of national revival. As Jews, Krochmal maintains, "the three-period cycle ... was duplicated and triplicated with us, and ... with the completion of the period of withering away and vanishing, there always emerged a new and reviving spirit; and if we fell, we arose and were fortified, and did not abandon our God."[37] The Jews are not outside of or beyond history, not free from the dynamic of growth and decay; but each time they go through a cycle, Krochmal asserts, a transcendental force blasts the biological rules of history and inspires them to begin a new odyssey of national life. The vulnerability of worldly, social existence and institutions is ultimately not inimical to the Jews, he writes, since their unencumbered spirit is interwoven with an eternal, universal force.

Krochmal's theory is an important attempt to heed the language of teleology and escape its implications for the Jews. But it does so at a

---

[36] For discussions of the relation between Krochmal, on the one hand, and Herder and Hegel, on the other, see Nathan Rotenstreich, *Jewish Philosophy in Modern Times: From Mendelssohn to Rosenzweig* (New York: Holt, Rinehart and Winston, 1968), Part I; and Shlomo Avineri, *The Making of Modern Zionism*.

[37] Nachman Krochmal, *Guide to the Perplexed of the Time* (Waltham, MA: Ararat Press, 1961), pp. 40–1. This book was first published in 1851, after Krochmal's death in 1840.

high price: It eschews the possibility of a humanly induced break in history and establishes monotheistic metaphysics and heightened spirituality as the lasting and constitutive elements of the Jews as a nation. This refusal to admit voluntaristic leaps in time and the equation of spirituality and nationhood were precisely what the Zionists, as virile and natural political actors, were forced to question. The semicyclical temporal imagination espoused by Zionists (as we saw in Chapter 1) was founded precisely on a deliberate choice to follow an opportunity and images from the distant past, and on the centrality of place and of sensual existence in human life. In other words, this temporal imagination involved a completely different conceptual world than the one Krochmal was engaged in, and it had nothing to do with the language of teleology.

To conclude, then, I suggested in this section (and in Chapter 1) that the Jews were able to choose the semicyclical imagination only after the grip of teleological narratives had become somewhat looser, when moderns had a greater sense that temporal imaginations are more a matter of choice than of necessity, that they could be shaped. We have seen, also, that the two meta-narratives of the nineteenth century – expanding universalism and organic nationalism – presented history as having a skeleton, an underlying structure that provides pregiven function and location to history's flesh – the actual, flowing events. In modernity, this skeleton of history must be deciphered by the reflective mind and must serve as the foundation for action or inaction; it is a tribunal that separates meaningful deeds from vain attempts to cast reality against the march of time. These meta-narratives of secular temporality were potentially more deadly for the Jews' yearning for communal revival than their former Messianic belief had been because these narratives presented (sometimes with scientific assurance) views of history as teleological and unaffected even by divine intervention. It was no accident, then, that Zionism did not appear earlier in the century, in the heyday of teleology; instead, this political movement signifies the dawn of a new era, the rise of a novel temporal consciousness that, side by side with its semicyclicality, zoomed in on the formless nature of history and enshrined the malleability of human affairs.

III. ZIONISM AND SUNDERED HISTORY

Yes, visions alone grip the souls of men. And anyone who does not know how to begin from them, may be an excellent, worthy, sober-minded person, even a philanthropist on a large scale; but he will not be a leader of men, and no trace of him will remain. Theodor Herzl, *Tagebücher* (1896)

No artist will paint his picture, no general achieve victory, nor any people its freedom, without first having desired and striven for it in ... an unhistorical condition. As the man of action, according to Goethe's phrase, is always without conscience, so he is without knowledge; he forgets a great deal to do one thing, he is unjust to what lies behind him, and knows only one right, that right of that which is to become. Friedrich Nietzsche, *On the Advantage and Disadvantage of History for Life* ([1874] 1985)

Around the turn of the century, when Zionism first emerged as a political movement, writers of very different intellectual stripes began to reject teleological concepts and to voice the notion of a fissure in history. For "Nietzschean" Zionists, the rupture in history expressed itself in the dissolution of one configuration of Jewish identity and the opportunity and need for creating a new one. Zionism and the evolving Hebrew culture answered the sense of meaninglessness and morbidity that came with the decline of Jewish religion and tradition. For this school, redemption was an individual affair, calling for creative and even idiosyncratic ways of forming the self within a new secular, cultural context. Socialist Zionists, in contrast, saw the fissure in history as represented by the economic and social sphere. In this reading, it was a specific historical stage of capitalism that had rendered the integration of Jews into European society impossible, since they had become a surplus population that constituted a burden to others. An amelioration of the Jewish predicament, according to this view, could not be achieved simply by a change of occupations or locations within Europe, or even by emigration to North America; rather, what was needed was a planned, collective action that would change the territory and economic foundations of Jewish life and, consequently, the totality of the community's social existence.

We may say, then, that Zionism emerged as a singular mixture of Nietzschean and Marxian themes; its success depended on a conscious reshaping of the self, as well as on new economic and social conditions. In clarifying this notion of a necessary rupture in self and society, I will examine the works of two prominent Zionist writers. The first is Micha Josef Berdyczewski (1865–1921), widely considered to be among the founders of contemporary Hebrew literature and the writer who gave it a modernist hue. As one commentator rightly observed, the importance of Berdyczewski's thinking "in the development of the Zionist pioneering ethos exceeds that of any other Hebrew author."[38] The second writer

---

[38] Ehud Luz, *Parallels Meet: Religion and Nationalism in the Early Zionist Movement, 1882–1904* (New York: Jewish Publication Society, 1985), p. 170.

to be examined in this context is Dov-Ber Borochov (1881–1917), one of
the most important thinkers of early socialist Zionism, whose ideological vision also significantly influenced the Labor leaders who founded
the State of Israel.[39] Both writers express the theme of sundered history,

Berdyczewski was born in the Russian Pale of Settlement, a descendent of a respected
family of Hassidic rabbis. Despite his religious education, the young Berdyczewski was
an avid reader of the emerging Hebrew literature, an interest that provoked those
around him and led to the collapse of his first marriage. Divorced, he emigrated to
Germany in 1890 and lived there for most of his adult life. His studies at German
universities exposed him to Western philosophy in general and to Schopenhauer and
Nietzsche in particular. In his writings (and life story), Berdyczewski displays the
ambiguities of Jewish life at the time, shifting from Yiddish to Hebrew and back, lion-
izing the creative and autonomous individual while concomitantly expressing anguish
over the collapse of the shtetl. During his life, he was well known as a gifted writer and
as an uncompromising critic of all the accepted schools and leading individuals: rabbinical Judaism, Haskala, Hibbat Zion, Ahad Ha'am, Herzl, and so on. He achieved
notoriety when he published (concomitantly) nine books of stories and essays near the
turn of the century, expressing in these works modernist themes, such as passion, longing for aesthetic experience, willpower, and ambivalence. But Berdyczewski's importance is only now recognized fully. Not only was his vast literary project a landmark
in modern Hebrew literature, but the themes of his stories and essays also seem to have
been critical in articulating and shaping the emerging Zionist ethos (although he was
not politically involved in that movement).
    For secondary literature on Berdyczewski, see Avner Holtzman, *Hakarat panim:
masot al Micha Josef Berdyczewski* (Holon: Reshafim Press, 1993); Alan Mintz,
Banished from Their Father's Table: Loss of Faith and Hebrew Autobiography
(Bloomington: Indiana University Press, 1988); and David Ohana, "Zarathustra in
Jerusalem," in *The Shaping of Israeli Identity: Myth, Memory, and Trauma*, ed. D.
Ohana and R. Wistrich (London: Frank Cass, 1995), pp. 268–89.
[39] Dov-Ber Borochov was born in the Ukraine and grew up in Poltava. He was mostly
self-educated, since like most Jews at this time he could not be admitted to a Russian
university. His importance to the Zionist movement lay in his work both as a politician
and as a theoretician. In the former role, he was the founder of the party Po'alei Zion,
which had a major role in shaping the Jewish labor movement in Palestine (see note 62).
He participated in a few Zionist congresses and lectured throughout Russia, Central
Europe, and the United States. As a theorist, he not only introduced the marriage of
socialism and Jewish nationalism but also insisted on seeing the Jewish problem as
fundamentally economic, and anti-Semitism as chiefly a symptom of material dependency and a distorted occupational structure. His many interests included philosophy,
economics, linguistics, and statistics, all of which he examined from his particular
position as a Zionist and a Jew. Between 1907 and 1917 Borochov lived in Central
Europe and the United States. He returned to Russia at the start of the Bolshevik
Revolution, but died soon after.
    For secondary literature on Borochov, see Matityahu Mintz, *Zmanim hadashim,
zmirot hadashot: Ber-Borochov 1914–1917* [New times, new tunes: Ber-Borochov
1914–1917] (Tel Aviv: Am Oved and Tel Aviv University, 1988); Allon Gal, *Socialist-
Zionism: Theory and Issues in Contemporary Jewish Nationalism* (Cambridge, MA:
Schenkman Press, 1973); Wistrich, *Socialism and the Jews*; and Jonathan Frankel,
Prophecy and Politics: Socialism, Nationalism, and the Russian Jews, 1862–1917
(Cambridge: Cambridge University Press, 1981).

particularly in works written around the turn of the century. Their works celebrate themes of historical discontinuity, the openness of human reality, and the urgency for action on both individual and collective levels.

"For every people," writes Berdyczewski, "nationality [or national culture] is the only treasure that contains human virtues. It is where the individual finds assurance for his actions and it is the necessary guardian of his [cultural] possessions. But with us [Jews], the individual perceives in nationality everything that opposes [the aspirations of] his heart."[40] For other nations, he explains, culture is an evolving whole, modified by circumstances and shifting needs; it is the realm in which the past is continuously reinterpreted, affirmed, and criticized, thus allowing individuals to respond to the challenges of the present. Moreover, national cultures lionize the distinct attributes and experiences of their peoples – their myths and stories, guiding values and spiritual quests, models of character and emotional fabric, attachment to landscape and environment – and tend to de-emphasize religion, especially when the latter has universalist orientation and appeal. The Jews, Berdyczewski felt, had cultivated a national culture that remained lifeless, extolling the frozen tenets of religion as its chief foundation. "For two thousand years," he writes, "we did not have a present at all. One long past engulfed us, a past devoid of a present or a future."[41]

For religious Jews, the Talmudic texts are a point of origin that holds absolute priority over the present; not only are they wholly accessible to the contemporary mind but they are also the only way to illuminate the perplexities of the here and now. The repetitive probing of the Talmud is performed not so much to provide new insights into the ancient texts, nor even to adapt them to the present. Rather, learning allows the student to immerse himself in the text until "its words and reasoning seem to be his own." The ritualistic reading of the old truths day after day "is a crucial step toward their reaffirmation."[42] But for the modern Jew who ponders how to integrate into civil society – wondering what clothes to wear, which holidays to observe, what foods to eat – this reciting of the past has become a temporal labyrinth, claims Berdyczewski:

The writers of every nation and language begin their life in the present, and are gradually progressing toward the past. This is like a tower that is wide at the

---

[40] Berdyczewski, *Kol ma'amarei*, p. 41.
[41] Ibid., p. 47.
[42] Samuel C. Heilman, *The People of the Book* (Chicago: University of Chicago Press, 1983), pp. 65, 72.

bottom and becomes narrow toward its head. The present is the foundation and the past is the roof. But the opposite is true for us. We will begin from the past and end in the present, and most often we will get lost and become weary midway and will not get to the present at all.[43]

Thus, in his view, the authority granted to the past prevents adaptability and rejuvenation, excluding individuals from having an impact on tradition, whether on its contents or its future course.

The past's authority also leads to the continuous reproduction of a certain type of self. Nietzsche famously claimed that "the Jews were a priestly nation of *ressentiment par excellence,* possessing an unparalleled genius for popular morality."[44] Berdyczewski, who read Nietzsche thoroughly, seems to agree with this statement, arguing that the Jew is still characterized by excessive morality and spirituality, a lack of earthliness and manliness, the repression of instincts and feelings, and too great a distance from Nature and aesthetic values. Many Jews, asserts Berdyczewski, think that "they realize the sense of national duty that lives in their hearts by preserving what has been transmitted to them by their forebears." In this way, Jews have become *"slaves of spirituality,* people without the habit of approaching life and the world around them in a natural way."[45] Christianity may also have similar repercussions, but in the eyes of Jews like Berdyczewski, the European is at the same time a citizen with a voice, an individual exposed to a blooming national culture, an independent agent in a free economy. In all of these spheres of life, non-Jewish Europeans opened domains of individual action and development that mitigated the Judeo-Christian slave morality/mentality. The Jew, in contrast, epitomizes for Berdyczewski the European malaise of morbidity and hatred of life that Nietzsche unmasked. The

---

[43] Berdyczewski, *Kol ma'amarei,* p. 37.

[44] Friedrich Nietzsche, *On the Genealogy of Morals* (Cambridge: Cambridge University Press, 1994), "First Essay," sec. 16. For a general discussion about Nietzsche's place in modern Hebrew literature, see Menahem Brinker, "Nietzsche's Influence on Hebrew Writers of the Russian Empire," in *Nietzsche and Soviet Culture: Ally and Adversary,* ed. B. G. Rosenthal (Cambridge: Cambridge University Press, 1994), pp. 393–413. For Nietzsche's influence on German Jewish writers such as Stefan Zweig, Franz Werfel, Jakob Wessermann, and others, see Jacob Golomb, "Nietzsche and the Marginal Jews," in *Nietzsche and Jewish Culture,* ed. Jacob Golomb (London: Routledge, 1997), pp. 158–92.

[45] Berdyczewski, *Kol ma'amarei,* p. 30. The idea that Zionists should regain their naturalness and manly strength was of course most pronounced in the writings of Max Nordau, the popular author of *Degeneration* (1892). George Mosse examined these aspects of Nordau's writings in *Confronting the Nation: Jewish and Western Nationalism* (Boston: Brandeis University Press, 1993).

modern Jew must therefore view the diasporic past as a cohesive, tainted whole – and reject it in toto. "Our soul is full of bitterness toward the past," writes Berdyczewski, "against all those who left us their own beliefs and thoughts. Our soul is burning in conjoining the past into one whole element, one that stands against our life and its foundations."[46]

In developing this consciousness of the necessity of a temporal rupture, Berdyczewski was rebelling against the writer Ahad Ha'am (Asher Zevi Ginsberg), who at the turn of the century was considered the most prominent Zionist theorist. Ahad Ha'am embraced the notion of Jewish cultural renewal but thought that such a project would be meaningful only if the fundamental spirit of Judaism was preserved and further elaborated. A radical departure from the past would leave Jews atomized, confused, and without an anchor, he opined (as we shall see in Chapter 4). Ahad Ha'am even wrote a disparaging essay ridiculing "our Nietzscheans." Certainly, he writes there, the Jews must embrace the idea of an *Übermensch*, but such an individual should be true to the Jewish tradition, embodying its ethical values in their highest form. We may be correct in speculating, he continues, that "Nietzsche himself, if he had a Hebraic taste, would have then changed his moral criteria. While still presenting the overman as an end in himself, he [Nietzsche] would have ascribed to this overman very different characteristics: the strengthening of the moral faculties, the overcoming of the bestial instinct, the search for justice and truth in thought and in action, and a world war against lies and evil."[47] Giving a paradoxical twist to the *Genealogy of Morals*, Ahad Ha'am claims that the Jewish *Übermensch* is therefore the *tzadik*, the moral saint.

In Berdyczewski's lights, Ahad Ha'am's judgment was off course. The latter forged an untenable concept of national identity, since it was grounded in an essentialist and monolithic depiction of the Jewish tradition as centered on an intensified moral consciousness and the rejection of self-assertion. Ahad Ha'am was unable to see that a merely secularized version of the diasporic culture would not be enough to energize a national revival, and that moral saints cannot be founders and settlers, even on a limited scale; Berdyczewski, in contrast, believed in the adaptability of culture to circumstances, and the latter now demanded new ingredients – libido, will, power. To be sure, Berdyczewski also

[46] Berdyczewski, *Kol ma'amarei*, p. 41.
[47] Ahad Ha'am, *Kol ma'amarei Ahad Ha'am* (Tel Aviv: Dvir, 1947), p. 155. For a recent study of Ahad Ha'am, see Steven Zipperstein, *Elusive Prophet: Ah'ad Ha'am and the Origins of Zionism* (Berkeley: University of California Press, 1993).

recognized that his generation was doomed to live with ambivalence, with "a split in the heart," as he famously coined it.[48] The tradition was too near, its allure not yet wholly overcome. The Jew was at a strange junction, existing in a temporal vacuum in which the past had ended but the future was still unknown. "We don't have a sky or an earth,"[49] says Berdyczewski – no fixed hook to pull us toward the future, no foundation to ground us in the past. The temporal experience of Zionism could therefore lead to confusion and paralysis, feelings that humans encounter on realizing that history is undetermined and malleable to their wills and imaginations. The answer to these feelings, according to Berdyczewski, is not to find a middle ground, to change one's geographic location and remain the same person morally. No, one must overcome the trepidation and stand up for the moment. As mentioned previously, he warned that the choice is "to be or to vanish!" and, even more specifically, "to be the last Jews or the first Hebrews."[50]

Berdyczewski's Hebrews would display a novel combination of the ancient and the new (exemplifying the semicyclical temporal imagination), a union whose imprints were to become evident in the Zionist ethos. Berdyczewski was among the first to revive and glorify biblical legends of self-sacrifice and courage (such as that of Samson), as well as stories of Jewish resistance to the Romans during and after the destruction of the Second Temple (e.g., the events at Masada).[51] The fascination of people like Ben-Gurion with Joshua, the biblical military leader who conquered the Land of Israel, was a continuation of this revival.[52]

Berdyczewski was also distinctive in that he joined the ancient heroic ethos with contemporary Nietzschean notions. For him, the creative will is the highest human attribute, and by allowing its expression we affirm life and realize our personal autonomy: "The will to live characterizes every being and is the essence of every living creature," he writes. "There is no life without will, without aspiration and without expansion."[53] Will is the wish to grow, to become something that we are not; it introduces a

---

[48] Berdyczewski, *Kol ma'amarei*, p. 63.

[49] Ibid., p. 41.

[50] Ibid., p. 29.

[51] For a discussion of these themes in Berdyczewski and of their significance for the Zionist attitude toward the use of force, see Anita Shapira, *Land and Power*, Chap. 1.

[52] Ben-Gurion's preoccupation with biblical heroes and his special relationships with biblical scholars fostered the popularization of biblical studies in Israel. Michael Keren discusses this phenomenon in his *Ben-Gurion and the Intellectuals: Power, Knowledge, and Charisma* (Dekalb: Northern Illinois University Press, 1983).

[53] Berdyczewski, *Kol ma'amarei*, p. 17.

perpetual experience of lack and aspiration. To be sure, he says, the Jews have always cultivated a sound will, which allowed them to preserve their religious identity and reenact the past. But this will measured itself by its ability to obey outer commands; it demanded the negation of the self. The new will of the Jew should be redirected toward self-formation, and growth should be redefined according to an individually chosen principle. Berdyzcewski argues that personal growth should be seen aesthetically, as the creative shaping of the emotional and spiritual material of the self. "We perceive the moral question of freedom and slavery," he writes, "not in a rational fashion, but in an artistic and poetic one. Surely the uncarved marble that changes naturally is freer than the one that bears the imprints of an artist ... but exactly because of its shape, the latter acquires true, internal freedom. The moral power of genuine man is only the power of a creator, a creator in soul and spirit, a creator in deeds and their arrangement."[54] Zionism offers a grand and exciting opportunity for the self to remold itself as a citizen in a new polity, as a warrior guarding a new territory, as a shaper of space in an exciting natural environment, as a speaker and cultural agent in a new language. By combining the biblical spirit of courage and dignity with aesthetic creativity, he claims, modern Jews can realize their true humanity: They can introduce something heroic and novel to the world, something that "did not exist before in the same shape and stamp."[55]

This sense of omnipotence allows the Zionist to welcome the task of making a break in history. In contrast to the rule-governed notion of time – whether in line with Herderian organic development, with Kantian linearism, historical materialism, and so forth – Berdyczewski demands a recognition of the openness of history, of its responsiveness to human deeds and aspirations. This recognition may not come easily. "They say," he writes, "if we believe in the sciences, that causal laws [in human affairs] rule similarly to natural laws, and who can therefore hope to alter them?" *But this notion of historical causality is the archenemy of the Zionist, teleology his foe.* Change in history is brought about by individuals, by people "working with the people and the nation, within its language, as the artist will do to the material at hand." These people, he continues, "are the heroes of deeds and thought, they are the ones who force society, who bend the direction of things."[56] Observing the

---

[54] Ibid., p. 349.
[55] Ibid., p. 41.
[56] Ibid., p. 61.

dynamic of historical change, he writes, we comprehend that time has no underlying structure and necessity working within it, but is, rather, composed of continuity and discontinuity, including moments in which events can be grasped and molded. Accordingly, human life cannot be perceived only as a continuum of interrelated, homogeneous time units: "One moment could contain a whole life, one deed and one significant phrase could be equal to many deeds and many phrases; one great hour in life could be equivalent to a person's entire existence."[57]

This view of time, we may say, fosters a consciousness of urgency, an eagerness to seize the moment in line with the present-centered temporal imagination. The Jews – who made patience and procrastination their national traits, who suffered from a lengthy repression of instincts – must now heal themselves by allowing their inner forces to erupt freely, Berdyczewski explains: "The conquest of the land [of Israel] certainly did not come through patience." The making of the Jew into an earthly, political being involves "a complete change and radical new beginning; and it is the nature of change not to be patient, it is the nature of change to reject and conquer truly."[58] Opportunities come and go, and decisive crossroads may be missed by those entangled in the dream of tradition; thus, he holds, Zionists must illuminate the potential for radical departure hidden in the moment, cultivating a will that interposes in history, swiftly and unmercifully.

The sense of Jews as being at a decisive historical juncture also animates the works of Borochov, a Labor Zionist who grappled with articulating a new conception of Marxism that would be compatible with the temporal experience of Zionism. Unlike Berdyczewski, who directed a fair amount of his intellectual effort at rejecting the Jewish tradition and the identity it enshrined, Borochov worked at confronting social theories that could have deemed Zionism illegitimate and irrational from a historical perspective.

One of Borochov's first targets was the teleological notion of time, especially the belief in (dialectical) progress, which most Marxists accepted. He believed that while other nations might hold such convictions, progress was a dangerous chimera for the Jews. "We do not rely on progress; we know that its over-pious proponents inflate its achievements out of all proportion," he writes. "Progress is an important factor

57 Ibid., p. 344.
58 Ibid., p. 87.

in the rapid development of technology, science, perhaps even of the arts, but certainly [also] in the development of neurosis, hysteria, and prostitution. It is too soon to speak about the moral progress of nations, of the termination of that destructive, national egoism. Progress is a double-edged sword; if the good angel within man advances, the Satan within him advances too." Elsewhere he adds that "no one has seriously proven the statements that progress entails salvation and has examined its real value.... It has not been demonstrated that the development of history, of nations and societies, contains any progress. And it is [therefore] entirely unfair to come to the Jewish people ... and ask them to put their stakes on progress."[59]

For Borochov, one may say, Jews are the best readers of omens. As marginal and dispensable, they were the first to experience the ominous European ambiance that further developed later in the twentieth century. Jews in particular could no longer think in teleological and deterministic ways, aspiring to be integrated into a European nation-state or to become part of a cosmopolitan human community. Borochov believed that anti-Semitism was unavoidable because it served economic interests; he understood expulsions of Jews from Western European countries such as England and France mainly in functional terms. As for modernity, he heeded Marx's view that the Jewish middle class fulfilled its historical role by enhancing cross-national trade and financing the first stages of mechanized capitalism; but unlike Marx, he believed in the importance of national differences and identifications, predicting that the Jews would constitute a growing economic threat to the evolving, local middle classes in Eastern Europe. Similarly, he reasoned, as industrialization and mass production advanced in countries such as Poland and Russia, and machines replaced workers, the lower strata of the Jewish community would gradually become superfluous, and the local proletariat – their potential competitors rather than comrades – would reject them. Jews never succeeded in becoming a part of the workforce in heavy industry, and even in light industry and unskilled jobs their position was uncertain. For Borochov, then, the advent of capitalism meant the deterioration of the Jew as worker, trader, shopkeeper, and even banker – a phenomenon that he believed would engender the eruption of ethnic malice.

[59] Dov-Ber Borochov, *Class Struggle and the Jewish Nation* (New Brunswick, NJ: Transaction Publishers, 1984), p. 36; followed by Borochov, "Questions Concerning Zionist Theory," in *Ketavim nivcharim* [Selected writings], vol. 1 (Tel Aviv: Am Oved, 1944), pp. 2–3 (Hebrew edition).

Borochov encouraged Jews, especially those committed to socialism, to think in national terms of their own and eschew the empty slogans of equal citizenship and universalism. In agreement with Austro-Marxists (who did not support, as we have seen, Jewish nationalism) and the pioneering socialist-Zionist Nahman Syrkin,[60] Borochov argued that "the national question must be considered more deeply and honestly; it is imperative to break once and for all with unfounded prejudices. We must understand that class consciousness cannot develop normally unless the national problem, in whatever form it may exist, has been solved."[61] Political independence is a precondition for the victory of socialism in any given group, since national and ethnic divisions tend to overshadow conflicts among classes. The quest for collective identity must be answered before material concerns can take precedence; struggle over the means of production develops only in well-defined social units where these means could be seen as belonging to the people (and not to the relatively few individuals who own them) who developed them through their collective history. To join the socialist revolution, then, the Jews must possess a territory of their own, self-governing bodies, and a distinct language and culture (all of which Borochov designates as "conditions of production").

After 1905, Borochov strove to demonstrate (in essays such as "Our Platform") that this process of forming independent conditions of production would be wholly *stychic*, that is, an inevitable and natural process immune to the human will and which stems from the material predicament of the Jews in the *Galut* (Diaspora). While his early writings also mention the external forces driving the Jews out of Europe, his conception of historical transformation at that stage highlights the role of human volition. This conviction is epitomized in his concept of "therapeutic" change, which he contrasts with the "evolutionary" one.[62]

---

[60] See Nachman Syrkin, *Kitvei Nachman Syrkin* [The writings of Nachman Syrkin], (Tel Aviv: Davar, 1939), Chap. 1.

[61] Borochov, *Class Struggle and the Jewish Nation*, p. 69.

[62] Borochov's main influence on socialist Zionism was his overall conceptual scheme presented here, which saw nationalism and socialism as compatible and emphasized the importance of developing an independent Jewish economy and a large working class. Yet Borochov's legacy is varied. Groups to the left of the Labor movement, such as Hashomer Hatza'ir, embraced the Marxist strand of his thought, as epitomized by "Our Platform." But Borochov was also espoused by those who ennobled the national cause and had little interest in class war and a universal revolution of the proletariat. In the context of this essay, of particular importance is his influence on the young Ben-Gurion, who was a member of the Palestinian branch of the party Po'alei Zion. As Ben-Gurion's biographer Shabtai Teveth notes, Ben-Gurion "was attracted by Borochov's

In the evolutionary type of change as defined by Borochov, events unfold gradually, employing forces that are immanent in a given social unit. In this notion of formation, the present contains the seeds of the future, and there is no need to "obtain assistance from any special means, but rather to shoulder the development of those forces that brought about the existing situation." In the transition to socialism, this means that "everything that supports the rapid maturation of capitalism and the opposition of class interests within it brings the problem to its ultimate resolution."[63] In such circumstances, human agency has the limited role of identifying the progressive elements in society and promoting them by intellectual critique, forging class consciousness and alliances, establishing political parties, and so on. There is no need to create a global, detailed blueprint of action; the communist vision serves only as a regulative idea, and intervention is determined according to the internal dynamic of the existing socioeconomic order and the specific developments in society and the market. In the evolutionary model, emancipation requires the ability to acutely observe the present, not the capacity to dream of, and then actualize, the nonexistent.

The second type of social change, according to Borochov, is called for in "pathological situations" – situations lacking any corrective elements in their present configurations. In such cases an anomaly exists, one that "is born not from the [natural] growth of society, but from destructive, external pressures. The solution to the impasse lies in healing, that is, in joining means aimed at a thorough extinction of the causes and forces that brought about the pain." This healing demands rapid external intervention and "should always bring to life new forces that have not existed before and that would not have appeared by themselves."[64]

idea that a pioneering movement to Palestine of young men and women was a prerequisite for rebuilding *Eretz Israel*," but he rejected "out of hand Borochov's fundamental maxim that historical necessity would in itself ensure a Jewish flight from exile to Palestine." In other words, Ben-Gurion embraced Borochov's voluntaristic, early conception of Zionism, and eschewed the wholly stychic, later one of "Our Platform." See Shabtai Teveth, *Ben-Gurion: The Burning Ground, 1886–1948* (Boston: Houghton Mifflin, 1987), p. 29. It should also be noted that toward the end of his life, Borochov seemed to have come full circle, championing his early ideas of 1903–5. See Frankel, *Prophecy and Politics*, Chap. 7.

[63] This paper has not been translated into English, and my references here are to the Hebrew edition and to the original Russian publication. See Dov-Ber Borochov, "On the Question of Zion and Territory," in *Ketavim nivcharim*, vol. 1, p. 46 (Hebrew edition); Borochov, "K voprosu o sione i territorii," *Evreiskaia zhizn* (hereafter *Ez*) 7 (July 1905): 70. I would like to thank Bella Barmak for making the translations from Russian to English.

[64] Borochov, "On the Question of Zion and Territory," p. 46; Part I, *Ez* 7 (July 1905): 70.

Therapy (or healing) is not the art of amending the given but a radical act that destroys what exists, promptly and decisively. Here, one cannot defer to empirical facts since the nature of correction demands a break from them; the healer is characterized not by strategic play in the present but by the ability to enliven the imagination, master unexpected powers, and render novel images palpable. Social therapy, argues Borochov, is an "enterprise," whereby the human will successfully establishes an all-engulfing, new mode of existence based on an inspiring ideal. This ideal should "sharpen the interested will, incite it to action, and prevent it from being … aloof from anything it encounters in objective reality." The "*combative* [*boevovo*, in Russian] value"[65] of the ideal is determined according to its ability to induce an ethos of forcefulness in individuals and to energize their confrontation with the environment. Those inspired by the combative ideal should act in concert, their actions being "organized according to a given and predetermined plan"[66] that would calculate necessary means and resources and leave as little room as possible for actual conditions to intervene in the erection of a new social order. With Borochov, "the plan" becomes a necessary means of intervention, a tool to be inserted in the hiatus of history and that will steer events onto a new course.

Borochov argues that Zionism belongs to the second, therapeutic type of social change. For him, those Jews who see Zionism as a mass movement of an evolutionary nature rightly conclude that "under no circumstances could Zionism become a reality, that it is an absolute utopia."[67] They search in vain for a tradition of audacious political deeds among the Jews, and all they find is a people who have made adaptability into an art of living and who are reluctant to embark on an unfamiliar course. But we live in an era in which today is a poor indicator of tomorrow, argues Borochov. Zionism would be possible once the Jews realized that discontinuity in history was both possible and necessary: "The Zionist movement is one of the clearest examples of a therapeutic movement for whom the *ideal is something totally new and separate from the existing orders of life*"[68] (my emphasis). Making Zionism real would necessitate

---

[65] My emphasis. See Borochov, "On the Question of Zion and Territory," p. 78; Part II, *Ez* 8 (August 1905): 40.

[66] Borochov, "On the Question of Zion and Territory," p. 47; *Ez* 7: 70.

[67] Borochov, "On the Question of Zion and Territory," p. 51; *Ez* 7: 76.

[68] Borochov, "On the Question of Zion and Territory," p. 52; *Ez* 7: 78. Borochov anticipates that after Zionism has successfully established its own independent conditions of production, it will become an evolutionary movement.

a change of landscape and climate, of familiar vocations and careers, of language and culture, of comfort and material conditions; it would succeed only if Jews deliberately distanced themselves from the *totality* of their current ways, if they welcomed the destruction.

In the movement's beginnings, only a small number of people could withstand such personal sacrifice. Consequently, according to Borochov, in Zionism "the individual element plays a huge role; for us it is not the quantity of members that is important. Rather, we desire that they should possess a high quality of consciousness and devotion. They will be the pioneering foundation of the movement."[69] This avant-garde elite must be able to envision a fictional future and give it absolute priority over adverse empirical conditions, he writes; it must methodically translate into reality a detailed political and economic plan that lacks even an anchor. He thus demands that the usual heroic figure in Judaism, the person willing to die in order to preserve the integrity of his or her faith in God, be displaced by a new type of hero, one characterized by a willingness to accept "sacrifices and the danger of personal extinction"[70] for the sake of the nation's cause.

Berdyczewski and Borochov represent opposing poles of Zionist thought. The former sought redemption through the aesthetic transformation of the self, the latter through the erection of a new socioeconomic reality. Berdyczewski was concerned with identity and meaning, Borochov with material existence and social justice. Despite these and other differences, however, their visions were complementary in practice. For the success of Zionism hinged upon a novel fusion – a fusion of a creative notion of the self with the quest for collective therapy. It hinged upon presenting normative metamorphosis as an individual achievement that also fosters grand collective action. In fact, even from a theoretical viewpoint, Borochov and Berdyczewski shared much more than first meets the eye. They concurred in the temporal ontology they advanced and in their celebration of similar themes of sundered history, including the amorphous nature of social life; the opportunity for transfiguration offered at unique historical junctures; the inadequacy of reform and other gradual processes; the valorization of risk and discontinuity; the power of the will to begin something unprecedented; and, finally, the decisive role of selected individuals in revolutionary times.

---

[69] Borochov, "On the Question of Zion and Territory," p. 52; *Ez* 7: 78.
[70] Borochov, "On the Question of Zionism and Territory," p. 60; *Ez* 7: 87.

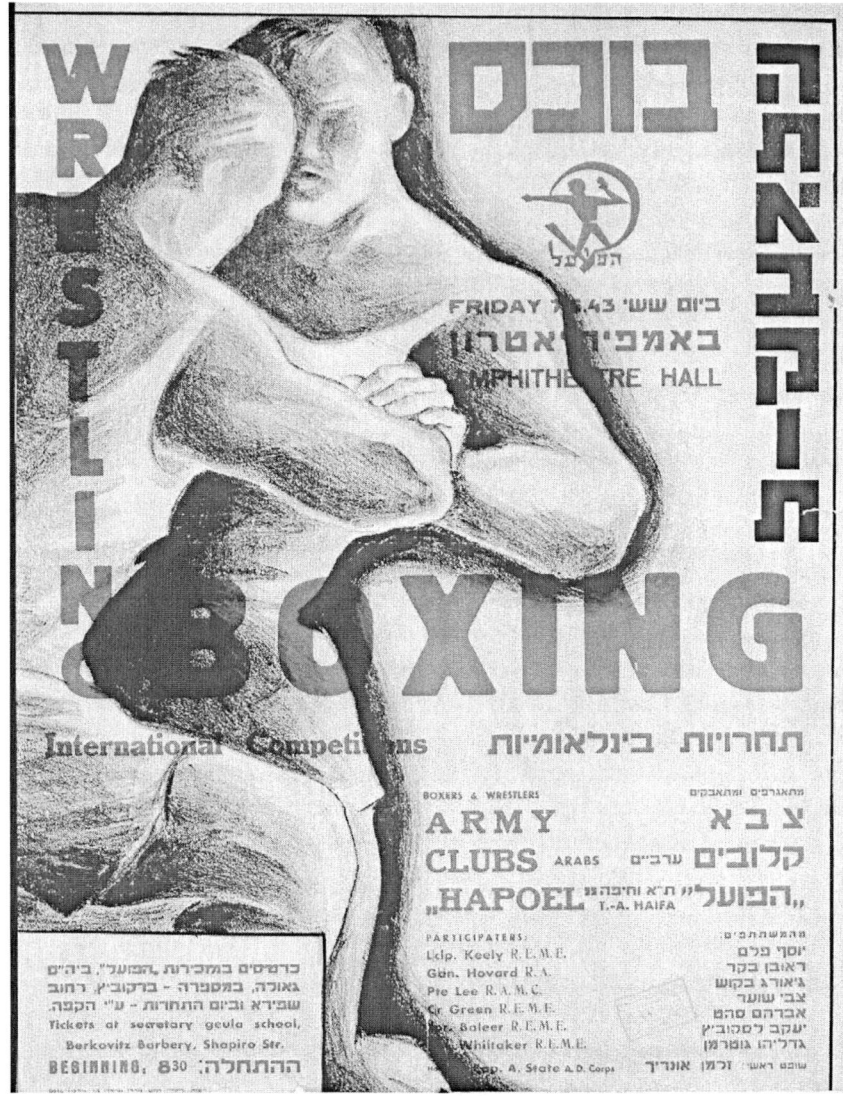

PHOTO 4. A poster announcing a boxing competition (1943). The participants included the British Army, the Arab Clubs, and Hapoel (a Jewish sport club). Photo courtesy of The Central Zionist Archives.

To be sure, Zionism was and is a modernist movement, aspiring to erect a nation-state that possesses the nexus of institutions characterizing this body since the sixteenth and seventeenth centuries. But if the Western European nation-states that emerged from that period did so in a piecemeal fashion, with monarchies and other central institutions gradually imposing their authority upon preexisting populations, in Zionism there existed at first neither an organizational foundation nor a geographically concentrated population to undertake such a project. Hence, in establishing political, legal, military, economic, and other institutions, as well as in bringing people to Palestine and making them citizens, the Zionist endeavor required a temporal consciousness of discontinuity and a celebration of the inaugurating "event" for its realization. The establishment of the State of Israel may have been an exemplary attempt at fulfilling a modernist dream through a postmodern temporal insight – one that accentuates the openness of history, its lack of confining metanarratives.

IV. FROM SUNDERED HISTORY TO BUILDING

The temporal consciousness of Zionism that we have explored had important consequences not only for the emergence of the movement but also for its future ideology and political practice. This was already evident when the first political leaders of the country preserved the revolutionary temporal imagination of early Zionism, professing that social reality is wholly open to willful intervention and is formed according to visionary human design. "The expectation of stychic process is nothing but a hypocritical apology for impotence and weakness," writes David Ben-Gurion. "It is not fatalistic destiny that governs history, and life is not merely a game of blind forces. The intentional and long-sighted intervention of the active, creative, and conscious will in history is one of the elements affecting the stychic process."[71] In this Ben-Gurionian vista, obstacles are either minor facts to be ignored or challenges that call for higher and more vigorous deeds.

Zionism became increasingly dependent upon, and enamored with, the ability of human beings to shape the existing geographical and demographic environments according to their will, to impose new, tangible "facts" where none had existed, to think of the environment and circumstances as essentially undefined and little restricted. While the desire of a group (tribe, nation, or empire) to expand its territory and might is perhaps the rule in history rather than the exception, for Ben-Gurion and many of his followers it seemed as if Zionist existence itself is unbound – in fact, is defined by this unboundedness – and limits (even self-imposed

[71] David Ben-Gurion, *Mima'amad le'am* (Tel Aviv: Ayanot, 1955), p. 24.

ones, such as a constitution) are thus pretentious and dangerous: "[O]ur state is the most dynamic state in the entire world," avers Ben Gurion. "Each day it is being created anew. Each day more Jews are liberated by emigrating to the Land of Israel. Each day, new pieces of land are being cultivated and are salvaged from neglect and bareness. Such dynamism cannot tolerate a fixed framework and artificial chains."[72]

Moreover, Zionism could never be sure of how long this transformative ability would last, and it preserves even today the dual and somewhat contradictory beliefs that a) humans can willfully craft events in light of their interests and dreams and that b) they must act with urgency before the window of opportunity is slammed shut by an unexpected gale. This duality, symptomatic of the consciousness of sundered history, helped Zionism become arguably the most successful revolution of the last century. But it also had some less laudable effects. Patterns of thinking and acting formed during the childhood of the movement became constitutive of its ethos, functioning as an inured foundation in its approach to the world. Many Zionists have gradually discovered that their source of strength is also their source of malaise, that (as is often the case) what was crucial in the formation of the movement became problematic later on.

These troubling political aspects of the Zionist conception of sundered history are exemplified by an almost mythic incident from the relatively recent history of Palestine, one that reflects the duality of Zionist temporal consciousness. In the 1930s, recounts Baruch Kimmerling, "conquering groups" (*kvutzot kibush*) used to erect instant settlements in which the parts needed for construction were prefabricated and only required assembling at the site. Within one day, such a group would have "built a wall, surrounded by a barbed-wire fence, which enclosed an area (about 40 by 40 yards) that included lodging cabins, a public mess hall, and a tower with a spotlight. Thus, within a few hours, with the help of a large manpower force ... an entire settlement was established, ready to defend itself against Arab attack."[73] Between 1936 and 1939, about 50 settlements were established in Palestine using this method, called in Hebrew *Homa Umigdal* (tower and stockade). The

[72] David Ben-Gurion, "Speech to the Provional State Council," September 30, 1948. Quoted here from Asaf Sagiv, "The Sabra's Lawless Legacy," *Azure* 33 (Spring 2008), http://www.azure.org.il/article.php?id=412.

[73] Baruch Kimmerling, *Zionism and Territory: The Socio-Territorial Dimensions of Zionist Politics* (Berkeley: University of California Institute of International Studies Press, 1983), p. 88.

operation was meant to secure the hold of Jews in areas where their claim to sovereignty was in question (despite their ownership of the lands in which they settled), and in order to create a continuity of Jewish communities before the British plan for the partition of Palestine (which would have given the Jews only a minute state) could be implemented. (It never was.) The architectonic model aimed to serve a distinct Zionist combination of agricultural community and military compound, and the swift method of construction, based on detailed planning and coordination, were so innovative that Homa Umigdal was chosen to represent Palestine in the World Exposition in Paris (1937).[74]

Homa Umigdal reflects the degree to which Zionists rejected limits on action (legal, political) and their increasing belief that physical edifices are incomparably more potent than words in shaping reality. Homa Umigdal also conveys the sense of urgency characterizing many Zionist actions, as well as the perception that shifting political circumstances might render future operations unfeasible. More than 60 years later (in March 1997), when the Likud government wanted to ensure Israeli control over the areas surrounding Jerusalem prior to any further implementation of the Oslo Accords, it accepted a plan to swiftly build a neighborhood on Har Homa (Wall Mountain).

In both time periods, this expansion strategy generated a profound crisis in the relationship between Jews and Arabs. The entire settlement project in the West Bank, in fact, demonstrates that in Israel, the enterprise of building is often associated with the nation's political goals, since it is the most tangible way to change the landscape, both physically and demographically. Building is an act of claiming ownership, not on behalf of the individual but for the community; it marks the borders of state territory. Hence, even architecture has often tended to follow political exigencies, rather than aesthetic and housing considerations. (This tendency is epitomized perhaps by the mobile homes and shipping containers being used by young settlers in the West Bank – especially since 1993 and the advent of the Oslo Accords – in their struggle to swiftly erect outposts on the hilltops, thus establishing an unauthorized reality that both the Israeli government and certainly the Palestinians find difficult to cope with.) In the State of Israel and the West Bank, a building's location, contour, materials, and hour of construction often reveal how an urgent relationship to time begets a conquering attitude toward space.

[74] See Sharon Rotbard, "Wall and Tower [Homa Umigdal]," in *A Civilian Occupation*, ed. Rafi Segal and Eyal Weitzman (Tel Aviv, New York: Verso, 2003).

More generally, and as will be argued in the next chapter, the Zionist (especially the socialist Zionist) could be seen as an urgent builder: a *homo faber* oriented toward reshaping the human and material worlds according to national aims and plans. Zionism was not carried out according to a prior, clear, and detailed plan to be executed (although the First Zionist Congress accepted the Basel Program already in 1897); constant improvisation and piecemeal progression were inherent to its modus operandi. But it is nevertheless true that at the core of this movement is a notion resembling that of the builder, who begins the formation of a project from abstract plans that have little to support them in (social) reality, with only a model conceived of in the mind according to which fabrication is executed[75] (see my discussion in the Conclusion). Put differently, Zionism is not a movement of people who lived on a certain territory, interacted among themselves for generations, and decided at one point to become a nation, but rather a movement in which both the nation and its home had to be formed and built – mostly through the Yishuv's (i.e., the Jewish community in Palestine prior to Independence) institutional planning and execution – and thus constantly imaged and planned before materializing. By insisting on the priority of the mind over "what is," however, humans tend to become less interested in dialogue with what already exists independent of their thoughts and actions; knowledge and models are conceived prior to engagement with the environment in which they are supposed to be implemented,[76] and may involve self-enclosure. At certain points, something like this happened in Palestine and shaped the relations between Jews and Arabs. As Walter Laqueur remarks, "being totally absorbed in their own national movement, they [Zionists] did not recognize that their cousins, too, are undergoing national revival, and they sometimes seemed to deny them the right to do so."[77]

Now, the ability to generate a new environment and to live with and within our physical and social creations grounds us and establishes spaces we can claim as our own; the things we bring about (fields, buildings, language, culture, social institutions) boost, in turn, our self-regard as potent beings. To live in a world that, for the most part, has been created by oneself and by contemporary co-builders is a unique feeling – a Promethean dream, perhaps – and at times could be

---

[75] Hannah Arendt, *The Human Condition* (Chicago: University of Chicago Press, 1958), p. 140.

[76] See James Scott, *Seeing Like A State: How Certain Schemes to Improve the Human Condition Have Failed* (New Haven, CT: Yale University Press, 1998).

[77] Laqueur, *A History of Zionism*, p. 230.

intoxicating despite the great difficulties along the way. Yet the combination of homo faber and politics that permeates the Zionist experience
could be problematic. "Homo faber," notes Arendt, is "a lord and master not only because he is the master or has set himself up as the master
of all nature, but because he is master of himself and his doings." This
mastery could be dangerous, since the "element of violation and violence is present in all fabrication, and homo faber, the creator of human
artifice, has always been a destroyer of nature."[78] More specifically, the
repercussions of and limits on violence vary according to the sphere of
application.

The designer of a house has extensive freedom in envisioning the
architectonic model and even in changing the landscape. Mountains can
be leveled; nowadays, even an island can be artificially made. Still, he or
she must negotiate with the existing geography and environment, taking
note of the path of the sun and the direction of the breeze, the shifting sandy soil and the frequent storms. The architect is also limited by
the qualities of the materials he or she is using; concrete can be given
almost any shape, but none will turn it into a "warm" material. But if
the context and physicality of matter still play some role in architectonic
designs, in the political sphere there are few visible or fixed constraints
on preexisting models: In that sphere there are no mountains to be seen,
no oceans to behold. Political obstacles and pressures may be formidable,
but they are not tangible. The limits of what can be achieved by political means are rather blurred because humans may be coaxed, shifted,
ignored, manipulated, silenced – and worse. This quality of politics is
especially ominous when no prior, human-social-cultural context exists
before the political vision is formed. The political model of therapeutic
movements, as Borochov notes, does not necessarily evolve gradually –
out of social reality – nor is it in dialogue with the individuals and communities inhabiting its space, especially when no such space exists. And
the more imaginary the character of the social model – the more focused
on the novelty and beauty of its own scheme, and the more driven by the
urgent exigencies of the initiators – the more violence toward oneself and
others it could engender.

With this understanding of both the novelty and risk of translating
the imagination into political praxis, it is hard to regard Herzl's con-
fessional words as merely of biographical interest: "*Vielleicht sind es
übrigens gar keine praktischen Ideen, und ich mache mich zum Gespött*

[78] Arendt, *The Human Condition*, pp. 144, 139.

PHOTO 5. Jewish laborers on the shore near Tel Aviv loading camels with sand for building. Photo by Zoltan Kluger, August 1, 1939. Courtesy of the Government Press Office, Israel.

der Leute, mit denen ich ernst rede. Und ich wandle nor im Roman?"[79]
(Perhaps these ideas are not practical ones at all and I am only making myself the laughing-stock of the people to whom I talk about it seriously. Could I be merely walking within my own novel?)[80]

---

[79] Theodor Herzl, *Theodor Herzl Zionistisches Tagebücher* II (Berlin: Verlag Ullstein, 1983), p. 52.
[80] *The Complete Diaries of Theodor Herzl*, vol. 1 (New York: Thomas Yoseloff, 1960), p. 13.

3

The End of Building

Any piece of land on which your feet shall tread, to you it shall be given,
as I have spoken (*dibarti*) with Moses.

Joshua 1:3

In regard to the disengagement from the territories of Judea and Samaria,
I am moved to the verge of tears whenever I stand on the northern slope
of the Ebal Mountain [where Joshua, according to biblical tradition, built
a shrine].

Ehud Barak, June 1999

In 1958, biblical study groups sprang up all over Israel. A society governed by revolutionary socialists was enchanted by the ancient text. These self-proclaimed atheists read the Bible somewhat as the ardent Luther studied the New Testament: without the mediation of thousands of years of interpretation and established authorities. The most famous group convened regularly at the home of Prime Minister David Ben-Gurion. These meetings brought together members of the young state's elite, including the president of Israel, Yitzhak Ben-Zevi; a future president, Zalman Shazar; the former chief-of-staff, later an archaeologist, Professor Yigael Yadin; the rector and president of the Hebrew University, Professor Benjamin Mazar; the deputy of the Chief Justice of the Supreme Court, Shneor Cheshin; and other academics and dignitaries. This group chose to study an often neglected book of the Bible, the Book of Joshua, which describes the conquest of the Land of Israel by the Hebrews who came from Egypt after the exodus. The discussions that ensued in this esteemed group concerned Joshua's military methods, the logistical problems he faced, the recent archaeological debates on the locations of biblical cities, the social and economic challenges faced by the conquering tribes, and more. In other words, the participants were attempting to fathom a moment in ancient history, one which they felt was akin to theirs and could serve as a source for inspiration.

The prime minister opened the last discussion in this series. Ben-Gurion presented a bold thesis that questioned the prevailing interpretations of biblical stories related to both Abraham and Joshua. According to these traditional interpretations, God revealed himself to Abraham, chose him as the first Hebrew, and ordered him to leave his home in Ur-Kasdim for Canaan. But Ben-Gurion turned this familiar genealogy and chronology on its head. In his opinion, a certain group had already embraced monotheism prior to Abraham's visitation by God. This group, averred Ben-Gurion, already lived in Shechem (Nablus), Canaan. Thus, the "Jewish people preceded Abraham,"[1] and the latter emigrated to Canaan because he had heard about the Hebrews and was drawn to their distinct religion. (There is no other way to explain, Ben-Gurion argues, why a well-off person would leave his native home in Ur-Kasdim, which was far more advanced economically and culturally than Canaan.) Moreover, suggests Ben-Gurion, this tribe never vacated Canaan when Abraham's great-grandchildren (Jacob's offspring) emigrated to Egypt; they remained in Shechem, cleaving to their language and religious creed. This city then served as the critical strategic base that helped Joshua conquer Canaan after the exodus from Egypt. "Only a few families – the most esteemed and well-bred – emigrated to Egypt," writes Ben-Gurion. "The rest stayed and lived in Canaan among other tribes, and their language was Hebrew."[2]

In Ben-Gurion's reading, then, the Hebrew people sprang from the earth of Canaan, as it were – they had never been immigrants who came

---

[1] David Ben-Gurion, *Iyunim besefer yehoshua* [Studies in the Book of Joshua] (Jerusalem: Kiryat Sefer, 1960), p. 321. For a discussion of Ben-Gurion's attitude toward the Bible, see Anita Shapira, "Ben-Gurion and the Bible: The Creation of a Historical Narrative," in her *New Jews, Old Jews* (Tel Aviv: Am Oved, 1997), pp. 213–47 (in Hebrew). For Ben-Gurion's relations with the intellectual elite of the young state, see Michael Keren, *Ben-Gurion and the Intellectuals*. For general discussions of Ben-Gurion, see Michael Bar-Zohar, *The Armed Prophet: A Biography of Ben-Gurion* (London: Barker, 1967); and Shabtai Teveth, *Ben-Gurion: The Burning Ground*.

[2] Ben-Gurion, *Iyunim besefer yehoshua*, p. 323. Ben-Gurion argues that other tribes in Canaan may also have spoken Hebrew, but that the Hebrew tribe was unique because it joined this language with monotheistic belief and thereby turned Hebrew into a holy language.

to a new land, nor ever left their land, as the tradition taught. He saw them as standing at the edge beyond which no historiography is possible, where there is no way to sever language from geography, identity from land. Some may read the prime minister's story as a dubious attempt to boost the legitimacy of certain territorial claims; on a deeper level, perhaps, Ben-Gurion testifies to the Zionists' longing to overcome their homelessness. His interpretation aims to subdue homelessness by presenting an almost atemporal, irrevocable bond between people and their land. Other Zionists expressed a similar desire to wholly belong to a certain terrain and place. "The human being," wrote the early Hebrew poet Shaul Tchernichovsky in his most famous poem, "is nothing but a small piece of land; the human being is nothing but the imprint of his homeland's landscape."[3] It is the insouciant dwelling of our childhood – and the openness we have then to the ways in which Nature discloses itself – that shapes our identity. The eagle and the rock, the grass and the fountains affect us more than mountains of words contained in any canon. While Jews in the Diaspora were characteristically ambivalent about their attachment to their place of residence, Zionists (at least those who were committed to the Holy Land) wished to bind themselves to a particular landscape, and they presented this bond as the heart of their identity. What could be heard in Palestine, wrote Berl Katznelson, was "a bitter, solemn roar of a nation without land ... [a nation] that seeks to amend the distortion of history by once again mooring itself, with its innermost being, to the land of its origins."[4]

[3] Shaul Tchernichovsky, *Shirim* [Poems] (Tel Aviv: Schocken, 1950), p. 466. This unidirectional view of the relation between Nature and the human soul led the poet to a melancholic conclusion that as someone born in the Diaspora, he is destined to feel eternal estrangement from Palestine. The pioneers of the Second *Aliya*, however, embraced a more active and dialectic attitude toward the land in their attempt to overcome this estrangement.

[4] Berl Katznelson, *Kitvei B. Katznelson* [The writings of Berl Katznelson], vol. 2 (Tel Aviv: Davar, 1946), p. 197. Such pronouncements express the Zionists' belief that their project in space is fueled by a craving they cultivated for two thousand years. Yet this craving must be seen in a wider cultural context, not merely in terms of Jewish history. As discussed in Chapters 2 and 4, by picturing an essentialist connection to the land, Zionists embraced Herder's view that a people cannot exist as a nation without a bond to a particular land. Herder's conception of nationalism was highly influential in Central and Eastern Europe, where most Jews lived. It should also be mentioned that in their relation to the land, Zionists were influenced by other modern schools, such as physiocracy, Russian populism, and English romanticism. See Ruth Kark, "Land-God-Man: Concepts of Land Ownership in Traditional Cultures in Eretz-Israel," in *Ideology and*

Since the second half of the nineteenth century, homelessness has emerged as a central theme in various contexts. Marx laments that workers are estranged from their bodies and from the world of objects they have created; Hardy writes about rootless existence in an age of massive demographic dislocations and social mobility; Weber beholds a disenchanted, objectivized natural world that is no longer meaningfully related to us. While each of these types of homelessness may have contributed to the emergence of Zionism, another experience of homelessness was more critical for the birth of this movement: the homelessness of a tradition and its language. As mentioned previously, during the Diaspora, tradition held sway over the individual's life and allowed Jews to mitigate the influence of frequent spatial dislocations. The study of the Bible, Mishnah, Talmud, and later canons (as well as the rituals and practices associated with these texts) established a continuity of identity from one place to another, from one generation to the next. Belonging was language based, formed in believers who read the same sacred texts, presupposed their timeless truth and enduring relevancy, and sought ways to contribute to a vast universe of interpretations. Throughout many generations, Jews understood that while communities may be forced to disperse and houses may have to be abandoned on the spur of the moment, a mind shaped by the language of tradition is ultimately never homeless.

The homelessness of the Jew was born when tradition and its language no longer functioned as a substitute homeland. As we saw in Chapter 2, for many Jews of the late nineteenth century the past became an unwelcome and even destructive force: Tradition was turned into a separate, devitalizing department within the self, and it was seen as hampering the aesthetic and creative will of the individual in his or her attempts to transform life and adapt to modern circumstances. Tradition suddenly meant passivity, lack of singularity, unnaturalness, unproductiveness, excessive spirituality. Most importantly, tradition signified a false faith in the shared world of meanings established and transmitted by words. Words of prayer and learning prevented no pogroms, assured no political rights, and answered no economic wants. It is certainly true that Hebrew writers of fiction and poetry played a major role in the Zionist revolution, creating vital cultural substance for the revived nation, reflecting the new challenges, options, doubts, and so on in modern Jewish

Landscape in Historical Perspective, ed. A. Baker and G. Biger (Cambridge: Cambridge University Press, 1992), pp. 63–82.

life – even serving sometimes as heroes and models for the people.[5] Still, even for one of the major figures in the new Hebrew literature (and probably the central writer of the Zionist labor movement), language was destined to become subservient to work: According to Y. H. Brenner, one should not trust the "the beauty of the new Hebrew terms" for their own sake, but rather should develop a language that expresses life – that is, expresses "working life and thought about work."[6] Only a language based on the concrete could be trusted and respected (luckily, Brenner was hardly loyal to his own recommendation).

This mistrust in language is not solely Zionist.[7] As George Steiner notes, we witness in Western culture (even prior to the Internet) a "retreat from the word." "Until the seventeenth century," he argues, "the sphere of language encompassed nearly the whole experience and reality; today it comprises a narrower domain. It no longer articulates or is relevant to all major modes of action, thought, and sensibility. Large areas of meaning and praxis now belong to such nonverbal languages as mathematics, symbolic logic, and formulas of chemical or electronic relations."[8] Moreover, the two great philosophers who shaped the intellectual climate of the late nineteenth century also mistrusted language:

[5] See Orsion Bartana, "The Brenner School and the Agnon School in Hebrew Literature of the Twentieth Century," *Hebrew Studies* 45 (2004): 49–69.

[6] See Y. H. Brenner's 1919 essay *"Adama* [Soil]," reprinted in *Kol kitvei Y. H. Brenner*, vol. 3 (Tel Aviv: Hakibbutz Hameuhad, 1967), p. 481.

[7] Neither is it wholly new: Hobbes, for example, expressed great mistrust in the common use of words.

[8] George Steiner, "The Retreat from the Word," in *Language and Silence* (London: Penguin Books, 1969), pp. 44–5. The diminishing role of ordinary language in modern life affects the role of the temporal dimension of human existence, since language is vital for creating a sense of narrativity and continuity. However, while Steiner underscores the roles of science and technology in this development, there are other ways to understand why moderns find it difficult to experience the full richness of time. Lukács, for example, argues that time (which is inherently qualitative and particular) has lost its allure in the age of capitalism, an economic system whose internal logic is based on calculability and commensurability. In capitalism, writes Lukács, "time sheds its qualitative, variable, flowing nature; it freezes into an exactly delimited, quantifiable continuum ... (the reified, mechanically objectified performance of the worker, wholly separated from his total human personality); in short, it becomes space" (Lukács, *History and Class Consciousness: Studies in Marxist Dialectics* [London: Merlin Press, 1968], p. 90). Henri Lefebvre agrees with this observation, contending that "the manifest expulsion of time is arguably one of the hallmarks of modernity" (Lefebvre, *The Production of Space*, trans. Donald Nicholson-Smith [Oxford: Blackwell, 1991], p. 96). According to this logic, it is the crisis in the way we experience time in capitalism that devalues language, not vice versa. See also my discussion of present-centeredness in Chapter 1.

PHOTO 6. A construction worker, Rothschild Boulevard, Tel Aviv. Photo by
Ze'ev Aleksandrowicz, 1933.

Marx presented the prevailing cultural, legalistic, political, and other
discourses as parts of the superstructure and as embodying a certain
ideology; Nietzsche suggested that language may be shaped by the naive
human desire to control the world through knowledge. ("Very belat-
edly [only now]" he writes, "is it dawning on men that in their belief in
language they have propagated a monstrous error.")[9]

The implications of this retreat from and suspicion toward the words
by which people historically formed their interactions were especially
momentous for secularized Jews, however. For without the linguistic-
textual world of their tradition, they had little existential ground or ability to maintain a continuity in time. To summarize, then, the alienation
of modern Jews from the sphere of language generally (similarly to other
moderns) and from the words and texts of tradition, in particular, contributed to the Zionists' search for a new, corporeal ground for their
identity. This led them to overcome their homelessness in a novel way:
through building.

[9] Friedrich Nietzsche, *Human, All Too Human* (Lincoln: University of Nebraska Press,
1996), p. 19.

I. BUILDING AS AN END IN ITSELF

"Historical events are not possible without linguistic activity; the experience gained from these events cannot be communicated except through language," argues Koselleck.[10] History is surely something different from, and much larger than, its expression in language. Yet we have no way of grasping history without the words, terms, and speech acts that articulate a certain historical moment – that is, the hopes and ideals, emotions and fears, mind-set and ethos of those engaged in it. Without language, the meanings of past events and of individual and collective actions are sealed to us. Now inquiring into the evolution of certain Hebrew words (as I am about to do) in order to understand the Zionist mind-set is somewhat paradoxical inasmuch as it occurs in a society that was inclined to devalue the sphere of language and its ontological and constitutive status. Nevertheless, the attempt to grasp essential dimensions of the movement necessitates such study. Possibly it is no accident that the Hebrew word that best expresses the Zionist frame of mind is a word that points to the most formidable objects created by men and women: *binyan* (building). *It is this word that bridges the linguistically oriented and matter-oriented worlds that some Jews traversed in the early twentieth century.*

The aim of this chapter is to explore the ways by which Zionists attempted to overcome their homelessness, cement their bond to the land, and create a new society and state through what could be termed *building*. In fact, "building" – both as a verb (an activity) and as a noun (an object) – occupies a profound metaphoric and heuristic position in the Zionist imagination, since it communicates the notion of belonging, of deliberately establishing connectedness. In Zionism as it evolved in Palestine, building signifies belonging on many levels but mainly on these three: a) in the material world produced by human beings; b) in a historically meaningful and humanized space; and c) in a community of constructors that willfully reshapes both space and matter. Since the Enlightenment, various political movements (noted in the following sections) have used the idea and practice of building to elucidate their projects and aspirations; the case of Zionism perhaps epitomizes the use of this metaphor in modernity, since in this national movement everything had to be invented and "built" (land, people, culture, language, social

---

[10] Koselleck, *Futures Past*, p. 222.

and political institutions, economy, and more). In other words, Zionism may offer an exemplary opportunity to reflect upon the potentials and failures of building as a *civic and public concept*, one that embodies the willful and premeditated aspects of modern politics.

In the Hebrew language of nineteenth-century Europe, *binyan* (building) was already used metaphorically to apply to tangible, whole systems. Shimshon Bloch, for example, writes about "the building of their bodies, which is healthy and solid" (1822), and Mendele Moykher Sfarim writes about "the building of the cosmos" (1867). The poet H. N. Bialik later proclaims that the tradition of the *Aggada* (the part of the canonical texts that is not concerned with law and rules) should be recovered, claiming that "it should be built as a building entire, ready and standing in its complete frame and height, in its details and abstractions, from the foundations up" (1918).[11] But other Zionists took this concept further, describing their entire project as *"binyan leumi"* (national building). One of the first writers to use this term was Ahad Ha'am in his famous essay "This Is Not the Way" (*Lo zo haderech*, 1889),[12] a critique of the first Zionist settlers and their earthly motivations. Due to this and other essays, Ahad Ha'am was paradoxically accused of engaging in *stira* or "destroying," as opposed to genuine *beniya* or "building."[13] (The early Zionist internal debate was often coined in terms of who was building and who was demolishing the collective project.)

Even more important were the different uses of the metaphor that came soon after those early days: While Ahad Ha'am portrayed the national building as composed mainly of new Jewish spiritual substance, the pioneers who shaped the Zionist ethos in Palestine thought in rather different terms.[14] They described the biblical land as the foundation of

---

[11] Chaim Nahman Bialik, *Kol kitvei Chaim Nahman Bialik* [The collected writings of Chaim Nahman Bialik] (Tel Aviv: Dvir, 1943), p. 206.

[12] See, e.g., Ahad Ha'am, *Al parashat derachim* [At the crossroads] (Berlin: Jüdischer Verlag, 1921), p. 6.

[13] See, e.g. Shmaryahu Levin, *Habinyan vehastira* [The building and the destruction], 1903, at http://benyehuda.org/shmaryahu/index.html.

[14] In trying to answer the questions posed here, I will not refer (for the most part) to building in its political and instrumental functions. It is well known that since its inception, Zionist politics has perceived construction as the ultimate assurance of ownership over land; even today, as noted in Chapter 2, the settlements in the West Bank are used to redraw the boundaries of the Israeli state. Massive construction, moreover, was an urgent solution to the housing problems of an immigrant society and had a critical role in the new economy. Indeed, the Jewish economy in Palestine was shaped, to a large extent, by the ups and downs in the construction industry, and this economy was thereby greatly influenced by the influx of newcomers. (To some extent, this is still the

the national building, and its edifice as including the immigrant population, economic and civic organizations, national culture and language, as well as state and military institutions; they presented, in other words, the entire national project as semipalpable. But why did Zionists find it necessary to picture their national endeavor as consisting of "one building"[15] and to use building metaphors and their collaterals so often, referring to their project as involving the activity of "building" or as "a building"? What were the implications of their highly functionalist and holistic political language? ["Each sensible Zionist," writes Chaim Arlosoroff, "appreciates the small achievements that, while from the perspective of our great building are like a grain of sand, nevertheless establish in their amalgamation the foundation upon which we would be able to continue the building."] How did the use of building as a chief concept shape the view of the individual in Zionism and what were the long-term effects of this view on Israeli citizenship? ["Anyone who builds," writes M. L. Lilienblum, "must select whole, solid stones and posit them as the foundations of the building.... [T]he individuals who now immigrate into the Holy Land are the foundations of the

case today.) In the years 1932–3, for example, investment in the construction industry comprised 45 percent of the total investments in the Jewish economy in Palestine (see Shlomo Levi, ed., *Bishnat hashloshim* [In the 1930s] [Tel Aviv: Davar, 1952], p. 331). While these practical motivations for building are essential for grasping why construction occupies such a prominent place in the Zionist imagination, my interest here is mostly limited to the meaning of building from a philosophical-political perspective.

[15] Aharon David Gordon, "Achariot hayachid" [The Individual's Responsibility], in *Sefer A. D. Gordon: Mishnato udvaro*, ed. Yehuda Iges (Tel Aviv: Ha'oved Hatzioni, 1943), p. 116. See also his uses of this term in "Land and Its Redemption," *Sefer*, p. 109.

Gordon (1856–1922) came to Palestine from Russia when he was 46. He became an important figure in the Second *Aliya*, partly because his writings and reflections are grounded in his own experience as a hardworking pioneer who was undeterred by barriers of age and poor health. Gordon was not a socialist or a Marxist, but he celebrated the capacity of human beings to labor with their own hands as their highest quality. He believed that the revival of the individual Jew would demand taxing physical work, since only such work could reconnect the Jew with Nature and the cosmic, spiritual dimension of existence; this mode of life, moreover, would grant Jews the economic independence and dignity that they lacked in the Diaspora. While Gordon was interested in the fate of the individual Jew, his thought is organic and perceives single men and women as inseparable from the national group. However, in contrast to Ben-Gurion, he was not particularly concerned with political issues and the project of state formation; his organic nationalism was part of a worldview that was chiefly spiritual and existential.

For a general discussion of Gordon's work, see Eliezer Schwied, *Hayachid: olamo shel A. D. Gordon* [The individual: The world of A. D. Gordon] (Tel Aviv: Am Oved, 1970); and Gideon Shimoni, *The Zionist Ideology* (Hanover, NH: Brandeis University Press, 1995), pp. 208–16.

building."][16] More generally, what can the Zionists' language and dominant metaphor teach us about their political philosophy in general and conception of democracy in particular?

I will explore these questions by examining the place of building in various writings of Zionists from the Second and Third *Aliya* (i.e., wave of immigration). I will pay particular attention to the writings of A. D. Gordon, the chief ideologist of the Second Aliya (which took place from 1904 to 1914), and to the writings of the young Ben-Gurion,[17] the major political leader who emerged from that Aliya.

Before we probe into the use of "building" in Zionism, however, it is worth noting that the desirability of human attachment to a particular place and the celebration of building in establishing such an attachment are controversial, both politically and otherwise. In his well-known essay "Building, Dwelling, Thinking," Heidegger explores the notion of building in its relation to a primary predicament of homelessness (*Unheimlichkeit*). Homelessness has a positive facet, he claims, since it "calls mortals into their dwelling"; the lack of home or feeling that we have a place of our own in the world raises the understanding that we

---

[16] See: Chaim Arlosoroff, "Haproblemot hafinanssiot bebinyan Eretz Israel [The financial problems in building Eretz Israel]" (1931), at http://benyehuda.org/arlosoroff/014. html, and M. L. Lilienblum, "Avanim lebinyan [Stones for the building]" (1891), at http://benyehuda.org/malal/mll102.html. Another common term used to describe the aim of the Zionist project was *bayit leumi* (national home). Yet the Hebrew word *bayit* means not only a home but also building or house – the actual object in which one may feel at home. Thus, the metaphor of *bayit leumi* maintains the tangible and object-like character of the Zionist language in describing the overarching goal of the movement.

[17] David Ben-Gurion (1886–1973), the first prime minister of Israel and its foremost politician in the age leading up to independence and after, also had a formative influence on Israel's ideology and practice. I cannot explore his thought at any length here but will mention a few ideas pertinent to this chapter. While a labor leader and a self-proclaimed socialist, Ben-Gurion also believed that the goal of building a Jewish state was more important than that of realizing a socialist vision; notions such as collective ownership over the means of production or just distribution of wealth, he claimed, were secondary compared to the central, national goal of Zionism (as he interpreted this movement). As prime minister, he pushed this position a step further, suggesting that citizens in the young nation should overcome their group and party loyalties and act according to the general interests of the state. Ben-Gurion held that the fate of the Zionist movement would be determined in Palestine, not in the political arena of the Diaspora; in fact, he epitomizes the activist strand of Zionism that was committed to concentrating efforts on creating a new social, economic, demographic, and military reality in Palestine before it was too late. Though an atheist, he saw the Bible as the most important source for shaping the new Hebrew's identity; and despite his firm realism, he held a utopian vision of the Zionist movement and later of the State of Israel. See note 1 above for relevant bibliography.

need to overcome this predicament.[18] To dwell, however, does not mean merely to inhabit a certain structure. Heidegger suggests that humans dwell when they save the environment from objectification and remain open to Being; he insists, however, that building is imperative for achieving such a mode of existence. To overcome their homelessness, he posits, human beings must build, not simply to find shelter but in order to merge with their surroundings in a proper way (a way that acknowledges what he calls "the fourfold"). In contrast to modernists such as Le Corbusier, Heidegger calls for humans to shape space and become integrated with it through properly made artifacts (in terms of form, location, materials, and so on) and the ensuing creation of "oneness" between humans and their habitat. Thus, he suggests, building leads to dwelling. But in fact, to build properly is already to understand Being, to take part in a form (or stage) of dwelling that is prior to the building itself and is expressed by the latter. He claims that the etymology of the word *bauen* (to build) reveals this inherent connection between building and dwelling, since in the old German language, *bauen* means also to dwell. It is conceptually erroneous, he avers, to disengage dwelling from building: "Building is not merely a means and a way toward dwelling – to build is in itself already to dwell."[19] Building completes our sense of dwelling and is essential to it; *it allows for existential wholeness and rootedness, which no other human activity can offer.*

In contrast to Heidegger's noninstrumental and apolitical view of building, Aristotle criticizes the disposition of human beings to bind

---

[18] Martin Heidegger, "Building, Dwelling, Thinking," in *Basic Writings*, ed. D. E. Krell (New York: Harper and Row, 1977), p. 339. For a discussion of the connection between homelessness and architecture in Heidegger, see Krell's essay "Das Unheimliche: Architectural Sections of Heidegger and Freud," *Research in Phenomenology* 22 (1992): 43–61.

[19] Heidegger, *Basic Writings*, p. 324. As noted, Heidegger embraces a noninstrumental view of building, believing that in building, humans learn to dwell and acquire a sense of "being-in-the-world." He suggests that in those houses and other structures that are built appropriately (such as the old farmhouses in the Black Forest), we see "the power to let earth and heaven, divinities and mortals enter a simple oneness into things" (p. 338). Within this "fourfold," Heidegger is concerned particularly with the earth. He argues that "mortals dwell in that they save the earth.... To save really means to set something free into its essence" (p. 328). A building helps human beings free and save the earth when its wooden walls evoke in them the nearby forest, when its location on the hillside reminds them of the hill's sheltering potential against winds and storms, and so on. The house both articulates preexisting aspects of the environment and shapes the way we experience and behold the surroundings in return. By helping the earth to emerge in such a way, the building allows mortals to begin relating to and caring for the earth, rather than seeing it as a mere object and resource.

themselves to the visible world of their creations and to the earth that bears them. While Heidegger is motivated by a hunger for existential wholeness, Aristotle seeks to separate the end from the means, the immaterial from the material, the citizen from the builder, and the polis from a particular piece of land. "There is nothing in common between the builder and the dwelling-house he builds," Aristotle writes. "The builder's skill is simply a means and the dwelling-house is the end. On this it follows that, if states need property [as a dwelling-house needs building tools and workmen to use them], property nevertheless is not a part of the state.... [T]he state is an association of equals, and only of equals; and its object is the best and highest life possible."[20] Despite our impressive skills in humanizing Nature and making it our property, Aristotle believes that the good life inheres in our capacity to be citizens in a democratic polity, as measured by the individual's *eudaimonia*. To achieve the latter, the citizen must be freed from the allure of the material-spatial world and the dexterity this world fosters; only participation in the political community, unconfined by any particular terrain, allows the cultivation of excellence and the goodness that comes with its ongoing practice. Good citizenship is threatened when people become too attached to the land they have amassed and the things they have erected upon it. Thus, in contrast to Heidegger, Aristotle suggests that genuine human fulfillment (for which the moral-political sphere is essential) calls for extreme caution in our relations to building – both the activity and the product itself.

Zionists were disposed to embrace a modernist, decontextualized architecture (which we will examine below) that was at odds with Heidegger's vision of architecture; but the meaning they gave to building has an important affinity with the existentialist philosopher's notion of it.[21] While they were motivated by genuine political, economic, and other pressing concerns, they also tended to posit homelessness, as they understood it, as a central problem of modern Jewish men and women and strove to combat this predicament through a shared project of

---

[20] Aristotle, *The Politics of Aristotle*, trans. Ernest Barker (Oxford: Oxford University Press, 1946), 1328a30.

[21] This resemblance between Heidegger's thought and Zionism in the sphere of building does not suggest that they had much else in common. Zionism contains a strong Promethean aspect that is not shared by Heidegger, and, needless to say, Heidegger's leader centeredness and other disturbing political ideas have nothing to do with the political vision of Zionism.

construction. This attempt to ground themselves in space led them to view building not merely as an instrumental activity necessary for establishing a polity; it also turned building and the transformation of space into an end in itself. With a few exceptions such as Herzl – who said that "a state is formed, not by pieces of land, but rather by a number of men united under sovereign rule," and that "the people is the subjective [*persönliche*], land the objective [*dingliche*] foundation of a State, and the subjective basis is the more important of the two" – the Aristotelian notion of the state (as a separate entity from the particular land it happens to be located in) did not take hold.[22] The identity of the citizen as founded on political institutions and norms was not separated in the minds of people from the notion of identity as based on place; the possibility of a conflict between these two foundations of Zionist identity had not, for the most part, even been contemplated. A certain "*oneness*" crept into early Zionist political thinking, in which people, land, culture, human constructions, political community, and state institutions were often thought to comprise together a monolithic, single building.

Aristotle may have been wrong in denying that building is an important human good and a vehicle for high aesthetic expression, as well as in denying that merging with one's natural environment in a proper and meaningful way is a worthy goal. But as the case of Zionism exemplifies, he was correct in insisting that the inability to distinguish conceptually between a political community and its vision of the good, on the one hand, and a certain land and the human artifacts on that land, on the other, may ultimately confuse the means with the ends, or the lesser ends with the higher ones. The activity and products of building could be dangerous, suggests Aristotle, since they could attach human beings to space in ways that propel them to prize the earth they dwell on and cultivate over their bonds with and commitment to their fellow citizens. Moreover, Aristotle insists that the practical skills required by builders and craftsmen have little to do with the virtues required of the citizen (such as capacity for deliberation, sense of justice, and independence of mind), and that the (nonverbal and nonpluralistic) solidarity among builders is different in kind from the solidarity required by citizens. With these general observations in mind, we could better examine the relations between building and politics in Zionism.

[22] Theodor Herzl, *The Jewish State*, trans. Sylvie D'Avigdor, at http://www.jewishvirtuallibrary.org/jsource/Zionism/herzl2.html.

PHOTO 7. A worker at a brick manufacturing factory in Tel Aviv. Photo by Hans Pinn, June 1, 1946. Courtesy of the Government Press Office, Israel.

II. ZIONISM, DISCONTINUITY, AND MODERNIST
ARCHITECTURE

Said Israel: Would you lay down the instruments of building and their practice; would you step down from the scaffold on which you stood with other prominent builders?

And he would reply: I relinquished the instruments and stepped down from the high scaffold to become myself lime, matter, and a brick.

Nathan Alterman, "A Citizen of the State of Israel: David Ben-Gurion" (a poem written on the occasion of Ben-Gurion's resignation from the prime ministership), November 1953

During the nineteenth century, the marriage of building projects and nationalism was taking place all over Europe – especially through monuments. In Germany, for example, Ernst von Bandel constructed the *Hermannsdenkmal* (completed in 1875) in honor of the Barbarian victory over the Roman legions. Youths all over Germany played a central role in this episode (by financing, for example), and the monument was therefore perceived as belonging to and expressing the spirit of the people, serving as a site for various national festivals. In fact, as the historian George Mosse claims, because of the participatory process of construction and the public functions of the place, "the history of the *Hermannsdenkmal* mirrors the course of German nationalism in the nineteenth century."[23] Later monuments, such as the *Niederwalddenkmal* (1885), heightened this bond between national identity and symbolic buildings in Germany.

Yet the metaphor of building and the practice of architecture are also alluring for revolutionary societies and avant-garde movements. The Soviets often used expressions such as *stroitel`stvo sotsializma* and *stroitel`stvo kommunizma* (building socialism and building communism, respectively); in the "Manifesto of Futurist Architecture" (1914), it is said that "architecture cannot be subjected to the laws of historical continuity" and that "each generation must build its own city."[24] Those who erect buildings are generally perceived as audacious initiators who interrupt the existing order. Building is a discontinuous activity: Constructions are (most often) not elaborations or continuations of previous ones; neighboring structures – and their stories, styles, or materials – do not bind a new construction. In fact, buildings tend to ignore previous ones; they announce their architectonic autonomy and are functionally self-sufficient. Moreover, buildings are not the fruit of a natural causation or a hidden teleology at work in human reality: They come into being only because individuals choose to become the architects of space and the absolute originators of action. "Every construction," writes Mircea Eliade, "is an absolute beginning, that is, it tends to restore the initial instant, the plenitude of a present that contains no

---

[23] George Mosse, *The Nationalization of the Masses* (New York: American Library, 1975), p. 59.

[24] Quoted here from C. Tisdall and A. Bozzolla, *Futurism* (London: Thames and Hudson, 1972), p. 130. The manifesto was written by the architect Sant'Elia. In Russian, the word *stroitel'stvo* means "to build and construct," but also to put something into order. For a discussion of building metaphors in Soviet discourse, see Richard Anderson, "Metaphors of Dictatorship and Democracy: Changes in the Russian Political Lexicon and the Transformation of Russian Politics," *Slavic Review* 60, no. 2 (2001): 212–335. For a general discussion of spatial metaphors, see George Lakoff and Mark Johnson, *Metaphors We Live By* (Chicago: University of Chicago Press, 1980), esp. p. 17.

trace of history." Early man felt that "this reproduction made him contemporary with the mythical moment of the beginning of the world and
... he felt the need of returning to that movement as often as possible in
order to regenerate himself."[25] Nietzsche makes this point about the connection between architecture and a sense of human power even stronger, suggesting that "in the architectural structure, man's pride, man's
triumph over gravitation, man's will to power, assume a visible form.
Architecture is a sort of oratory of power by means of forms."[26]

Buildings (at least symbolic ones) have, then, a significant role to play
in the rise of national consciousness and in recovering the past (this is
obviously also true in Zionism), but from ancient times to modern revolutions, they also represent the notion of new beginnings from scratch,
and they exemplify the Promethean powers of human beings.

The perception of discontinuity and the wish for new beginnings was
particularly strong among the originators of the Zionist revolution. As
Gordon observes, "[W]hen we come to build the building of our life anew,
we have an advantage. We are severed from any piece of land, without
national independence, and scattered in all countries. In other words, we
have nothing to destroy or to fight against yet. *We can begin by building,
creating, and laboring from scratch*"[27] (my emphasis). Building became
an all-engulfing and dominant metaphor in Zionism, since this movement had to shape the entire national project: its geographic location
and relation to the human environment, its general outlines and intricate
details, its dwellers and their medium of interaction. The metaphor of
building testifies to the conviction of many Zionists that they can erect
the totality of their world autonomously and in an innovative manner.
"We will build in the most daring and exquisite manner," writes Herzl,
"more than ever happened before, because we have means that have
never before existed in history."[28] These bold convictions are reflected by
the architectonic style taken up by the movement.

Since the early 1930s, when building became more intense among the
Jewish community in Palestine due to growing immigration, modernist
styles of architecture were increasingly espoused by Zionist architects – a

[25] Mircea Eliade, *Cosmos and History: The Myth of the Eternal Return* (New York:
   Harper Torchbooks, 1959), pp. 76–7.
[26] Friedrich Nietzsche, *The Twilight of the Idols*, trans. Antonym Ludovici (Hertfordshire,
   England: Woodsworth Editions Limited, 2007), p. 54.
[27] Gordon, "Geula vtzedek [Redemption and justice]," in *Sefer*, p. 32.
[28] Herzl, *The Jewish State*. Quoted here from Zvi Efrat, ed., *The Israeli Project: Building
   and Architecture, 1948–1973* (Tel Aviv: Tel Aviv Museum of Art, 2004), p. 47.

choice affirmed by the emerging socialist movement and establishment and reflected in the style of official and nonofficial buildings in both city and country (e.g., in the public buildings of *kibbutzim* and *moshavim*, the two predominant agricultural forms of settlements of the movement). In the Diaspora, there was no Jewish national style of building that could serve as a starting point, and these architects (among them Arieh Sharon, Shmuel Mestachkin, Zeev Rechter, Julius Posener, Dov Karmi, and Oskar Kaufmann)[29] rejected both the traditional building styles of their countries of origin and the local Arab style of building they found in Palestine. (Erich Mendelsohn, who came to Palestine in 1935 after a very successful career in Germany was among the notable exceptions; he recognized the importance of the local architectural-cultural context and saw the emerging architecture in Palestine as an opportunity for a creative synthesis of modernist and Middle Eastern styles and traditions. He preformed such a synthesis at the Hadassah Hospital, which is part of the Hebrew University and is located on Mount Scopus, Jerusalem. Mendelsohn, perhaps the only renowned architect working in Palestine at that time, refused to build in Tel Aviv, which he considered to be too influenced by the modernist styles he helped to form while working in Germany.)[30] Bold conceptions of architecture, with influences including the Bauhaus, the international style, and Le Corbusier, were seen as apt for the new society: As the senior Israeli architect Ram Karmi notes, "the young people who rebelled in the diaspora and chose the new, ivrit way of life viewed the Zionist revolution as the foundation for modern life generally; the radical sprit of the white architecture that was blowing from Europe fitted them like a glove fits a hand."[31] ("White architecture" refers to the habit of using white plaster on the external walls, an aesthetic preference of Le Corbusier.)

The revolution in modernist architecture complemented the Zionists' own all-encompassing experiment, and the two shared some important values: Both asserted human autonomy in relation to transcendental

[29] Both Sharon and Mestachkin were in fact graduates of the Bauhaus, and the former became responsible for the master plan of settlement, infrastructure, population distribution, and so on in the new state (see note 64, this chapter) while the latter became the chief architect of Hakibbutz Ha'artzi.

[30] See Alona Nitzan-Shiftan, "Contested Zionism: Alternative Modernism: Erich Mendelsohn and the Tel-Aviv Chug in Mandate Palestine," in Haim Yacobi, ed., *Constructing a Sense of Place: Architecture and the Zionist Discourse* (Hants, England: Ashgate, 2004)

[31] Ram Karmi, *Lyric Architecture* (Tel Aviv: Ministry of Defense Publications, 2001), p. 12.

forces; both aspired to leave the past behind and start a literal or metaphoric building from scratch. Julius Posener even suggested that, by using the right architecture in Palestine, one could create for the Jew "an apartment free from past memories."[32] While Zionist architects adapted modernist notions of building to suit the local conditions of Palestine (especially the light and climate), they held onto the universal and decontextualized spirit of modern architecture. "Constructive form is not peculiar to any country; it is cosmopolitan and the expression of an international philosophy of building," said Hannes Meyer (1926), the director of the Bauhaus School.[33] Paradoxically, perhaps, the cosmopolitan style of architecture became a part of the ethos of a national movement asserting its distinctiveness, and this style was at odds with the embeddedness in the distinctive ancient land Zionism aspired to achieve.

Tel Aviv was the first modern Hebrew city, and its modernist architects embraced new ideas such as horizontal-strip windows, flat roofs, and an overall horizontal focus – a new style that displaced the traditional emphasis on the vertical aspects of the building (which had been said to place it in relation to the sky and the divine). In some buildings, the autonomy of the builder in relation to Nature was also evidenced by features that followed Le Corbusier's style of using columns (pilotis) and establishing a significant open space below the structure. New technologies and materials (e.g., steel, fortified concrete) facilitated the separation of the mass of the building from its volume, or its structure from its inner and outer walls, allowing for significant playfulness and innovative searches for geometrical beauty (especially of façades) without using ornaments and decorations of the past. The new architectonic spirit in Palestine aimed to be functional, to use space rationally, to be coherent and clean; it celebrated the self-sufficiency of the human spirit, its use of reason, its directness and boldness, and its aesthetic and practical inventiveness. The modernist architects in Palestine were also seeking to establish a new relationship between the individual and the community, and thus they underscored the pubic dimensions of buildings. This was epitomized by the cooperative housing blocks built for city workers in Tel Aviv (for example, those designed by the architect Sharon in 1934),

[32] Julius Posener, "One-Family House in Palestine," *Habinyan* 2 (1937): 1. Quoted here from Alona Nitzan-Shiftan, "Contested Zionism," p. 30.
[33] Frank Whitford, ed., *The Bauhaus, Masters and Students by Themselves* (Woodstock, NY: Overlook Press, 1992), p. 250.

which offered low-cost apartments with a shared yard, grocery store, library, laundry room, kindergarten, and so on, but was also evident in the emphasis on porches in the entire young city. The porch faced the street and served as a private space open to dialogue with the public one; it helped foster the informal and light spirit of society and its strong sense of community.

The revolutionary and bold style of building embraced by Zionists echoes the temporal imagination of "sundered history" we discussed earlier. This vision, to repeat, depicted time as open and containing no binding meta-narratives: Since time was seen as formless, some Zionists in Palestine could take the Promethean aspect of modernity to the extreme; from some of their pronouncements, it seems that there was little to stop or guide them, to suggest a limit to their actions. They became, through their colossal project of building, perhaps the exemplary moderns. In their understanding at least, their world (a rough and demanding one, to be sure) was created mainly in their own image, little confined by preexisting reality – especially not by their own past, or by the presence of the Arabs in the country; the notion of building with its inherent self-sufficiency and assertiveness, both expressed and supported this conviction. International politics, the shared world established among nations, and even conventions and words generally, had questionable meaning in this self-made world of Zionists in Palestine. "The Land of Israel will be ours," said Ben-Gurion, "not when the Turks, British, or the next peace council will allow this and ratify a diplomatic agreement but when we, the Jews, will build [*nivneh*] it.... The aim of our revival effort is the building of the Land [*binyan ha'aretz*]."[34]

III. BELONGING AND THE WORLD OF MATTER

We should, however, probe more deeply into the meaning of building in Zionism where it involves a change in relation to the entire world of matter. For Zionists, the national building was not merely a necessity but also an opportunity to attach Jews to the phenomenal sphere of existence. The Zionist building included "paving roads, establishing means of communication, uncovering natural treasures, constructing industry, and so on. This is what it means to create a homeland."[35] Their view

---

[34] David Ben-Gurion, *Mima'amad le'am* [From class to nation] (Tel Aviv: Iyanot, 1955), pp. 23–4.
[35] Ibid.

was that Zionists should be disposed to champion productive activity
and be invested in the durable transformations of tangible reality. "We
must," writes Gordon, "position work at the center of our goals" and
"base upon it [the] entire building."[36] The cherished, traditional Jewish
activities had always been studying and dwelling in the ocean of words;
the new Hebrew individual was supposed to generate a world of objects
as evidence of his or her existence. Life in Palestine was to be based on
"earthly foundations"; these were said to be the "only foundations that
we [Zionists] are building our lives on, and not upon individual, spiritual foundations."[37]

Zionists, then, embraced work not merely because humans are compelled to do so, because without work they would lack the means to
preserve and reproduce life. Gordon, Ben-Gurion, and other socialist
Zionists who founded Palestinian Zionism viewed work as articulating homo faber's highest qualities and as providing the gifts of self-
realization and existential affirmation. Through productive interaction
with Nature, human beings palpably express their originality and imagination, tenacity and dedication. "The object of work," writes Marx, "is
the objectification of the species-life of man; for he duplicates himself
not only intellectually, in his mind, but also actively in reality and thus
can look at his image in a world he has created."[38] One could argue,
then, that the socialist Zionists' mistrust of their own tradition and the
rabbinical mode of life found an echo and a supporting shoulder in the
Marxist mistrust of minds that solely reproduce themselves, minds that
do not seek perceptible proof for their inner activity.

The Zionists' desire for the self to express itself by begetting objects –
along with their quest to establish a unity between subject and object –
led some of them to seek the exclusion of non-Jews from the project of
national revival. Without Hebrew work (or work by Jewish pioneers),
"the whole Zionist building totters," avers Ben-Gurion.[39] This is why
Zionists should rejoice, he wrote, that "Tel Aviv is being built entirely
by Jews," and that "new, large neighborhoods in Jerusalem, Tiberias,
and Haifa are being built wholly, from the foundations up, by Jewish

[36] Gordon, "Work," in *Kitzur kitvei A. D. Gordon* [Selected writings of A. D. Gordon]
(Tel Aviv: Shtible, 1936), pp. 50–1.

[37] Ben-Gurion, *Mima'amad le'am*, p. 85.

[38] Karl Marx, "Economic and Philosophical Manuscripts," in *Karl Marx: Early Texts*,
ed. David McLennan (Oxford: Basil Blackwell, 1971), p. 140.

[39] Ben-Gurion, *Mima'amad le'am*, p. 41.

workers."[40] The national building would be "ours" only by insisting on Jewish workers alone, since only then would the building be an authentic extension of the builders and symbolize their national unity. I may not have built this house myself, or paved this road, but if my brothers and sisters – fellow members of the national unit, the unit that really counts – did the work, then this house and road belong to me, too; they are an extension of myself. While there were also economic reasons to demand that Arabs not be involved in building projects or agriculture,[41] such involvement would have also threatened the entire picture of the merging of self and material world that Zionists sought. (In practice, Jews never achieved full control of the labor market, in construction or in other spheres of the economy.)[42]

Since only Jews – few in number, impoverished, and inexperienced – were hastily erecting a new world, they tended to celebrate the active and productive will. Any construction is an act of will, and constructing grandly necessitates a grand will. (As Nietzsche suggests, the architect's work is expressing "a great act of will, the will that moves mountains.")[43] The builders of the nation defy existing circumstances, shaping history in their own hands: As Gordon remarks, "in the name of 'historical necessity,' we will not achieve anything in the Land of Israel. Historical necessity is working against, not for us."[44] The builder breaks free from the present predicament; the critical issue for this individual is the moment of transition, of finding the impudence to cross the gulf between nothing and something. "For such a great project – the revival

---

[40] Ibid., p. 188. Needless to say, the unity of subject and object, of individual builders and a collective project, was strongest in the kibbutzim.

[41] Gershon Shafir, for example, argues that while early Zionist pioneers were interested in promoting the national goal, they also advanced their economic interests by creating "an ethnic plantation colony" (Shafir, *Land, Labor, and the Origins of the Israeli-Palestinian Conflict, 1882–1914* [Cambridge: Cambridge University Press, 1989], p. 79) that distinguished between skilled (Jewish) and unskilled (Arab) workers. This ethnic distinction allowed Jewish workers to monopolize certain professions and therefore to demand higher wages from their Jewish employers (p. 60).

[42] The celebration of Hebrew work and the notion of a unified national subject (people) with the national building no longer holds as an ideal. Since 1967, most of the workforce in construction and agriculture has been comprised of Palestinians. During the 1990s, many migrant workers from various countries joined this workforce and replaced some of the Palestinians. In addition, construction and agricultural work lost their normative value in Israeli society.

[43] See Nietzsche, *The Twilight of the Idols*, p. 54.

[44] Gordon, "Derachim legeula [Paths of redemption]," in *Sefer*, p. 22.

of a dead land, for example – the essential thing is the beginning, the birth into life," he explains.[45] Will is necessary, then, not to enable us to avoid tempting options or even to help us sustain a given course of action (the two purposes traditionally attached to the will). The essential point for the builder is the capacity to begin, to envision the future as a horizon of continuous inaugurations, and to thereby deny the gap between thinking and doing. This creates a dependency on action: Since the builders conceive of themselves as the originators of projects and their self-affirmation as hinging upon the scope and greatness of their deeds, they acquire a sense of existential uncertainty that can be alleviated only by perpetual construction and evidence of action. As Arendt notes, "[T]he normal mood of the willing ego is impatience, disquiet, and worry [*Sorge*] ... because the will's project presupposes an I-can that is by no means guaranteed. The will's worrying disquiet can be stilled only by the I-can and I-do."[46]

Since Zionism combined this notion of the impatient, active will with its disposition to beget the concrete, it committed itself to continuously challenging existing material circumstances; the expansionist strands in Zionism were by no means inevitable, but they were fed by this fateful union. Gradually, moreover, Zionism became a movement defined by continuous action, as if the lack of it threatened its identity. A few years ago, a sign put up by the Jewish Agency read, *"Zionism is about doing – yesterday, today, and tomorrow."* The sign was located near the entrance to Mount Herzl in Jerusalem, where both Herzl and Yitzhak Rabin, among others, are buried. As this message indicates, the production and transformation of tangible collective reality – and perhaps the expansion of its domain – has often become in Zionism an end in itself, the cement of collective life, rather than an auxiliary of it.

IV. BELONGING AND THE HUMANIZATION OF SPACE

The notion of building is inherently dialectic: It suggests that humans can freely begin a stupendous project, but it also testifies to their desire to belong and to find a safe haven. By using building metaphors, numerous Zionists evoked the most common function of buildings and conveyed that their deeds were aimed at constructing a state that would be a

---

[45] Ibid., p. 21.
[46] Hannah Arendt, *The Life of the Mind.* Vol. 2: *Willing* (New York: Harcourt Brace Jovanovich, 1978), p. 37.

shelter for the Jews. Human beings build because they seek refuge from the sun and wind, rain and cold. The building, because it is relatively immune to the changes of environment and climate, allows humans to feel comfortable and to fulfill certain vital functions, such as working, resting, cooking, and reproducing. The building may also protect human beings from other human beings, as well as from beasts, guarding against both penetrating gazes and potential physical harm; it is a barrier against others, both psychologically and practically. By employing the metaphor of national building for their project, early Zionists desired to connote a similar idea: Such building would be a refuge for Jews from the hardships they had experienced in Europe and elsewhere. It would involve a circumscribed territory where people can hide from deliberate economic deprivation and recurrent manifestations of hatred and harm;[47] in this shelter, their dignity and self-respect would finally lose the fragility and dependence on the goodwill of others that had characterized Jewish existence in the Diaspora.

It was not shelter alone that Zionists were seeking, however: They yearned for a wholly new relation to space and place. According to Gordon, the Zionist wishes "to release himself from rationality, mechanics, and get back to nature, to space, to the limitless."[48] Eretz Israel offers relief from both the traditional small-town life of Jews in Eastern Europe and the pressing, urban-modernized life of Jews in Western Europe. For Gordon, indeed, the Jewish national revolution is also a revolt against destructive features of modern life generally, such as distance from nature, other-dependency, and heightened intellectualism; the Jews epitomize these ills, but have been given a singular opportunity to overcome them and begin from scratch. To feel at home in the new-old open space, however, the Jew must turn this space into his or her distinct place, and do so through unmediated attachment to nature, hard physical labor, and even purifying suffering. For Gordon, it is not space as such that lies at the center of Jewish national revival but the particular soil of the Holy Land with its unique connotations and qualities, which would be disclosed only to those who open themselves wholly to their environment. Indeed, the pioneers habitually touched and tasted the soil, kissed it, and described it in erotic terms (mountains as a woman's breasts, spring

---

[47] Despite their long-term plans, it is important to remember that for the pioneers of the Second Aliya the notion of Palestine as a physical shelter was still distant: They were politically powerless and wholly impoverished. Many pioneers left the country, and those who remained were often on the verge of despair.

[48] Gordon, *Kitzur kitvei A. D. Gordon*, p. 9.

water as God's milk, etc.). They contemplated and praised its beauty and generally were in awe of it; as Boaz Neumann observes, they cultivated a profound "desire" for the land.[49]

This is in accord with the semicyclical imagination (see Chapter 1), which is based on the valorization of our *sensual experience* in relation to a specific place, since only such an experience brings back memories – personal or collective – that are associated with that place. The poet Rachel, among the pioneers who settled near Lake Kinneret (Sea of Galilee) and who was influenced by and was close to Gordon, expresses this point: "We were walking on the soil that retains the sound of Abraham's footsteps. We were hearing God's words from bygone days 'and I shall glorify your name.'" And she adds, "they say, these waters have miraculous qualities: whoever drank from them even once would return to them. Isn't the reason why the sons in the Diaspora yearn for the quiet shores of the Kinneret the fact that their fathers slaked their thirst just here?" In fact, Rachel observes, "the Kinneret is not just scenery, not simply a piece of nature – the fate of an entire people is attached to its name. With thousands of eyes, our past will look at us from its [the sea's] midst, with thousands of lips this past would speak to the heart."[50] The place, Eretz Israel, retains sounds, tastes, and pictures from the ancient past, guards them for the present, activating and alluring the individuals living in this present through sensual experiences; a lively dialogue is established across generations between a past that lives on and a present complete with revolutionary energies.

The soil, in particular, is an essential source of rejuvenation: "We are renewing the earth, and the earth renews our spirit," Gordon writes.[51] This mutual renewal occurs through mutual construction, as explained by S. Y. Agnon in *In the Heart of the Seas*: "As did others among our brothers, people of the Second *Aliya*, Yitzhak Komar [the novel's hero] left his country, homeland, and city and immigrated to *Eretz Israel* to build it from its ruins and to be built by it."[52] (Agnon echoes a very popular song of the pioneers, according to which "we came to this land to

[49] See Boaz Neumann, *Teshukat hahalutzim* [Land and desire in early Zionism] (Tel Aviv: Am Oved, 2009).

[50] Rachel, "Al seffat haKinneret [On the shore of the Kinneret]" (1929), at http://benyehuda.org/rachel/alsfat.html. I am indebted to Neumann's *Teshukat hahalutzim* for making me aware of this source.

[51] Gordon, "Our Rights in Palestine," in *Sefer*, p. 108.

[52] S. Y. Agnon, *Temol shilshom* [In the heart of the seas] (Tel Aviv: Schocken, 1993), p. 1 (Hebrew version). Agnon, of course, is alluding here to Abraham.

build it and be built by it" [*Anu banu artza livnot ulehibanot ba*].) The pioneer is motivated by a deep emotional connection to the biblical land and a sense of obligation to salvage it from its historical destruction.[53] When Western colonialists approached a new terrain, they tended to follow their forerunner Columbus, who saw America as echoing the Garden of Eden, a place that was not yet corrupted by human endeavors and greed like his own. Most Zionists, in contrast, saw Palestine as a demolished edifice that could be restored only by a novel, vast project of construction. They were mostly blind to the efforts made by the indigenous Palestinian inhabitants to cultivate and maintain the land, to their well-kept terraces and *bustanim* (orchards), to their great care in situating their houses and fitting them to the preexisting landscape. Zionists tended not to perceive the Land of Israel as virgin and innocent, yet neither did they see it as an already inhabited space; rather, they saw it as pregnant with ancient historical import and memories that would remain unredeemed if Jews did not cultivate the land, erect houses, establish industry, and pave roads.

Abraham Shlonsky's 1928 poem "Toil" (translated by Leah Goldberg) expresses many of these sentiments:

Dress me, good mother, in a splendrous coat of many colors/ And with dawn lead me to toil/ My land wraps in light like a prayer shawl./ Houses stand like phylacteries./ And like bands of phylacteries glide hand-laid asphalt roads./ Thus a beautiful city offers her morning prayer to her creator./ And among the creators, your son Abraham, Poet-roadbuilder in Israel./ And toward evening, at dusk, father returns from his labors/ And like prayer whispers with pleasure:/ A dear son of mine is Abraham: Skin, sinew, and bones. Hallelujah! Dress me, good mother, in a splendrous coat of many colors/ And at dawn lead me to toil.

In this well-known poem, charged with biblical allusions in which the original meanings are reversed, toil becomes a new mode of worship or,

---

[53] Gordon, for example, says that "the land of Israel is the land of the people, and they should revive it – and revive their claim upon it – through their work, creation, and life" (Gordon, "Politika tzionit [Zionist politics]," in *Sefer*, p. 41). Moreover, the commitment to the biblical space is still an important feature of Zionism – and not only among those on the political Right. Even prominent speakers on the Left, such as Amos Oz, cherish this commitment. Oz, for example, says that precisely with the Oslo agreement, it may be "indeed appropriate to renew this settlement [in Hebron]." He adds that one should take care that this renewal is done by Jews who respect the Palestinian population and their rights. See Amos Oz, "To Renew the Jewish Settlement in Hebron," in "24 Hours," *Yediot Aharonot*, January 16, 1997, p. 5. The conviction that the land belongs to the "people" – who have moral claim upon it and are committed to it – led Zionists to keep the land in the state's hands. Until recently, the state owned more than 90 percent of the lands in Israel.

rather, an altar at which to worship.[54] The worker self-consciously and happily sacrifices himself on this altar. The biblical father (Abraham) is now the son (the poet Abraham), who chooses to be sacrificed for the sake of a human cause: the building of the land. To be sure, the land is presented in religious terms – it is light like a prayer shawl, dressed with square, small houses that resemble the boxes of the *tefillin* (phylacteries) and with roads that glide like the straps of the tefillin. But space has been essentially humanized: The land is marked with man-made artifacts, with a beautiful new city. Thus, the land is worshiping its creator – the pioneer (not God, who according to the tradition promised the land) – who is also being sacrificed because he transforms that land with his physical labor.

The constant dialogue between the ancient, biblical past (and the theological-symbolic meanings of the land) and the contemporary projects of the builders is never absent from the Zionist relation to space. But for the most part this dialogue, contrary to what one may have expected, never led to a mode of thinking that has sought to preserve and cultivate the preexisting landscape and scenery. Genuine attachment to the ancient soil is formed not by guarding it against radical transformation and saving the environment, but rather by an ongoing intensification of efforts to transform it.[55]

The Zionist reenchanted space: Just when others, such as Weber, were proclaiming that modern space (and the universe as a whole) was irrevocably objectified and barren of import, Zionists sought to make space speak. They rejected the notion of what Lefebvre calls "abstract space," one that is formal, homogeneous, quantitative, Nature negating, and asensual.[56] While one cannot ignore the possessive and utilitarian interests of the Zionists' attitude toward the land, perhaps their deeper motive was a longing to feel at home in an environment that emitted historical pictures with which they could identify on their own terms. In Giveon, they thought of Joshua and the sun that obeyed his order and stopped its movement until he had completed his war, Nature and man cooperating

---

[54] See Leah Goldberg, in *The Modern Hebrew Poem Itself*, ed. Stanley Burnshaw (Detroit, MI: Wayne State University Press, 2003), p. 83.

[55] Exceptions are poems written by women. Such early Zionist poets as Rachel, Bat-Miriam, and Esther Raab, who wrote during the first decades of the twentieth century, express great care toward the natural environment and landscape of Palestine. See Revital Amiran-Sapir, "Al Em Haderech [On the road]" (Master's thesis, Political Science Department, Tel Aviv University, 1999).

[56] Lefebvre, *The Production of Space*, pp. 49–51.

in the conquest of the land; in the Kishon River, they thought of Elijah, who slaughtered there hundreds of false prophets, illustrating the brutal fate awaiting those who oppose the true faith. For many Zionists, the spots where heroes (such as Judah the Maccabee, Bar Kochba, or Samson) conducted their wars were of particular meaning, but almost every spot of the land contained a story, one that injected purpose into, and provided a model for, their own lives.

In contrast to settlers in the New World, who preserved native names such as Connecticut and Massachusetts, the Zionists' quest to give ancient meaning to the land led them to ignore the Arabic names of places in Palestine. The new Hebrew map used mostly biblical names, translated Arabic names into Hebrew, or invented new Hebrew names. The process of naming locations in the State of Israel was a part of a deliberate plan that erased the Palestinian map and facilitated the intended marriage of the present with the past through language (as we will see in Chapter 4).[57]

In their quest to "build" themselves, many Zionists recognized, then, that merely dwelling on the biblical land was insufficient and that they would acquire a sense of belonging only when they humanized nature, leaving upon it the marks of their imagination, work, and language. Buildings, in particular, facilitate such humanization: They circumscribe regions, render them distinct, and relate them to one another. As Karsten Harries notes, we feel differently near a field or an orchard, near a villa or an industrial plant; a properly shaped, built space becomes "heterogeneous."[58] This diversity allows us to orient ourselves – and not merely in the literal sense. We can navigate in life because of the specificity of places: Here we rest and enjoy intimacy, there we work, and over there we gather and meet others. We narrate our lives and gain a sense of identity through our experiences in and recollections of particular locations. In the Land of Israel, contemporary and ancient locations mingled – at certain spots being almost fused and at others residing side by

---

[57] See Meron Benvenisti, "Hamapa haivirit [The Hebrew map]," *Theory and Criticism* 11 (1997): 7–30.

[58] I was greatly helped in this section by Karsten Harries. See his *The Ethical Function of Architecture* (Cambridge, MA: MIT Press, 1998), p. 156. For the importance of place in human experience, at least as expressed in modern literature and philosophy, see J. E. Malpas, *Place and Experience: A Philosophical Topography* (Cambridge: Cambridge University Press, 1999). On the increasing disappearance of place and the implications of this development for our sense of self, see Marc Augé, *Non-Places: An Introduction to an Anthropology of Supermodernity* (London: Verso, 1995).

side – creating a unique map through which the Zionist self navigated, in constant conversation between the then and the now.

V. COMMUNITY OF BUILDERS

Thus, we see that the Zionist, Hebraically inspired individual was "built" in relation to matter and the self-produced phenomenal world. He and she also reconnected with the ancient meanings of the land and personally transformed this land. The sense of homelessness was alleviated through these new attachments to matter and place, and thus building was not viewed merely instrumentally but (in a way that resembles Heidegger's argument) as essential to the core ideas of the movement. However, the Zionist individual was a part of a community with a purpose, a community of builders: This was the third dimension to which he or she became attached in striving to overcome a sense of homelessness.

To be sure, the Zionist community in Palestine was highly diverse from a political point of view (incorporating, for example, Marxists and ultra-nationalists, radical secularists and pious believers); it always knew demonstrations, strikes, harsh public arguments. Impressive democratic decision-making practices and free elections were respected by the Zionist movement in Palestine and abroad even before the establishment of the state (e.g., in the kibbutzim, in the various political parties, in the representative body of Jews in Palestine called *Asefat Hanivharim*, in the World Zionist Organization). Nevertheless, many thinkers and leaders of this rather democratic community underscored the need for uncompromising unity, acted under the presupposition of a shared national project, and allowed the socialist Zionists to shape its contours. While the nature of the project initially demanded daring, nonconformist men and women, eventually the institutions they created downplayed the status of the individual within both the movement and the state. Self-realization, *Hagshama*, meant serving the collective's goals, such as settlement and defense, rather than realizing a life of an individual qua individual.

The demand for social cohesion was expressed in the call to join together the creative wills of individuals – their wills being their distinct feature as initiators of something new – into one effective force of action. "Instead of a central will, guiding and powerful," laments Ben-Gurion, "we [Zionists] still have wandering, separate wills, broken and impaired."[59] Shared building was used to correct this human diversity, since in this activity, wills are augmented and merged – not in the Rousseauian sense of a general, political-legal will, but in the sense of an inaugurating and productive will.[60] Building, we learn from the biblical story of the tower of Babel, is a tempting venue through which people can express their solidarity: The tower reflects to the builders their capacity to possess a shared end and testifies palpably to their alliance. Large building projects have the capacity to introduce a feeling of oneness among a plurality of human beings; they turn them into co-builders who form horizontal relationships. Building is possible only by mitigating divisions among classes, parties, or individuals; at the same time, the act of building itself protects against frictions.[61] Workers are cemented as they install a structure that relates them to one another, absorbs their scattered energies, and allows them to share the rapture reserved for makers on a grand scale.

In national building projects, each act finds its meaning by being a part of a continuous chain. The brick that one person lays should be placed appropriately beside another's; the wall they erect together must meet the walls erected by others. Only then will the structure stand. As builders of the nation, individuals similarly agree that their practical actions have an overarching, collective effect: One builder takes on public service; another engages in industries critical for the nation. One works in the fields; another serves in the military. These are not merely the choices of men and women seeking the best ways to fulfill themselves individually;

---

[59] Ben-Gurion, *Mima'amad le'am*, p. 224. Gordon expresses a similar idea: "We, who are coming to build a new building, would certainly not be able to build much on the basis of divisions among us" (Gordon, "Pioneering and the Union of the Nation," in *Sefer*, p. 14).

[60] Gordon complains that "the fundamental thing that a national creation requires – a creation that is great, liberating, and reviving – we [Zionists] are missing. We lack the union of wills and forces vital for a collective creation" (Gordon, "Achdot leumit [National unity], in *Sefer*, p. 25).

[61] The notion of "one building," or one national project, shaped the type of socialism that evolved in Palestine. This socialism, which is often termed *constructive socialism*, embraced socialist ideas, such as the cooperatives and hegemony of the working class, but denied the notion of class war. The picture of shared building limited, from the outset, any idea of civil conflict over power and resources. Nahman Syrkin was the first to use the term "constructive socialism" in the Zionist context (1919), and Berl Katznelson later elaborated it. For a discussion of the term, see Shimoni, *The Zionist Ideology*, pp. 194–201; and Zeev Sternhell, *The Founding Myths of Israel: Nationalism, Socialism, and the Making of the Jewish State* (Princeton, NJ: Princeton University Press, 1998).

they also find meaning and justification in reference to community goals, and individuals are evaluated according to their relative contribution to the advancement of these goals. When we describe buildings, we often speak of functional unity, of the fact that the house succeeds when it performs and harmonizes different functions. The same presupposition of functional unity – of viewing the parts chiefly in terms of their contribution to the whole – holds for the way Zionists understood their shared project and their desire to erect "one building." Builders do not relate to one another as a community of *speech*, a community that hinges on their capacity to invent shared meanings through public words; what joins them are productive deeds joined to other productive deeds, a continuous sequence that progressively transforms their collective existence. (In this vista, even the free search for knowledge is evaluated from a national viewpoint, with the Hebrew University being described as "a stone in the building of the future."[62] Rather than being a relatively neutral space incorporating students from different nations, and embracing the international and universalist aspect that is the hallmark of at least some European universities, this Hebrew University was harnessed from the beginning with contributing to the overall project, although many of its early leaders supported Brit Shalom, the Zionist association that supported a binational state and the cultivation of Arab-Jewish relations based on mutual respect and shared interests.[63] After the establishment

---

[62] Chaim Weizmann, *Devarim* [Speeches], vol. 1 (Tel Aviv: Mitzpe, 1936), p. 68.

[63] Brit Shalom was a small but well-known Jewish association in Palestine. It argued that Jews should relinquish their insistence on being a majority in Palestine and embrace instead a binational state in which Arabs and Jews would keep some autonomy as separate communities but share central political institutions. Most of the members of this group were of Western and Central European origins, appalled by the nationalism that had propelled World War I. Yet they were committed Zionists, and some of them had strong religious backgrounds and were reluctant to see the Holy Land divided. In their refusal to envision a Jewish, sovereign, national state as the main goal of Zionism, they combined a liberal faith in equality and toleration, some universalist notions of socialism, and anti-imperialism, on the one hand, with profound roots in the Jewish moral tradition, on the other. (Many of them were influenced by Ahad Ha'am, although he had reservations about them, and considered their program unrealistic and dishonest.) See Steven Aschheim, *Beyond the Border: The German-Jewish Legacy Abroad* (Princeton, NJ: Princeton University Press, 2007), pp. 6–45. See also Chapter 4. Yoram Hazony, then, argues that the Hebrew University became the main bastion of intellectual forces that opposed the idea of a Jewish state. Both Labor Zionists and Revisionists, he argues, failed to grasp the power of the critical ideas that sprang from this institution and that shape much of Israeli political thought today, because "neither movement believed much in the power of ideas." See Yoram Hazony, *The Jewish State: The Struggle for Israel's Soul* (New York: Basic Books, 2000), p. 79.

of the state, incidentally, the fields of sociology and political science at the Hebrew University were dominated by functionalist theories.)

This vista also holds that the functional unity of the building should not be left to chance. "Without a building plan," writes Ben-Gurion, "the fulfillment of Zionism would be impossible. A program is needed that will master and unite forces aimed at action and construction; this great project cannot be accomplished by chance, blindly, as an afterthought."[64] In envisioning their project as a building, Zionists embraced the fundamental maxim of architecture since Brunelleschi: the need for an overarching plan and for methodological thinking in materializing it. Herzl, Borochov, Ben-Gurion, and many other Zionists had little faith in "evolutionary" or organic change. They approached the future as something that should be premeditated, organized, and actualized through human action. Amid much improvisation in the Yishuv, there were also plans for collecting funds and for buying lands, for attracting immigrants and for securing their livelihood, for acquiring weapons and for creating military forces, and much more. After the War of Independence, with housing in short supply, the architect A. Sharon was called to form a plan that would determine the location of new mass-housing projects, their urban planning, and their architectonic style; building, indeed, became a national project to an unprecedented degree.[65]

This ongoing search for a planned construction of social reality could arise from public deliberation, yet more often it emerges from a hierarchical political order. Building plans necessitate architects; they tend to introduce a division of labor between those who make blueprints and those who follow, between those who see the overall picture and those who passively accept a given concept.[66] By introducing such a division, building projects ingrain a long-term nonparticipatory ethos; debate, critique, and the individual innovation of builders are inimical to their construction. In fact, buildings impose a particular vision not only upon

---

[64] Ben-Gurion, *Mima'amad le'am*, p. 224.

[65] For the most part, Sharon's plan called for creating small agricultural settlements and intimate towns that would be spread throughout the unpopulated parts of the country and would transfer the immigrant population to these undesirable areas. Sharon's town was designed like a big kibbutz, with significant distances between houses, a lot of green areas, and a central area of services. From an architectonic, economic, and demographic point of view, these towns are (for the most part) a failure. See Zevi Efrat, "The Plan," *Theory and Criticism* 16 (2000): 203–10.

[66] It is interesting to note that in 1962, Ben-Gurion was awarded the honorary degree of "Doctor of Architecture" by the esteemed Technion, the only person to win this title in the history of this higher education institute.

those who make them but also upon the future inhabitants of the building. Roger Scruton (who follows Ruskin) therefore argues that architecture "is the most political of arts, in that it imposes a vision of man and his aims independently of any personal agreement on the part of those who live with it."[67] Buildings, in other words, are typically not democratic in their underlying vision, in their construction process, or in the type of dwelling they habituate; hence, their problematic nature as a metaphor for a state in which citizens allegedly practice self-government.

Builders make poor citizens – not only because their bond is mediated through matter rather than through language, and not only because their activity tends to downplay pluralism rather than cultivate it, but also because their role does not involve an ongoing, critical reflection on, and responsibility toward, the overall scheme. Citizens as builders are not empowered as individuals but as members of a construction team; for this reason, they lack the sense that it is precisely their *cultivated individuality* and sense of freedom that must be brought to bear upon the political.[68] ("All the complaints in the name of personal freedom," avers Ben-Gurion, "are simply a cover-up for anarchy, rebelliousness, and irresponsibility in regard to public affairs.")[69]

Because of the widespread conception of the Zionist as a builder, an alarming instrumental language about human beings has developed in Zionist politics. Fascinated by their capacity to produce the concrete, early Zionists tended to perceive human beings as a part of the palpable universe they were constructing; they pictured themselves and others as *malleable material*. "The human being, the nation ... everything is one primordial substance," writes Gordon. "Everything is being born in a new creation."[70] Thus, the entire human realm is seen as raw material that can be shaped at will to fit nonpersonal functions. "As long as the building process of the Jewish State continues," writes Vladimir Jabotinsky, "then the owner of capital is not an owner of capital, and the worker is not a worker. Both are for us nothing but material for the building that we are erecting."[71] Yosef Trumpeldor, a Zionist legend,

---

[67] Roger Scruton, *The Aesthetics of Architecture* (London: Methuen, 1979), p. 15.

[68] On the lack of genuine individuality in the early days of Israeli society, see Yaron Ezrahi, *Rubber Bullets: Power and Conscience in Modern Israel*.

[69] David Ben-Gurion, October 1921; see *Labor Archive*, file no. 1, quoted here from Dan Horowitz and Moshe Lissak, *Mi-yishuv li-medinah* [The origins of the Israeli polity] (Tel Aviv: Am Oved, 1986), p. 208 (in Hebrew).

[70] Gordon, *Kitzur kitvei A. D. Gordon*, p. 103.

[71] V. Jabotinsky, *Olamo shel Jabotinsky* [The world of Jabotinsky: A selection of his works and the essentials of his teaching], ed. Moshe Bella (Tel Aviv: Dfusim, 1972), p. 232.

PHOTO 8. Chief of Staff Yitzhak Rabin speaking at the Mount Scopus Amphitheatre after receiving an honorary doctorate from the Hebrew University at the end of the Six Day War. Photo by Ilan Bruner June 28, 1967. Courtesy of the Government Press Office, Israel.

was already arguing in 1916 that "we should create a generation that would have no interests and no habits. A bar of iron with no purpose. Flexible, but iron. A metal that one could form according to whatever is needed for the national machine. A wheel is missing – I am the wheel.... It is necessary to dig in the soil? I am digging. It is necessary to shout, to be a soldier? I am a soldier.... I have no face, no psychology, no emotion, I don't even have a name: I am the pure Idea of service, ready for all, not attached to anything; I know only one command: to build."[72]

Rather than taking the (future) citizen as an end in herself, as the prime goal of the revival project, the building-oriented Zionist gradually fostered a politics that views citizens predominantly as facilitators of the collective project. Instead of valuing the moral-religious saint of former times, Zionism relished the work and military related skills required for nation building; it even presented the exemplary cultivation of these skills as an expression of laudable *spiritual character*. "We always demanded the best for service in the IDF," declares Chief of General Staff Yitzhak Rabin in his celebrated speech at Mount Scopus in June 1967. "When we said the best for the air force ... we did not mean those who are best in the technical or skillful sense." Rather, he continues, in order to defeat the entire enemy forces of four states in just a few hours, pilots must possess "values of moral goodness, values of human goodness." In general, the manifestations of valor and professionalism by soldiers during the Six Day War "begin in the spirit and end in the spirit."[73] With these words, Zionism arrived at an ironic point, since with them the IDF soldier replaced the traditional righteous "*tzadik*" (who was characterized by the adamant shunning of violence) as the possessor of unsurpassed spirit. Given the ongoing conflicted relations they faced with the Arab population, mainstream Zionists were unable and perhaps uninterested in cultivating an ethos underscoring the citizens' ability to explore the good and moral life in ways that could challenge and disturb the collective good.

VI. TELISHUT

This discussion may help to explain the distinct feature of the Jewish State in its early decades: the relative fusion of this institution with society. Despite the fact that Western European, democratic politics

---

[72] Yosef Trumpeldor (1916) in Vladimir Jabotinsky, *Megilat hagedud* (Jerusalem: Ari Jabotinsky Press, 1947), pp. 205–6.
[73] See Yitzhak Rabin's speech in *Neum lekol et* [A speech for every occasion], ed. Tamar Brosh (Tel Aviv: The Open University, 1993), p. 63.

(especially Britain's) served as a model for Zionists, Zionism seems to have developed a holistic concept of politics whereby state, civil society, and individuals were seen as profoundly integrated. In general, the state was not conceived as detached from the community, as having its own singular logic and interests, an embodiment of the art of accumulating and exercising power; rather, the state was most often viewed as wholly continuous with the community – fully expressing and responding to its needs, fears, preferences, values – and thus as having the legitimacy to call on the individual to be incorporated into collective ends.[74]

To be sure, as the State of Israel was being formed, there were attempts to introduce new conceptions of citizenship that highlighted the new type of political vision associated with a state. In particular, Ben-Gurion advanced the notion of *Mamlachtiut*, by which he meant that instead of seeing themselves as primarily members of particular parties and factions, individuals should embrace a spirit of public-mindedness, think about the general good of the state as a whole rather than on their sectarian interest, and conceive of themselves as law-abiding citizens with equal rights and duties under one sovereign body that deserves legitimacy regardless of who holds power.[75] But even this important political notion of Ben-Gurion's did not suggest that the community and the state are separate; the state merely became the pinnacle of the building project as a whole. The political history supported this lack of separateness: From its inception, the Yishuv in Palestine was shaped by political institutions that preceded the mass immigration and thus took the role of integrating the newcomers into society; later, the army was not understood as a professional army but as a citizen's army, deeply rooted in communal life and culture; and the party that dominated the political system (*Mapai*) also controlled the *Histadrut* (the hegemonic workers' union), which owned a considerable portion of the economy, thus further blurring the line between state and civil society. In fact, when people use the term *medina* (the Hebrew word for state) they often mean the "entire thing": government institutions, a certain territory, and society combined;[76] in line with the notion of national building, the state does not exist as a distinct institution but as part of a whole.

[74] See Charles S. Liebman, "Conceptions of the 'State of Israel' in Israeli Society," *Jerusalem Quarterly*, 47 (Summer 1988): 95–107.
[75] See Alan Dowty, *The Jewish State: A Century Later* (Berkeley: University of California Press, 1998), Chap. 4.
[76] In the German language, for example, *Staatsgebäude* is also a semiobject, but this term does not assume that the nation is a part of that object (i.e., the state apparatus).

The national building was a solution to the Jews' growing exclusion from European nation-states and their dire economic predicament, especially in Eastern Europe. But the Zionist vision, we have seen in this chapter, was more than an attempt to answer such problems, and it searched for new grounds for Jewish existence and the overcoming of homelessness. Perhaps, in fact, the aim of the Zionist pioneer could be described as overcoming something more than is generally understood by "homelessness": he or she was trying to surmount *telishut*, which could be translated as disconnectedness and being apart. Literally, it means being separated from something, as when a leaf is detached from a tree. *Telishut* is the Hebrew word most resembling homelessness, but it does not evoke directly the idea of a home but rather being apart, alone, disconnected, nonembedded; it is more all-engulfing than homelessness.

It is striking that people who have often experienced dislocation in their history did not invent a word for homelessness in the immediate sense. Perhaps this is because God (who in the Talmud is also called *hamakom*, or "the place") is supposed to be the "container" of our world and could be revealed everywhere. Thus, the Jewish believer, even in the Diaspora, is never without a place or a home, nor is he baffled about who he is. But once secularization set in and the language of tradition lost its grip, things were different. "The Jew could be found in each and every place, and yet no place was his own," as Pinsker put it.[77] The Jew did not assimilate well into European national cultures and remained a permanent stranger. Most of the attachments of this individual to the world were severed – and the Jew acquired the status of *talush*. He became not only without a sense of secured home and native land – but also without a clear identity. Not only was Zionism an attempt simply to solve homelessness in the sense of having a land of one's own, but it also aimed to ground the self in all spheres of existence: in relation to nature, manmade objects, political community.

Yet as we shall see, Zionists gradually discovered that finding a genuine answer to *telishut* cannot be accomplished solely within the framework of building, and that such an answer necessitates the creation and reproduction of a shared world of meanings. Such a task, however, cannot be reached when the status of language is fragile – as it had become, owing to their own revolution.

---

[77] Leo Pinsker, *Auto-Emancipation*.

PHOTO 9. Lord Arthur Balfour addressing the audience at the opening ceremony of the Hebrew University (1925). The speakers sitting on the podium include C. N. Bialik and Rabbi Kook. Unknown photographer; photo courtesy of The Central Zionist Archives, Jerusalem.

PHOTO 10. Notrim (or Gafirim, members of the Jewish police force set up by the British administration in Mandatory Palestine) guarding the Hebrew University on Mount Scopus (1947). Photo by Ya'akov Ben-Dov, courtesy of The Central Zionist Archives, Jerusalem.

PHOTO 11. A donkey carrying books for the National Library at the Hebrew University. Unknown photographer and year; photo courtesy of The Central Zionist Archives.

4

Hebrew and Politics

The tribes of the Diaspora are now being fused into one people, united and unique. For the renewed Jewish nation, Hebrew is the cultural cement, as the land is the material cement and independence the political one.

Prime Minster David Ben-Gurion, 1952

David Ben-Gurion, the first prime minister of the State of Israel, once told the story of his first encounter with H. N. Bialik, the great national poet of the Zionist movement. Bialik came in 1909 to visit the young socialist Zionist pioneers (who numbered only a few thousand at the time) in Sejera, one of their villages. The pioneers requested that he deliver a speech; the humble poet adamantly refused. But, continues Ben-Gurion,

after he heard our crazy songs and saw our ludicrous dances, a mixture of Arab and Hasidic songs, he stood, totally shocked.... He exploded, talking to us about the sorrows of speechlessness. Not our hard work, wants, or loneliness impressed his soul – but rather our inability to express ourselves properly, in a manner that is true and authentic to our hearts. The distress of these secluded individuals, who threw their entire past behind them ... who plowed during the day and were on guard with a rifle during the starless nights – the restless spirit of those entrapped in their muteness because they lacked reliable and precise words to articulate the drama of their hearts and souls, and who hungered to silence their sorrow even with foreign songs and borrowed dances – in short, the sorrow of speechlessness that he saw in a small village in the mountainous Galilee was the most difficult and painful thing for him.[1]

---

[1] David Ben-Gurion, *Zichronot* [Recollections], vol. 3 (Tel Aviv: Am Oved, 1973), p. 5 (in Hebrew).

Bialik understood that Zionism is an odd revolution: Not only did those who advanced it lack the proper words to describe their own actions – and were therefore unable to give an adequate account to themselves or others of their deeds – but the essence of this revolution was the transformation of the phenomenal world, the creation of a palpable new reality that could be seen and measured, numbered and quantified.

In this anecdote about early Zionism in Palestine, an important feature of this movement is exemplified: In Zionism (especially its dominant socialist strand), collective action preceded language, and the latter became an auxiliary to praxis rather than a precondition for its formation. The difficulty in cultivating Hebrew as a vernacular was understandable, but as late as 1929, Bialik suspected that the problem was not the lack of a rich vocabulary per se, but rather something deeper – a lack of respect for the role of language and reflection in public life. He noted that "a nation that lacks clear, correct, and healthy thought ... is unable to do the appropriate thing; it will always be diverted from the right path."[2] Moreover, if the public and reflective use of words had a questionable place during the dawn of Zionism, surely the last few decades have not witnessed a transformation of language's status: Settlements and construction, roads and bulldozers, barriers and fences, the size of territory and measure of populations – numbers and facts on the ground still shape the substance of Israeli politics. The realm of public discourse continues to lag, limping and faltering behind a reality shaped, for the most part, by other means.

It is perhaps impossible to measure, with the quantitative methods of the social sciences, the "standing" of language: the place it holds in a people's public life, the degree to which it is constitutive of social reality. Nevertheless, to reflect on such standing in a certain political culture (which in the case of the State of Israel has been shaped mostly by Jews) is not a minor or meaningless endeavor. The weight we ascribe to the words spoken in public concerning shared affairs, the faith we may feel in the power of spoken and written words to expose a truth about reality and to form the political community as a reality – these are *essential* to political life. The notion that language is critical for achieving consensus on strategic-utilitarian issues and especially on notions of right and good has obviously been a major

---

[2] H. N. Bialik, *Devarim shebe'al peh* [Speeches and lectures], vol. 2 (Tel Aviv: Dvir, 1935), p. 137 (in Hebrew).

preoccupation of political theory in recent decades, with the ascent of Habermas's theory of communicative action and theories of deliberative democracy. But the insight goes back to the Greeks. According to Isocrates, Athens

always honored eloquence which all men crave and envy in its possessors; for she realized that this is the one endowment of our nature which singles us out from all living creatures.... She saw that in other activities the fortunes of life are so capricious that in them frequently the wise fail and the foolish succeed; whereas the art of beautiful speech is never allotted to ordinary men, but is the work of an intelligent mind, and that it is in this respect that men who are accounted wise or ignorant present the strongest contrast.

In fact, *Hellenes* "signifies no longer a race but an intelligence," a bond created by education and a certain vision of humans, rather than by "common blood."[3] Aristotle also famously noted that "language serves to declare what is advantageous and what is the reverse, and it therefore serves to declare what is just and what is unjust.... It is the peculiarity of man ... and it is association in these things which makes a family and a *polis*."[4] In *The Politics* (Book VII), Aristotle further suggests that a significant difference exists between a polis whose sense of confidence and even raison d'être is based on its achievements in the phenomenal world (which he associates with imperialistic politics) and a polis that values most the virtue of its individual citizens and thereby its character as a political body. The first type of city would measure its achievements in terms of wealth, territory, population and the like; the second – in hoping to cultivate the character and happiness of its citizens – would have to overcome its mistrust in the ephemeral nature of language and anchor itself in a world created through shared words. A mixture of the politics animating each of the two cities is probably needed for any political entity, yet one may speak of two distinct ideal types.

It is common today to examine the revival of Hebrew as a vernacular mostly in the context of nineteenth-century nationalism and the attempts of many emerging nations to revive their historical languages (the celebration of Italian and German was essential to the rise of nationalism in

---

[3] Isocrates, in Harold Goad, *Language in History* (Harmondsworth, UK: Penguin, 1958), p. 38.
[4] Aristotle, *The Politics of Aristotle*, trans. Ernest Barker (Oxford: Oxford University Press, 1946), p. 6.

these two countries, for example). This comparative perspective is useful for obvious historical reasons, but it is also misleading. In reviving this language (that was never really dead), Zionists transported into the sphere of language a dense, intense confrontation between the divine and the secular realms. In no other national movement in modernity did the revival of a national language also involve such a complete and swift transfiguration of its theological and ontological status. To express private and public life, Hebrew had to be wrested from its role as a holy language and made ordinary. Yet precisely this radical change left the Hebrew language flat and weak, and fostered the Zionist inclination to embrace tangibly oriented politics; the Jewish polity that evolved in Palestine approximated Aristotle's ideal type of one that evaluates its power and success chiefly in light of what can be seen, measured, numbered, and augmented.

Bialik, who, like Aristotle, identified the human being as a "speaking creature" (*hai medaber*), noted with concern this character of the emerging Jewish polity. He differentiated between two types of human action, one based on the use of exact numbers and calculations in order to erect concrete artifacts in the phenomenal world, and the other based on invisible, spiritual creations made by letters and words. There are times, he noted, "that history enchants and fools us ... directing our attention to palpable actions that are made in full daylight, and which we celebrate thinking that we are hastening our redemption, while in fact the truly great deeds – which lead to the explosion of the nation's energies – are invisibly conducted, and they are the hidden secret."[5]

I begin this chapter by discussing briefly the meaning of the attempt to secularize the Hebrew language, and will point to the immense challenges facing the effort to use Hebrew effectively in the public sphere. Later in the chapter, I will explore how the two (probably) most important conceptions of language suggested by the Zionist "cultural school" – those of Ahad Ha'am and of Bialik – viewed the role of language in national life, and the problems their conceptions pose for a viable place for Hebrew in democratic politics. As we shall see, *the poor status of Hebrew in Zionist and Israeli political life stems not only from the dominance of socialist ideology and building-oriented philosophy, but also from the fact that those who championed the role of language failed to adequately address pivotal issues for democratic politics*, issues such as the relationship between morality and power in language, the role and

[5] See *Devarim*, vol. 1, p. 37.

value of the individual speaker, the place of truth in communal communication – and even the value of public speech and discussion as such. (Bialik, the poet, of course could not have been expected to reflect on these issues directly, but he presents a view of language that has troubling political implications.)

I. CAN MAN BE THE MEASURE OF ALL THINGS IN HEBREW?

As we have seen, Zionism involved a critical departure from the culture of the Diaspora since it conceived of collective action as the transformation of the material-visible world and measured its achievements mostly in these terms (as for secularization, however, the revolution was less radical than initially seemed and religion was not separated from the state). Building and marshaling the means necessary for this grand project were its main goals. This national movement was a rebellion against life in the Diaspora, which was depicted as involving various undesirable aspects. These included outdated religious beliefs and practices, self-enclosed and suffocating communities, political dependency and an ethos of submissiveness, heightened spiritualism, and the neglect of Nature (including one's body); the list is long. *But Zionism as it evolved in Palestine was also a repudiation of word-based communal life in the deepest sense.* This feature of the Zionist revolution is mostly implicit; it is somewhat overshadowed by the fact that Zionism championed the renewal of Hebrew as a language of everyday life and today rightly celebrates the achievements of contemporary Hebrew literature. Moreover, this revolution was conceived through words (Herzl's *The Jewish State* being the most famous example, but think also of the writings of Nordau, Ahad Ha'am, Gordon, and Jabotinsky). Writers of all sorts played not only a major cultural role in its history but also a major political role, and almost every home in the kibbutzim, for example, had a respectable library. (Indeed, the kibbutzim were the home of some of Israel's best writers, poets, composers, artists, and so on, and an important part of the attempt to create a fresh Hebrew-based culture.) Nevertheless, an earth-shattering transformation in the status of words occurred during this revolution.

For the early Zionists (especially, but not only, the socialists), *the failure of the diasporic way of life was also a failure of the word in general,* for faith in the power of words was perhaps the very foundation of the world of the Diaspora and of Jewish identity during that long period; once this way of existence had collapsed, its foundation was profoundly demolished. So when language was revived for the sake of creating a national identity and an attachment to the land (the "cultural cement" of the people, as Ben-Gurion referred to it in the epigraph of this chapter), it was conceived of mostly in instrumental terms; it was no longer viewed as the bearer of truth and revelation.

The celebrated figure of the socialists was the *halutz*, an individual (as we saw in Chapter 3) characterized by the capacity for hard work and attachment to the land, the desired figure of Jabotinsky's Revisionist movement, an individual capable of upholding the Iron Wall, someone who is "proud, generous, and ruthless."[6] Later, the celebrated character of the young Israeli culture – the *Sabra* – was depicted as one who uses words economically, expressing him- or herself in action rather than in speech. The multilayered and biblically inspired language of the first generation of *halutzim* – not to mention the ironic and idiomatically rich Yiddish of the Diaspora – were progressively displaced by a more direct and instrumental language. Key words used by the generation leading the struggle for independence included *dugri* (דוגרי, direct, simple manner of speaking, without fear and unnecessary linguistic ornaments; the word is borrowed from Arabic), and *tachles* (תכלס, practically, bottom line. The word is borrowed from Yiddish).[7] In the words of Ben-Gurion, "not by the power of literature, but by the power of intrepid people of action … is this enchanted castle being erected."[8]

In spite of the avalanche of words about political affairs, both written and spoken, during the history of the movement, to this day there is hardly a political text, a document, or a public speech (with the possible exception of the 1948 Declaration of Independence) that has

---

[6] See V. Jabotinsky, at: betar.org.il.

[7] I am following here Oz Almog, *The Sabra – A Profile* (Tel Aviv: Am Oved, 1997), pp. 230–1 (in Hebrew).

[8] I owe this quote to Anita Shapira. See her "Ben Gurion and the Bible: The Creation of a New Historical Narrative?" in *New Jews, Old Jews*, p. 239 (in Hebrew). To be sure, one can find conflicting proclamations by Ben-Gurion on this matter (not to mention the fact that he was an avid reader himself). As a prime minster in the late 1950s, he initiated and pushed for a grand endeavor of translating into Hebrew classic and important books from all over the world – China, India, and the Muslim world included. He proclaimed at the time that "since our independence, I felt that together with the [political] state we must establish the state of the spirit, a state that is not limited by territory. We must give our generation all the treasures of the human spirit in Hebrew, in our language, since each one of us is a citizen of the world." See Mordechai Naor, "We Must Establish the State of the Spirit," published in *Ha'aretz*, April 24, 2011, available at: http://www.haaretz.co.il/hasite/spages/1225785.html.

become entrenched in Israeli political culture and serves as a shared reference point – a foundation for discussing beliefs, goals, or events. Few phrases exist that are familiar to all and that could provide the basis of a shared world of connotations; hardly any interpretive debates are conducted over past documents or speeches. Each text or speech begins from scratch, as it were, and descends into the void that awaits it, there to be forgotten. Nor is there a work in political philosophy that performs a function analogous to, say, the Federalist Papers (not to mention the writings of a Rousseau or a Marx); in fact (as mentioned), until recent decades there have been few works of political philosophy at all, despite the relative strength of the philosophical tradition in Israel and among Jews in general. (As for the status of Hebrew prose and especially poetry, including their relation to politics, I shall discuss this subject in this chapter and the next.)

I would not like to be understood as suggesting that there have been no worthy speeches on political affairs, although there haven't been too many of those either. (Among the notable exceptions, one could mention Israeli Defense Forces Chief of Staff Moshe Dayan's eulogy of Roy Rotenberg, a young Israeli killed in 1956 near the border with Gaza; IDF Chief of Staff Yitzhak Rabin's speech when he was awarded an honorary doctoral degree by the Hebrew University soon after the 1967 war; and Menachem Begin's 1952 speech against the reparations agreement between Israel and Germany.) As we shall see, the reasons for the predicament of Hebrew in public life are mainly twofold: a) the low status of language in a civic culture based on other foundations and b) some of the characteristics of the new Hebrew language, which evolved hand in hand with Zionism and the Jewish state, and remained partly caught up in its political functions.

However, in the Diaspora – and still for ultraorthodox Jewish believers today – the very same language had an altogether different religious status, regardless of the vernacular Jews happened to be using throughout the generations (and in this sense, incidentally, the status of Hebrew in Judaism resembles the status of Arabic in Islam, rather than the status of any language in Christianity).[9] To begin with, for the observant Jew,

---

[9] As Adrian Hastings notes, for the religious Muslim, the *Qur'an* "has to be read, recited out loud five times a day in Arabic," and thus it was almost impossible to translate this sacred text. In Christianity, by contrast, "neither Hebrew, Greek, nor Latin had any special claim on its loyalty, and it was quickly recognized that sacred texts remained equally sacred in translation." See Hastings, *The Construction of Nationhood*.

the Torah (which was given in Hebrew), represents permanent and fixed metaphysical and ontological truths about the author of the world (a wholly spiritual, monotheistic, and self-contained Being) and about how this world was created (as told in the Book of Genesis). The Torah, however, also contains ethical-legal duties, obligations, and rights (both in regard to God and to one's fellow man) that are absolute but must be adapted to the times and to concrete situations. Hence, a rich tradition of interpretation (spanning thousands of years) was created to bridge the fixed past with the present and its changing needs.[10] Part of this tradition of interpretation is in languages other than Hebrew (the Talmud's Aramaic, for example), but in order to be able to interpret rightly the original canonical text, one must know Hebrew well; otherwise the study and interpretation could be misleading and inaccurate. Contribution to the tradition of commentary became the highest activity open to the believer, and *all* male members of the community were supposed to have some basic knowledge of it. However, in addition to the importance of Hebrew to the observant Jew in deciphering the law (or Halacha) as well as the secrets of creation, he also communicates with God through prayers; it is the language in which the soul intimately expresses itself in its search for transcendent consolation and communication with God. "For in the utterance of prayer, it is Hebrew words which fully express the purpose of the heart, and thus help to attain the desired goal,"[11] the *Zohar* tells us. The Book, then, is the anchor of identity for both the community and the individual, a "mobile homeland" (to use Heinrich Heine's phrase). It is an "alternative reality"[12] that trumped any contingent territorial or political association the Jews happened to find themselves in as part of the Diaspora. This was true at least until modern times when the wish of many Jews to integrate into their native nation-states arose and the pressures to relinquish their distinct language grew as well.

Within a tradition centered on texts and words and the endless interpretations they allow, Hebrew, then, has a privileged place: It is called *leshon hakodesh*, the language of holiness, both because the sacred texts were originally written in this language and because the language

[10] See Gershom Scholem, *Od Davar*, pp. 153–61.
[11] I owe this citation and some of the insights in this paragraph to Lewis Glinert. See his essay "Hebrew," in *Contemporary Jewish Religious Thought*, ed. Arthur A. Cohen and Paul Mendes-Flohr (New York: Charles Scribner's Sons, 1987), p. 326.
[12] As Bialik notes, "The notion of the Torah was elevated in the eyes of the people in unmeasured ways. In the people's imagination, the Torah was almost like a second reality; in fact, a more abstract and higher reality that stands alongside or even instead of actual reality" (*Devarim*, vol. 1, p. 50).

itself, its letters and words, are considered holy (and not only by Jewish mystics). "Just as the Torah was given in *leshon hakodesh*," it is written in the Aggada, "so the world was created with *leshon hakodesh*"; in fact, "God looked into the Torah and created the world" (Gen. R. 18:4).[13] God first created the letters and words, and then created the world, "without toil and effort, only through His Word" (ibid.); thus, the best way to understand Creation and render it transparent – to fathom the metaphysical Truth about things, as it were – is by understanding the underlying matrix, Hebrew.[14] The name Adam is just a name when translated, but in Hebrew it contains the word *dam*, blood, which is the fluid that dominates the human body and is vital to its existence, and this name is also associated with *adama*, soil, the matter from which Adam was created; the Hebrew word, then, is thought not to be merely an arbitrary signifier but to reveal the essence and origin of things, their ultimate truth.

Hebrew, for the believer, is thus not merely a natural language that evolves historically, the invention of a nation of speakers that reflects this nation's passage through time; rather, many of its speakers understand themselves to use a language that was given to them and that is not primarily their own: They are the keepers of language, not its masters. The language of Creation situates the speaker in a transcendental and cosmic context, elevating the individual to higher spheres, while also humbling him or her. Of course, Hebrew can be used, and has been used throughout the ages, for daily affairs, including wills, correspondence, contracts, community records, scientific writings, and the like; sometimes Jews used it among themselves when they did not want noncommunity members to understand them. And there is no agreement in the tradition about the necessity of using it, even in the study of and writing about the Torah. The Talmud, as mentioned, is mostly in Aramaic, and Maimonides's *Guide for the Perplexed* was originally written in Arabic. In fact, Jews did not insist on speaking and using Hebrew; although this language began to be seen as holy probably in the rabbinical era, in this same period Jews were no doubt using other languages as well, especially Aramaic, Greek,

---

[13] See Glinert, "Hebrew," in *Contemporary Jewish Religious Thought*, p. 326. See also, Judah Halevi, *Book of Kuzari*, trans. Hartwig Hirschfeld (Whitefish: Kessinger Publishing, 2003), p. 109.

[14] This understanding of Hebrew was widespread, and not only among Jews, of course. Dante, for example, believed that before Babel the "*modi essendi* of things were identical with the *modi significandi*. The Hebrew of Eden was the perfect and unrepeatable example of such a language." See Umberto Eco, *Serendipities: Language and Lunacy* (New York: Orion, 1999), p. 51.

and Latin.[15] Nevertheless, from a theological point of view, the language's holiness is rarely contested among believers.

The word *davar* demonstrates the relation between the holiness of language and human action, and between words and deeds generally. *Davar* bridges different realms, since it has two interrelated meanings: on the one hand, a word, and on the other, a deed or event (*davar* could also mean a thing). In biblical Hebrew, *davar* (which stems from *dibber*, i.e., spoke) often means the Word of God: words that are sublime and powerful – and that generate action and create events in the world or prohibit them[16] (e.g., the fifth, legalistic book of the Torah, or Pentateuch [Deuteronomy], is called in Hebrew *Devarim* [דברים], and the Ten Commandments are called *aseret hadiberot*). Whether spoken or written, however, the order is clear: God is an intentional and separate being who begins his intervention in the world through the effective words, epitomized by *davar*. Humans, when they use words, share this understanding concerning the priority and potency of language in relation to conduct and objects. But it is not only the order from speech to action that is important but also the lack of a clear distinction between them. In the Bible, "the word is the highest and noblest function of man and is, for that reason, identical with his action." In this view, words "cannot be inconsequential" – or be a cover-up for a reality divorced from their meaning – since "the word is connected to its accomplishments."[17] Indeed, the last book of the Bible (Chronicles), a narration of past words and deeds, does not distinguish between the two and is called *Divrei hayamim* (דברי הימים).

This veneration of the word of God propelled the Kabbalists, the Jewish mystics, to develop their theory of language, in which the world is transparent and has a symbolic character. For them, according to Gershom Scholem, "everything, beyond its own meaning, has something more, something which is part of that which shines into it or, as if in some devious way, that which has left its mark behind in it, forever."[18] Whatever exists in the world was not only created through language but also contains a distinct soul, or *pneuma*, that is revealed in its name.

---

[15] See: Angel Sáenz-Badillos, *A History of the Hebrew Language*, trans. John Elwolde (Cambridge: Cambridge University Press, 1993).

[16] I am greatly indebted in my discussion of Davar to Thorleif Boman, *Hebrew Thought Compared with Greek* esp. p. 65.

[17] Ibid, pp. 65, 66.

[18] Gershom Scholem, "The Name of God and the Linguistic Theory of the Kabbala," *Diogenes* 80 (Winter 1972): 165.

This symbolic character of created beings and things is the upshot of the movement and proliferation of a language that originates in the name of God. The name of God is a major concern for the Kabbalists (as it was for many other medieval commentators), with some suggesting that it includes only a few letters or even one letter, and others suggesting that the entire Torah is actually the name of God. The name (or names) of God is seen as expressing symbolically an extremely potent and creative abyss that is inexpressible and noncommunicable; the name appears in the finite realm but points to the mysterious infinite. For Isaac the Blind (born circa 1160), one of the first known Kabbalists, the name of God, uttered first by God himself, is the source of all language and things (*devarim*). As Scholem explains, for Isaac "all *devarim* take form, and all forms issue (finally) only from the one name, just as the twig issues from the root." "It therefore follows," continues Scholem, "that everything is contained in the root, which is the one name."[19] The name and the language itself were understood to be in a kind of exile while Jews were in the Diaspora; the return to the Holy Land, therefore, created a new challenge and an exciting opportunity for the holy language.

The revival of Hebrew in modern times, especially the unity of language, land, and people – a triangle of holiness, according to Judaism – suggested essentially two radical, internally consistent options: the return of the theological meanings imbued in the language or its complete secularization and "normalization." These radically opposed options were famously articulated by the young Scholem.

Of the first option, he wrote that "a language is composed of names. The power of the language is bound up in the name and its abyss is sealed within the name. Having conjured up the ancient names day after day, we can no longer suppress their potencies. We rouse them, and they will manifest themselves, for we have conjured them up with very great power."[20]

---

[19] Ibid., p. 168. On Scholem's analysis of the name of God in the Kabbala, see Eric Jacobson, *Metaphysics of the Profane: The Political Theology of Walter Benjamin and Gershom Scholem* (New York: Columbia University Press, 2003), Chap. 4.

[20] See Robert Alter, *Necessary Angels: Tradition and Modernity in Kafka, Benjamin, and Scholem* (Cambridge, MA: Harvard University Press, 1991), p. 36. See also Alter, "Scholem and Modernism," *Poetics Today* 15, no. 3 (1994): 429–42. According to Alter, Scholem, like many others at the time (especially in Germany and Russia), embraced the dramatic theme of oncoming apocalypse and was inspired by the modernist Zeitgeist in fathoming the unique predicament of language in Zionism. Clearly, the passage quoted here also raises the question of the extent to which Scholem followed Benjamin in his understanding of time and history. On the one hand, Scholem was very concerned about bold leaps into the past, which he did not see as possible or desirable; it seems that the

Scholem believed that God "will not remain silent in His own language," a language (and history) that reveals a God that is not benign and merciful, but is rather unpredictable and prone to the apocalyptic. The new reality in Palestine – the land that is in fact "a volcano" of meanings and connotations – might breathe new life into the names that have been dormant in the Diaspora: names of places, names referring to political life, names of religious practices, institutions, and rules. For the diasporic Jew, Jerusalem, for example, is a place of the imagination, a locus of a distant redemption; for the new Jew in Palestine, however, the name invokes something concrete that has political implications. As Psalm 122 puts it, "our feet were standing at your gates, Jerusalem; Jerusalem that is built as a city that was put together, united"[21]; in the context of Eretz Israel, this could be interpreted as a demand for action regarding the status, expansion, and unity of the city. The Jew was never the master of the Hebrew language, and the new Jew would be no different: The language might overwhelm him or her, shaping deeds and intentions, because words such as "Knesset Israel" or "Medinat Israel" have non-acknowledged yet profound theological and even messianic meanings.[22] The Zionists' semicyclical temporal imagination allowed potent words to be reborn in their native land; this time around, however, the names, expressions, and idioms would have *not only the theological allure but also the force of tradition and history*, the longing and the background chant of the many generations that uttered them. The cry of oppressed, desperate, yearning Jews of the past could awaken the weak Messianic powers (to use Benjamin's term) of those who are alive in the present and who are responsible for respecting the aspirations and dreams of the dead; this responsibility, however, would mean, in the Zionist context, that redemption would have a national rather than a universal-ethical character. It would consist of a commitment to build the land and the

Benjaminian "time of the now" did not appeal to him. On the other hand, Scholem's vision of history was clearly inspired by Benjamin. For example, in a 1946 lecture titled "Memory and Utopia in Jewish History," he suggested that there is no clear continuity of generations, symbols, or ideas, or even utopian aspirations in history, but rather a dialectical process whereby pictures from the past change, some being exhumed while others are assigned to forgetfulness; our consciousness and will play a prominent role in this selective approach to history and tradition. The resemblances to Benjamin's *Theses* are obvious. See Scholem, *Od Davar*, pp. 119–22. I am also indebted to William Cutter; see his "Ghostly Hebrew, Ghastly Speech: Scholem to Rosenzweig, 1926," *Prooftexts* 10 (1990): 413–33.

[21] עומדות היו רגלינו בשעריך ירושלים; ירושלים הבנויה כעיר שחוברה לה יחדיו. תהילים, קכב

[22] See on this point Aviezer Ravitzky, *Haketz hameguleh umedinat hayehudim*, p. 14.

state, rather than salvage the memory of the exploited classes in the history of civilization.[23]

The other path open to the Zionist conception of the Hebrew language – secularization – was no less dangerous because of its relative vacuity and flatness. To Scholem, Hebrew could be viewed as a purely contemporary human construct, without the depth and weight of tradition, without connotations, meanings, and obligations evoked by the ancient words; such a vision of Hebrew would complement, in the sphere of language, the preference for the international style seen in the sphere of architecture. Put differently, the new society that would use this "built" language and would build itself from scratch would suffer from extreme cultural impoverishment and shallow identity. To take his point further, in this case Hebrew would become a "normal" language that suited various functions: communication, individual expression, the storing of information, and the like. It would help create a nation from people who have come from all corners of the earth, who had only this language as a shared foundation, one that differentiated them from both the nearby Arabs and the Yiddish-speaking Jews of the Diaspora.[24] In this purely functional view of Hebrew, there is even no essential connection between Zionism and the revival of Hebrew, as Herzl himself recognized.[25] Indeed, since the biblical vocabulary was hardly fitting for modern science, natural history, technology, produced objects, sensibilities, and the psyche, many words in modern Hebrew have borrowed their new meanings from foreign languages, have been invented by drawing

[23] To be sure, the leap to the past could have other implications, closer to Benjamin's. Buber, for example, believed that only by using the original, Hebrew biblical words and embracing the semicyclical temporal imagination would Zionists be able to emulate the ancient, Hebraic thought and restore humanistic values, such as the pursuit of justice, truthfulness, and heightened conscience. (These values originated in the distinct history of the nation, but they must be applied universally.) According to Buber, "one must overcome the shallow vision of time, a vision according to which the world of faith which these [original, biblical] words convey is today merely something to be contemplated in consciousness rather than a reality. Only the entrance into that reality infuses life with meaning and makes it worthwhile." See Martin Buber, *Tuda ve-yehud*, vol. 2 (Jerusalem: World Zionist Organization Press, 1984), p. 395.

[24] The differentiation between the European Diaspora and the Hebrew-speaking community in Palestine was also expressed in the choice of Sephardic pronunciation over Ashkenazic. On this point, see Itamar Even-Zohar, "The Emergence of a Native Hebrew Culture in Palestine, 1882–1948," *Cathedra* 16 (1980): 165–89 (in Hebrew).

[25] On Herzl's attitude toward Hebrew and the discussions about the language in the early years of the Zionist movement, see Michael Berkowitz, *Zionist Culture and West European Jewry before the First World War* (Cambridge: Cambridge University Press, 1993), Chap. 2.

on the flexibility of the Hebrew root, or have been adopted from external sources altogether. For example, the influences of Yiddish, Russian, Arabic, and (today) English on modern Hebrew are most significant.[26] At the dawn of Zionism, some scholars even claimed that there was no such unified language as "Hebrew": This name did, in fact, represent a number of languages that should be differentiated according to their historical period.[27] This *artificial*, borrowed component of the Hebrew language could color the entire language, manifesting its arbitrary and superficial character, both historically and linguistically. Hebrew could be viewed then as being anchored fundamentally to the present, unsentimentally galloping forward with the times, deaf to the meanings embedded in its own history, attracted to and needful of foreign languages, armed with a self-understanding dominated by *functionality*. The self-reflexivity of the modern mind – which after Nietzsche, Marx, and Freud was suspicious of language and the way it shapes reality – could be put fully to work upon the concoction of the Hebrew language. According to Scholem, seeing Hebrew in this way would make it an unstable "language of ghosts": impoverished, unable to maintain the bond of a people with their land and their past, or to nourish the creation of a new communal identity.

By deciding to make Hebrew the national language, then, Zionists – according to Scholem – took on an almost impossible balancing act: reviving a language while trying to suppress its apocalyptic vision and Messianic aspirations, or, to put it another way, cultivating a vocabulary suited to life in the present and immediate future while seeking legitimacy in names and expressions anchored in the distant past and permeated with theological meanings. One day, warned Scholem, the people would have to choose between these two options: "succumb to the [holiness of the] language, or deteriorate to their extinction" because of the hollowness of their words.

Yet if we take Scholem's observations a step forward, it could be argued that the challenge of modern Hebrew, especially in the public arena, *has been exactly the repudiation of these two extreme options.*

---

[26] On the history of Hebrew, see William Chomsky, *Hebrew: The Eternal Language* (Jerusalem: Rubin Mass, 1967); Chaim Rosen, *Ivrit shelanu* [Our Hebrew] (Tel Aviv: Am Oved, 1955); and Ron Kuzar, *Hebrew and Zionism: A Discourse Analytic Cultural Study* (Berlin: Mouton, 2001).

[27] For a recent study of the influence of Yiddish on contemporary Hebrew, see Ghil'ad Zuckermann, "Israeli, daber israelit – muflaut hasafa haisraelit [Israeli, speak Israeli! – The marvels of the Israeli language]," *Iton 77*, no. 318 (2007): 16–21. Zuckermann suggests that Yiddish (as well as other languages) influenced modern Hebrew decisively, and thus the latter should be viewed as a new language, "Israelit."

The revived Hebrew could have shaped itself according to a human measure that nevertheless maintains an open dialogue with tradition. It could
have created a new sphere in which to dwell, one that lies between instru-
mentality and Revelation, as well as between the private and the epic;
a language in which words convey meaning and depth, possess weight
and truth despite being a human creation alone that lacks the holiness
ascribed to them by tradition. In particular, there was a need for such a
language in the public sphere, the sphere through which modern Jews
began to conduct their lives. This sphere did not exist in the Diaspora, during which Jews were dispersed and did not exercise autonomous political
power, and it did not exist in the mostly monarchic Hebraic antiquity.

Because of the unique status of Hebrew in the tradition, however, the
opportunity for words to be potent in the political sphere was immense,
and Zionism could have transformed the language and text-centered culture of Judaism into a political life in which language has a privileged
place – one even more privileged perhaps than is customary in contemporary liberal democracies. Hebrew could have regained its position as
constitutive of action (in the sense of *davar*) and remain central to the
way citizens conduct themselves in their political world; it could have
been a language that is not merely a medium of communication but also
a source for generating rich meanings and public import. To be sure, this
usage in the public sphere would have demanded a few critical changes
in the language and its understanding (changes that cannot be "planned"
and decided upon but, rather, reflect complex cultural, intellectual, social,
and other processes). Let me mention these briefly.

First, a new view of tradition would have been required in which it
is conceived of not as an orderly, coherent, hierarchical, and teleological body of thought and law but as a vast container of interrelated parts
and arguments. This human-made container – its form as well as content – would be full of tensions and contradictions, and the speaker who
dives within could approach it playfully and sacrilegiously. The spirit of
Judaism – of argumentativeness and ongoing dispute, of tolerating different points of view without necessarily resolving the tensions between
them – suggests a view of tradition that could be useful politically. More
generally, rather than seeing tradition as irrelevant (which sometimes it
is) and hopelessly destroyed, it should be thought of as an opportunity
for creativity and for helping form a fresh outlook (I will say more about
this point later).

Second, a novel vocabulary would have been needed, one suited to political affairs and democratic concepts that did not exist in the language's

earlier periods of use. These include such concepts as the right to free speech or assembly, separation of powers, minority rights, and gender equality. The problem was (and is) not the invention of this vocabulary, but rather granting it cultural and linguistic depth: Political concepts are always contested; when no shared linguistic tradition exists, however, their use tends to become wholly strategic. Moreover, in this vocabulary the bond between effective words, deeds, and actual things in the world would have had to be reestablished. The use of Hebrew in the Diaspora was mostly limited to learning and liturgy and did not shape collective action; *politically*, the union of words and deeds did not exist, certainly not in the holy language. The revival of the language in the modern era would have had to aspire to an emulation of the strong bond of language and reality in the Bible, only this time with man and woman as the principal authoritative speakers.

A third change that would have been required to make Hebrew politically more meaningful is that the Hebrew-speaking individual would have had to feel spontaneity, flexibility, and a sense of freedom within the language. For the early Zionists, the word had to be freed from the biblical phrase in which it was locked, and the self had to be freed from the emotional and existential horizon circumscribed by the past and its limited vocabulary. The modern notions of selfhood, as they developed in early modernity and were expanded upon by Rousseau and the Romantic movement, had a very limited influence on the development of Hebrew in the nineteenth century. A rich concept of the self – with a vocabulary able to express emotional depth and complexity, and informal and intimate aspects of existence, detached from pompous declarations or ideological slogans – was critical in conceiving a substantial notion of democratic citizenship.[28]

Finally, to achieve political effectiveness, the renewed language would have had to replace the theological notion of Truth and Revelation – or at least establish alongside it a new, valid, human-based notion of truth. From a political-democratic perspective, the Hebrew language can no longer be viewed as the bridge between the other-worldly and the this-worldly spheres, no longer be the embodiment of transcendent light. Rather, arguments and expressions of the finite individual about the world and about his or her inner world, about what is right and what is useful to do, should

---

[28] On the formalistic and majestic character of Hebrew in the early decades of Zionism and the Israeli state, see Yaron Ezrahi, *Rubber Bullets*, pp. 19–30. As Ezrahi notes, the shift toward the exploration of the Israeli self occurred in the 1950s, with poets such as Nathan Zach, Yehuda Amichai, Dalia Rabikovitch, Dan Avidan, and others; however, the origin of the personal and subjective voice could already be found in Bialik and some of his contemporaries.

be viewed as articulating a limited perspective that is nevertheless a valid truth about the world. This truth can only express the way in which a situated human evaluates and judges political circumstances.

The political audacity concealed in the revival of Hebrew, accordingly, is the attempt *to position humans as the origin of truth claims about the world*,[29] in a language that belongs to a "great truth" and in which humans had always been, essentially, mere interpreters.

Mainstream Zionism in Palestine was not very interested in this project because it was preoccupied with building (although some writers, such as Agnon, were working in this direction of bridging the different layers of Hebrew and enriching the vocabulary of the self, albeit not in the political context.)[30] Socialist Zionists tended to devalue language's place

---

[29] The weight and truth value of words indeed remain fragile in the Israeli public sphere. Simcha Ehrlich, Israel's former deputy prime minister, once said "I don't mean what I say, and I don't say what I mean." Ehrlich's candid words seem to reflect the attitude of many Israeli leaders toward their own public words, even regarding critical issues. Recent examples of this attitude include the following: In April 2002, Prime Minister Ariel Sharon declared that "the fate of Netzarim [a Jewish settlement in the Gaza strip] is the fate of Tel Aviv." He was later elected again to the prime ministership (early 2003) vehemently opposing the disengagement plan from Gaza; less than a year later, he espoused and executed this disengagement. Ehud Barak, during the run-up to Labor's leadership primaries (May 2007), vowed that if Prime Minister Ehud Olmert would not leave office when the Winograd committee published its final report (on the second Lebanon war), he would press for early elections; later, when he became defense minister in Olmert's government, Barak renounced his earlier commitment and kept the Labor Party in the government (January 2008). Benjamin Netanyahu declared before the elections (February 2009) that he would not abide by Olmert's commitments to withdraw and would not evacuate settlements (from the West Bank), and generally talked about "economic peace" with the Palestinians, rather than about substantial political moves. After the elections, when he was prime minister, he accepted a two-state solution (in his Bar-Ilan speech, June 2009), which of course would lead to such withdrawals and evacuations.

As Professor Yuli Tamir, a former minster of education and a political theorist noted, in Israel, "no one says the truth. If no one stands behind his words and commitments, why should anyone listen or become politically involved? When it becomes impossible to believe anyone, then there is nothing to talk about, and there is no way to say what you believe in.... Now when there is no political discourse, there is no democracy, or just a semblance of one" (available at: http://www.ynet.co.il; accessed March 25, 2009).

[30] In 1967, Scholem agreed that the two visions of the Hebrew language could be mediated. In writing about Agnon, he noted that this writer was perhaps the last great artist able to bridge the past layers of Hebrew with the contemporary vernacular. Scholem even acknowledged that "the Hebrew words have acquired a new virginity" and that "it is possible to mold them to fit new contexts, without the odor of holiness – which is sometimes heavy and cumbersome – emanating from them." See *Od Davar*, p. 343. In general, he refused to "pick sides" and to see Judaism (and Hebrew) either as wholly a secular-historical creation or as hostage to its theological origins; secularism, it seems, was a stage within the dialectical development of Jewish existence in time, and the next stage might be different. He noted that he was not a "secular person" and warned that "if Jews would try to explain themselves only historically, they would be propelled to a mode of thinking of annihilation and complete destruction." See G. Scholem, *Devarim Bego*, p. 41.

PHOTO 12. A "youth Aliya" girl on guard duty at the "Ayanot" agriculture school. Photo by Zoltan Kluger, April 4, 1948. Courtesy of the Government Press Office, Israel.

in shaping the phenomenal world, not always consciously, and after two or three generations the dialogue (of the *Sabra*) with tradition became minor. It is interesting, however, to examine the vision of language among those *who did* celebrate its role in Zionism and who saw its renewal as the principal task, for *their* ultimate failure to advance a viable political role for the Hebrew language (or a picture of it that would indirectly promote such a role) boosted the tendency of socialist Zionists and others to focus on their material and quantitative achievements. Indeed, there was an important "cultural" strand in Zionist political thought that celebrated the role of language in national life (this line of thought began with Rabbi Yehuda Hai Alkalai in the middle of the nineteenth century). It was led by Ahad Ha'am, and it suggested that the furtherance of the national culture – especially its spiritual, philosophical, and moral aspects as they evolved historically – would be the most important achievement of Zionism. But even this school, often discussed today as a source of inspiration for contemporary Israel (at least for the Jewish community in the country), failed to suggest a conception of language conducive to democratic life and supportive of a viable political sphere.

II. LANGUAGE, COLLECTIVE SPIRIT, AND TELEOLOGICAL TIME: AHAD HA'AM

The first major attempt to think about the role of language in Zionism was carried out by Ahad Ha'am. During the first decades of Zionism, when various incompatible visions of the movement competed fiercely, he presented a clear and articulate voice calling for the revival of the Hebrew language and literature as perhaps the most critical goals of Zionism. Ahad Ha'am underscored the thought-oriented, soul-searching, and moral characteristics of Jewish literature and demanded a Zionist politics and Hebrew culture that continued in this tradition. The Zionism that ultimately developed in Palestine, however, rejected his conception of a predetermined collective narrative that is language centered, spiritually guided, and evolving gradually and without temporal leaps. In fact, the marginal place that Ahad Ha'am occupied in the actual development of the movement underscores my earlier point that other characteristics have dominated Zionism to date. Yet his vision of a national identity as grounded in language is still relevant today, when we are evaluating the achievements and failures of Zionism as a building-centered philosophy and praxis. He presents us with a viable option as Jews and Israelis (with Jewish origins) enter the twenty-first century and address pressing concerns about the meaning of Jewish identity, the best ways of preserving and cultivating this identity, and the overall place of literary culture in contemporary life.

In reflecting on the role of language in the nation's life, Ahad Ha'am seems to follow the Herderian tradition. While a direct link cannot be proven, in his intellectual autobiography Ahad Ha'am remarks that he read German literature at an early stage and that he especially admired "books written by Enlightenment thinkers, such as Herder and the like."[31]

---

[31] See Ahad Ha'am, "*Pirkei zichronot*," in *Kol kitvei Ahad Ha'am* ["Recollections," in The collected writings of Ahad Ha'am] (Jerusalem: Ahuza Ivrit, 1947), p. 495. (Hereafter, I shall refer to this text as *Kk*.) Despite this revealing statement, Ahad Ha'am rarely refers explicitly (let alone in any detail) to Herder in his writings. Thus, it is difficult

So let us begin by noting, in brief, Herder's understanding of language and its interdependence with nationalism. (See also the discussion on Herder in Chapter 2.)

Herder celebrates language as the most important feature of both individual and collective life. For individuals, language is a testimony to the ways we experience and reflect upon the external world. In contrast to Condillac and Rousseau, Herder claims that language is intrinsic to human existence – that *we cannot think without it*, be conscious of the world or ourselves without words; to think, he says, is to speak with oneself, and dialogue is essential to our internal existence as well as our existence with others. Nor can we remain related as a people (*Volk*) without sharing a language: He suggests that a correspondence exists between the history of national life and that of language, and that the liveliness of a language reflects the intensity of collective life and culture. A lifeless language (one frozen in rules and conventions) is an ominous sign for a culture, and the more "vitality it [language] has, the less it can be written at all."[32] (Hence, the critical role Herder assigns to poetry, which lends itself to be recited, and to oral folk culture.) Both the mentality of the nation and this mentality's narration are preserved in language: "The language is its [the nation's] collective treasure, the source of its social wisdom." Most nations guard their national language and see it as the source of their "communal self-respect,"[33] not because of narrow-minded tribalism but, rather, because of the cultural achievements that languages contain and shelter.

To lose the language of our ancestors, therefore, is to lose our anchor and orientation: "Our mother tongue embodies the first universe we saw, the first sensations we felt, the first activities and pleasure we enjoyed. Secondary ideas of time and place, of love and hate, and all the flaming impetuous thoughts of youth are perpetuated by it. This perpetuation of

---

to prove conclusively that he conceived his main ideas under the direct influence of the German philosopher (the secondary literature, indeed, hardly mentions them together). But reading the two thinkers, one nevertheless must note the deep-seated similarities in their thinking about language and culture, time and nationalism. It should be noted that Ahad Ha'am was also influenced by nineteenth-century writers such as Spencer and Krochmal, whose organic-biological and idealist philosophies (respectively) partly resemble Herder's. This resemblance points to the difficulty in distinguishing the exact sources of influence on Ahad Ha'am and in mapping their genealogy.

[32] "Essay on the Origin of Language," in *J. G. Herder on Social and Political Culture*, edited by F. M. Barnard (Cambridge: Cambridge University Press, 1969), p. 120. See also Barnard, *Herder's Social and Political Thought: From Enlightenment to Nationalism*.

[33] "Ideas for a Philosophy of History," in *J. G. Herder on Social and Political Culture*, p. 165.

thoughts and feelings through language is the essence of tradition."[34] It is not only tradition in general that is preserved in language, however, but also the tradition of our relation to a particular environment. In Herder's vision, spirit (*Geist*), language, and land are essentially interdependent, since language (and spirit) spring in part from an interaction with the environment as its foundation and vital force; language, in turn, contains ideas, emotions, myths, and memories that shape the nation's relation to the environment. In contrast to state institutions (which Herder, a well-known critic of Frederick the Great and Prussia, views as often being merely machines of power and homogenizing forces), the language of tradition provides continuity of time and space – it expresses a lasting identity that sustains the *Volk* and provides a meaningful context for the lives of the nation's members.

Ahad Ha'am's conception of nationalism and his celebration of language as epitomizing the nation's spirit manifest a deep affinity to these aspects of the Herderian thought.[35] For Ahad Ha'am, modernity had a

---

[34] Ibid, p. 164.

[35] In his acclaimed study of nationalism, Hans Kohn distinguishes between two types. The first type (modeled after the French Revolution and liberal thought) presents the nation as a political entity born at a definite moment: A number of individuals rationally decide to join their fates and establish a set of institutions, a constitution, and laws to regulate their shared lives. The members of this polity are citizens who preserve their natural rights; their bond does not negate their individuality but rather guards it. Kohn's second type of nationalism (modeled after the German experience and Herderian thought) pictures the nation as a prepolitical entity, distinguished by shared soil and landscape, language and literature, and ethnic origins and folk culture. Human beings do not choose to join such an organic body; they are born into and inescapably shaped by it. In fact, individuals cannot comprehend themselves without this engulfing whole and its collective meanings and purposes. Naturally, in this vision, the nation has no distinct moment of formation; it is a creature that gradually unfolds in history according to its distinct and incommensurable spirit and character. See Hans Kohn, *The Idea of Nationalism* (New York: Collier Books, 1967); Elie Kedourie, *Nationalism* (Oxford: Blackwell, 1993).

It should be mentioned that Eric Hobsbawm and Zeev Sternhell have argued that Zionism wholly espoused the (Herderian) nationalism that dominated Eastern and Central Europe. Sternhell in particular claims that Herder's organic nationalism is much more relevant to our understanding of Zionism than liberalism or even socialism. In Sternhell's view, the appeal of Herder's thought to Zionists lay in "the definition of the nation not in political or judicial terms but cultural, historical, linguistic, and religious terms." This definition "raised the stature of all those peoples who had lost their political independence hundreds of years earlier. The idea that the individual owed his being to the nation, that unique cultural unit which derived its existence from nature and was rooted in the soil of the motherland, created a human identity independent of a person's political or social status." This interpretation of the affinity between Zionism (as it evolved in practice) and Herderianism is questionable. In order to establish a Jewish state, Zionists had to reject central tenets of Herder's and Ahad Ha'am's thinking. These included the notion that identity is cultivated through language, the conception of social change as

centrifugal effect on Jews. On a demographic level, communities dispersed because the Jewish population moved from the country to the city, from the enclosed community to urban anonymity, from the European *shtetl* to roomy America and elsewhere. Worse was the spiritual confusion: There were religious Jews and ambivalent *maskilim*, cautious traditionalists and ardent Nietzscheans, socialists who rejected their Jewishness as well as those who embraced it, a multiplicity of nationalists adhering to their adopted countries and cultures, and more. Ahad Ha'am believed that, in this context, the main problem of the Jews was a breakdown of identity and the impending collapse of the entire diasporic way of life. It was not economic impoverishment or political insecurity that concerned him most but the evaporation of Jewish culture in an increasingly unfenced, secular world freed from the ghetto's walls. His response was to espouse a centripetal strategy that pictured two centers in need of reconstruction: a physical one in Palestine and a spiritual one at the heart of the nation. In his view, these two centers could not be separated; spiritual invigoration could take place only on the original soil of the Jews, and no settlement project in Palestine would be possible without the prior recognition of the national spirit and self.

In his view of the nation, Ahad Ha'am highlights the role of the *Volksgeist* (*ruach ha'am*) as the central characteristic, or supra-subject, of this body of people. In Judaism, he writes, the Hebrew language – confined to writing and hardly spoken, limited in subject matter, known almost exclusively to men, increasingly under siege from the local languages of various nations as well as from Yiddish – is nevertheless the principal guardian of this spirit. Ahad Ha'am argues that the people have an "instinct" for perpetuation. To him, the source of the power that allows people to further Zionist causes "is not in reason, but rather in the lower department of the soul," a place where the national instinct propels a person to fulfill the nation's interests regardless of his or her own good. This driving power or instinct is in fact "a national sense of preservation (*hush kiyum leumi*) that induces us to do whatever is needed for safeguarding our national existence,"[36] sometimes unintentionally and unconsciously.

---

occurring through slow evolution, the faith that time is ontologically continuous, and the belief in an essential *Volksgeist* that dominates the nation's life and binds it to a particular ethos (an ethos that, according to Ahad Ha'am, involved, in the Jewish case, heightened moral norms and the spurning of force in human interaction). See Zeev Sternhell, *The Founding Myths of Israel*, p. 55; Eric Hobsbawm, *Nations and Nationalism since 1780*. See also my disscussion in section II, Chapter 2, this volume.

[36] Ahad Ha'am, "Sach hakol [The sum total]," *Kk*, p. 421.

Individuals may think that they attempt to satisfy their own narrow goals and ostentatious, rational designs, but their individual actions unknowingly combine to steer the community away from harm and promote its existence. Moreover, communal continuity and unity are also preserved by the irrational fabric of emotions: Ahad Ha'am insists that membership in a (national) community does not result from considerations of utility and necessity but from a profound passion for the community, from a complex of emotions that belies calculations.[37]

These instincts and emotions are the forces that assiduously maintain the integrity and consistency of something higher: the nation's shared consciousness. In the same manner that individual identity is secured by continuity in time – by the ability to hold together past impressions, existence in the moment, and hopes for and fears of the future – the national ego (*ani leumi*) secures an identity throughout the ages. Yet the national ego is able to transcend the limited temporality that binds the individual body. For Ahad Ha'am, it is this national ego, "in its historical shape, that wishes to exist, this ego and not another, entirely as it is, with all its memories and hopes."[38]

In these and other pronouncements about instincts, emotions, and consciousness, Ahad Ha'am emerges as one of the most essentialist and collectivist Zionist thinkers. To him, the nation is like a person, possessing a core (ego) that is critical for its identity. Moreover, while even Herder gave a prominent place to the individual – seriously contemplating how this individual could best materialize his or her authenticity, happiness, and freedom – for Ahad Ha'am the individual is, for the most part, a passing moment in the life of the nation's collective semibody: "*Individuals that come and go in each generation are like those diminutive parts in the living body, which are renewed every day, without having any ability to unsettle the overall unity of the entire body.*"[39]

Despite these biological metaphors, to Ahad Ha'am the essential living force of the nation is its spirit, and he posits a dual relation whereby the spirit is disclosed in language and language shapes the spirit. In agreement with Herder ("What is the whole structure of language," the German thinker asks, "but a mode of development of man's spirit, the

---

[37] Ahad Ha'am, "Lo zo haderech [This is not the way]," *Kk*, p. 12.

[38] Ahad Ha'am, "Avar ve'atid [Past and Future]," *Kk*, p. 82.

[39] Ahad Ha'am, "Lo zo haderech," *Kk*, p. 12. Moreover, the important redemption is of the collective: "In the Jewish religion, the end is not the redemption of the private human being, but rather the success and perfection of the 'public' dimension of the nation – and ultimately of the entire human race" (p. 372).

history of his discoveries?"),[40] Ahad Ha'am suggests that language is the
vast container of culture and meanings, and that the intricate record of
words reflects the history of a nation's mentality. "Language is on many
occasions the finest key for fathoming the nation's spirit,"[41] he writes,
since the thoughts and souls of the people urge them to choose a certain
vocabulary to express themselves. Corresponding to the development of
the Jewish spirit, the history of Hebrew reveals a steady movement from
the poetic and emotional elements predominant during its ancient, independent political life toward a more abstract and reflective language (ever
since the destruction of the Second Temple and the composition of the
Mishna and the Talmud). Such modifications of the language's vocabulary, grammar, morphology, and so on are seen as inevitable because
language is intertwined with both the movement of the nation in time
and the progress of its spirit.[42]

Even more decisive for Jews was the overall alteration in the status of
language in the nation's life. Ahad Ha'am believes that, in the absence
of a fixed territory and a shared public life, language became the sole
bond of the Jewish people: In fact, "we barely have any remnant; *only
our language itself still shows signs of life*"[43] (my emphasis). Thus, in his
view, whoever longs to revitalize the Jewish culture must pay heed to
language.

Language mirrors the spirit, according to Ahad Ha'am, but it is also
the main sphere through which this spirit advances: Through language,
the nation's culture can be revived, its identity cemented, its self-respect
enshrined. This renewal is not a mere technical one: He rebukes both the
artificial invention of words (the path partly embarked on, for example,
by the great linguist and Zionist hero Eliezer Ben-Yehuda) and the emulation of European modern literature, with its preoccupation with the
individual's conflicted soul and aesthetics (as practiced, for example, by
Berdyczewski). For Ahad Ha'am, language has an integrity all of its own:
It is not a political tool, an ideological means, an entity to be constructed
at will. Words are to be added in a natural, spontaneous way, each very

---

[40] Ibid., p. 142.
[41] "Al devar otzar hayhadut belashon ivrit [Concerning the treasures of Judaism in
Hebrew]," *Kk*, p. 113. "It cannot be said," Ahad Ha'am adds, "that there is a nation,
either living today or already vanished, that existed, temporally speaking, prior to its
national language" (p. 179).
[42] Like Herder, Ahad Ha'am criticizes the tendency to freeze the Hebrew language into outdated grammatical structures and vocabulary and rejects the notion of "pure" language.
See "Halashon vedikduka [The language and its grammar]," *Kk*, p. 99.
[43] Ahad Ha'am, "Etza tova [A good advice]," *Kk*, p. 133.

gradually enlarging the potentially spacious terrain we call human experience. Moreover, the integrity of language requires that these new words and phrases be in line with the nation's spirit.[44] In the case of the Jewish people, this means that literature – the arena, for Ahad Ha'am, where language is truly renewed – should be preoccupied with giving ourselves a probing account about our unfolding collective life, hence, with *philosophical, moral, and contemplative* discussions: "In Israel, literature must submit to reflective thought if it wishes to be respected by the people." Therefore, "if you desire to enliven the language, strive to enliven the literature; and if you would like to enliven the literature, inject it with living thoughts."[45]

In his Zionist vision, Ahad Ha'am is haunted by the impression that the elements that preserved the Jewish people in the past may not hold. As noted, he was particularly concerned that the Hebrew language was under siege: The German Reform movement suggested that prayer could be conducted in languages other than Hebrew and that there is no inherent connection between Jewish faith and the biblical language; many writers of the younger generation preferred to write prose and other types of works in the "relevant" languages of the surrounding cultures; modern Hebrew itself had little to offer in terms of important works on science, economics, politics, and the like; and even the prophet of Hebrew nationalism, Herzl, initially preferred German for the popular language of the future state. The crisis of the Jewish people is reflected in the predicament of its language, then, and for Ahad Ha'am the revival of this people as a nation would come through the revitalization of this language[46] – in part through the reestablishment of an intimate relation between language and soil and a reversal of the impoverishment of the former due to exile:

At the time when our ... fathers felt that the "ground" was receding from under the nation's feet, they decided to reduce the "moveable goods" of the "national foundation," thus avoiding the loss of this foundation in its entirety. Religion,

---

[44] To be sure, translations from other languages are important (since no nation should be immune to the teachings of others), but all the new material should be "absorbed" by the nation and made germane to its spirit. See "Chikui vehitbolelut [Imitation and assimilation]," *Kk*, pp. 88–9.

[45] Ahad Ha'am, "Halashon vedikduka," *Kk*, p. 97. This view, incidentally, led Ahad Ha'am to invest immense energies in editing the journal *Hashiloah*. It also explains his (unfulfilled) desire to write a major book that would be a sort of *Guide for the Perplexed* for modern times.

[46] This is in contrast to others, such as Simon Dubnov, who was also concerned with preserving the Jewish culture, but who thought this could be done by achieving some sort of communal autonomy within European states.

literature – and the keystone of both, language – were the interdependent triangle of the nation.... These three national treasures were from the onset "attached to the soil," and in order to carry them from place to place it was necessary to forgo some of their roots – that is, those that could not be severed from their natural habitat. Religion had to relinquish the Temple and all the commandments hinging on [physical] existence in Eretz Israel, literature had to abandon living works that were nurtured by the scents of the fields in our fatherland, and language had to forgo the use of speech, which cannot be exercised in a foreign environment and an alien land.[47]

The bond between "living" literature and speech, on the one hand, and the nation's homeland, on the other, is one of the main reasons Ahad Ha'am considered Eretz Israel essential to Zionism. Indeed, his attitude toward it perplexed many in the movement: Why, they wondered, does he insist on a Jewish community in Palestine if he takes every opportunity to ridicule their grand plans of settlement and their political aspirations? Ahad Ha'am did not have any illusions about Palestine becoming a home for the entire Jewish people.[48] Yet in line with the *Volkisch* tradition, he saw the union of the people and the land as critical for the new movement. A Jewish elite that would live on the ancient land and breathe its history would create a spiritual center, one that would inject new substance into Jewish identity everywhere: "The predicament of our nation ... propels us to recognize the need to return and join the coalesced elements that have been divorced, the two critical pillars of our national life, both of which are so close to us yet so remote: our country and our language. By establishing a true literary center in Palestine, we would marry them into a national horn of plenty, one that would overflow into all the countries of our dispersion."[49]

The land, for Ahad Ha'am, is the womb of language: Topography, climate, flora, associations, and memories that the place begets all shape the character of the language and enliven it. The renewal of the attachment to Nature would, he believed, gradually reintroduce into Hebrew emotional, poetic, naturalistic, this-worldly, and other types of vocabularies

---

[47] Ahad Ha'am, "Riv leshonot [dispute over languages]," *Kk*, p. 403.

[48] Ahad Ha'am adamantly criticizes the belief that a Jewish state can be established in the foreseeable future. Among the stumbling blocks, in his view, are the facts that Jews control only a small segment of the territory in Palestine; that the land is not empty of inhabitants (in contrast to what many Zionists professed) and so one must respect the Arab population and its rights; and that the economic infrastructure, resources, and potential for growth are severely limited. For these and other reasons, then, Ahad Ha'am does not see Palestine as a solution for the Jewish masses.

[49] Ahad Ha'am, "Higia hasha'a [The time has come]," *Kk*, p. 379.

that had been missing for many generations. A community of workers, farmers, craftspeople, scientists, intellectuals – Jews occupying all
the "normal" professions of modern life – would expand the horizons
of Hebrew and generate writings in these fields. He saw this literature
being spread through holistic national education and as benefiting Jews
everywhere by allowing them to experience the universal challenges they
face as human beings and moderns from "within" their national spirit or
"from the perspective of their relation to Judaism and Judaism's relation
to them"[50] – that is, through vocabulary and concepts that formulate
the quandaries, achievements, and thoughts of a modern people in distinctively national terms. The significance and attractiveness of Hebrew
would substantially increase once it was spoken in daily life again, he
averred, allowing its speakers to think and experience the world through
its unique, holistic prism. In contrast to Scholem – who, as we saw, feared
that Hebrew words "are about to explode" and that the mooring of language and land would open up a catastrophic abyss for future Israelis –
Ahad Ha'am believed that cultural revival, the essence of Zionism to him,
must begin by rebinding the Jews to the only place where their language
could truly be alive.

Part of the reason why Scholem and Ahad Ha'am differ is that the
latter viewed the development of language in a continuous, evolutionary manner and did not fear semicyclical leaps into the ancient, virile
models of Hebraic existence; in his organic temporal ontology, Jewish
culture was moving precisely toward a deepening of the characteristics it
acquired in the Diaspora – not breaking away from them. The reintroduc-
tion of aesthetic vocabularies and writings into modern Hebrew (to be
expected in Palestine) would not mean a transformation or displacement
of the central characteristics of the language and spirit as they evolved
in the Diaspora; rather, to Ahad Ha'am these new vocabularies would be
like energizers that propel the national spirit forward.[51] For him, the most
important products of the Jewish national spirit were the Jewish religion
and its literary tradition, yet he was adamant that this religion should be
seen as a *cultural achievement*, not as the gift of God.[52]

This interpretative move of secularizing selected contents of religion allows Ahad Ha'am to construct a cultural continuity between the

---

[50] Ibid., p. 134.
[51] "If in other nations poetic creation is considered as a high end in itself ... in Israel the
creation must be subjugated to abstract thought if it were to be respected by the people"
(ibid., p. 97).
[52] Ahad Ha'am, "*Hamusar haleumi* [The morality of the nation]," *Kk*, p. 161.

normative tenets of the Jewish religion as they gradually evolved in history and the normative world he foresaw for modern Judaism. At the center of both stand a limited number of critical *moral convictions*, including an uncompromising search for justice and a faith in its supremacy over all other considerations; a disposition toward abstract thinking that leads Jews to espouse a "view from nowhere" (to use Thomas Nagel's phrase to describe ethical deliberations that are conducted irrespective of personal interests, communal membership, and any particular situatedness); a reluctance to glorify human beings or to view them as Promethean demigods; and a spurning of altruism as well as uncritical forgiveness (in contrast to Christianity, as Ahad Ha'am understands it) when it could endanger oneself.

Most importantly for Ahad Ha'am, these moral convictions also included the commitment to avoid the use of force in human conflict:

Ever since the days of the prophets, our fathers learned to scorn in their hearts the power of the fist, and respect only spiritual power.[53]

Moreover,

There should be in the world one nation whose national attributes will prepare it for moral development, more than any other nation.[54]

He sees the Jewish *Volksgeist* as advancing a heightened morality that would serve as an example, as a light for other nations. The moral codes of this nation are not subject to radical changes, just as its language is not open to these changes: "[O]ne cannot make with one's hands a new moral theory, just as it is impossible to create a new language. Both the rules of language and moral rules are the fruits of a national spirit."[55] Indeed language and morality are profoundly interrelated, since the former preserves the moral codes by establishing and ingraining certain key and potent concepts, idioms, phrases (e.g., "Have you murdered and also taken possession?");[56] by fostering a certain tradition of describing moral dilemmas and situations; and by enhancing the idea that persons' behavior toward each other is subject to rules, just as human speech and communication are.

Ahad Ha'am, then, constructed an essentialist picture of Jewish culture that celebrated high moral standards reflected in the practices, literature,

---

[53] Ahad Ha'am, "*Hikui vehitbolelut*," *Kk*, p. 88.
[54] Ahad Ha'am, "*Shinui arachim* [A change of values]," *Kk*, p. 156.
[55] Ibid., p. 158.
[56] "הרצחת וגם ירשת", מלכים א, פרק כ"א, פסוק י"ט

and language of the nation. (As noted, he was not alone in reconstructing Jewish culture in this fashion; the German Reform movement presented a similar position during the nineteenth century, as have Jewish scholars throughout the ages.) This made him the first major critic of Jewish attitudes toward the Arabs and their lands. Early on, he noticed the unbridgeable gap between the Jewish spirit and cultural nationalism, on the one hand, and the practices required by state-centered politics, on the other. "If Palestinian Jewry is unable to exercise restraint and decency now that it holds a little power," he asked, "*how much worse will it be when we control the land and its Arab inhabitants?*"[57] (my emphasis).

Contrary to Ahad Ha'am's notion that land is first and foremost a means to cultural inspiration and linguistic reinvigoration – hence, he believed that academic and literary institutions in Eretz Israel would be far more important than agricultural colonies[58] – most Zionists saw territory as a political resource whose control and integrity constitute necessary preconditions for sovereignty and so for security and normalcy. This political anchoring to the land propelled (Jewish) Israelis to invent an ethos of virile citizenship, naturalness, and heroism – which was only reinforced by the increasingly difficult nature of Arab-Jewish relations in Palestine. In other words, the emerging Israeli ethos neglected precisely what Ahad Ha'am considered most critical – the distinctive Jewish moral spirit. It should be underscored that he did not oppose the future emergence of a Jewish state in Palestine (although it was secondary to his interest in spiritual revival). However, he thought that a state should be the fruition of a long project aimed at ensuring not only the revival of organic, whole, Jewish life in Palestine but also the strengthening of Jewish identity to ensure that *state power was subject to the spiritual-moral tenets of Judaism as he understood them.*

The second feature of Ahad Ha'am's Herderianism that brought it into conflict with mainstream Zionism as it evolved in Palestine at the time was its view of language as the theater of cultural preservation and elaboration. To be sure, Zionists in Palestine (especially the pioneers of the Second Aliya) were also highly committed to promoting the Hebrew language as

---

[57] Ahad Ha'am, *Igrot Ahad Ha'am* 5 [The letters of Ahad Ha'am] (February 12, 1914): 160–1. Quoted here from Steven J. Zipperstein, *Elusive Prophet: Ahad Ha'am and the Origins of Zionism* (Berkeley: University of California Press, 1993), pp. 246–7.

[58] "The establishment of one great school [*beit-midrash*] in *Eretz Israel* for philosophy [*hochma*] or Arts, the foundation of one academe for literature and language – that, in my mind, is a considerable and sublime national endeavor that advances us toward our ends more than a hundred colonies of agricultural workers." See Ahad Ha'am, "Techiat haroach [the revival of the spirit],"K*k*, p. 181.

the sole vernacular, as they demonstrated by teaching it in schools and kindergartens, by using it in their political debates and public spaces, by writing literature and journalism in Hebrew, and more. Nevertheless, it could be argued that many in the new Hebrew society that emerged in the Yishuv perceived its language, partly at least, in instrumental terms. For example, this language supported the claims of Jews to sovereignty over the land by evoking ancient names, it distinguished the Jews in Palestine from the Yiddish-speaking Jews of the Diaspora (as well as from the Arab population), and it promised a "neutral" and widely acceptable means of communication among Jews who spoke the numerous languages of the Diaspora. "The existence of the new Hebrew society had nothing but an ideological justification," writes Benjamin Harshav. "That ideology saw *Eretz Israel* as an embryo Jewish state belonging to the immigrants and sanctioned as a Jewish 'homeland' by the League of Nations."[59]

Ahad Ha'am, as we saw, held a rather different conception. According to him, language should not create a gulf between Palestinian Jews and Diaspora Jews but, on the contrary, it should serve as a bridge between them by encouraging a gradual expansion of Hebrew among Diaspora Jews. Similarly, language (especially its vocabulary) should bridge the present and the past and so establish an unbroken cultural chain. For Ahad Ha'am, language is not a tool subject to the human will, one that can be used to distinguish a political community from other such communities through words invented by linguists; rather, it constantly exhumes what has transpired into the present, transmuting the "has been" into a continuous "becoming." New words must be added in a natural way to accommodate the needs of the present, but they must be introduced by people who are situated "within" the language and its continuous flow, not by experts who have mastered it from "above." In short, unlike the socialist Zionists, Ahad Ha'am affirmed the intrinsic value of the intangible world established by words. He was interested not in the sphere in which human beings compete for power and resources but, rather, in the sphere that

[59] Benjamin Harshav, *Language in Time of Revolution* (Berkeley: University of California Press, 1993), p. 142. For an excellent testimony regarding the relation between language and ideology in early Zionism, see Y. H. Brenner's essay, "Tzarat haleshonot [The quandary of languages]." Brenner, a pivotal figure in the literary life of Zionism during the first two decades of the twentieth century, refused to choose between Hebrew and Yiddish. Why, he asked, should we "disturb each other, contradict, destroy? With us ... there is nothing to destroy – everything is in ruins.... [W]ith us, blessed be any hand that enriches our lives with something, since our lives, gentlemen, are very, very poor." See "Tzarat haleshonot [The quandary of the languages]" (1909–11), at http://benyehuda. org./brenner/baaaretz.

human beings constitute among themselves by writing and reading, speaking and debating – by interacting with one another as interpretive beings in search of meaning and understanding, as *homo-hermeneut*.[60]

The vital role that Ahad Ha'am ascribes to language in forming a national community suggests an affinity between his thought and the Aristotelian republican tradition, a democratic tradition that sees the search for shared notions of the good and of identity as central to politics – and that celebrates linguistic interaction in the public sphere as essential to this project. In many respects, he was more perceptive and accurate in his understanding of Zionism and of external circumstances than were his rival contemporaries, and questions of Jewish identity in general and in relation to tradition still haunt Israeli society today. But did he suggest *a viable political option* – at least as far as public language is concerned – one that has been neglected by Zionism as it evolved in Palestine? Despite his celebration of language, Ahad Ha'am's vision of its nature and place in Jewish life is problematic from a political point of view. The purist vision he advanced – which sought, among other things, to guard Hebrew from outside influences and needs not compatible with its main tenets – presents fundamental problems from the perspective of democracy and its language.

How so? Because when Ahad Ha'am advanced the notion that heightened morality is the gist of Jewish culture and language, he opened an unbridgeable rift between this-worldly politics and the national language as he saw it. A language devoted to abstract thought and ethical deliberations that did not take seriously the problem of the use of violence in human interaction is hardly helpful *politically*. In fact, one could argue that Ahad Ha'am *exemplifies the rift between morality and politics in modernity*, a rift that was elucidated by his near contemporary, Max Weber.

Weber advanced the notion that in secular modernity, different "value-spheres" acquire new autonomy and their own distinct internal logic. These value-spheres (economy, politics, morality, culture, eroticism, art) are objective-social worlds that have evolved in Western history while the old Christian (and Jewish) prospect of harmony among them has been gradually lost. The parting of the political and moral spheres was particularly significant, and Weber argues that

[t]he position of the Gospels is absolutely unambiguous on the decisive points. They are in opposition not just to war, of which they make no specific mention,

---

[60] See Eyal Chowers, *The Modern Self in the Labyrinth*, Chap. 2.

but ultimately to each and every law of the social world ... if this seeks to be a place of worldly culture, one devoted to the beauty, dignity, honor, and greatness of man as a creature of this earth. Anyone unwilling to go this far ... should know that he is bound by the laws of this earthly world, and that these include, for the foreseeable future, the possibility and inevitability of wars fought for power, and that he can only fulfill the "demand of the day," whatever it may be, within the limits of these laws.[61]

At least since Machiavelli's *The Prince*, a mode of thought in the West viewed politics as a distinct sphere of human activity, with its own goals, rules, and means; it is a sphere of *raison d'état* characterized by ongoing struggle among competing interests, and one can survive politically only by accepting the particular demands of this sphere. States vie for power, prestige, resources, and other earthly goods; they often evaluate their actions according to amoral if not immoral criteria. Their ultimate goal, to Weber, is the preservation and development of their own culture and language (in this respect, he and Ahad Ha'am concur); the ultimate threat to the modern, he believed, is the meaninglessness of the bureaucratic iron cage and of being dominated by instrumental rationality. Culture is the only sphere that offers a refuge, a horizon of significance from which meaning can be injected into our lives through *individual* choices. But this elevated or worthy goal of politics stands in contrast to the means it employs: not only deception or disciplinary techniques but also violence, which is inherent to politics. However, violence is diabolic, often bringing about the opposite result than what was intended. Politics does not leave souls intact or whole. The responsible use of violence, the ability to measure the human and other costs of the means in relation to the desired ends, and the ability to make fine distinctions in the exercise of violence are at the very heart of politics.

In Weber's view, in fact, the demands of the political sphere have become more distinct and harsh in modernity because of the unprecedented power of Leviathan, and because of the rise of nationalism and the growing competition among secularized nation-states (free from adherence to Christian norms). Corresponding to these political developments, Weber suggests, are the demands of the ethical value-sphere, which have intensified as well. A process of abstraction has taken place: The commitment to apply moral norms to one's own community's members has been

---

[61] Max Weber, *Weber: Political Writings*, ed. P. Lassman and Ronald Speirs (Cambridge: Cambridge University Press, 1994), p. 78.

eclipsed by a commitment to apply these norms to human beings as such, without regard to their religion, race, sex, and so forth. Moreover, the refusal to use violent means has extended, moving from the reluctance to use them within the bounds of the community to the total rejection of these means in any human interaction; as the nation-state has become more exclusionary, religion and ethical-moral theories (such as Kant's) have pointed elsewhere. Weber's analysis of ethical universalization and pacifism is based on his understanding of Christianity and how it evolved with Protestantism, yet the same development, as we have seen, applies to Judaism and Ahad Ha'am's vision of it.

Indeed, Ahad Ha'am's thinking epitomizes this crisis of the value-spheres, and he was totally uninterested in mediating between them. Weber seems to suggest that the fate of modern men and women is to move among the value-spheres according to circumstances and personal choices; Ahad Ha'am, as we have seen, affirmed an essentialism that committed the entire nation to a single sphere. His conviction that Judaism has a distinct spirit, a heightened moral life with a universal outlook, did little to help bridge the gap between the moral sphere and the political one.[62] His writings suggest a scant contemplation of power, what it is composed of and how to augment it; nor did he much consider the occasions on which it is justified to use organized violence, the responsibilities involved, and the dangers inherent in its use. Of course in the Diaspora, Jews participated in wars (and had some prominent warriors, such as the medieval poet Shmuel Hanagid). But the community as a whole did not. Moreover, in Judaism the shaping of a moral individual does not hinge on participation in a public sphere and on an active life of citizenship (in contrast to the Aristotelian model of *areté*, for example); communal life is important for moral perfection, to be sure, but political life is not – as the sages understood since the destruction of the Second Temple. So Ahad Ha'am's presentation of the diasporic tradition as centered on an elevated morality divorced from politics was shared by many at the time and had a sound basis in history; as we have seen, non-Zionist Jews, such as Herman Cohen, Abraham Geiger, and Léon Cahun, depicted the Jewish tradition in similar terms. But while these non-Zionists could uphold such positions relatively without strain, the same could not be said of adherents of the project of national revival.

[62] See Ahad Ha'am, "pitze'e ohev [A Lover's Wounds]," *Kk*, pp. 20–22.

One might even say that because Ahad Ha'am believed that tradition and language are inseparable, he concluded that Judaism does not and should not contain any significant vocabulary and literature to cope with power and the exercise of force. Indeed, while the commentators writing on the Torah occasionally refer to questions of justice and war, for example, the Jewish tradition nevertheless has no writers like Hugo Grotius or Carl von Clausewitz; it was preoccupied, moreover, mainly with the role of the unarmed victim, not with the role of the one exercising violence.[63] ("There is no Jewish theory of war and peace" notes Michael Walzer, "and until modern times, there were no theories produced by individual Jews.")[64] Power and violence have their own conceptual world: the goals to be achieved by war, legitimate and illegitimate actions, self-defense and aggression, inhuman and humane behavior in war, proportional and superfluous response, soldier and noncombatant, and so forth. Ahad Ha'am's position meant that Jewish thought and the Hebrew language should not be concerned with these matters: He firmly positioned language within the ethical sphere, and *the upshot was that Hebrew could hardly be brought to bear upon the emerging state institutions* and, more specifically, upon the use of violence by Jews in advancing their causes.

So we might say that the essence of the Hebrew language as Ahad Ha'am conceived of it cannot cohere with the goals and practices of the modern state. Indeed when Zionists were beginning to think of a modern nation-state of their own, they found that their tradition as it evolved from the time of the late prophets and of the Talmud – and especially the way the tradition came to be understood during the nineteenth century – was contradicting this project and, hence, of little use as far as the employment of forceful means is concerned. Ahad Ha'am denied this conclusion, of course, saying that the spirit has to "elevate" the domain of the flesh, including the state; this institution could be shaped, he believed, according to the taxing moral demands of tradition.[65] That is, continued to think, as Jews always did, about the need to shape earthly, mundane life in light of the moral force, and not to try to achieve moral perfection through rejection and seclusion from this life. Yet Ahad Ha'am's philosophy isolates language from serious thought about violence and

---

[63] See on this point Ezrahi's illuminating discussion in *Rubber Bullets*, Part III.

[64] See Michael Walzer, "Commanded and Permitted Wars," in *Law, Politics, and Morality in Judaism*, ed. by Michael Walzer (Princeton, NJ: Princeton University Press, 2006), p. 149.

[65] It should be mentioned, however, that Ahad Ha'am advocated Jewish self-defense in Eastern Europe after the Kishinev pogrom of 1903, thus relaxing his demand that Jews not resolve conflicts through the use of force.

power: At the outset, it seems, he allowed national politics to in fact take an independent path and refused to see the constant need to negotiate between the political and ethical spheres, a negotiation and deliberation that require appropriate language.

Those who were later influenced by Ahad Ha'am, such as the members of Brit Shalom (a group that included distinguished names such as Judah Magnes, Hans Kohn, Arthur Ruppin, Martin Buber, Samuel Hugo Bergmann, Gershom Scholem, and Henrietta Szold) indeed concluded (after World War I, which seemed to have affirmed the dangers inherent in nationalism and imperialism and their interrelatedness) that the rift between the Jewish tradition, on the one hand, and the demands of the nation-state, on the other, is unbridgeable. Zionism, according to them, should therefore aspire to a binational state with the Arabs in Palestine. This solution would allow Jews a cultural form of nationalism that would preserve their identity and moral character but would also demand that they relinquish the quest for political independence in the form of a sovereign Jewish state.

Ahad Ha'am conducted various battles throughout his life, many of them with his fellow writers. Some of them he accused of introducing foreign elements into Jewish culture and literature, such as Nietzscheanism; others he accused of shallowness and meager literary talents. In general, he preferred what he called "literary workers"[66] devoted to reviving and secularizing the Hebrew tradition and narrating the history of the nation – taking part, he hoped, in a great project of collecting and selecting works from the tradition and organizing them for the use of laypeople. He did not value creative writers committed to exploring the complexity of the individual (nothing was more foreign to Ahad Ha'am than the preoccupation of his Jewish contemporary Freud with the psyche of the self). More generally, his view of language as a *national treasure*, joined with his diminished regard for the unique individual, led him to ignore the role of language in forming the self and its singular voice – both as an individual and as an active citizen in the public sphere.

Ahad Ha'am rebuked such writers as Berdyczewski for seeking an aesthetic vocabulary that delves into the modern soul, with its frustrations and fears, chaos and inner conflicts, desires and irrational drives, inexplicable and insatiable longings. He saw this modernist probing into the self and its glorification as non-Jewish and as too attached to poetic,

---

[66] Ahad Ha'am, *Kk*, p. 329.

essentially audible forms of expression, rather than to the written word. Since the Romantic movement, he thought, a culture of subjectivity has evolved in modernity – one more concerned with questions of taste and style, beauty and desire, than with justice and probing social critique.

Now for Ahad Ha'am, the unprecedented emphasis of Western culture on poetry – especially when centered on the emotional fabric of the self and questions of aesthetic judgment – had a surprising elective affinity with parliamentarianism as a leading political philosophy and practice. The same modern self, with its heightened emotional predispositions and evocative rather than reflective and measured language, appeared on the political stage. So Ahad Ha'am's skepticism toward the individual in literary and aesthetic forms was also expressed politically: He was especially suspicious of speech in deliberative bodies because he believed that these bodies serve mainly to foster a mind-set of a crowd and to generate irrational emotional reactions: "Any great assembly of the people's representatives – whether it is called parliament or congress or any other name – is in essence an emotional crowd, or, as Sighele termed it, 'hysterical women.'"[67] While deliberative bodies are perhaps inevitable, he conceded, they are most often characterized by a depressing superficiality, actually reducing the quality and abilities of each of the participants; rather than allowing wisdom and truth to emerge through collective effort, they merely raise unreflective passions: "All the decisions that are made by a majority of one assembly or another are necessarily of a lesser value than those that spring from the mind and heart of one excellent man."[68] The rift between the moral and political spheres in his philosophy is thus complemented by a rift between the written-reflective language and the rhetorical, dangerous speech of public deliberation.

Ahad Ha'am exemplifies the low status of this type of deliberation both in Judaism and, to some extent, in Zionism. Michael Walzer suggests that the roots of this attitude toward deliberation are ancient: "[P]erhaps because of the profound impression left by the prophets [who voiced divine truth] on Jewish political thinking, their disappearance did not open the way for any explicit defense of worldly deliberation."[69] Ahad Ha'am merely continues here a long Jewish way of thinking about the

---

[67] Ibid., p. 297. Ahad Ha'am does see the parliaments as inevitable nevertheless; he only wishes there would be strong leaders to guide them.

[68] Ibid.

[69] See Michael Walzer, in *The Jewish Political Tradition*, ed. Michael Walzer et al., vol. 1: *Authority* (New Haven, CT: Yale University Press, 2000), p. 205.

origins of truth and of sound political judgment. For him, moreover, the ascent of subjective expressivism and oral public dialogue is also at odds with the rational, careful, and written-based language that characterizes the Jewish tradition. The moral, conceptual vocabulary of this tradition is not the fruit of egalitarian practices but of the writings of great scholars and rabbis, great figures whose *personalities* were, in his view, completely irrelevant to their work and remain enigmas to us.[70] Political greatness, the greatness of the person who acts in the world and expresses him- or herself in public, and who influences others with words, had nothing to do with the spirit of Judaism.

Nowadays, many people see Ahad Ha'am as someone who offered an attractive path for Zionism. Numerous contemporary Israelis, including secular men and women, seek to renew their bond with and knowledge of the Jewish tradition: its practices, its customs, and especially its classic texts. Study groups and innovative *batei-midrash* are blossoming everywhere; even popular musicians and singers are part of this search (reviving, for example, medieval Jewish poetry). Ahad Ha'am is indeed a hero for those interested in making tradition relevant for contemporary Israeli life and in reinvigorating a rich Jewish identity that is based on the Hebrew language. It must be acknowledged, however, that as far as the ills of the Israeli political sphere are concerned, he offers limited help. The foremost champion of Hebrew language in early Zionism (and the greatest thinker and writer of the movement) profoundly devalued its political potential: Neither in content nor in form was this language suited to democratic life.

III. LANGUAGE, TIME, AND REVOLUTION: CHAIM NACHMAN BIALIK

Through our examination of Ahad Ha'am's views, we see that the first major attempt to adapt modern Hebrew to the human measure, to rescue it from the theological domain, on the one hand, and the threat of artificiality and shallowness, on the other, proved politically lacking.

---

[70] The "young" writers, such as Brenner, believed that Ahad Ha'am did not understand the contemporary Jewish predicament: "People complain that our literature ... does not educate; however, there is no other option. All our literature is individualistic, every writer among the young a world unto itself.... The Jewish street has been dispersed, the small town had moved to America, the collective Jew is different ... only individuals have been left, Hebrew-Europeans with distinct psyches, and each and every one has his own soul, desperation, dreams." See "Tzarat haleshonot."

PHOTO 13. David Ben-Gurion and the late poet Chaim Nachman Bialik aboard the S.S. *Martha Washington* on a cruise. Unknown photographer, October 1, 1933. Courtesy of the Government Press Office, Israel.

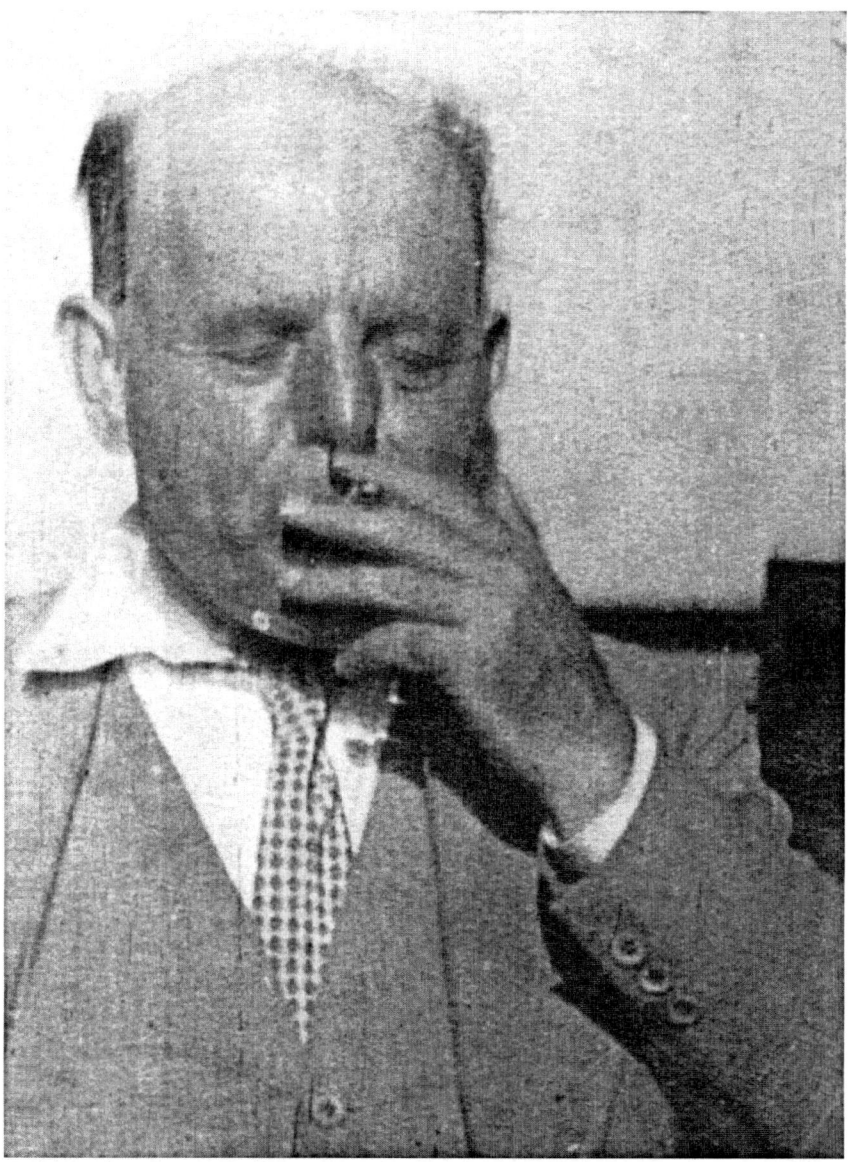

PHOTO 14. Chaim Nachman Bialik (1925). Unknown photographer; photo courtesy of The Central Zionist Archives, Jerusalem.

Although Chaim Nachman Bialik (1873–1934)[71] – the first and most important national poet of Zionism and the man Ben-Gurion considered to be the "spiritual leader of his people" and the most influential Jew of his generation[72] – was not a political thinker, his work offered a far better opportunity for Hebrew-speaking men and women by proposing a less dogmatic dialogue with tradition and granting greater significance to the individual speaker. To begin with, there was considerable continuity between Ahad Ha'am and Bialik: The poet considered Ahad Ha'am to be his mentor and followed him in many respects, thinking of him as the "sage" of Zionism; Ahad Ha'am, in turn, considered Bialik to be perhaps the only poet whose work had national, not only aesthetic, significance. For not only did Bialik write about such subjects as the modern crisis of Judaism, the longing for Zion, and the pogroms in Eastern Europe, but his work also played an important role in the renewal of the Hebrew language, and he participated in various Zionist political activities (beginning in his youth in the Ukraine and later in Palestine).

For Bialik, as for Ahad Ha'am, the Jewish crisis was not merely one of economic and political (material) conditions, but it was, especially, one of identity due to secularization and the destruction of former ways of life and due lack of Jewish national self-consciousness in an age when European nationalism conquered all other political forms. The great Zionist project, in his view, was therefore to mold a new identity based on the vast literary tradition of Judaism (which Bialik mastered). The goals were to turn religious texts into cultural products, to enliven and redefine old concepts, and to create a lasting canon before total forgetfulness of tradition would set in. Bialik saw the rebuilding of Palestine as essential for this project, but more important was the infusion of new life into the Hebrew language – the essence of the new nation's identity. "Language is the soil of the spirit, the dwelling-house of the spirit, and that is why I call it the land of the spirit," he writes.[73] Elsewhere, he adds that "language distinguishes one nation from another.... [T]he 'I' of the nation is written on its back. Everything flows and changes, [is] taken away, robbed, removed, even the soil is robbed – everything except language.

---

[71] In addition to his rich poetry, prose, and essays, Bialik translated various European classics, such as Shakespeare's *Julius Caesar*, Schiller's *Wilhelm Tell*, Cervantes's *Don Quixote*, and Heine's poems. In collaboration with Yehoshua Hana Ravnitzky, Bialik published *Sefer haaggada* [The book of legends] (1908–11), a three-volume edition of the folk tales and proverbs scattered throughout the Talmud.

[72] David Ben-Gurion, *Zichronot*, vol. 2 (1934–35), (Tel Aviv: Am Oved, 1974), p. 476. I owe this reference to Shmuel Avneri.

[73] Bialik, *Devarim*, vol. 1, p. 69.

The contents all change and pass away, and the form [language] stands: she is the eternal, cosmic."[74] Language is the heart of tradition, flexible enough to withstand the inevitable changes in the contents of tradition while preserving continuity, too. This emphasis on the "form" as distinct from the "content" renders language the bridge between the long period of the Diaspora and the coming age of Zionism.

Throughout the generations, Bialik observed, only those who retained the Hebrew language remained Jews, and those who attempted to uphold the faith without it eventually lost their communal identity altogether. Jews long deeply for their language and are invested in it both spiritually and emotionally, he claimed, and Zionists have to take advantage of this fact. Accordingly, he believed that the task of his generation was to expand the horizons of language, to make it a part of everyday life, to transform Hebrew from a stock of written words into genuine *living speech*. Given these great expectations, however, what Bialik witnessed in Palestine was not encouraging. He felt that "the entire official Hebrew language [in Palestine] is not really Hebrew and in fact is a disgrace to Hebrew, it is coarse barbarism." This desperation propelled him at times to suggest Rousseau-like solutions: "I told our leader [Chaim Weizmann] ... that if the people are not willing to understand the culture, then they must be forced to do so through coercion. The few are allowed to impose their will upon the people even through compulsion."[75]

Bialik was not merely a national poet and a public persona, however; he was a rather complex and profound person, thinker, and writer who was preoccupied with exploring his own self. His lyrical poetry reveals unresolved tensions and ambivalence in his own individual soul as a Jew, a modern, a man. Among other things, one can see in this poetry (which was influenced by romanticism and symbolism) a longing for transcendent consolation as well as for the comfort offered by erotic love; for surrendering to sexual desire as well as fear of the spiritual and existential implications of this surrender; a hunger for having a home and a sense

---

[74] Ibid., p. 15.

[75] Ibid., pp. 134, 135. Bialik's frustration was perhaps exaggerated. In many respects, the revival of the Hebrew language has been relatively successful surely (compared with Gaeilge, for example). The challenges to this revival were numerous: creation of new vocabulary, domains of knowledge, and genres; the freeing of the individual word from phrases entrenched in classical texts; the transition from being merely a written language to a vernacular; and more. See Benjamin Harshav, *Language in Time of Revolution*, Chap. 25. One should also note that these days, ironically, many contemporary writers have similar complaints about speechlessness – only they feel that the Hebrew language actually deteriorated during the last few decades.

of unresolved homelessness and aloneness; bursts of profound hope and lightness and of irredeemable despair and guilt (as well as an ongoing preoccupation with death); a desperate search for the private self and a willingness to carry the nation's yoke; admiration for the communal past and utter rejection of the collective passivity represented by this past; deep respect for tradition and its ancient texts, yet revulsion from these very same texts and the people that worshiped them.[76] Regarding this last point, he writes: "Once more. Look: a spent old scarecrow/ shriveled face/ straw-dry shadow/ swaying like a leaf/ bending and swaying over books.... You've not changed: All old as the hills/ Nothing new/ I'll join you, old cronies!/ Together we'll rot till we stink."[77] There is indeed a deep sense of crisis in Bialik's writings, of moving between two incompatible worlds, of being attached to the diasporic culture of books and learning while recognizing that *a break* with this culture must take place.

For Bialik (as for Berdyczewski), there was no clear continuity in time; instead, he saw an existential rift between Diaspora and Zion, a rift that must be bridged *creatively* through language. To begin with, he says, Jews must restore "the words, idioms, and expressions of the ancient language ... all the significance and connotations that they used to have in the past." At the same time, these speakers must fit to the salvaged words – "in an organic and natural manner" – "the new meanings and conceptions of the age."[78] For example, Bialik suggested that the newspaper of the Hebrew workers in Palestine be called *Davar* (meaning, as we have seen, "the word," "a deed," and "a thing"), alluding to the biblical prophets who said, "And the Word [*davar*] of the Lord came unto me." (This newspaper, which was so named and which used to be probably the leading daily in the new state, no longer exists, and the same can be said of the socialist world of which it was a part.) Following Ahad Ha'am, Bialik advocated the creation of a new canon based on selected texts from the Jewish tradition, and he actually contributed to this project through a collection of Aggada stories in *The Book of Legends* (which he edited with Y. H. Ravnitzky). And yet, in contrast to Ahad Ha'am, Bialik did not adhere to an essentialist view of the Jewish tradition; he recognized not only its richness and complexity but also the need to adapt it to new circumstances without always submitting to the authority of the past.

[76] See on this point, Ruth Nevo at http://israel.poetryinternationalweb.org.
[77] C. N. Bialik, "Return," trans. Ruth Nevo, at http://israel.poetryinternationalweb.org.
[78] C. N. Bialik, *Bialik Speaks: Words from the Poet's Lips, Clues to the Man* (New York: Herzl, 1969), pp. 47–8.

"Every generation," he suggests, "proceeds and submerges the preceding buildings in its own edifice."[79] While recognizing that Judaism was historically focused on molding a moral person, his Judaism included also the Maccabees (who rebelled against the ancient Greeks).[80]

For Bialik, linguistic creativity, imagination, and originality preserve and adapt the tradition; he would have agreed with T. S. Eliot that tradition "cannot be inherited, and if you want it you must obtain it by great labor."[81] The recognition of the historically unique and creative role of the poet with respect to the (literary) past generates fascinating tensions present throughout Bialik's work. With him, the new Hebrew individual becomes someone with a distinct voice, a creator in the vast ocean of ancient words, moved not only by abstract ideas but also by emotions and the beauty of Nature, committed to written texts as well as to living, powerful speech (in these points he strongly differed from Ahad Ha'am).[82] This individual sees tradition not as a solid building or as an oasis of stability but as something pregnant with frictions, ruptures, formlessness – it embodies the creations of living beings with their constant struggle to impose order on their lives and their tendency to fail in fulfilling this task.

The emergence of the speaking, linguistically innovative individual advocated by Bialik could have fostered the notion of political actors in the Aristotelian sense and effected the use of language in the public

---

[79] Bialik, *Devarim*, vol. 1, p. 185.

[80] In contrast to his mentor, Bialik seems to have embraced Zionist values such as valor and virile citizenship, which for many Zionists were represented by the Maccabees. During a public celebration of *Hanukka*, Bialik noted that "there is no doubt that for this *Hanukka* holiday, which was neglected in our history because the original book [in the Hebrew language] has been lost, its time has come; the great deeds and upheavals that occurred in our nation should be attached to it. And we should thank those who ... designated this holiday for the most eternal occurrence in our history.... All the events associated with redemption will be linked with this national holiday, and because of it a few historical moments that have been relegated to forgetfulness will be salvaged." See *Devarim*, vol. 1, p. 107.

[81] T. S. Eliot, "Tradition and the Individual Talent" (1919), at http://www.english.illinois.edu/maps/poets/a_f/eliot/tradition.htm.

[82] The desire to create original things pertains both to the individual and to the nation: "In our Diasporic existence we did not participate in the original making of things, from their roots and the soil; this has been our greatest disaster. We did not partake in the genesis of creations but joined in later.... However, the main right a human being may gain over his creations, as well as his enjoyment from them, comes about only as a natural reward for the initial exertions, which are also the most difficult and dangerous ones." *Devarim*, vol. 1, p. 137.

sphere; but, for the most part, his vision of language and the poet had problematic implications for the relation between language and politics. Moreover, despite his repeated complaints about the status of language in the public sphere, one could argue that his own vision of language indirectly contributed to that status.

Bialik's understanding of language is best expressed in his seminal, short essay, "Revealment and Concealment in Language"[83] (1915). He begins this essay by suggesting that behind every human existence lurks *Tohu* (תוהו). This biblical word, which appears in the second verse of Genesis, has conflicting meanings: It connotes both formless matter and the void or nothingness; it both animates and terrifies us, being the source from which life springs and the nothingness into which this life eventually dissipates. In Bialik's picture, as God overcame the abyss of Tohu by creating the world through his Divine Words, so human beings escape Tohu by endlessly inventing their own words:

> It is clear that language in all its forms does not admit us to the essence of things; on the contrary, it serves as a barrier against this essence.... [T]he spirit of a human being, naked, without its speaking shell, is always wondering. No words exist, only cosmic perplexity; an eternal "what" is frozen on the lips. And, in fact, there is no place even for "what," since it contains the hope for an answer. But what is out there? silence, the mouth is arrested. And if a human being begins to speak and feels calmer, this is only because this person dreads dwelling one instant with that dark Tohu, with silence face to face, without a curtain.

The purpose of language, in Bialik's view, is to cover up our fundamental reality: We invent words in order to express an endless stream of questions and as a way to position ourselves away from and distinguish ourselves from Being (or Nothingness) – instead of bearing the proximity

---

[83] C. N. Bialik, "Revealment and Concealment in Language [Gilui vekisui balashon]," trans. Jacob Sloan, *Commentary* 9, no. 2 (1950): 171–5. Bialik wrote this essay as a *reflection on language as such*, without specific references to Judaism, Hebrew, Zionism, or indeed modernity; one should not, therefore, reduce it to an historical context or the circumstances of its author. Nevertheless, the fact that the text was written in Hebrew by someone who was strongly involved in a national project of linguistic renewal and who explicitly connected the themes of this essay with his own poetic work should not be ignored either. I will discuss this point later on in the chapter.

Unless otherwise noted, all references in my discussion are to this text (although some of the translations have been substantially modified). It should be noted that this is a most difficult piece to "summarize," to say nothing of translating it from the original Hebrew, since it contains many allusions to the languages of the Bible, Talmud, and Kabbala. There have been numerous interpretations of this essay. See, in particular, Z. Luz and Z. Shamir, eds., *Al gilui vkisui balashon* [On the explicit and the allusive in language: Studies on Bialik's essay] (Ramat Gan: Bar-Ilan University, 2001).

of this source and end of all things. Words are valuable to the extent that they occupy a space – to the extent that they evoke a rich enough import to help humans weave the necessary veil. For Bialik, language as a whole is the fruit of continuous and piecemeal efforts to weave this veil, and the efforts involve the invention or augmentation of "spacious" or "strong" words that may effectively conceal. "As bodies become visible and their lines demarcated when they stand against the light, so the being of a word is disclosed when it fills up a small cavity in fencing Tohu, when it protects against Tohu's darkness," he writes. As people forget their troubles by investing themselves in various deeds and undertakings, they also rush to "build in their own mouths" linguistic walls and divert their minds from what lies beyond their anthropocentric existence. By wondering, questioning, answering, writing, naming, conversing, debating, and so forth, human beings establish a rich ocean of words; each word leads to another in a self-perpetuating and endless labyrinth: "The main thing is that in man's thought no space will be vacant, not for one single minute left without a dense, uninterrupted chain of words, one upon another like an armor, without a gap that is even a hair's breadth between them."

The meaning of Bialik's claim here cannot be underestimated; *it is a Copernican Revolution of sorts within Jewish thought*. Traditionally, as we have seen, Hebrew was thought of not simply as representing the Truth about the world – a perfect transparent medium, if you will – but also as being itself the source of Truth and Reality, as the "substance" from which everything has been created. Bialik undermines Hebrew's ontological and divine status altogether: Humans gain an inkling of their aloneness and acquire self-recognition through their first use of words; the more words they use, however, the more distant they become from Being, the less "home" they have in the nonhuman world and the less transparent this world becomes for them. Bialik's idea is very different even from a postmodernist claim, such as Richard Rorty's, that "where there are no sentences there is no truth, that sentences are elements of human languages, and that human languages are human creations."[84] In Bialik's understanding, rather, language *is not supposed* to reveal the world or the nature of God and does not aspire to disclose intentions or moral precepts. Rather, its raison d'être, its foremost reason for existence, is to cover up formlessness in a pile of words and metaphors, descriptions and conventions. Language engulfs humans in a world of meanings they

---

[84] Richard Rorty, *Contingency, Irony, and Solidarity* (Cambridge: Cambridge University Press, 1989), p. 5.

have developed in order to deny Tohu, or the abyss. The accumulation of this collective attempt to suppress the infinite darkness is what is called tradition.

Yet this description does not encompass Bialik's whole theory, for in his view the nature of language is dynamic. As he expresses it, words at their creation evoke a sense of awe, but they become flat by being constantly exchanged in common use, like paper money. The spirit and idea evoked by a new word are gradually lost through its continuous employment, and the word becomes an empty shell. The same, of course, could happen to a whole system of words, to a whole language. "A word, a system declines and yields to another ... because the word or system has been worn out after being manipulated and used," he writes, "and then it is no longer able to conceal and hide adequately." Language is thus destined to become lifeless, lacking the power to renew itself. At those times, it matters little what individuals say, what convictions and pictures they may master when they think and converse: The old words betray them, unable to conceal their existential void. A new shelter has to be hastily invented, for there is nothing worse than being in between, exposed. Those who realize early the need for a new shelter are not only perceptive but also brave, and Bialik states that *"the first leap, the primary decision to create something from scratch – this is the moment of the utmost danger and supreme heroism"* (my emphasis).[85]

We might view these moments of language as losing its blocking power and needing to be reinvented as moments of "sundered history," of a lack in meta-narrative and direction (see Chapter 2). In Bialik's view, the poet (and each one of us to the extent that he or she lives poetically) plays a critical role in confronting this chaotic time. Most people (even prose writers) use words as if they can be taken for granted and are secure in their customary usage; they deny the mortality of words and are unaware of the miracle that is reenacted each time a word successfully conveys a meaning and conceals. But for Bialik, the poet, who is attracted to the "Life" (and perhaps light) emanating from Tohu and who seeks to expose its "secret," stands precisely on the circumference delineated by language. From this dangerous position, he or she can listen carefully to the spirit that animates words, but also use them to construct an effective bulwark against the abyss. On the one hand, poets seek a glimpse of Tohu, and they do so by inducing in words "constant movement, new constellations and arrangements. The words dance under their hands, they die and are

---

[85] Bialik, *Devarim*, vol 1, p. 137.

being revived, they sink and shine.... [T]hey lose their soul and regain it." On the other hand, while the poets enliven the language by experimenting with it, they also stretch the space that fresh words occupy. Powerful words, like the word "I," change our perceptions and stabilize our existence. Thus, poets are the *ultimate builders*, the ones who construct and attend to the walls of the linguistic shelter.

As is true of many of his poems, Bialik's vision of language is both distinctively Jewish and distinctively modern contemporaneously. On the one hand, his vision echoes the Jewish culture of study, of ongoing dialogue composed of questions and answers related to ancient texts, of men learning together day after day and assaying the creation of an alternative, word-based reality into which the external world of the present cannot easily penetrate. Yet Bialik's vision of language is also highly modern, picturing an epoch characterized by an avalanche of words in literature, science, therapy, journalism, and more, one in which the degree of "noise," or distraction these words are able to induce in the mind, is incomparably higher than in any other period.[86] Bialik's attunement to modernity is in fact even more profound than this; in advancing a skeptical perception of language in relation to Being or truth, and in underscoring the self's dread of existence without solid foundations, Bialik echoes Nietzsche. The German philosopher/philologist saw language as an attempt to conceal the chaos of existence and introduce a semblance of order (for example, by categorizing objects into chairs and desks, spoons and knives, or by inventing notions such as causality and time). Moreover, Nietzsche believed that European culture is nihilistic and in total disarray, since all foundations of certainty (religion, Nature, science) and their corresponding vocabularies have collapsed, leaving the self in an existential void. This void reverberates in Bialik. Yet the Jewish moment of living in the abyss and coping with nihilism is unique, both because of language's significance in shaping this group's identity and because of the heightened predicament of groundlessness faced by the modern Jew.

While Bialik's reflections are intended as ahistorical and universal – and their great appeal partly stems from this characteristic – it must also be then said that the collapse of the diasporic way of life and of the

---

[86] A somewhat similar argument is made by Martin Heidegger. *Dasein*, he suggests, has a sudden sense of uncanniness, of not being at home, when it experiences itself as being-in-the-world. *Dasein* attempts to escape this state by losing itself in an environment it considers familiar and safe: the world of everyday concerns, of the "they" and its distracting language. See Martin Heidegger, *Being and Time*, trans. J. Macquarrie and E. Robinson (New York: Harper and Row, 1962), p. 233.

languages associated with this life (e.g, Yiddish and the religion-laden Hebrew) exposed a certain Tohu with all its threatening potential: a life without a home to belong to in space, without a meta-narrative to locate oneself in time, without firm beliefs to hold onto, without a political community to imagine, and, in short, without an anchored identity either for the self or the community. "We were born," wrote Bialik to Ahad Ha'am, "under some unknown star, at dusk, among piles of rubble, as the sons of the old age of our hoary people.... *It was a time of primeval chaos, of erased boundaries, of end and beginning, of destruction and building, of age and youth*. And we, the children of transition, were both wittingly and unwittingly bowing before and worshiping both these realms ... [s]uspended between these two magnets" (my emphasis).[87]

The threat of being left in empty space was not an imaginary one. Bialik's general statement in "Revealment and Concealment in Language" – that "*the most dangerous moment, in speech as well as in life, is nothing but that moment between one veil and another, when Tohu flickers*" – can be seen as particularly relevant to his own generation's predicament. This generation attempted to mold an identity and a language in a rush; no one understood better than Bialik the irredeemable exhaustion of the diasporic understanding of language and its vocabulary and the need to reinvent a new one (that also reaches out to the past). But seen in this historical context, the role of language (as Bialik understands it) as concealing, distracting, and shielding the community and the individual from disturbing truths can be *politically* dangerous. One wonders, that is, if Bialik's general theory and his understanding of modern Hebrew is echoed in the actual political uses of this language in Zionist history. Does modern Hebrew serve to entomb the chaos and violence involved in the implementation of Zionism, concealing existential truths that should be seen and discussed? Consider the following example:

In 1949, just a few months after the War of Independence, David Ben-Gurion, Israel's first prime minister, established a committee of scholars (cartographers, historians, archeologists) to suggest new names for the Negev region in southern Israel; this region had just been occupied, and most of the native Bedouin population either fled or were expelled. As Meron Benvenisti argues, rather than "representing" given geographical and human spaces with scientific validity, the new map and names

---

[87] H. N. Bialik's letter to Ahad Ha'am, in *The Collected Writings*, vol. 1 (Tel Aviv, 1935), p. 117 (in Hebrew). Here quoted from Arthur Hertzberg, ed., *The Zionist Idea: A Historical Analysis and Reader* (New York: Atheneum, 1971), p. 73.

suggested by the committee were expected to create a certain symbolic and political reality. After laborious work, the committee offered a report in which "no fewer than 333 of the 533 new names were either translations [into Hebrew] of Arabic names or Hebrew names that had been decided upon on the basis of their similarity in sound to Arabic names"; only eight original Arabic names were transliterated untouched. Names that had originated in Arabic were converted into semibiblical names (Bir Abu Auda into Be'er Ada, Rakhma to Yeroham, and so on). Villages and towns, historic sites and roads, hills and valleys acquired new names and therefore meanings. The upshot has been that "generations of Israelis became familiar with the names of the historical sites and geographical features of the Negev without it ever occurring to them that these were nothing but distortions of Arabic names."[88]

The same process has taken place in other parts of Palestine, so that the entire history of the Arab civilization and settlement in the country has been concealed.[89] This tendency still exists in Israeli public language

---

[88] Meron Benvenisti, *Sacred Landscape: The Buried History of the Holy Land since 1949* (Berkeley: University of California Press, 2000), p. 19. As noted, the same phenomenon of inventing a Hebrew map existed all over the country, with a few exceptions (such as Wadi Ara, Wadi Milek, or Tzomet Qastina, which are used by the Hebrew-speaking Jews in Israel and not only by the Arab citizens of the country).

   Bialik, who died in 1934, had nothing to do with this project of name displacement. Yet one should note that his own vision of territorial expansion in Palestine did not suggest self-restraint. "How much land does an individual need?" he asked in one of his public appearances. Once, he told the audience, he heard a professor saying that in order to feel safe, a man needs soil in direct proportion to his height, or rather the full measure of his height, so that if he stumbles and collapses for some reason, this man would be certain that no part of his body would remain in midair. "I have listened to the numbers given by the Keren Kayemeth Le-Israel" [Jewish National Fund, responsible for acquiring territory in Palestine], continued Bialik. "And I ask: is the redeemed territory fitting to the entire height of the Jewish people, is it sufficient for our sense of security and for alleviating our fear of falling down? One must answer: no, a nation of sixteen million with a world stature of 4,000 years – for this type of nation this small segment of territory is not even enough to lay its foot on" (*Devarim*, vol. 1, p. 109). Bialik depicted Palestine as an empty, undeveloped country, full of poverty and hunger, and the Jews as the redeemers of the land and of the Arabs as well (*Devarim*, vol. 1, p. 154). Nevertheless, he also proclaimed that there is enough territory in Palestine for both Jews and Arabs, and he called for peaceful and cooperative relations between the two nations. In general, he seemed to support the pragmatic political solutions of the labor movement. (On Bialik's positive attitude toward the labor movement, see Shmuel Avneri, "Bialik vteno'at hapoalim [Bialik and the labor movement]," in *Haaretz* (Culture and Literature section), Friday, July 2, 2010, p. 4.

[89] In the Israeli map, there is no equivalent to Massachusetts and Connecticut, or Ontario and Quebec – extended regions that retain aboriginal words and names. What stands out in the Israeli case is not that the conqueror gives new names to places – this has

and influences the way Israelis view their moral debt (or lack thereof) to the Palestinian people. Nor is the fate of contemporary Hebrew much better. A number of commentators have pointed out that modern Hebrew tends to obscure the full meaning of military acts and facts. Hence, for example, the 1982 war in Lebanon was officially called *milhemet shelom hagalil*, or war for the safety/peace of the Galilee, thereby turning the meaning of the highly potent word *shalom* on its head; the term *hisul memukad*, which can be translated as "focused liquidation" – a kind of marriage between the detached surgical term *memukad* and the language of commercial sales – is in fact "targeted assassination"; the word *hisuf* (an odd twist on the word *lahsof*) means the act of revealing or exposing something, but it is used by the army to signify a military action in which the orchards, gardens, buildings, fences, and so on of Palestinians are removed for "security reasons." The territories that have been occupied by Israel since 1967 are called by adherents of the Right Judea and Samaria, rather than "occupied territories" (as they used to be called soon after the war) or the West Bank, and Jerusalem has been "united" by the war, rather than annexed. Palestinians who are demonstrating against the occupation are "violating public order," rather than protesting against the imposition of an Israeli order and rule to begin with, and if a demonstrator happens to be killed by the army, this is not because a soldier aimed and fired but, rather, because "shots have been fired."[90] From the other political direction, the Israeli pullout from Gaza (2005) has been termed by the government *hitnatkut*, which means self-chosen separation and disengagement from something one was attached to – an act of growth and sign of maturity, perhaps – rather than the humiliating word "withdrawal" (which could have been used in reference to the Israeli army in Gaza) or the harsh notion of "evacuation" or even "forced displacement" (of the Jewish settlers).

In these and many other examples, one sees that precisely in the most important issues – those of life and death and of bitter national conflict – the official language too often becomes vague, abstract, detached, cleared of the blood, horror, and brutality of actions and their tangible meanings. Perhaps these characteristics of the official Hebrew are not unique and

been done throughout history everywhere, and often in Palestine itself – but rather the systemic, thorough, and all-engulfing way this naming project has been done. (See also note 88.)

[90] Shulamit Har-Even, "The Limits of My Language, the Limits of My World," in *Hebrew Writers on Writing*, ed. Peter Cole (San Antonio, TX: Trinity University Press, 2008), p. 198.

are evident in other official languages as well (and existed well before modernity); yet given the long history of the conflict between Israel and its neighbors, its centrality to public life, and the IDF being perhaps the most important institution of Israeli society, these characteristics have become well entrenched and have influenced the language as a whole. Indeed, the writer Shulamit Har-Even has expressed fear that the Hebrew language is losing some of its concise, active, and especially direct and bold nature.[91] And David Grossman famously wrote some years ago that "bit by bit a new type of recruited words emerge here, words that are treacherous, that have lost their original meaning, that do not describe reality but rather assay to conceal it."[92]

Certainly Bialik had no role in forming the political-linguistic reality that Har-Even and Grossman refer to, and he would probably have been a harsh critic of it. Yet as Quentin Skinner argues, texts cannot be understood in isolation from the context in which they have been written. Their full meaning comes to light if we see them as an answer to a specific question that does not necessarily appear in the text and is not necessarily acknowledged by the writer (who may not even be aware of the set of questions he or she is answering). While we tend to see some texts as "classic" and "timeless," in fact they should primarily be understood in the context of the time and space in which they appear, and the way they operate in an entire semantic field.[93] Similarly, Hans-Georg Gadamer observes that "not just occasionally but always, the meaning of a text goes beyond its author,"[94] partly because a text contains meanings that are not accessible to the author, who is embedded in his or her intellectual and cultural horizons, or may take certain problems for granted – and these meanings may come to light only for the temporally distant interpreter.

The vision of language that emerges from "Revealment and Concealment in Language" is troubling. Bialik's understanding of language as an ongoing, collective project of concealment in the face of the danger of Being often sits too well with modern Hebrew and its reactions to threats to collective self-image and identity. A language that was

---

[91] Ibid.

[92] David Grossman, "Machbesat milim [Word laundromat]," in his *Hazeman hatsahov* [The yellow wind] (Tel Aviv: Hakibbutz Hameuhad, 1987), p. 44 (in Hebrew). I am also helped here by Robik Rozenthal, "*Hisufim batzariah*," *Ma'ariv*, October 3, 2005 (in Hebrew).

[93] See Quentin Skinner, *Meaning and Understanding in the History of Ideas* (Middletown, CT: Wesleyan University Press, 1969).

[94] Hans-Georg Gadamer, *Truth and Method* (New York: Continuum, 2004), p. 296.

composed in flight – created to overcome the existential void and speech-lessness of the modern Jew in Zion – seems to have retained or repro-duced its original constitution as a sheltering entity in the face of the ongoing challenges posed by the political and conflictual world outside its bounds (not to mention the horrors of the Holocaust, which were not widely discussed or written about in Israel for many years; the Hebrew language, wholly divorced from the Diaspora, offered – for survivors and for a traumatized community as a whole – a partial refuge from mem-ories related to those horrors). More generally, since modern Hebrew and Zionism were deeply intertwined from the beginning – and since Hebrew was disseminated largely through kindergartens and the school system (which were controlled by the state) – this language was always enmeshed in Zionist and Israeli politics, having little *relevant*, independent, and prior tradition of how to name and describe things and phe-nomena in the world in a way that could elude and challenge this politics (although the first, literary steps for the renewal of the language began in the nineteenth century, before Zionism and even the Hibbat Zion move-ment emerged). The fact that Israeli Jews were the only Hebrew-speaking people in the entire region, and that Israel is the only place in the world where Hebrew became the vernacular, did not help to challenge this ten-dency for self-enclosure.

Now, there is little in Bialik to suggest that the role of the poet, or any other speaker for that matter, is to question the shielding role of lan-guage; on the contrary, he seems to suggest that poets (despite their fasci-nation with Tohu) are measured by the degree to which they are able to produce potent words and word combinations that thicken the wall, that constitute effective building blocks. For him, poets face Tohu with their backs to their community, instead of facing the community and pointing to the Tohu that is concealed beneath its patches.

I have argued thus far that in identifying the nub of language as conceal-ing and sheltering, rather than as truth driven and committed to accurate descriptions, Bialik presents a potentially dangerous vision, politically speaking; sound politics begins with the will to see reality as it is (how-ever limited our abilities in this matter may be), not only as one wishes it to be, and meaningful public deliberation commences when citizens dis-cuss and explore the truths about the world and are not preoccupied with finding the best means of evading these truths (unless one succumbs to the sorry claim that all descriptions of reality have the same truth value, of course).

Yet another major danger for language in the public sphere that emerges from Bialik's essay concerns his distinction between two types of languages: a prized, inward one and a hollow, public one. Bialik writes that:

[t]heir [the words'] core is consumed and their spiritual strength fades or is hidden, and only their husks, cast out from the private domain to the public, still persist in language, doing slack service within the limited boundaries of logic and social intercourse, as external signs and abstractions for objects and images. It has come to the point where the human language has become two languages, built upon one another's destruction: one, an internal language, that of solitude and the soul [poetry] ... the other, the external language, that of abstraction and generalization.

The language of the individual's soul is vibrant and innovative; it is in constant motion since the basic materials of life and the world are in motion.[95] While society, in order to function and coordinate, needs stability and fixed signs, the individual – both in order to be true to the nature of things and to affirm the life within him or her – must be responsive to the unknown and unpredictable, to the ever-changing and ever-different; poetry, which is attuned to the inner self, its surroundings, and the relation between the two, best addresses and heightens this changeability and celebrates the singularity of the moment (although the poem itself endures). The internal conversation of the self is a nonutilitarian one: In it, we do not try to communicate with others, to introduce joint action into the world, or to achieve practical advantage and take control of our environment. The inner dialogue is also not about rationally and methodically inquiring into our surroundings and finding "facts" and "laws" or about solving taxing moral dilemmas.[96] Rather, according to Bialik, this dialogue is emotional and expressive, having no goal beyond itself except diversion.

This creative dialogue helps human beings to face Being and the sublime (Tohu) by articulating the primal experience of wonder and fear in confronting something that transcends them and is impenetrable to them. In part, language here is merely a distraction from aloneness and smallness, an inner conversation being proof of existence to oneself and a way of keeping oneself company. Yet more importantly, private language

---

[95] See C. N. Bialik, "Chevlei lashon [The birth pangs of language]," in *Sipurim vedevri safrrot* [Stories and other writings] (Tel Aviv: Devir, 1975), p. 10.

[96] I am helped here by Michael Oakeshott, "The Voice of Poetry in the Conversation of Mankind," in *Rationalism in Politics and Other Essays* (Indianapolis: Liberty Fund, 1991), pp. 488–542.

is where individuality truly expresses and asserts itself, suggests Bialik, since each individual must find his or her own images and mental pictures in describing authentic primary existential, emotional, and spiritual experiences that others cannot express for that individual. To think poetically is to think freely, not being chained to any necessary and logical route of thought nor to rules and habits, and to find unexpected connections between what seems frozen in its separateness. Natural language is essential here, since in the poem *there is no gulf between content and form*, and it is impossible to conduct this kind of conversation through arbitrarily chosen signs, as in mathematics. What we say is interwoven with how we express it, and asserting our person means being innovative on both levels. To be sure, there is no equality among individuals as creators of images and fresh language; yet while the poets surely excel in this regard, ultimately each individual must be capable of some measure of poetic conversation in order to form him- or herself as an individual; it seems that for Bialik, as for Hölderlin (and Heidegger) "poetically man dwells."

To sum, then, in contrast to the Jewish tradition (especially the Kabbala), which avers that the Hebrew language originated with God and that men and women – through their endless interpretations – may only disclose a truth that has already been pregiven in the text, Bialik proclaims the autonomy and creativity of the speaker (although he believes that in terms of the *form* or poetic style in which speakers choose to express themselves, they should take note of national conventions, too).[97] And in contrast to the Jewish tradition, in which the emotional expressiveness of the devotee is balanced by a rational voice that follows the Law and God's commands despite one's feelings (e.g., Abraham's willingness to sacrifice Isaac) while tirelessly seeking to fathom God's reason and intentions, Bialik seems to attach the revival of Hebrew in modernity mostly to the former aspect of language. He believes that this revival must come from the heart of the essentially Romantic (yet tamed and responsible) individual before it can become the medium through which the nation communicates with itself. (As Ariel Hirschfeld notes, with Bialik, "Hebrew turned, unknowingly but with great force, from a language of the mind to a language of the emotions and the senses.")[98]

Throughout his life, Bialik was preoccupied with searching for his poetic voice, and he reflects on its sources and meaning in poems such as

---

[97] See Bialik's speech on Yehuda Halevi in Odessa, 1913, at http://www.benyehuda.org/bialik/dvarim_shebeal_peh68.html.
[98] Ariel Hirschfeld, "He Had a Garden and He Still Has One," *Ha'aretz*, March 6, 2008.

"Zohar," "My Poetry," and "I Didn't Win Light in a Windfall." As a young poet, Dan Meron observes, Bialik rejected the lyrical style of the Hibbat Zion movement, which he considered too sentimental and locked within conventions. Instead, he was influenced by the Odessa style of *Hashiloah* and attempted to write poetry that was emotionally restrained, coherent, clear, and concerned with illuminating the predicament of the Jew and Judaism in modern times, rather than the internal drama of the private self. This Odessa style "was not imposed upon him, but confirmed his own deepest intuitions"[99] about the direction Hebrew poetry should embrace. Gradually, his voice became more autobiographical and realistic, and his own life became the anchor of his national allegories and historic references: "I didn't win light in a windfall/ nor by deed of a father's will. I hewed my light from granite. It quarried my heart. In the mine of my heart a spark hides/ not large, but wholly my own. Neither hired, nor borrowed, nor stolen – my very own."[100]

In situating himself as the source and center of his poetry, Bialik rejected familiar poetic traditions within Judaism. In particular, according to Meron, he shunned the tradition of the prophets, in which the speaker's role is limited to delivering the orderly and coherent words of God (which are being "introduced" into his mouth), as well as the tradition of prayer, which involves repetitive, collective singing (led by a cantor) at the synagogue and in which private prayer is conducted within pregiven historic and collective contexts. Indeed, Bialik attempted to salvage the multilayered vocabulary of Hebrew but sought the liberty to write about the world (and himself as a part of this world) from his unique experience and perspective, wholly self-reliant, giving birth to his own imagination – unhindered by customs, expectations, or religion.[101]

---

[99] See Dan Meron, *Taking Leave of the Impoverished Self: H. N. Bialik's Early Poetry* (Tel Aviv: Open University, 1986), p. 98 (in Hebrew).

[100] Bialik, "I Didn't Win Light in a Windfall," trans. Ruth Nevo. The poem continues as follows: "Sorrow wields huge hammer blows/ the rock of endurance cracks/ blinding my eye with flashes/ I catch in verse. They fly from my lines to your breast/ to vanish in kindled flame. While I, with heart's blood and marrow/ pay the price of the blaze."

[101] At times, however, Bialik seems to seek limits, or at least a binding context, to individual creativity. "The intention and aim of the writers' association," he notes, "is not to mold the writers into a flock wherein all are dancing to the same flute and grazing, subject to the whip of one shepherd. On the contrary, we aspire to multiplicity, to the happiness of abundance. Each one seeking his unique path, his singular way as God blessed him.... However, we only ask that all would share one understanding: that writers are the retainers of the nation and its eternal needs. We must sing, each with his own instrument and vocalizing his own segment, but ultimately all this must come together, and ... become one symphony.... If one hears melodies from a thousand different operas, this is not only irritating to the ear and upsetting to the nerves – this should not even be

"His words present poetry not only as a human non-religious creation, but in a sense as a human anti-religious creation that is aimed at displacing the secret wisdom"[102] of poetry that originates with God, explains Meron.

Bialik argues, however, that in the public sphere (*Reshut harabim*) there is yet another type of language, one composed of the "husks" (a Kabbalistic term) of words and lacking the liveliness and creativity of the private language. It is used for communicating and negotiating while seeking to achieve tangible goals, or for constructing abstractions and generalizations necessary for the formation of knowledge. Public speech is based on the "permanent and static" aspects of language: The import of signs is wholly nonpersonal, each word having one meaning only, fixed and widely known in advance.[103] One could reasonably expect, avers Bialik, that ordinary language would easily provide us with all those names, adjectives, verbs, and so on that are needed for daily use and smooth interactions. But as in mathematics, in which the number is an abstraction that can represent a multiplicity of things, so in public language the word is devoid of concreteness and is detached from things or events themselves. Words are used as mere signs, ones that could be arbitrarily replaced since no inherent relation exists in this language between the word and the phenomena it describes. The human soul remains indifferent to this use of language, written or oral, since no emotional and existential power animates the word, but only the demands of utility and reason. As language becomes more distant from Tohu and the moment of its birth in the individual, then, it loses its weight and substance, meaning and authenticity. Politics is perhaps the most distant of spheres, because it is not only removed from the creative self and preoccupied with master plans of collective building, the mobilization of entire populations and the like, but it is also aloof from the *spiritual forces animating the nation and its culture* (forces that essentially originate in individuals and their inward languages).

At times, Bialik sees politics as a type of game conducted by a few professional leaders, distant from the sovereign spirit of the people and conducted in an opaque language. "The complete happiness of a people,"

---

regarded as singing. It is better if such music never came into existence in the first place." *Devarim*, vol. 1, p. 128.

[102] Meron, *Taking Leave of the Impoverished Self*, pp. 374–5.

[103] C. N. Bialik, "Chevlei lashon," p. 10.

he writes, "is not dependent on the fruitful actions and valor of its leaders, but rather on the free development – entirely free development – of
all the powers within its soul and entire life. The spirit of the people is
the sole master and legislator, and politics is merely a servant, content to
perform the will of its master, and not the reverse."[104] In this strong vision
of cultural nationalism, politics – actions as well as words, leaders but
also one's political persona generally – are of secondary and subservient
position. Politics is about protecting and cultivating culture and collective spirit, not a sphere with its own ways of reasoning and demands;
surely it has no claim of being an important part of the good life for men
and women alike.[105] At other times, Bialik suggests a Sisyphean struggle
aimed at elevating ordinary speech: Even trivial "political truths," such as
Hebrew signs in the streets, could and must become "truths of the soul,"
he believes (I will return to this point in the next chapter). Yet Bialik's
more principled position as expressed in his essays is that the contents
of the soul, on the one hand, and social (especially perhaps political)
discourse, on the other, belong to two related but essentially different
linguistic spheres that serve different needs and mirror different aspects
of our being, and that these two languages are "built upon one another's
destruction."[106]

This strong linguistic distinction between poetry and public-political
language is questionable. To begin with, Bialik's view is at odds with
the biblical conception of language, in which the prophet's words –
which often have political and social significance – are considered to
be persuasive and effective, constituting a performance for an audience
through a language that is full of poetic qualities, such as alluring imag-
ery and rhythm; the homily later continued this tradition, although the
status of the speaker was different in this case. In addition, since medieval times, a (small) Jewish literature of rhetoric emerged, hand in hand
with the blossoming of Hebrew poetry.[107] In the Hellenic tradition of

---

[104] See Bialik, "Tarbut vpolitika [Culture and politics]" (1918), at http://benyehuda.org/
bialik/tarpol.html.

[105] Bialik's attitude toward politics is expressed in the following humorous story he once
told. "When Noah opened the ark, the creatures stood in line. Among them was the lie.
When Noah said only couples could go on board, the lie immediately summoned his
wife, flattery, and they were allowed to board the ark. When the time came to leave the
ark, however, they were already three: lie, flattery, and their daughter – politics." Quoted
here from Shmuel Avneri, *Ha'aretz*, July 2, 2010.

[106] Ibid.

[107] See Isaac Rabinowitz, "Pre-Modern Jewish Study of Rhetoric: An Introductory
Bibliography," *Rhetorica* 3, no. 2 (Spring 1985): 137–43. According to Rabinowitz,

antiquity, moreover, there was no sharp separation between poetry and rhetoric. Aristotle, for example, noted this connection, suggesting that "words express ideas, and therefore those words are the most agreeable that enable us to get hold of new ideas. Now strange words simply puzzle us; ordinary words convey only what we know already; it is from metaphor that we best get hold of something fresh, ... [B]oth speech and reasoning are lively in proportion as they make us seize a new idea promptly."[108]

To be sure, poetry and public speech are not identical: The latter is concerned with statements about evidence and factual truth, with logical arguments and coherence, with the creation of an engaging narrative that balances emotions and reason – none of which is characteristic of poetry. The gist of rhetoric, moreover, is the ability to articulate a *Doxa* that will convince one's peers to undertake collective action and shape the common world and the public good; poetry, in contrast, most often has no goal beyond itself and the pleasure or relief it can offer. Despite these and other differences, however, poetry and public speech share the need for originality and creativity in language, and both require the ability to make innovative connections, to shed new light on circumstances, to address the specificity of the moment, to cultivate the imagination. Poetry perhaps celebrates emotional expressiveness, but effective politics cannot ignore this dimension either. Moreover, both poetry and politics must share a profound faith in the power of words, whether one seeks to convey oneself or shape the world one shares with others. Images, finally, play a significant role in both: Zionism, in fact, greatly benefited from the aesthetic and poetic element in language, the playwright Herzl submitting (in addition to his detailed plans) an imaginative picture of the Jewish

---

Moses ibn Ezra, for example, both wrote poetry and examined rhetoric in the twelfth century. It should be mentioned, however, that the first comprehensive treatment of rhetoric by a Jew is apparently the fifteenth-century study by Judah Messer Leon, *The Book of the Honeycomb's Flow*. In general, reflections on rhetoric occurred in the context of considerable communal (legal, judicial, monetary, and more) autonomy and inspiring developments in political thought by Maimonides and Rabbi Nissim ben Reuven of Gerondi, for instance. On this last point, see Menachem Lorberbaum, *Politics and the Limits of Law: Secularizing the Political in Medieval Jewish Thought* (Stanford, CA: Stanford University Press, 2002). Lorberbaum's study is part of an attempt to retrieve and reexamine the Jewish political tradition. In this context, see also the two volumes of the *Jewish Political Tradition* (published by Yale University Press and edited by M. Walzer, M. Lorberbaum, N. Zohar, and Y. Loberbaum), as well as the various publications of the Shalem Center in Jerusalem.

[108] Aristotle, 1410b10.

state in his speeches and writings, a picture so powerful as to become a force in its own right.

Bialik, however, describes (as noted) a gulf between potent poetic language, on the one hand, and abstract, flat, and fixed public (not only political) language, on the other, apparently distrustful of the possibility for inventiveness in the public use of words and skeptical of the power inherent in these words (although some of his poems, notably "In the City of Slaughter" [1903], had profound political influence, and although he gave many public speeches throughout his life).[109] This view of language in *Reshut harabim* is however understandable: Due to the lack of a Jewish public sphere and independent political life generally – and the absence of communal *political* memory – public speech and political discourse could not have become central features of the Jewish tradition in the Diaspora; Jews have nothing equivalent to Napoleon Bonaparte's "Farewell to the Old Guard" or to Queen Elizabeth's "Against the Spanish Armada," to Cromwell's "Dismissal of the Rump Parliament," or to Patrick Henry's "Give me Liberty or give me Death" speeches. Bialik's vision of public language merely reflects this status and reinforces it: The dramas in our lives, the great forces that move them, have little to do with the political world we share and the words spoken in that world. In fact, one may argue that while developing his distinct and independent voice as a poet, Bialik, in his reflections on language, nevertheless exults a vision of it that remains attached to certain religious-liturgical categories, since not only is its chief concern and propelling energy the relation between humans and Tohu but this relation is also based on fear and awe (as is often the case in Jewish prayers). The primary experience of humans, the one that injects life into their words and speech, is the relation between them and what is beyond them (Tohu, God) – and not their relation to each other. Human beings, who (as noted) are for Bialik *hai medaber*, are not then Aristotelian *zōon politikon* or *zōon logon* echon after all, despite the shared belief of both writers in language as the chief characteristic of these beings: Bialik seems to suggest that the creative, linguistic energies of humans flourish at a distance from the public sphere; their interpretations of the world are less concrete and original, less meaningful and holy-like, the more they embrace their roles as citizens.

[109] For an illuminating discussion about this poem and its role in shaping the Zionist ethos of self-defense, see Michael Gluzman, Hannan Hever, and Dan Meron, *Beir hahariga: bikur meuchar* [In the city of slaughter – A visit at twilight] (Tel Aviv: Resling, 2005) (in Hebrew).

I have previously noted (see Chapter 3) that Zionism displaced the language-based world of the Jewish believer with the materially based world of homo faber, the builder; Bialik represents perhaps the most significant attempt, within Zionism, to oppose this displacement. Since he was not only a national poet and cultural icon but also deeply involved in Zionist public affairs (especially in the last decades of his life), his influence in general and on the understanding of modern Hebrew in particular was immense. Thus, his failure to link the notion of *hai med-aber* with citizenship and to picture politics as a critical arena of speech and linguistic innovation is unfortunate. However, Bialik is important for understanding the relation between Hebrew and politics, not only because of his stature but also because the actual developments in Eretz Israel uncannily followed his vision. On the one hand, poetry (and literature in general) has blossomed with immense creativity and become central to the young state's culture and identity (see next chapter); on the other, the political uses of language have been of questionable importance and have most often demonstrated little imagination and ingenuity.

Despite the radical new experiences of the *halutzim* and other Jews in Palestine – a life led with a renewed bond to an ancient land in the context of a fresh meeting between West and (Near) East, with collective experimentation in the kibbutzim and novel moral codes and notions of distributive justice, with aspirations for new gender roles, and with a need to shape cooperative relations with the native Arab population – no new political vision or vocabulary emerged in Palestine in general and among the socialist Zionists in particular (the marginal Brit Shalom was an exception). The need to integrate yet respect multiple diasporas, each with its own rich cultural background, did not generate an appropriate vision of the state either. Furthermore, Zionism added almost nothing original to the two dominant ideologies that influenced it – nationalism and socialism – nor was there an attempt to think creatively about the challenges facing Jews elsewhere in the world and about a growing anti-Semitism, especially in Europe (this is still the case today).[110] Later, Israeli society became highly innovative – in the arts, in advanced technologies,

---

[110] As Arendt commented (in 1945), "and so it has come to pass that this new class of Jews, who possess such a rich new experience in social relationships, have not uttered a single fresh word, have not offered a single new slogan, in the wide field of Jewish politics ... content merely with repeating the old socialist or the new nationalist banalities." See Hannah Arendt, "Zionism Reconsidered," *The Menorah Journal* (1945): 170–1.

PHOTO 15. A poster issued during the 1950s by Haifa's city council as part of a national effort to teach the new Jewish immigrants Hebrew. The Yiddish-speaking immigrant asks: "Excuse me, how do I get to the city council?" To which the sabra responds with an uncomprehending "What?" Photo courtesy of The Central Zionist Archives.

in agriculture, in (inescapably) military strategies, and in much more – but its politics, both conceptual and actual, has not been one of these spheres of innovation.

My main argument in this chapter has been that the great challenges – of envisioning, in the public sphere, a language that is neither holy nor artificial and instrumental, a language that is neither hostage to transcendental truths nor a diminisher of human-made truths and the status of the individuals articulating these truths – have not been resolved. Ahad Ha'am and Bialik advanced the cause of Hebrew in many ways, yet their contribution to a viable vision of Hebrew in a democratic context has been minor. This chapter manifested the difficulties that the individual Hebrew speaker meets in the public sphere, and it might be worthwhile to look for models that bridge language and democratic politics more successfully. In this regard, the work of Hannah Arendt is a good place to start.

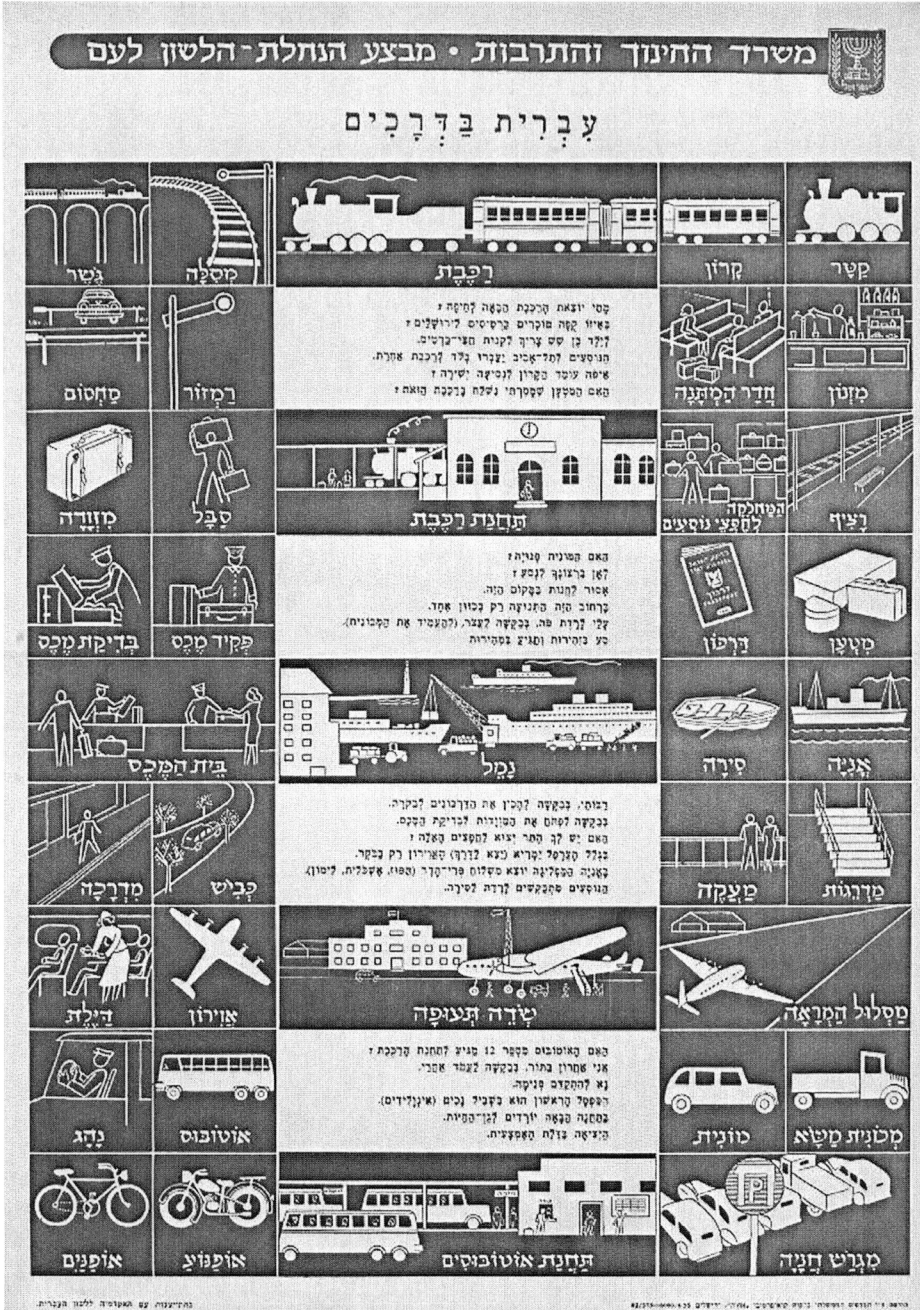

PHOTO 16. A poster issued by the Ministry of Education during the 1950s explaining basic concepts regarding transportation and travel to new immigrants. Similar posters dealt with professions, equipment, tools, military commands, and much more. Photo courtesy of The Central Zionist Archives.

5

Democratic Language and Zionism

Words can be relied upon only so long as one is sure that their function is to reveal and not to conceal.

Hannah Arendt, "Reflections on Violence" (1969)

In 1935, when Arendt was working as secretary general of the Paris office of the Youth Aliyah organization, dedicated to preparing Jewish children for emigration to Palestine, she visited the Yishuv. She was particularly impressed with the kibbutzim. She saw their members as a "new aristocracy" of halutzim, who were not concerned with material wealth and individual self-interest, who successfully combined labor with culture, who were committed to equality and social justice, and who practiced self-government in council-like form. In her understanding, the halutzim were indeed a new type of Jew, self-reliant, attached to the soil, unsullied, and unapologetic. But as time went by, and the Arab-Israeli conflict became more apparent and the crisis of European Jewry more acute, Arendt became increasingly aware of the shortcomings of the new aristocracy. She began to accuse the socialist-Zionist movement of being "self-centered" and "too decent for politics"; the halutzim, she observed, left politics to professional politicians, who were supposed to advance their interests, and cared little about local or international politics as long as they were left alone to advance their dream.

"The national aim of the socialist Zionists," writes Arendt, "was attained when they settled in Palestine. Beyond that they had no national aspirations. Absurd as it may sound today, they had not the slightest suspicion of any national conflict with the present inhabitants of the Promised Land; they didn't even stop to *think* of the very existence of the Arabs" (my emphasis). Arendt continues, claiming that "nothing could better prove the entirely un-political character of the new movement than this innocent obliviousness." Arendt's judgment is obviously exaggerated, and at least since the Faisal-Weizmann agreement of 1919, and especially after the events of 1929, some pioneers (perhaps not the majority) realized that a fierce national conflict might be in the making. But it must be admitted that even the spiritual leader of the halutzim, A. D. Gordon, thought that the new settlers were too absorbed in their own world. "And what is our attitude toward the Arabs," he once asked, "who, whether we like it or not, are our partners in social-political life? What do we know about them and would we like to know more than the anti-Semites know about us?"[1]

For Arendt, the new Jew's lack of ability to "think" – specifically, in this case, to better understand the others' point of view and national aspirations, to grasp where things are heading, to imagine possible consequences, and to come up with fresh ideas for averting this scenario – was disastrous. The establishment of a Jewish nation-state perhaps resolved the homelessness of some Jews, but it also led to the creation of a vast number of new stateless people (the Palestinian refugees) and an Arab minority destined to be second-class citizens. The lack of thinking was also evident, in her mind, in the Yishuv's insufficient interest in the fate of European Jewry and its legitimate struggle for collective political rights, and in the defeat of anti-Semitism (not to mention the low involvement of the Yishuv in World War II; Arendt, similarly to Jabotinsky, interestingly, believed that a Jewish army should have been established to fight in this war).

The ability to "think" acquires increasing weight in Arendt's writings, partly because it is the basis for having an "opinion" on political matters, one that may play a part in a democratic public sphere. For her, *the capacity to think is intimately linked to language* and the ability of human beings to open up the world, and themselves to the world, through it. More specifically, to think seriously necessarily leads the individual, at least at critical times, to act politically through deed and speech; to use the latter properly, however, means to understand

---

[1] See A. D. Gordon, "Avodateno meha'ta [Our Future Work]" (1918), at http://benyehuda. org/gordon_ad/our_work_henceforth.html. Other Zionists, such as Ben-Gurion, even believed (in 1930) that it would be possible to join forces with the Arabs and expel the British forces from Palestine. Ben-Gurion remained hopeful concerning Arab-Jewish cooperation at least until 1936. For the Zionists' response to Palestinian nationalism, see Laqueur, *A History of Zionism*, Chap. 5.

language as a medium that probes the shared human reality and propels one to transcend self-enclosure with given horizons.[2] Now, since mental and linguistic enclosure is a threat to the political use of Hebrew (as we have seen in the previous chapter), Arendt's vision of democratic language may help us better comprehend what has been missing in the Zionist understanding of this language. Four of Arendt's arguments seem particularly important in this context:

(a) The ability to form an individual language or voice is essential to thinking and critical reflection, and hence is conducive to democratic citizenship.

(b) Private and public languages are different, but they also have much in common (e.g., plurality, disclosure) and should hence be seen as a continuum.

(c) Language promotes democratic life to the extent that it is understood as a medium through which we endeavor to open up reality – which itself is partly established by words – rather than conceal it or flee from it.

(d) Citizens can create a shared public world only if they use language and have faith in the words spoken in public. Language in the public sphere – which is not just a pale echo of private language – is essential for providing a fuller sense of existence because it involves appearing before others and the formation of a political persona.

---

[2] While Arendt criticized the relatively "pure," early halutzim, whom she admired for not thinking hard enough in political matters, she used (after many years) similar terms to describe the failings of a totally different sort of human being, whom she despised. In the introduction to her book *The Life of the Mind*, Arendt explains that she was motivated to consider the meaning of thinking and its relation to language after the Eichmann trial, which she witnessed in Jerusalem. What was remarkable about Adolf Eichmann, she suggests, was not his "stupidity," but rather his "thoughtlessness." This characteristic was reflected in his language: "In the setting of the Israeli court and prison procedures he functioned as well as he had functioned under the Nazi regime, but when confronted with situations for which such routine procedures did not exist, he was helpless, and his cliché-ridden language produced on the stand, as it had evidently done in his official life, a kind of macabre comedy. Clichés, stock phrases, adherence to conventional, standardized codes of expression and conduct have the social recognized function of protecting us against reality, that is, against the claim on our thinking attention that all events and facts make by virtue of their existence." See Hannah Arendt, *The Life of the Mind* (New York: Harcourt Brace Jovanovich, 1978), p. 4.

Partly because of his language, Eichmann was unable to develop an "enlarged mentality" and to "go visiting," two Arendtian concepts that call for engaging others' point of view before making judgments and choosing a course of action in the world. See on this point Leora Bilsky, "When Actor and Spectator Meet in the Courtroom: Reflections on Hannah Arendt's Concept of Judgment," *History and Memory* 8, no. 2 (1996): 137–73.

I. LANGUAGE AND REVEALMENT

We have seen that for Bialik, private conversation evolves within the self as an authentic and aesthetic response to feelings of wonder and fear in the face of the frightening sublime. The origin of the inner dialogue of the self, one that is unique to it, is emotional and expressive (and is epitomized in poetry). Arendt, too, values the inner conversation within the self and sees this use of language as essential to our being; however, there are important differences between her view and Bialik's, especially concerning the place of thinking in human existence and the purpose of this human activity. For Arendt, our personal and inward use of language is intertwined with our deep-seated, drivelike, need to think. Thinking, according to Arendt, is essential for our humanity; it is a spontaneous, non-goal-oriented, and somewhat wandering activity of the mind. Thinking does not set out to transform the phenomenal world or to boost our power in and instrumental control over our surroundings. The motivation for thinking comes instead from our constant wonder toward the world and our yearning to infuse the world with meaning. Thinking is not motivated by the search for truth, certainly not for scientific truth: "[I]mplicit in the urge to speak is the quest for meaning, not necessarily the quest for truth."[3] The realistic, Platonic notion of truth is, in fact, dangerous to thinking (and to politics), she notes, because it is fixed and decontextualized and because it presupposes unanimity. Instead of this truth, the thinking self is seeking *a story* that will render reality meaningful and sensible, allowing this self to overcome alienation between itself and the world, and within itself.

There is a Hegelian echo in Arendt: Thinking, she suggests, commences with an unsettling of the self's pregiven sense of belonging to place and community, parents and friends, tradition and conceptual vocabulary – an unsettling that leaves the self strange to the world and to itself due to the breakdown of the everyday and the "taken-for-granted." But as it proceeds and develops, thinking involves the self's ability to transcend these feelings of nonbelonging through rich, coherent narratives about its relation to people, places, convictions. Stories locate us in the world: They connect events and make sense of their unfolding; they situate the self's story with the stories of others and within a preexisting web of relations and meanings.[4] Thinking is thus destructive and constructive.

---

[3] Arendt, *The Life of the Mind*, p. 99.
[4] See Seyla Benhabib, *The Reluctant Modernism of Hannah Arendt* (Oxford: Rowman and Littlefield, 2003), pp. 107–13.

It first generates alienation but then turns the self into a conscious and reflective denizen in the world; a meaningful sense of being at home is something to be acquired, chosen, narrated – and is therefore distinctive for every self. According to Arendt, this dialectic is ongoing: Since both self and world change, the acquired sense of belonging ebbs; the sense of being at home that was created by thought is again replaced by estrangement, which leads in turn to new ways of thinking when fresh words and stories are called for. In any case, the sense of home we have in the world is dependent less on the artifacts we make and the building we erect on the surface of the earth than on the quality of the stories we come up with and how these stories attach us to objects, places, and especially people.

Thinking, indeed, occurs in and through language: The Greeks already noted that we can only think in words and that words inescapably shape our thinking. If we feel growing estrangement from the pregiven world as we become aware of ourselves as distinct selves – including the pregiven linguistic descriptions of this world – any thought that would salvage us from this predicament would have to employ a vocabulary that does not accept as a matter of course any conventions of expression and meaning; language must undergo a personal and internal reformation that parallels the journey of thought. ("Above all," writes Proust, "I had ... to exclude words spoken by the lips but not by the mind; those ... colloquialisms which after much social intercourse we get accustomed to using artificially, which fill the mind with lies, those purely physical words.") Thinking and tradition are thus in constant tension. While the latter asserts its authority through conventions ingrained in idioms, verses, or slogans, thinking must shun this dimension of language. In shaping its personal language, then, the self employs creative analogies and metaphors; these elucidate and familiarize the surroundings, forging meaningful relationships between things and events that do not present any such relationship to the naked eye. Arendt emphasizes that thought can be exercised quietly, consisting of an internal dialogue of the self – but it can be carried out only through language. The Greek word *logos* refers to this phenomenon, since it encompasses both speech (which might be internal) and thought, thus relating the coherent and orderly shape of words and sentences to meaningful and substantial thought.

The self's distinct vocabulary is associated, in Arendt's mind, with the role of the reflective and somewhat aloof spectator, not with the role of the doer and engaged political actor. Nevertheless, while the private or inward use of language is not essentially political, there are profound relations between this language and public speech – and between the self as a thinking and observing being, on the one hand, and the citizen as action oriented in the phenomenal-communal world, on the other. For Arendt, three important points seem to emerge in explicating these relations.

Firstly, thinking is an internal dialogue between me and myself. In this dialogue, I am the one asking the questions and also the other providing the answers. I espouse a certain point of view and then another; without this ongoing, restless dynamic of the mind, thinking would not be a critical endeavor and would not possess its open character. Thinking, claims Arendt, is not launched by a monolithic entity facing the world and expecting answers from outside. Rather, it presupposes a duality within the self, the containment of at least two different voices that are in a constant state of wonder toward the world and of questioning in relation to each other. There is a noticeable continuity between this vision of the thinking self and Arendt's well-known claim concerning the inherent plurality of the political sphere. The interiority of the self also contains innate plurality and difference, and in this sense the engulfing human world and the internal structure of consciousness reflect and echo each other. *Thinking is in a certain sense always political*, since it enlivens and affirms the plurality of human communal existence. Just as politics requires the ability of the citizen to view the world through an "enlarged mentality," to examine the world from his or her peers' point of view, so thinking takes place by inviting a few perspectives to take part in the internal dialogue of the self.

Secondly, however, Arendt suggests that plurality would be dangerous if a friendship did not exist between one's interior voices. She goes beyond Aristotle (who claims that a polis requires good partnership and friendship among citizens)[5] in suggesting that friendship within the political community is associated with companionship within the self: It should be practiced in the private realm before it can be practiced among citizens. To begin with, internal conversation does not aim at unity and the longing to be One: This type of longing tends to flatten diversity and to remove the need for exploring it through language. In a political community, if we make sure that we are all similar to one another, we would perhaps be able to establish a strong bond among us, but our conversation with each other will be almost superfluous and the language will

[5] Aristotle, *The Politics*, 1295b24.

eventually decline. The same attempt to flee significant, diverse inner voices – because we desire to maintain a peaceful selfhood – may happen to each and every one of us if we are not sufficiently alert.

Genuine inner friendship leads elsewhere: It is based on plurality, which expresses itself in language, and on the willingness to enter into dialogue. This dialogue is aimed at achieving inner solidarity (rather than unity), but only once I welcome and esteem the other voice within myself. For Socrates, Arendt writes, "the duality of the two-in-one meant not more than that if you want to think, you must do it so that the two who carry on the dialogue be in good shape, that the partners be *friends*."[6] Internal friendship is the most fundamental and lasting friendship, and it molds one's life as the Demon formed Socrates' life.

In this context, Arendt explains the famous Socratic claim – "that it is better to be wronged than to do wrong" – thus: Moral deliberation involves a comprehension not only of the effects that our actions may have upon others, but, even more fundamentally, of the effects these actions may have upon ourselves. (An individual who, for example, slaughters another may have to live after this act with a vicious, violent voice within him- or herself – and to see the world from the perspective of that voice.) Consciousness of one's duality and the need for inner friendship has moral import because it leads one to cultivate a conscience, a moral voice necessary for sharing a life with oneself and others. In fact, the friendship among the voices within the self is also a precondition for other friendships, since only a person who knows how to be a friend to him- or herself may form good friendships with others, and since the foundation of both friendships is plurality expressed through language. Awareness of the need for internal friendship establishes lasting practices and qualities necessary to live with others, such as curiosity, listening, generosity, forgiveness, and truthfulness.[7]

---

[6] Arendt, *The Life of the Mind*, pp. 187–8.

[7] Surely, Arendt is not the first theorist to underscore the dualistic and dialogical nature of the self. The Freudian picture of the self, in particular, similarly involves a dualistic existence and constant conversation between ego and superego within the psyche. For Freud, however, these are contradictory voices, the former representing reality and its taxing demands in the present, the latter a heightened morality and the cultural ideals of the past; these aspects of the psyche, moreover, are entangled with emotions and instincts, and rational deliberation is always endangered by these forces. For Arendt, however, the internal conversation is first and foremost an expression of wonder regarding the world outside oneself, not an attempt to resolve psychosexual and emotional conflicts. Inner dialogue does not spring from our emotions, needs, or unconscious drives, but rather from the desire to think: "It is not our soul but our mind that demands speech," she writes. Her view also resembles Gadamer's. See the appendix to his *Truth and Method*.

The third facet of Arendt's view of thinking that has political import concerns the *outcome* of the mind's plural, friendly conversation. As mentioned, for Arendt, ceaseless wonder and an attempt to find our home or location in the world propel this conversation; hence, this conversation is dynamic, not goal oriented, and mostly noncommittal in judgment. Yet this conversation could also become the anchor or springboard for our public selves; in fact, it is vital for shaping the way we present ourselves to others. Thus, when the self seeks to become an actor in the public sphere, at a certain point its multivocal, inner conversation must arrive at one voice with a judgment, an argument, a *Doxa* (see below); its public speech must be devoid of contradiction, confusion, or incoherence.

The meaning of the Greek word *Doxa*, notes Arendt, is a reasoned opinion that does not presume to be based on external and universal truth but, rather, articulates the manner in which a self, from its unique perspective, grasps and understands the shared reality. Doxa does not connote relativism; rather, it reflects a coherent interpretation of the world from one perspective within it, expressing the belief both in the existence of a shared reality and in a singular viewpoint that interprets this reality. Doxa is an attempt to form my own vista and to express it in such a way that its truth value and sincerity are evident to all – without denying the truth value of other arguments and alternative narratives. In its journey from the internal life of the self to the public world of the citizen, then, thought's search for meaning is increasingly complemented by the search for this type of truth. Internal contradiction and dogmatic positions are fatal for this project, since they signify my inability to explain to myself and others the manner in which the world opens itself toward me. For Arendt, the lack of mental coherence and the laziness of mind underlying a contradiction or an unreasoned opinion mean that I am not fulfilling my role as citizen as well as I should.

Socrates is again illustrative: Philosophy, in his vision, is a conversation among friends, presupposing an equality of and openness to all participants; its main end is confined to the human measure, to clarifying to ourselves and our peers who we are and what our Doxa is. The Socratic conversation renders a prejudice, an uncritical conviction, into an articulate argument with an internal logic, thereby fostering a correspondence of thought and action, words and deeds. Thinking, as a practice of questions and answers within the realm of words, ripens the self (unintentionally perhaps) for political life: It provokes the formation of consciousness and conscience, of an ethical self-recognition without which no significant entry into a more public life is possible. The Socratic way of life, as Arendt understands it, bridges the internal conversation stemming from a need to think with the political language of citizenship and the need to act. (Socrates was, in this sense, a political philosopher.) In fact, Arendt claims, in the ancient Greek language, Doxa does not mean merely *opinion*; it also implies prestige and having a good name, thereby integrating beliefs and arguments with their practical consequences. When uttered in the public sphere, my opinions could become a rhetorical act with political import, earning me a certain position in my community – depending on the content of my arguments, the manner in which they were articulated, the timing and context of their expression, and especially the way they affected others and thus the world.

Language may spring from probing thought, but it may end with perilous political action. At a certain juncture, the aimless and wondering thought of the spectator may meet the political world and turn speech into deeds, rhetoric into collective action. This juncture is especially called for in times of danger; without attending to the political during these times, thought will lose its standing and relevance and will endanger the conditions necessary for its own weight and blossoming. "When everybody is swept away unthinkingly by what everybody else does and believes in, those who think are drawn out of hiding because their refusal to join in is conspicuous and thereby becomes a kind of action," writes Arendt. "In such emergencies, it turns out that the purging component of thinking (Socrates' midwifery, which brings out the implications of unexamined options and thereby destroys them – values, doctrines, theories, and even convictions) is political by implication."[8] Karl Jaspers (who, in contrast to Heidegger, boldly opposed the Nazi regime) represents, in Arendt's opinion, a more general phenomenon: When private words and thoughts become public – particularly when weighty matters are at stake – they may disclose the individual in unexpected ways and force him or her to confront people, worldviews, and even powerful regimes.

Arendt echoes Aristotle's claim in the *Rhetoric*: There is an inherent connection between the persuasive weight of words and the character of the speaker (ethos). While for Aristotle this use of words is mostly premeditated, for Arendt there is something profoundly unguarded, improvised, and spontaneous in our public expressions. Choice of words,

---

[8] Arendt, *The Life of the Mind*, p. 192.

constructed arguments, tone, and style may be used sometimes as a camouflage, but ultimately public speech discloses who we are. This speech tends to strip the self naked like nothing else could; in unsettled times, this exposure is even more pronounced. The chair I produced, the rules I followed, the tasks I performed, the building I constructed – these say little about me; they would add up to an impoverished narrative of selfhood. In contrast, public words, in themselves and as giving meaning to our actions, may disclose the individual and answer the question of who one is, what one is loyal to, what one finds tolerable and intolerable or just and unjust, and what risks one is willing to take in upholding certain positions. *The political sphere forces upon us unexpected circumstances that belie an attempt to hide behind conventions*: It "reveals" who we are because it calls for new, individual responses to an ever-changing environment (especially in modernity), rending precedents only partially helpful and inviting us to suggest and model something novel in the world. More generally, language plays a critical role in Arendt's vision of political action as a second birth and a new beginning, less because it expresses our pregiven distinction and difference than because it allows the formation of this distinction and plurality. [9]

Arendt's celebration of thought is not without shortcomings. She fails, for example, to give an adequate account of the relation of thought to character and of thought to emotions, [10] and one wonders if her picture of the

---

[9] Arendt explains, "If action as beginning corresponds to the fact of birth, if it is the actualization of the human condition of natality, then speech corresponds to the fact of distinctness and is the actualization of the human condition of plurality, that is, of living as a distinct and unique being among equals." See Hannah Arendt, *The Human Condition* (Chicago: University of Chicago Press, 1958), p. 178.

[10] Arendt seems to indicate that thought is predominant in shaping character, but does not systematically explicate such a bold view. Equally troubling, she refuses to contemplate the role of human emotions in shaping the way we think, speak, and act in the world. "Whatever the passions and emotions may be," she writes, "and whatever their true connection with thought and reason, they certainly are located in the human heart, and not only is the human heart a place of darkness, which, with certainty, no human eye can penetrate; the qualities of the heart need darkness and protection against the light of the public to grow and to remain what they are meant to be, innermost motives which are not for public display." See Hannah Arendt, *On Revolution* (London: Penguin, 1990), pp. 95–6. (I owe this quotation to Rolando Vazquez, "Thinking the Event with Hannah Arendt," *European Journal of Social Theory* 9, no. 1 [2006]: 4–5.)

It is not clear how such a position would have made poetry possible at all. Worse, by suggesting a dichotomy between the public potential of thought, on the one hand, and the eternally hidden and impenetrable realm of emotions, on the other, Arendt risks rendering decisive human motivations unintelligible, and political action sterile and radically different from the way it appears in the world. If Bialik was wrong in presenting inner conversation as based solely on emotions and desire for poetic expression, Arendt presents an equally one-dimensional and distorted picture of this conversation

self is plausible.[11] Nevertheless, her conception of language is important in claiming that the proper cultivation of democratic language involves attention to the role played by both the inner language of thought and the external, public language. (As noted, these languages complement each other: The plurality of voices within the self and the internal friendship among them foster plurality and companionship within the political community. The inner dialogue of thought fosters self-understanding and self-formation, and these in turn produce a whole individual who could express a distinct Doxa in the public sphere.) Without faith in the reality established by words, in their weight and substance, neither the inner conversation that illuminates the self for itself and narrates the world nor the formation of a political community as a part of that world would be possible. Words establish the world as a reality for me while establishing me as a reality for the (political) world.

The most important point, perhaps, is that Arendt pictures the essence of language as residing in its capacity to divulge: Language is primarily about revealing the world to me through the unsettling of ordinary linguistic conventions and clichés; it allows the unearthing of myself for myself through distinct vocabulary and conversation, and the exposure of myself to others in the political sphere through speech and deeds. *Words, for Arendt, involve a continuous movement of exposure, a course that ties the private to the public and inner language to public language.* The fundamental "drive" of language, which any viable democracy must embrace and cultivate (and that other types of regimes strive to suppress), is its power to reveal existing human reality and to reinvigorate this reality through this ongoing exposure. As Arendt states in a well-known essay, "Truth and Politics": "[N]o human world destined to outlast the short life span of mortals within it will ever be able to survive without men willing to do what Herodotus was the first to undertake consciously – namely ... to say what is."[12]

---

in which the place of emotions in human conversation remains hidden and unaccounted for. A rich human conversation, internal and public, must and in fact does contain both thought and emotions, reflection and expression.

[11] Arendt's picture of the inner dialogue within the self does not address the fact that most often this conversation is not very friendly, but is rather saturated with inner conflict and strife (as exemplified by the Freudian vista, whereby the ongoing dialogue between the ego and superego is about *modus vivendi*, not friendship). Moreover (as discussed in the following), Arendt unconvincingly presents the conversation within the self as occurring in words that owe little to history and tradition, as if the self could be understood as insulated from its situatedness.

[12] Hannah Arendt, "Truth and Politics," in *The Portable Hannah Arendt* (London: Penguin, 2000), p. 546.

II. DEMOCRATIC LANGUAGE AND TRADITION

I noted earlier (see Chapter 4), that Bialik offered a very different view of language: It is a veil that covers Tohu and the abyss; its basic instinct is concealment, not revealment. One could also reasonably argue that Bialik understood the revived Hebrew in this same light: as concealing the existential void that had appeared in the life of the new Jew who had suddenly become secular, socially and culturally alienated from his and her country of origin, a soil-bound pioneer in a distant country. Later (and with no direct connection to Bialik; see Chapter 4) the necessity of coping with unpleasant facts concerning the Arab-Israeli conflict may have fostered this concealing function of Hebrew: The official language transformed the native place-names and rewrote the map (revealing, as it were, the supposed original Hebraic names that had been buried), and too often it described very ambiguously the full meaning of violent acts and events. (The key Palestinian term *Nakba*, which was introduced only in 2007 into the textbooks of Arab-Israeli schoolchildren, was removed again by the government in 2009.[13] It has never appeared in the textbooks of the vast majority of Jewish-Israeli schoolchildren.) One wonders whether the dominant view of the Hebrew language as a "national treasure" (which was first advanced by Ahad Ha'am), and as the "cultural cement" of the people (as Ben-Gurion saw it), hindered (most) Hebrew speakers from performing the unveiling role that Arendt expected of language as such, and especially in the public sphere: When the language "belongs" to the collective and is seen as serving its ends (rather than inviting a "song of myself" to be written), it is difficult to use it in subversive ways and to challenge deep-seated, shared beliefs, narratives, and practices.

Democratic language demands that the individual be posited as an originator of valid truth about him- or herself and the world; this language, moreover, must support the individual's endeavor to open the world through fresh descriptions, narrations, metaphors. Yet, as we have seen previously, in the revived Hebrew language the place of the individual as the originator of truth remains problematic. This language had to overcome the traditional notion of Judaism, according to which truth is given to the believer, and does not originate with that person; the

---

[13] The education minister Gideon Sa'ar explained his decision by saying that there is no reason why the official curriculum should present the establishment of the State of Israel as a "catastrophe."

believer is an interpreter of texts, laws, and circumstances, and not the source of ultimate values and claims about the world. In Ahad Ha'am, the place of the individual is so diminished that his or her voice, at best, is subsumed within the unfolding Volksgeist; in any event, this voice is supposed to be concerned with the cultural life of the nation and its moral fabric – and only marginally with political affairs. In Bialik, who despite being a "national poet" represents a serious attempt to free the individual in relation to the collective, the expressive-aesthetic voice of the singular person is celebrated and is given proper significance; yet this voice seems to continue to pose the words that humans utter in relation to what is beyond them (Tohu instead of *Elohim*) as their chief, vivid conversation – and not the intracommunal one. And while for Arendt the inner dialogue of thought is the solid foundation for reasoned opinion in the public sphere, for a Doxa that would resonate with others, Bialik suggests a chasm between the two languages of human beings and sees the communicative language (which is necessary in the political sphere) as devouring words and thus thinning the substantiality of their speakers.

Yet Arendt's view of democratic language is devoid of any serious consideration of the issue of tradition, its potential and dangers, as far as language is concerned; after all, the meaning and power of the words we utter are not determined by us alone, but also by tradition and the customary uses of these words. While at times Arendt laments the destruction of tradition, at other times she sees this development as an opportunity. She writes, for example, that we are now able to "look upon the past with eyes undistracted by any tradition." She adds that

some past, not necessarily its essence, is … alive and present in every form of speech. But the point … is not the past but tradition, and the distinction between them. Tradition orders that past, hands it down [*tradere*], interprets it, omits, selects, and emphasizes according to a system of preestablished beliefs. If I say that no tradition can claim validity today, I do not say that the past is dead, but that we have no reliable guide through it anymore.[14]

Arendt recognizes that the past continues to live in our language but asserts that this past no longer presents us with clear distinctions between the positive and the negative, the orthodox and the heretical, the true

---

[14] Hannah Arendt, "Distinctions," *New York Review of Books* 13, no. 12, January 1, 1970. Elsewhere she repeats the same point: "The break in our tradition is now an accomplished fact. It is neither the result of anyone's deliberate choice, nor subject to further discussion." See her *Between Past and Future* (New York: Penguin, 1961), p. 26.

and the false.[15] What remain are fragments of words and thoughts that are evaluated in their own right, out of context: They no longer claim to be parts of a coherent narrative, one that possesses authority and accumulated wisdom.

Arendt thinks that Benjamin was correct in recognizing that the breakdown of tradition (European, German, and Jewish) was without remedy. He was also perceptive in suggesting that "the transmissibility of the past had been replaced by its citability"[16] – through quotations or expressions that must hold interest and originality in their own right in order to have any effect on the modern's mind. More generally (as we have seen in our discussion), both in *The Life of the Mind* and in *The Human Condition*, Arendt downplays the role of tradition in shaping language and, therefore, in shaping the modern individual's thought and action. Her commitment to new beginnings, natality, and revolution seems so profound, in fact, that it is precisely the breakdown of tradition that allows her to celebrate freedom of thought and of spontaneous, novel, human political action.

Zionists such as Ahad Ha'am and Bialik found this radical break with the language of tradition threatening and unacceptable. They realized (as the story in the opening pages of Chapter 4 demonstrates) that in the Zionist case, language is not simply "there," born hand in hand with the capacity to act, but in fact might lag behind the latter (deed and speech do not necessary rise together, as Arendt suggests). Ahad Ha'am and Bialik were concerned that without the language of tradition – properly cultivated and adapted to modern times – national identity would remain empty and superficial, marked by confusion and short of self-respect. Moreover, they seem to suggest that nothing is more dangerous *than a radical sense of potency and willfulness that lacks an equally potent language to check it,* than a people acting in the empty time of sundered history but lacking the reflexivity to use this freedom properly. They hoped for a Hebrew language that would gain at least part of its legitimacy and weight in virtue of its resonance with and inspiration by the vocabulary of the past – with its singular concepts, conventions, idioms, and names.

While Ahad Ha'am attempted to integrate tradition by presenting an uninterrupted continuity of the past and the present, one that allows the

---

[15] Hannah Arendt, "Introduction," in *Illuminations*, trans. Harry Zohn (New York: Schocken Books, 1968), p. 44.
[16] Ibid., p. 38.

"essence" of the Jewish nation to emerge, Bialik offered a more compelling vision. He did not think that tradition has an essence, but rather saw it as always shifting, each generation having somewhat different needs and concerns, values and goals. The main thing that should be guarded, then, is the "form" of tradition – mainly its vocabulary and manners of articulation – which each generation could creatively and playfully fill with contents streaming from its own heart. More specifically, for Bialik, the Jewish tradition is composed of the Halacha (law) and the Aggada (legends); both, he believes, should be viewed as great literary creations of the Jewish spirit. "The Halacha is an act of creation no less than the Aggada,"[17] he avers. These two elements of tradition are mixed in Jewish texts, and for good reason: They complement each other since both are aimed at the perfection of a just man,[18] and they display dialectic relations whereby in history "a live and healthy Halacha is a past or future Aggada, and vice versa." While in the Jewish tradition the two stand for concrete bodies of writing, they in fact represent two essential aspects of human existence that may have other manifestations as well. The Aggada represents the longings of the heart, the aspirations, the unbounded will, and the Halacha the point where these have been fashioned into detailed rules, sets of concrete obligations, actual social orders. "The Halacha," notes Bialik, "is in no event a repudiation of emotions, but their reining in."

Because the Halacha is presumably frozen in time, it could nowadays be considered distant, irrelevant, and foreign to those who hold nonreligious lives; in the age of secularization, the Aggada does not escape this fate either. If tradition is viewed as essentially the creation of God, and if it is beheld as a totality, we will not be able to relate it to our existence and circumstances. Only the anthropocentric and aesthetic perspective offers a way out of this alienation from the past, suggests Bialik. The "total artist ... that delves and imbibes from the depth of the great abyss in the nation's soul and the secrets of its life – such an artist, I say, will not be hindered in doing even in this material [the Halacha] great things, if only these things spring from his heart." The great achievements of the Jewish tradition, the aspiration to mold a moral person and to encompass everything, from minute rules of everyday life to uplifting spiritual

---

[17] All references are to Bialik's essay "Halacha and Aggada [Jewish Law and Legends]" (1917), at http://benyehuda.org/bialik/article06.html.

[18] For Bialik, the moral man is an ongoing "creation," which does not presuppose a core or an essence to be revealed.

prayers, are harvests of human inventiveness manifesting great imagination – and hence are near to us and open to fresh use.

This aestheticization of the religious-moral sphere also means that
tradition is no longer viewed only vertically but also horizontally, so to
speak: Great works of art do not become antiquated and anachronistic
but retain their capacity to speak and to move us across time. These
are the significant achievements of tradition. "The historical sense,"
writes T. S. Eliot, "involves a perception, not only of the pastness of the
past, but of its presence; the historical sense compels a man to write not
merely with his own generation in his bones but with a feeling that the
whole of the literature ... has a simultaneous existence and composes
a simultaneous order. This historical sense ... of the timeless and of
the temporal together, is what makes a writer traditional."[19] The different sculptures and paintings, as it were, are spread before us, or rather
alongside us; they are interrelated, presenting obvious references, secret
and open dialogues, a process of learning as well as freshness. These
works have no fixed hierarchy and the interpretation of their meaning
changes; they do not convey coherence of themes or values, or suggest,
when taken together, a certain "essence." In fact, as we have seen, Bialik
sees works of art (especially poetry), as springing from the need and
desire of humans to face Tohu: The chaos, the allure of the abyss, the
irrational, the destructive, the lurking death, and the awareness of our
finitude are all part of the forces animating the creation of tradition and
are expressed in its great literary works.

Surely this view of tradition is at odds with the way that most Jews
understood it in the past and is thus on shaky foundations; it is unclear to
what extent art can replace Revelation as the source of tradition. Thus,
the great project of Bialik is to achieve the nearness of tradition and its
presence in our lives primarily on the grounds of language; the latter is
elastic and flexible, being one step removed from the contents of tradition itself (but of course not divorced from it). As noted, he saw oft-used
words and idioms as empty shells that invite us to use them in creative
ways that breathe new life into them: The temporal distance between us
and the moment in which words were born or used in a certain way is an
invitation for creativity, for introducing our own self. Words house the
souls of those who preceded us and invite us to take shelter, too. Because

---

[19] T. S. Eliot, "Tradition and Individual Talent," in *Twentieth Century Literary Criticism: A Reader*, ed. David Lodge (London: Longman, 1972), p. 71.

they house past life they are essentially alive, even if dormant; our relation to them is like I to Thou, soul to soul, a relationship of conversation.
Not to take the vocabulary that has been handed down to us earnestly is
not to take the lives of those who preceded us seriously, and not to take
these lives seriously diminishes, among other things, our own lives and
our descriptions of them.

"The Ideal of Hebrew speech," writes Bialik, "should not be to render speech profane, but [to preserve] its holiness.... We must create and
beget within the language, *and elevate it into a holy speech.*"[20] This
notion of infusing the profane with the holy does not mean preserving
the theological meaning of words (as Scholem feared), but rather finding individual-innovative ways to animate preexisting words and expressions and rendering our speech powerful and meaningful. It aims to
achieve precisely that solid ground for modern Hebrew that I mentioned
at the beginning of the previous chapter as this language's greatest challenge – a place between the weight of transcendental origin and the sense
of contemporary concoction, of "a project." Yet for Bialik, as noted, this
elevation of the language does not concern the public sphere.

Bialik's understanding of the relation of contemporary speakers to a
given vocabulary is richer than the attempts of crude revolutionaries to
free political actors from the historical weight of words altogether, and
it does not abandon the language of tradition to those who preserve
their faith and employ this language in sometimes disastrous ways (while
advancing their Messianic visions). He believes there is enough room
for playfulness and flexibility in interpretation, so that we need neither
become the hostages of tradition nor tumble into the abyss of an artificial language. The language user may retrieve a forgotten meaning and
connotation, or boldly march into a new semantic field while expanding
the range of language. "The superior creator," writes Bialik, "first esti-
mates and grasps the entire power and scope of language – to its most
distant regions – and if he steps outside the existing boundaries of language, this step is also the expansion of these boundaries as he moves."[21]
Poetry and speech, then, allow innovation within a milieu, authenticity
within preexisting context. As mentioned, in order to fulfill this coming together, the poet must be immersed in tradition and be familiar
with the various uses of words and phrases in history: A simple word

[20] *Devarim*, vol. 2, p. 129.
[21] Bialik, "Chevlei lashon," p. 12.

combination in Hebrew can send one on a journey of a few thousand years' worth of allusions and associations. (To be sure, the use of old words will not always be successful, and sometimes it may seem forced, inexact, and burdened with excessive pathos – as in fact often happened in modern Hebrew, especially in the early days. See my discussion of Ben-Gurion and the Bible that follows).

Meaningful individuality and distinctiveness, Bialik believes, is an integral part of Judaism, and commenced with the Jewish-Spanish poets and philosophers in the medieval period. In line with this birth, *individuality in Judaism is married to language*: No significant individuality can exist if it is not articulated, and "the spirit of man always comes to a complete union with the spirit of his language."[22] Tradition, then, is the vast treasure of clay with which we can play, and the image-creating individual is the "king and master of language."[23] The latter individual, instead of being ensnared in the language that has been handed to him (as Scholem thought might happen) bends its rules and expands its boundaries, introduces innovations in its syntax and grammar, vocabulary and semantics – but out of knowledge, not out of superficiality and ignorance. Bialik's greatest legacy, perhaps, is that the two poles that seem to pull modern Jews apart – tradition and individuality – actually complement each other.

Bialik, we have seen, failed to join this complex and rich picture concerning the relation between the individual speaker and tradition with a viable notion of democracy. His vision of speech as essentially concealing and shielding does not foster democracy's need to let factual truth emerge publicly, or communal shared convictions and self-image to be questioned and challenged despite the embarrassment this may bring about. Later Israeli poets addressed this lack. In what is likely a direct reference to "Revealment and Concealment in Language," the greatest post-Independence Israeli poet, Yehuda Amichai, seems to both agree and disagree with Bialik: "What has been left to us? We must begin from scratch. We use utensils from the past – words, idioms, thoughts, and pictures – and hold onto them, just the way survivors of a drowning ship clutch the shipwrecks." Yet in contrast to Bialik, Amichai adds that "words no longer serve as a shield behind which one can do other things. Words are not a screen, or clouds that hide action and performance.... [W]ords are a new beginning with stones from the past. And the more

---

[22] Ibid., p. 9
[23] Ibid., p. 11.

tiny and broken these stones are, the stronger the new building will eventually become."[24] Amichai, whose poetry contains many allusions to the
Jewish tradition (for example, he famously wrote in reference to "El
male rachamim" [God full of mercy], a Jewish burial prayer, that "If
God was not full of mercy, Mercy would have been in the world, Not
just in Him") shares Bialik's general fascination with the ancient words
and celebrates the playfulness and creativity they allow. But his poetry
represents a break with the notion of the "we" and the taken-for-granted
collective that demands sacrifice and unity. Amichai calls on his generation to combine intense involvement with social reality with the use
of language in subversive ways that shake taken-for-granted beliefs and
that sustain doubt and critical distance.

Amichai and his generation were also less inclined to feel themselves
revolutionary creators, the "masters" of the language, as Bialik put it,
and the critical stance of the poet in relation to society is also joined in
later Israeli poetry with a more humble position generally and in regard
to tradition specifically. After all, each word belongs to an ocean of contexts and meanings, and hence any utterance is also an act of surrender,
of letting go of semantic control; while trying to express ourselves, we
are being led elsewhere despite ourselves. To say that we are a part of
tradition means that we can establish ourselves as selves only through
language, that this language is not our individual creation, that the more
language-savvy we are the more capable we are in using it to articulate
ourselves imaginatively and authentically – but that even then we are
always relegated to the status of participants in a conversation that is
both anterior and posterior to us. To be a historical being, or "to be
historically, means that knowledge of oneself can never be complete,"[25]
partly because the meanings of the descriptions we use to fathom ourselves and the world transcend us.

Of course, Israeli poetry has changed its character since Bialik's
days, but his understanding of poetry's place in the evolving Hebrew
culture seems to have been somewhat prophetic (and his pessimism
exaggerated).[26] One of my central arguments previously has been that

---

[24] Yehuda Amichai, "Dorot ba'aretz, [Generations in the Land]" (May 1968) in *We Hereby
Declare*, ed. Anita Shapira (Tel Aviv: Dvir, 2008), p. 142.

[25] Gadamar, *Truth and Method*, p. 302

[26] Bialik was wrong in his assessment regarding the future of Hebrew, which today flour-
ishes (among certain groups at least) in terms of the number of speakers, the variety of
works written in Hebrew, the range of vocabulary, the numbers of translations from
Hebrew to other languages, etc. I thank Professor Moshe Florentin for making this point
to me. (See also note 75 in Chapter 4).

in Zionism, language lost the constitutive role it had had in Jewish tradition and in the life of Diaspora Jews, and that this national movement increasingly prized "doing" and the transformation of the phenomenal world over the creation of a shared language-based world. Yet to the extent that language was celebrated in Zionism and Israeli society, it was first and foremost the poetic language that achieved this status. To be sure, the distinction between poetic language and political language is not always clear (and, as I have argued, Bialik was wrong in assuming a deep gulf between them); in Israel's history there is at least one important case – that of Nathan Alterman and his famous column "Hator hashevi'i" – in which some of the most important political statements have been formulated by a leading poet who wrote in a poetic language about current events. However, even Alterman's political stature was based on the fact that he was an important and influential poet, and not a politician writing poetry.

Indeed, while there were also impressive writers such as Chaim Hazaz, Moshe Shamir, Yizhar Smilansky, and of course Shmuel Yosef Agnon who expanded the range of Hebrew early on, the highest cultural achievement of the Jewish national revival project in Palestine has been its poetry. Some of these poets (in addition to Alterman and Amichai) may be familiar: David Avidan, Uri Zvi Greenberg, Chaim Gouri, Leah Goldberg, Rachel Bluwstein, Dahlia Ravikovitch, Nathan Zach, Avraham Shlonsky, Shaul Tchernichovsky, Yona Wallach, Agi Mishol, T. Carmi – the list goes on. These poets wrote works at the highest level and have been recognized both in Israel and in the international world of letters. Generally speaking, poetry has been admired in Israel, and many poems have been turned into popular songs, blurring the borders between high and low culture (as epitomized perhaps in the person of the poet-singer Meir Ariel). Some of the poems written in Hebrew since the late nineteenth century have become perhaps the most significant canon of Israel (e.g., Alterman's "Magash hakesef," Amichai's "Elohim merahem al yaldei hagan," Gouri's "Hare'ut," Shemer's "Yerushalayim shel zahav," Rachel's "Rak al atzmi," Pagis's "Katuv be'iparon bekaron hatum").These poems (and many others) are widely familiar; they are considered to be eloquently articulating dimensions of the Israeli (and Jewish) experience, they are taught in schools and recited in public ceremonies, and they serve as shared points of reference (at least, this was true in the past, before the fragmentation of Israeli society took hold).

To be sure, poets everywhere – from Byron to Yeats, from Mickiewicz to D'Annunzio – have been involved in the formation of national movements; Herder, the "father" of cultural nationalism, believed that poetry is the essential fountain of national identity, best expressing the collective's vitality, its experiences and aspirations.[27] But in addition to the general importance of poetry for national movements that has evolved since the French Revolution, there seem to be particular reasons for its central position in Israeli culture.

First, the high status of poetry in Zionism could be explained in light of the significant place of poetry in Jewish tradition, commencing with biblical poems, such as the Song of Deborah and the Psalms, and continuing with the Piyutim, medieval Jewish poetry, Hazanut, Hasidic Nigunim, and more.[28] Second, poetry has been able to acquire its influence in modern Hebrew culture in part because it often serves as a bridge between the present and the ancient past. Certain words, symbols, and phrases from the old texts economically evoke a whole avalanche of connotations and meanings that embody the semicyclical temporal imagination that has been so central to Zionism. Poetry could best point to unseen connections between the now and moments from distant eras, thus exploring the almost erotic attraction between events, predicaments, or pictures that are separated by temporal oceans (see my discussion about the semicyclical temporal imagination in Chapter 1).

Third, the privileged place of poetry in Israel also springs from a poetic aspect of the early Zionist self. While the mentality of building and the notion of using rational plans to shape reality were important to Zionism, for Bialik (as for Scholem and Buber, among others), Zionism was first and foremost a project of the heart. Poetry was the prime echo of this heart and its fuel: It reflected the aesthetic dimension of Zionism and its belief in making something out of nothing, in taking history as raw material to be crafted through the creative imagination, in shaping a *distinct* and *enchanted* world to which one could be attached. As the poem exemplifies the notion that words can be assembled to convey something singular that did not exist before and that was not goaded into being by necessity or causality – a sheer display of human freedom and

---

[27] See Revital Amiran, "Cultural Nationalism and the Formulation of the Political: Reflections on the Jewish National Movement," forthcoming.

[28] Furthermore, some of the Jewish prayers, as well as the Book of Psalms itself, contain a strong expressive element that speaks to the individual's heart. In other words, both in terms of genre and to some extent content, modern Hebrew poetry has deep roots in Jewish culture that contributed to its acceptance and popularity (although concern with the law and a rational approach to religion generally have been the dominant facet of Judaism).

creativity – so the whole Zionist experience is evidence of this absence of necessity that operates in human affairs generally and in politics in particular.

There is simply no political text that has anything resembling the status of poetry, as noted in Chapter 4. Which texts can become canonical? Most often constitutions or legal documents, declarations of independence or of rights, speeches by leaders and public figures, certain letters and books. But in the Israeli public sphere one rarely hears "as was written in our Declaration of Independence"; "as X once said in her speech on the eve of that defining moment" is even less likely. It is impossible to hear, of course, "as is written in our Constitution." This lack of a political canon in Israel is odd since there have certainly been the occasions to develop such a canon and the public need to use it. Some (singular) political texts acquire canonical status especially after a revolution when there is a need to establish and legitimize a new order or in the aftermath of a war, when a great challenge faces the nation, or when fragmentation of society looms and it needs to redefine itself in a way that appeals to its different parts.[29] All of these apply to the State of Israel, but they did not lead to the canonization of texts. To the extent that there is such a canon in Israel, it is perhaps poems such as Alterman's "Magash hakesef" that serve in this function (and even then, only for a part of the Jewish community); one can hardly say, however, that poems can offer a coherent vision or provide an elaborate argument.

More specifically, political canons are important since they articulate shared goals and values, sift the past for what is significant and should live on, identify major problems and things to be overcome, define or invent shared layers of identity and the desired relations among the various groups in society, elevate the image of the political community and help it celebrate itself, specify the rules and procedures citizens would like to abide by. Political canonical texts are critical, moreover, because they allow a community to develop a rich culture of interpretation and argumentation, and to address conflicts through words rather than through other means; surely the Jewish culture made this way of resolving internal conflicts and tensions one of its distinguishing marks. But in Israel, there are no shared texts that remain alive in the citizens' memory and are seen as their own, texts that serve as established anchors of

---

[29] My discussion of political canons is greatly helped by Yaeli Elam, "Deciphering Political Canonical Texts: A Promise to Be Experienced," Master's thesis, Tel Aviv University, 2007.

reference – and which citizens approach when they attempt to understand not only the past but also the challenges of the present and what should be done in the future.

To be more precise, there was an attempt, during the first decades after Independence, to use the Bible in such a manner. The Bible (in contrast to the Talmud) inspired many among the (predominantly secular) generation that established the state: For them, it was a history book, a geography guide, a mediator in forming their bond to the land, a source-book for speech. Ben-Gurion, who understood and supported this unique role of the Bible, wanted to go one step further and establish the Bible as a political canon. He realized that there was a need to find a text that would be appealing to the Jewish immigrants from Arab countries and to the vast number of immigrants who came to Palestine after World War II (who were not, for the most part, committed Zionists), and that would underscore the distinction between Israel and the Diaspora. His use of the Bible was not religiously motivated, and his Messianic language was not aimed at achieving, through political means, Messianic time here and now; he mainly saw the Bible as the spiritual, historical, and political source of the nation (echoing what Gandhi attempted to do with the *Arthaśāstra*),[30] one that is shared by all Jews and could provide a moral framework that transcends the state.[31] Setting aside more or less the entire Jewish tradition except the Bible, as well as ignoring the meta-historical and metaphysical implications of the terms he used, Ben-Gurion (after 1948, and particularly after 1956) began to speak and write about the Messianic mission of the State of Israel as it was articulated by the prophets, a mission that included values such as "you shall love your neighbor as yourself," and that demanded that Israel become an exemplary people, society, and polity (*am segula*, and *or lagoyim*). Ben-Gurion, however, also used the Bible instrumentally, describing mundane political events of the labor movement as resonating with sublime biblical moments, as well as suggesting, for example, that the new IDF air force and navy were fulfilling prophecies articulated in the ancient texts.[32]

Yet this extensive attempt to use the Bible as a canonical text for political and social purposes failed completely. To begin with, many

---

[30] See Anthony J. Parel, "Gandhi and the Emergence of the Modern Indian Political Canon," *Review of Politics* 70 (2008): 40–63.

[31] See on this point Nir Kedar, *Mamlakhtiyut* (Jerusalem: Yad Izhak Ben-Zvi, 2009), Chap. 6 (in Hebrew).

[32] See Anita Shapira, *New Jews, Old Jews*, Chap. 9, and Naomi Mandel-Levy, "Ancient Language in a New Reality," Ph.D. diss., Hebrew University, 2009, Chap. 3.

intellectuals at the time (especially those from the Hebrew University) feared the possible union of the authoritative political style of Ben-Gurion, his military activism, and his call for strong republican values, on the one hand, with a Messianic vision whose sources are metaphysical and eternal, a vision not determined by the needs and goals of the living, on the other. But the biblical jargon used by Ben-Gurion and his followers also felt hopelessly artificial and forced: Its bombastic attempts to glorify the present ended up ridiculing current events (since the mundane present could never match the sublime source), it adopted an unacceptably selective approach to Judaism, and it was overly motivated by instrumental and immediate needs. The crude notion that the potent and resonating words of the Bible could be used to boost the language of the public sphere only exposed the linguistic abyss facing this sphere. In short, this experiment left no lasting marks on Israeli political discourse (although religious Zionists, without connection to Ben-Gurion, have always used it).

Without shared, elevated and taken-for-granted texts and vocabulary, the Israeli public sphere lacks the foundation necessary for developing debates and deliberations: In discussing the fate of the occupied territories, for example, some talk about divine rights and some about security concerns, some about economic interests and some about identity and soil, some about the meaning of the Holocaust as involving Jews' commitment to never harm others and some about never exposing the Jews again to any security threats, some about the human rights of Palestinians as individuals and some about their collective rights (or lack thereof) as a nation. And so on. The most important debate in Israel has been stalled for so many years partly because there are no agreed-upon foundations on which to conduct this debate. The demarcating line between welcomed plurality of thought and paralyzing cacophony probably cannot be defined – but it is evident once you see it.

In the last two chapters, I have attempted to explore what would have been needed to grant language a viable place in the Israeli public sphere, a democratic language that would not be conceived of as artificial, arbitrary, and self-serving, on the one hand, but neither chained to the metaphysical and theological meanings permeating Hebrew, on the other. I have mentioned a few features of this type of democratic language and a few premises that should be attached to it (for example, that it should be committed toward ongoing, truthful revealment of self and the world with less fear of the abysses it might disclose; that it should help deepen the plurality of citizens once conceived of as builders, and assist the formation of engaged, yet "thinking" individuals; that speakers should be seen as legitimate originators of truth statements and be released from the need to be measured in relation to the absolute, God-given truth; that in terms of style this language should be more inspired by poetic and rhetorical modes of expression; that it should include certain political canons; and more. Most of all, however, I pointed to the importance of tradition as an invaluable source of linguistic richness, as well as a world of meanings and experiences attached to words, expressions, idioms. Following Bialik, I argued that tradition should be viewed aesthetically and playfully and be salvaged from the monopoly of religious interpretation of it.)

Yes, there is always the danger that opening ourselves to tradition – and allowing it a greater place in shaping who we are and the political world we share – will lead to growing conservatism and religiosity, tribalism and intolerance. Non-Jews could be further excluded from a political sphere dominated by a Hebrew language that strengthens its bond to tradition. These are valid concerns, especially in Israel today: It seems that when traditions (Jewish as well as Islamic) are left exclusively to believers, some of these groups interpret them in an increasingly extreme and narrow fashion and in a way that tends to support nationalist worldviews. Yet in the case of Judaism and Israel, the dialogue with tradition could and also does lead elsewhere: to the marriage of Judaism with the liberalism and cosmopolitanism of the nineteenth century, to the formation of strong individuality through the language of medieval Judaism, to the text-based and language-savvy culture that emerged since the age of the Mishnah and Talmud, and so on.

It is, of course, essential that the State of Israel becomes a bilingual state so that mutually respectful conversation between Arabs and Jews becomes possible in everything from daily life to the highest human concerns, and so that the use of one language will not be seen as an exclusion of the other. But on a more profound level, it is wrong to assume that the neglect of a dialogue with one's past necessarily leads to a better dialogue with the others with whom one shares the present, that a vertical, culture-specific dialogue somehow excludes a horizontal, cross-cultural one. If we have to choose between a mode of living with others (Jews and non-Jews, believers and nonbelievers) that is based on the narrowest common dominator agreed upon through negotiations, and thereby accept an impoverished public sphere (and perhaps impoverished notions of selfhood and friendship, too), or a mode of living that is based on the assumption that there should be "more of us," that our cultural horizons

PHOTO 17. Jewish and Arab workers marching in the May Day parade in Ramle. Photo by Zoltan Kluger, May 1, 1949. Courtesy of the Government Press Office, Israel.

should become ever more far-reaching and our self-understanding ever richer, but precisely because it is richer and more encompassing it also allows greater possibilities for genuine conversation and agreement with others – then it seems to me that the latter option is vastly preferable.[33]

---

[33] For the distinction between negotiation and conversation, ad hoc and superficial agreements as opposed to more genuine and lasting ones, see Charles Blattberg, *Shall We Dance? A Patriotic Politics for Canada* (Montreal: McGill-Queen's University Press, 2003), p. 32.

Conclusion

Sabbath

Here, where this
tree is standing, we
were like dreamers;
in this spot where
the tree is standing,
sheep roamed, and
black goats.
Now this tree
is standing here,
and in the house
opposite, the
candles are
being lit.

B.

I went to seek the
stone's forgiveness:
Soon a gray house
will be raised here,
and for many years
this place will be
merely a wasteland of
debris and newspaper
fragments.
Who will recognize
you, my fair
mountains?
Among shabby shoes
and piles of rubble
boys are wandering
barefoot.

C.

The human being must
dwell, the human being
must dwell somewhere
or other; even in a very
ugly house the human
being must dwell –
with a roof and a floor
and a window, since
where else would a
human being dwell?
That is what a stone
said to me in the
mountains; a mute
stone spoke, and I
bowed my head.

"My Poem about Stones [*Shiri al haavanim*]," Leah Goldberg

Human beings must dwell somewhere or other, writes Goldberg, and
every human being has the right to have a place to call home – not a right
for a convenient or beautiful home, or for one expressing our taste and
vision, but for a simple, even ugly home that satisfies basic human needs.
"Right" is not the correct word perhaps, since even before one is legally

or politically entitled to dwell, the world as such – including the stone, that symbol of muteness and hardness – recognizes the human need to dwell as natural and prior to the norms we form with others. This poem, which proceeds from the present to the past, ends on an optimistic note: Eventually Sabbath, the day of rest and completion, will arrive, candles will be seen in the windows, and the wounds will heal.[1] But prior to that stage, it is acknowledged that dwelling has a dual, terrible price that the initial dreamers do not see: the tangible price of the mountains and the landscape, which have been disfigured by the violence of building and are blemished with the waste created by inattentive human action; and a hidden human price (not spoken of directly in the poem) since not only are the goats and sheep gone but the shepherd is, too. One wonders if it is his or her children who are wandering barefoot among the piles of rubble. Yet before returning to this fateful meeting of builders with mountains and goats, of new dwellings and stubborn rubble, we should recall the moment when a unique political movement was born far away from the place that Goldberg's poem seems to describe.

To understand this novelty of Zionism, we must understand its context. The breakdown of nineteenth-century conceptions of order and purpose in history – especially of the future-oriented, temporal imagination of incessant progress – raised various concerns among European thinkers. Max Weber, for example, believed that the lack of an overarching scheme that ruled human events meant that nothing could divert modernity from its destructive, dehumanizing track. The precise problem, in his view, was not the amorphous nature of history per se but the fact that moderns have established "life-orders" that dominate them and are immune to change; the actual conditions of life and institutions were the problem, not the ontological structure of history. In the past, Weber seems to suggest, the openness of history granted humans the ability to introduce radical transformations solely by the power of their beliefs and actions; prophets (such as Buddha, Moses, Jesus, and Muhammad), in particular, were able to steer history in novel directions by addressing human spiritual and emotional needs. But the last great religious revolution in the Occident (by Luther and Calvin) spawned unpredictable outcomes that put the human capacity for renewal in jeopardy. The Protestant worldview and its accompanying ethics helped generate social institutions, such as market capitalism and bureaucratic mass organizations, which became entrenched and uncontrollable. Instrumental

---

[1] I am indebted to Elisheva Hacohen for clarifying this point.

rationality increasingly threatens to level individual normative commitments, functional practices work to shape people to fit external necessities, and disciplinary techniques erode their perception of themselves as independent beings responsible for their convictions and deportment. Since, in Weber's view, there was and is no meaningful, benign narrative underlying historical time, he found it unlikely that the new type of person, the narrow professional, or *Fachmann*, would be able to break free from the overbearing, rationalized institutions of modernity. For Weber, history might in theory be malleable and undefined, but the reflective mind at the dawn of the twentieth century should have recognized – if this mind was courageous and mature enough – that, in practice, history was locked into an unstoppable course.[2]

Zionism emerged as the antithesis of this "entrapment" consciousness. Weber saw Western civilization as a ship without a pilot, steered by a chance event (the spiritual sea change of Protestantism) to the womb of the iron cage, where individuals remain baffled by the effects of their own creations. A small number of Jews, noticing the same undefined quality of history and its hazardous direction, chose to glorify the human capacity for self-assertion and mastery of events, to inject their lives with meaning and passion precisely by virtue of history's formlessness. Like Weber, Freud and other entrapment theorists – but for different reasons – they were skeptical about the ideology and practice of progress. Yet these early Zionists aimed to reappropriate the human capacity for a novel beginning, a capacity that Weber thought had been lost in the modern era.

In fact, we have seen that Zionism exemplifies the Promethean aspect of modernity, since in the rhetoric of this movement (in counterdistinction to the actual difficulties on the ground) the human imagination, will, and capacity for action are thought to be nearly boundless – truly unchained from the fetters of teleological and ontological interpretations of history. As we have seen in the first and second chapters, Zionists who began to act politically toward the end of the nineteenth century fully sensed the uniqueness of the moment: the freedom to choose a guiding temporal imagination in an era when no single imagination was hegemonic. Most of them embraced the semicyclical temporal imagination,

---

[2] I have explored these issues at length in the book *The Modern Self in the Labyrinth*. For a general overview of the changes in European historical and political consciousness around the turn of the century, see Jan Romein, *The Watershed of Two Eras: Europe in 1900* (Middletown, CT: Wesleyan University Press, 1978).

presenting the marriage of the present with the ancient Hebraic past as an opportunity that must be seized, rather than a necessity that must be obeyed. Yes, Zionists were often acting urgently and out of great concern for the fate of European Jews and later for the Jews living in Arab countries, and they had to deal with immense pressures both in Palestine and in relation to the world. But as we have seen time and again, for Zionist leaders and writers there was nothing stychic about the movement, and surely nothing forcing the choice of Eretz Israel. In acting boldly in the theater of history, however, the Zionists were also rebelling against their own tradition, in which the understanding that political action could radically alter human fate by itself had been absent for 1,800 years, ever since the Diaspora commenced. Perhaps the most important and enduring lesson of Zionism is indeed the possibility of human beings to turn – mostly through political action, with difficulty but also quite swiftly – despair into hope, powerlessness into dignified existence.

The Zionists' mistrust of the foundations of Jewish existence in the Diaspora (especially concerning the role of learning and language in shaping that existence), the genuine and urgent needs of an essentially "homeless" European Jews at the end of the nineteenth century, and the Zionists' sense of freedom in relation to (above all, teleological and organic) time led them to espouse a vision of politics as involving the "making" of a semipalpable, grand object – a national building (*binyan leumi*). This building and home incorporated everything: land, people, public institutions, culture, universities, language, and more. The downsides of this Zionist vision of politics were not only its holism (which, as we saw in Chapter 3, tended to exclude nongroup members) but also its instrumentalism, fixation on the ultimate ends, and the way it measured success.

Aristotle's distinctions might help elucidate this point: One could argue that leading figures in, and strands of, Zionism approached the formation of the Jewish State as involving *techne* (craft) and only marginally *phronesis* (practical reason). Aristotle suggests that "building is an art and is essentially a reasoned state of capacity to make"[3] (on this point, see also Chapter 3). Objects such as buildings, observes Aristotle,

---

[3] Aristotle, "Nicomachean Ethics," in *The Complete Works of Aristotle*, ed. J. Barnes, vol. 2 (Princeton, NJ: Princeton University Press, 1984), Book VI, p. 1799. I am also helped in this discussion by John Wall, "Phronesis as Poetic: Moral Creativity in Contemporary Aristotelianism," *Review of Metaphysics* 59 (December 2005): 313–31; and Gadamer, *Truth and Method*, pp. 312–24.

come into being not out of necessity, or by Nature, but rather by deliberate choice and the use of intelligence, and the activity they demand involves only a segment of time, a well-defined duration. In making them,[4] moreover, human beings act according to a clear, prior *eidos*, or image, they have in their minds and use a more or less preexisting body of knowledge about how to make them. In principle at least, the knowledge of how to make a building can be complete even before the first brick has been put in place. Both the way of achieving the end and especially the end itself are not dependent on circumstances and specific situations; the historical and evolving aspect of human existence is not relevant here. In making objects, suggests Aristotle, humans perceive raw materials instrumentally and as morally neutral resources, and are concerned especially with the final outcome – less with the path of getting there. Whether the floor is laid immediately after the foundations or only after the roof is completed, whether we use one method of construction or another, these things do not change the quality of the building as long as the final outcome remains true to the architectonic design. Finally, making is an activity that leaves something tangible behind, something that has a beginning and an ending determined by will, and that is separated from us even if it is in some way an expression of us. (Social Zionists, as noted, denied this separation of subject and object and the merely instrumental approach to building in general.)

Yet Aristotle notes that while "making has an end other than itself, action does not; for good action itself is its end."[5] We build houses in order to have shelter and feel we have a place of our own on this earth; in other words, we seek a good that is external to the building activity itself and view (or should view) this activity chiefly in terms of the other purposes it fulfils. Construction itself, because of the qualities it requires us to develop – ones that come at the expense of developing higher qualities – has something servile about it. But in moral-political action (praxis), to act well (say, in a courageous way) is an end in and of itself, although it could also bring us some external good (such as reputation). In moral-political action there is also a given end – achieving what we deem to be the good moral life (the life of the active and virtuous citizen in a polis, for example); yet here not only is nothing tangible

---

[4] The relevant Aristotelian term here is *poiesis*, which means to create something that lasts in the world and whose aim is beyond the activity of producing itself.

[5] "Nicomachean Ethics," p. 1800. I am helped here by H. G. Gadamer, "The Problem of Historical Consciousness," in *Interpretive Social Sciences: A Reader*, ed. P. Rabinow and W. Sullivan (Berkeley: University of California Press, 1979), pp. 137–45.

being "produced" but the means and path taken cannot be separated from the end as well. To act justly in each situation we come across is an end in itself and an exercise of an important human capacity, *as well as* a step in shaping a person toward becoming a good citizen; hence, the particular or singular action and the overarching end are inseparable. One cannot be expected to be civically courageous if the course of life displays the opposite characteristics. For Aristotle, our histories do not define us, but they are highly significant in shaping us and our ethos, and we are formed by the way in which we choose to interact with others throughout our lives.

This is why, as Gadamer notes, ongoing reflection and heightened awareness is needed not only concerning the ends of life but also with respect to the means and route leading to the accomplishment of these ends; the good moral-political person will therefore need to acquire a certain distance from the ultimate ends that were set in advance – so that he or she would be able to dispassionately evaluate the moral meaning of the means as well. Moreover, because moral and political action demands our finding the right course of action and for the right reasons in specific, mostly singular, and ever-changing circumstances, our vision of the good life is likely to be modified along the way (what it means to be a good citizen is not fixed in advance, once and for all). In contrast to the static nature of architectonic plans, as human beings we continuously revise and redefine ourselves and our goals, partly due to changes in circumstances in the world and in others inhabiting our environment, partly due to changes in ourselves. Finally, and as writers such as C. Taylor, H. G. Gadamer, and H. Arendt note, in order to be able to respond properly to this changeability and open-endedness of human affairs, we need to develop a nuanced and rich use of language so that we would be able to describe situations adequately, make the relevant distinctions among them, and consult others as well as our past about how to resolve ethical dilemmas (and ensure that our particular decisions cohere with our overall vision of the good).

Politics involves both craft and action, a search both for tangible, lasting ends and for preserving and cultivating a shared moral-cultural world; the differences between political communities is perhaps one of balance between these two facets of politics. It is difficult to generalize about a movement as complex and multifaceted as Zionism, but by and large it is fair to say that this movement conceived of politics mostly in terms of given ends to be achieved through correct planning and of things that need to be created and produced. This tendency had already begun with Herzl's *The Jewish State*. Not only is the final object – the state – boldly presented here (although there is nothing in reality to support this idea), but a considerable part of this short book is in fact a detailed plan about how to "construct" this state: acquiring lands, securing housing, establishing financial and government institutions, moving masses of people, and so on. The most important text in the history of Zionism is to a great extent a blueprint, a plan for setting up a state.

The same focus on the state (and land) is visible in Ben-Gurion's thinking. In 1937, during the debate about a British proposal to divide Palestine into two states, Jewish and Arab (the first, not a viable one), Ben-Gurion noted in a letter to his son, Amos:

> My assumption is – and that is why I am an enthusiastic proponent of the idea of a state, even if it involves division at this point – that a partial Jewish state is not the end, but rather the beginning.... We would establish sophisticated defense forces, a superb army – I have no doubt that our armed forces would be among the best in the world – and then I am sure that nothing will stop us from settling in other parts of the land, either through consent and mutual understanding with our Arab neighbors, or through other means.[6]

Leading Zionists, then, clearly understood the movement as goal oriented, and either did not sufficiently contemplate the means required for its achievement (Herzl) or were willing to use dubious ones if necessary (Ben-Gurion); they did not grasp that *how* this end would be accomplished might be constitutive of its final moral makeup. They perceived the formation of the *Medina* as something wholly new, as a *creation* of their thoughts and deeds, and less as something that involves a multiplicity of members and neighbors, and is thus other oriented and action based (in the Aristotelian sense). "Whoever is interested in building a new building must first demolish the old one," writes Herzl;[7] while the founding father was referring to the Jewish existence in the Diaspora (i.e., the "old building"), his logic also applies to what happened in Palestine, the metaphor of building (as something self-sufficient and whole) conveying the limits of dialogical politics in relation to the Jewish diasporic past as well as to the multinational and cultural reality in Palestine.

To be sure, most Zionist parties were not dogmatic or fanatic, and were attuned to changing circumstances. They were savvy in their

---

[6] Ben-Gurion, "Michtav le-Amos [Letter to Amos]," October 5, 1937, in David Ben-Gurion, *Michtavim le-Paula* [Letters to Paula] (Tel Aviv: Am Oved, 1968), p. 211 (in Hebrew). Quoted here from Tel Aviv Central Library, electronic reprint no. 001990445.

[7] Herzl, "The Jewish State," at http://benyehuda.org/herzl/herzl_003.html.

operative dimension – the socialist Zionists and labor movement (especially Mapai) made this flexibility their distinguishing mark[8] – yet their maneuvering was not sufficiently concerned with the moral meaning of some of their most important actions. (This was first epitomized perhaps by the terror used by Begin's Irgun before the War of Independence, acts to which most of the Yishuv were opposed, and later by the methods used by some of the Israeli forces during that war, methods aimed at expelling segments of the Arab population.[9]) The idea of forming a Jewish state (or commonwealth) and controlling as much territory as possible was hegemonic (especially after the Biltmore Program of 1942) and ultimately not open to question. It was not only the weight given to the predetermined end and vision that were problematic, however, but also the weakness of a moral language that could have checked it once the cosmopolitan hopes and the faith in the progress of humanity that characterized many Jews of the nineteenth century were discredited by history. Success and failure were thus determined according to the solidity and volume of the final object – the national building – and less in light of the means and path leading to this formation and the moral fabric of the builders constructing it. The territorial expansion and settlement project after the 1967 war – despite the enormous moral and political costs – has continued with the same logic of measuring success in terms of tangible results.

I have suggested throughout this book that achieving the *binyan* involved emphasizing certain virtues and capacities and downplaying others. Hard work, sacrifice, military valor, inventiveness, resourcefulness, simplicity, naturalness, engrossing public-mindedness, and (to a certain degree) conventionality were among the virtues and characteristics valued in advancing a certain vision of the good and worthy life, the

---

[8] Dan Horowitz and Moshe Lissak, *The Origins of the Israeli Polity* (Tel Aviv: Am Oved, 1986), p. 181.

[9] See Benny Morris, *1948 and After: Israel and the Palestinians*. This does not mean that the Yishuv and the young state did not have at times fierce moral debates about the means and methods employed in the conflict with the Palestinians. These debates were perhaps especially pronounced after the massacres of Palestinian civilians by Israeli forces in Deir Yassin (1948), Kibya (1953), and Kafr Kassem (1956). The events of 1948 also received harsh internal criticism, for example, by the important poet Nathan Alterman, who in his poem "Al zot" condemned, during the war, the deportation and killing of Arab civilians by Israeli forces in Lod and Ramla. Nevertheless, the deliberate killings of Palestinian civilians by Israeli forces during the War of Independence, especially those massacres done in the last stages of the war (for example, in Operation Hiram in the Galilee) were not often discussed in the decades that followed, either in the public sphere or in the schools, while the massacres performed by Arabs against Jews received much attention.

life of the nation builder. Yet democratic citizenship, I have suggested, requires other virtues and capacities. These include independence of thought and civic courage, truthfulness and love of truth (even when it unsettles social conventions), public-mindedness balanced by critical distance, participatory ethos and sense of empowerment, a cultivated sense of justice. The latter set of virtues were never absent from Zionist/ Israeli society, which was a democratic community since the days of the Yishuv, but they were of secondary importance in comparison to the virtues of the nation builder, at least until the 1960s. During the course of about a hundred years, Jews in Eretz Israel eschewed the traditional Jewish virtues of the *tzadik*, celebrated the virtues of the early pioneers and gradually turned away from them, and only in recent decades began to seriously contemplate the type of citizen required by a viable democracy.

We have also seen that language is essential for performing the tasks of the citizen. This understanding of the role of language is especially strong in the republican tradition. Cicero, for example, professes that through eloquent speech, "the most numerous advantages accrue to the republic":[10] He believes that such speech and language in general are essential for discussions among peers, for arguing about what is good and useful, and for reproducing a sense of commonality and shared practices. While cultural nationalists (such as Ahad Ha'am) may view language primarily as a collective treasure that preserves and cultivates a distinct national identity over time, republicans underscore the *political* significance of language and its importance not only for the community that wishes to act collectively in the world but also for the individual who searches for his or her voice as a critical, yet engaged, citizen. Zionism fostered a strong sense of shared purpose and demanded much sacrifice from its adherents in Eretz Israel, but it grounded itself on other foundations: It was materially and spatially oriented. Recent attempts to describe the State of Israel as embodying, at least in its early decades, republican ideals[11] are thus highly problematic: While Zionism called for a strong sense of common good and expected its members to fully engage in state building (although many of the new masses of immigrants had little such commitment and engagement and came only because they had no other option), the solidarity of its supporters became significantly

---

[10] Marcus Tullius Cicero, *De Inventione*, trans. C. D. Yonge (Whitefish, MT: Kessinger, 2004), p. 8.

[11] See Shafir and Peled, *Being Israeli: The Dynamics of Multiple Citizenship*, Chap. 2.

mediated through the land and the actions necessary for its control and reconstruction. These foundations, however, eventually created a fragile political community.

This fragility is evident in many spheres of contemporary Israeli life, but the growing inequality and poverty (especially child poverty) in the economic sphere and the diminished commitment of the state to the social dimension of citizenship stand out.[12] The swiftness and thoroughness with which the egalitarian and socialist ethos has crumbled now that the building phase is over do not mean that this ethos was not genuine, but that the ideas and language that supported it were weak and left unclear imprints on Zionist and Israeli political thought. To explain this point, it might be worthwhile to recall that during the pre-state period of the Yishuv, there was a considerable effort by the Histadrut (the workers' union) to expand the range of social rights to all Jews engaged in the project of state building. There was a need to lure immigrants, ensure their loyalty to the great project of state formation, and reduce the chances of inner strife in a country composed of multiple diasporas. Social rights thus included a right to subsidized housing, health care, employment, unemployment benefits, and education; after Independence, the National Insurance Institute added another tier of welfare payments, such as maternity leave support, compensation for accidents at work, and benefits for the relatively economically weak segments of the population (such as the elderly and the handicapped). Various institutions, policies, and legislation turned the young state into one of the most egalitarian states in the Western world. Even if socialist ideas served national purposes, there is no doubt that they were also ardently believed in and endlessly professed, that both the official ideology and practice were egalitarian, and that Israel was considered to be an almost model welfare state, akin to the Scandinavian countries.

In recent decades, however, the Israeli welfare state has been significantly weakened; the state now espouses a more neoliberal vision of economic life, and inequality has been rising. In 2006, according to the Central Bureau of Statistics, the income of the two upper deciles constituted almost "one half of the total gross income of the households in the population (44.9%), compared with the two lower deciles, whose

---

[12] My discussion of social rights is based on the discussion in *Being Israeli*, especially Chapters 2 and 11. I am also helped by Averham Doron, "Shaping Welfare Policy in Israel 2000–2005," at http://www.taubcenter.org.il/files/H2007_Welfare_Policy_2000–2005.pdf.

share of the total gross income of the households in the population [was] 5.7%." The report adds that "the share of the lower decile ... has not changed, whereas the share of the upper decile rose by 0.7%."[13] Most disturbing, in 2007 (according to the Bureau) about 40 percent of Israeli children lived below the poverty line, and about 30 percent of the Israeli population were in danger of poverty.[14] Contemporaneously, social rights have been shrinking and losing their universal application: For both health care and education, for example, the state increasingly provides or ensures only basic levels of service, and many among those who can afford it are opting for privatized schools, colleges, primary health care, and hospitals. The entitlement to welfare has been restricted, and welfare services have been privatized with little regulation and supervision by the state.

This process is, of course, not unique to Israel, and many countries have experienced similar developments.[15] What is striking about the Israeli case, however, is the rapid pace in which this process has occurred and the weakness of the political-institutional opposition to it: "In the 1960s, income distribution in Israel was among the most egalitarian in the Western world. In the middle of the 1990s, there existed few Western countries in which inequality is greater."[16] Since then, inequality has become even more pronounced, with the government in Israel – emboldened by the support of the media and prominent commentators, of business leaders and economists – advancing an expansive notion of neoliberalism in which various spheres of individual and social life are becoming subject to the mechanisms and logic of the free market (although considerable parts of the welfare state have not yet been demolished). The legislature (Knesset), the local governments, the universities, and the courts have offered little opposition to this policy.

Many workers no longer enjoy the protection of strong labor unions, are employed (often temporarily) through companies that offer human

---

[13] Central Bureau of Statistics, "Income Survey 2006," August 13, 2007, at http://www.cbs.gov.il/hodaot2007n/15_07_150e.pdf.

[14] Central Bureau of Statistics, "Objective & Subjective Indices of Poverty & Social Exclusion," October 9, 2009, at http://www.cbs.gov.il/www/hodaot2009n/23_09_211b.doc.

[15] The reasons for these neoliberal developments include globalization and fierce competition in open markets, policies imposed by the World Bank, structural changes in the workforce, demographic changes, taxation policies, hegemonic economic worldviews, symbiosis of political and financial elites, among other reasons; however, Israel, which tries to emulate the United States in many spheres, has been especially responsive to the economic model of that country since the days of Ronald Reagan.

[16] Report of Bank Hapoalim, 1996. Quoted here from *Being Israeli*, p. 286.

resources services, or are foreign workers and, hence, especially vulnerable. In 1961, the leading party, Mapai, declared:

The Histadrut, under the leadership of Mifleget Poalei Eretz Israel [Mapai], would continue to act, in substance and in spirit, toward the formation of the people until all become working people, without class differences and without the exploitation of their fellow man.[17]

The near collapse of this worldview cannot be attributed solely to the political weakness of the Labor Party in recent decades (a weakness that has many causes, and is only partly related to its socioeconomic policy). It seems, rather, that the very ideas animating the welfare state and social democracy have become alien, and the public sphere in Israel was almost devoid of them until the social protest movement tried to revive them in summer 2011 (these ideas include the notion that there are inborn social rights, that every individual deserves an equal chance, that the public benefits from the welfare and flourishing of its individual members, that loyalty to the state is related to social solidarity, that there is a relation between sound democracy and rough equality and/or a strong middle class, and so on).[18]

In fact, the type of *reasoning* that led to the creation of social rights and to the valuation of solidarity has become almost incomprehensible, as if representing a strange logic (a phenomenon that did not occur in other Western countries, such as Britain, France, and Germany, which were never as social-democratically oriented as Israel, but where these ideas still have significant political power). Such weakness signifies either that no appropriate language was created to defend these ideas in the past, or that if such language was created it left questionable marks. In a sense, perhaps, the Labor movement and its past values are victims of their own philosophy, which celebrated the role of "doing" and devalued the importance of the shared world of meanings that could only be formed by open, plural, and ongoing articulation and deliberation.

The fragility of Israeli democracy can also be demonstrated if we look more closely at what is happening in the actual sphere of building in this country. The State of Israel, at least during many periods, has resembled a large construction site. The relative density of its population and the huge number of immigrants from the former Soviet Union during the

---

[17] See Mapai's platform, August 1961, at http://www.archavoda.org.il/AvodaArch/matza/pdf/knesset5.pdf. The labor movement did not fully implement this vision, of course, but it did great things in promoting a relatively egalitarian society that respected working men and women.

[18] See Sternhell, *The Founding Myths of Israel*, Epilogue.

1990s have necessitated the building of new towns and the expansion of existing ones almost overnight. In addition, the flight of the middle class from the cities has resulted not only in the blossoming of the suburbs but also in new roads, highways, and railroads. The military's partial pull-out from the occupied territories and its decision to move away from the country's center have necessitated the construction of huge new bases in the periphery (especially in the Negev). And the expansion of consumerism has entailed the rapid emergence of new malls housing the latest brand names. While the intensive construction that has always characterized Israel thus continues, its spirit has drastically changed: Especially in Tel Aviv and its surroundings, new apartment buildings tower majestically over the city, affordable only to the very affluent, expressing exclusivity and impenetrability through aesthetic means; simultaneously, new gated communities promise their residents beautiful scenery, seclusion and security, and overall social homogeneity (e.g., Tel Andromeda in Jaffa). The architecture of the first decades after independence featured deliberate simplicity, relative humility, rough homogeneity, and public-mindedness. This has more recently been displaced by an architecture that relishes economic gaps and expresses the breakdown of communal solidarity.

One of the most striking phenomena has been the change in the small villages, which were built across the country just decades ago (in the late 1940s and 1950s) in a uniformly austere style. Over the years, a second ring of houses has emerged around the original houses in these villages, houses belonging to the sons and daughters of the founders. These houses betray a wholly different architectural universe. A village west of Jerusalem serves as a good example. In the new streets of this village, the visitor encounters a modern house made of white rectangular stones, its arched windows echoing a traditional Arab building style; a Norwegian wooden house, with its sharp angles meant to protect residents from the Scandinavian winter; a Moroccan-style, yellow-orange house with an interior courtyard that promises seclusion from an imaginary dense neighborhood; a house made of unpolished paving stones that intimates the utmost simplicity and embeddedness in the nearby landscape; a house made in part from vast, sunproofed glass panes that allude to a high-tech industry building; and so on.

The great care reflected in the designs and materials of this secondary ring of buildings stands in sharp contrast to the neglect of the street and public spaces, which lack even trees to protect pedestrians from the Mediterranean sun. The houses in this village, as in many such villages, are enveloped by high fences that skirt the very edge of the road, leaving no room for areas that would bridge the public and private spaces; moreover, the houses are huge, each occupying almost the entire lot reserved for it. Piles of discarded, decaying building materials engulf the village, and the mountain on which the lots have been leveled by bulldozers seems bare and maimed: What Leah Goldberg describes in "My Poem about Stones" as the inevitable damage building does to Nature has often turned, in recent decades, into a practice of environmental neglect. This microcosm evolves, it should be mentioned, while open spaces rapidly shrink throughout Israel, a country in which development is often prized over the preservation of green areas and the natural landscape (although movements and organizations concerned with the health and preservation of the environment, as well as the Ministry of the Environment, are gaining increasing weight).

This new architectural scene in Israel often betrays a perverse notion of individuality. Each house is a unit unto itself, unrelated to its surroundings; it fulfills a personal vision of style that is devoid of community and, for the most part, does not recognize others' existence. In their attempt to flee shared humble origins, the founders' children have concretized the threat of arbitrariness lurking behind an erroneous interpretation of individuality, one that does not recognize its indebtedness to tradition, context, and public-ness. Indeed, the lack of both a shared aesthetic language and any relatedness among buildings (especially single-family houses) is complemented by an inability to transcend the private, to conceive of the street and public areas as shared spaces that people are responsible for and which they could enjoy in concert. Israelis still express themselves in building, investing much of their energies and resources in projects of construction; only now these projects tend to be wholly personal, exhibiting Israelis' confusion about the nature of relatedness in an era in which the image of a shared building project has lost its grip.

There are some similarities between these radical shifts on the ground and recent developments in Israeli politics. In the beginning, the plurality of the Zionist movement was partial in practice because of the overbearing, dominant role of socialist Zionism in establishing and leading the state; now, however, fragmentation rules. The Israeli public scene is currently composed of multiple small-to-medium parties and public organizations, each representing a different worldview and identity: ultra-Orthodox, religious nationalists, radical secularists, religious Sephardim, Arab Israelis, soft communists, dovish peace seekers, nationalist hawks, and more. Some of these parties and groups aspire not only to purvey distinct policies but also to develop distinct myths, values, institutions, and practices.

Private schools, some of which care little for the good of society and for notions of shared citizenship, are mushrooming; even at state schools, however, children encounter few children who come from backgrounds different from their own. Group identity becomes thicker, leaving little place for overlap or even contact among communities beyond basic bargaining; in fact, as several scholars recently observed, "[T]he chief characteristic of the groups composing it [Israeli society] is that of mutual negation."[19] This negation (which is somewhat less pronounced when there is a clash between Israel and the Palestinians or others) is expressed in part through the deterioration of the public sphere, wherein interests are narrowed, turning issues that used to concern the entire society – such as the rule of law, the integrity of the judicial system, poverty and economic justice, the predicament of the elderly, education, science and research, religion, and immigration – into the "territory" of a single party or just a few of them. The basic notion of politics as oriented toward the public good has been displaced by a politics that, for the most part, is unable to articulate a common vision beyond the need for individual and national security. Given this predicament, election campaigns have become hollow and simplistic, negative in nature and devoid of substantial discussion about the grave issues facing the country.

As long as (the Jewish) citizens thought of themselves as engaged in the shared project of building a Jewish state, they were united by this idea and by their practical achievements; they possessed an overarching sense of purpose that overshadowed their differences and infused them with the joy of being together that is characteristic of makers on a grand scale. But the materialization of the national building manifested the limits of building as a political concept: Buildings incorporate the idea of completion; they are entities that presuppose an end. Buildings cannot reproduce themselves; political communities seek to do so perpetually. After completing, with impressive success, the critical elements of their

---

[19] M. Mautner, Avi Sagi, and Ronen Shamir, "Reflections on Multiculturalism in Israel," in *Multiculturalism in a Democratic and Jewish State* (Tel Aviv: Tel Aviv University Press, 1998), p. 75. See also Yossi Yonah, "Fifty Years Later: The Scope and Limits of Liberal Democracy in Israel," *Constellations* 6, no. 3 (1999): 411–28; and Uri Ram, "The State of the Nation: Contemporary Challenges to Zionism in Israel," *Constellations* 6, no. 3 (1999): 325–38.

building of the Israeli state (social and political institutions, a strong army, an advanced economy, a dense population, reasonable universities, and more), co-builders discovered that they possessed different visions of the good and worthy life. More precisely, they cleaved to mutually exclusive notions of identity once the experience of state formation could no longer unify them, turning to the cultivation of their enclosed group and individual identities while neglecting a public sphere that had little to offer them besides tangible achievements. Israelis realized, then, that the solidity intimated by the image of a national building was uncertain.

Actual, grand buildings are highly misleading; despite the awe that they inspire and the stability they are supposed to convey, ultimately they cannot escape the fragility that is the fate of any human artifact. National buildings are even more misleading since the production of a shared, concrete world does not create a genuine, lasting community. To be sure, words sometimes draw us apart, revealing profound gaps in worldviews that would otherwise have been overlooked; sometimes they even accelerate distance unjustifiably. Nevertheless, only certain uses of language can achieve an enduring community. Political leaders such as Pericles and Cato the Elder, Mazzini and Lincoln, Churchill and Obama have used language not only to mold themselves and advance their careers but also to communicate their ideas to the nation, to inspire and redirect its course, to generate solidarity and a sense of common purpose.[20] The future quality of Israeli democracy depends, to a large extent, on the degree to which its new generation of leaders and citizens will be able to promote such seemingly amorphous political and moral conversation, one that will help it transcend its building phase and render the past horizons of the language-based Jewish culture more accessible.

[20] See, for example, Fred Kaplan, *Lincoln: The Biography of a Writer* (New York: HarperCollins, 2008).

Bibliography

Adler, Anja. 2008. "Hannah Arendt and Zionism: An Unresolved Battle for Jewish Politics," Master's thesis, Tel-Aviv University.

Agnon, Shmuel Yossef. 1993. *Temol shilshom* [In the heart of the seas]. Tel Aviv: Schocken (in Hebrew).

Ahad Ha'am 1898. "Haprogress vsina'at Israel [Progress and the hatred of Israel]." At http://www.benyehuda.org/ginzburg/Gnz_048.html (in Hebrew).

1921. *Al parashat derachim* [At the crossroads]. Berlin: Jüdischer Verlag (in Hebrew).

1947a. *Kol ma'amarei Ahad Ha'am* [The collected essays of Ahad Ha'am]. Tel Aviv: Dvir (in Hebrew).

1947b. *Kol kitvei Ahad Ha'am (kk)* [The collected writings of Ahad Ha'am]. Jerusalem: Achuza Ivrit (in Hebrew)

Al-Azm, Sadik J. 1967. *Kant's Theory of Time.* New York: Philosophical Library.

Alkalai, Yehuda. 1974. *Kitvei harav Yehuda Alkalai* [The writings of Rabbi Yehuda Alkalai]. Ed. Y. Raphael. Jerusalem: Mosad Harav Kook.

Almog, Oz. 1997. *The Sabra – A Profile.* Tel Aviv: Am Oved (in Hebrew).

Alter, Robert. 1991. *Necessary Angels: Tradition and Modernity in Kafka, Benjamin, and Scholem.* Cambridge, MA: Harvard University Press.

1994. "Scholem and Modernism." *Poetics Today* 15, no. 3: 429–42.

Amichai, Yehuda. 2008. "Dorot ba'aretz [Generations in the land]." In *We Hereby Declare,* ed. Anita Shapira. Tel Aviv: Dvir (in Hebrew).

Amiran-Sapir, Revital. 1999. "Al em haderech [On the road]." Master's thesis, Tel Aviv University.

Forthcoming. "Cultural Nationalism and the Formulation of the Political Reflections on the Jewish National Movement."

Anderson, Benedict. 1983. *Imagined Communities: Reflections on the Origin and Spread of Nationalism.* London: Verso.

Anderson, Richard. 2001. "Metaphors of Dictatorship and Democracy: Changes in the Russian Political Lexicon and the Transformation of Russian Politics." *Slavic Review* 60, no. 2: 212–335.

Arendt, Hannah. 1945. "Zionism Reconsidered." *Menorah Journal* 32, no.2: 162–96.

　1958. *The Human Condition*. Chicago: University of Chicago Press.

　1961. *Between Past and Future*. New York: Penguin.

　1968. "Introduction" in *Illuminations*. Trans. Harry Zohn. New York: Schocken Books.

　1970. "Distinctions." *New York Review of Books* 13, no. 12, January 1.

　1978. *The Life of the Mind*. New York: Harcourt Brace Jovanovich.

　1990. *On Revolution*. London: Penguin.

　2000. *The Portable Hannah Arendt*. London: Penguin.

Aristotle. 1946. *The Politics of Aristotle*. Trans. Ernest Barker. Oxford: Oxford University Press.

　1984. *The Complete Works of Aristotle*. Ed. J. Barnes. Princeton, NJ: Princeton University Press.

Arlosoroff, Chaim. 1931. "Haproblemot hafinanssiot bebinyan Eretz Israel [The financial problems in building Eretz Israel]." At http://benyehuda.org/arlosoroff/014.html (in Hebrew).

Aschheim, Steven. 2007. *Beyond the Border: The German-Jewish Legacy Abroad*. Princeton, NJ: Princeton University Press.

Augé, Mark. 1995. *Non-Places: An Introduction to the Anthropology of Supermodernity*. London: Verso.

Augustine. 1961. *Confessions*. Trans. R. S. Pine-Coffin. New York: Penguin Books.

Avineri, Shlomo. 1981. *The Making of Modern Zionism: Intellectual Origins of the Jewish State*. New York: Basic Books.

Avneri, Shmuel. 2010. "Bialik vteno'at havoda [Bialik and the labor movement]." *Haaretz*, July 2 (in Hebrew).

Baer, Yitzhak. 1985. *Mehkarim umasot betoldot am yisrael* [Studies in the history of the Jewish people]. 2 vols. Jerusalem: Hachevra Hahistorit Haisraelit (in Hebrew).

　1988. *Galut*. New York: Schocken Books.

Barnard, Frederic. 1965. *Herder's Social and Political Thought: From Enlightenment to Nationalism*. Oxford: Clarendon.

　1988. *Self-Direction and Political Legitimacy: Rousseau and Herder*. New York: Oxford University Press.

Barrett, William. 1971. *Heidegger, Kant, and Time*. Bloomington: Indiana University Press.

Bartal, Israel. 2007. "Secularization of Time and the Culture of Recreation." In *New Jewish Time*, ed. Y. Yovel et al. Tel Aviv: Keter (in Hebrew).

Bartana, Orsion. 2004. "The Brenner School and the Agnon School in Hebrew Literature of the Twentieth Century." *Hebrew Studies* 45: 49–69.

Bar-Zohar, Michael. 1967. *The Armed Prophet: A Biography of Ben-Gurion*. London: Barker.

Bauer, Otto. 2000. *The Question of Nationalities and Social Democracy*. Trans. Joseph O'Donnell. Minneapolis: University of Minnesota Press.

Bauman, Zygmunt. 2000. *Liquid Modernity*. Cambridge: Polity.

Ben-Gurion, David. [1937] 1968. "Michtav le-Amos [Letter to Amos]," October 5, 1937. In David Ben-Gurion, *Michtavim le-Paula* [Letters to Paula]. Tel

Aviv: Am Oved. Tel Aviv University Central Library, electronic reprint no. 001990445 (in Hebrew).

1955. *Mima'amad le'am* [From class to nation]. Tel Aviv: Ayanot (in Hebrew).

1957. *Netzah Israel* [The eternity of Israel]. Tel Aviv: Ayanot (in Hebrew).

1960. *Iyunim besefer yehoshua* [Studies in the Book of Joshua]. Jerusalem: Kiryat Sefer (in Hebrew).

1971–6. *Zichronot* [Recollections]. 6 vols. Tel Aviv: Am Oved (in Hebrew).

Benhabib, Seyla. 2003. *The Reluctant Modernism of Hannah Arendt*. Oxford: Rowman and Littlefield.

Benjamin, Walter. 1976. *Illuminations*. Ed. with Introduction by Hannah Arendt. New York: Schocken Books.

1986. *Reflections: Essays, Aphorisms, Autobiographical Writings*. Ed. Peter Demetz. Trans. Edmund Jephcott. New York: Schocken Books.

1989. *Benjamin: Philosophy, History, Aesthetics*. Ed. Gary Smith. Chicago: University of Chicago Press.

1996. *Selected Writings*. Cambridge, MA: Harvard University Press.

Ben-Sasson, Hayim, ed. 1976. *A History of the Jewish People*. Cambridge, MA: Harvard University Press.

Benvenisti, Meron. 1997. "Hamapa haivirit [The Hebrew map]." *Theory and Criticism* 11: 7–30 (in Hebrew).

2000. *Sacred Landscape: The Buried History of the Holy Land since 1949*. Berkeley: University of California Press.

Berdyczewski, Micha Josef. 1954. *Kol ma'amarei Micha Josef Berdyczewski* [The collected essays of Micha Josef Berdyczewski]. Tel Aviv: Am Oved (in Hebrew).

Bergman, Shmuel Hugo. 1976. *Bamish'ol* [On the path]. Tel Aviv: Am Oved.

Berkowitz, Michael. 1993. *Zionist Culture and West European Jewry before the First World War*. Cambridge: Cambridge University Press.

Biale, David. 1986. *Power and Powerlessness in Jewish History*. New York: Schocken Books.

Bialik, Chaim Nahman. 1913. "On Rabbi Yehuda Halevi." At http://benyehuda. org/bialik/dvarim_shebeal_peh68.html (in Hebrew).

1917. "Halacha and Aggada [Law and legends]." At http:www//benyehuda. org/bialik/article06.html (in Hebrew).

1918. "Tarbut vpolitika [Culture and politics]." At http://www. benyehuda. org/bialik/tarpol/html (in Hebrew).

1935. *Devarim shebe'al peh* [Speeches and lectures]. 2 vols. Tel Aviv: Dvir (in Hebrew).

1943. *Kol kitvei Chaim Nahman Bialik* [The collected writings of Chaim Nahman Bialik]. Tel Aviv: Dvir (in Hebrew).

1950. "Revealment and Concealment in Language [Gilui vekisui balashon]." Trans. Jacob Sloan. *Commentary* 9, no. 2: 171–5

1969. *Bialik Speaks: Words from the Poet's Lips, Clues to the Man*. New York: Herzl.

1975. *Sipurim vedevri safrrot* [Stories and other writings]. Tel-Aviv: Dvir (in Hebrew).

1981. *Chaim Nachman Bialik: The Selected Poems.* Trans. Ruth Nevo. Tel Aviv: Dvir.

Bilsky, Leora. 1996. "When Actor and Spectator Meet in the Courtroom: Reflections on Hannah Arendt's Concept of Judgment." *History and Memory* 8, no. 2: 137–73.

Blattberg Charles. 2000. *From Pluralist to Patriotic Politics: Putting Practice First.* Oxford: Oxford University Press.

2003. *Shall We Dance? A Patriotic Politics for Canada.* Montreal: McGill-Queen's University Press.

Bluwstein, Rachel. 1985. *Shirim, michtavim, reshimot* [*Poems, letters, writings*]. Tel Aviv: Dvir (in Hebrew).

Boman, Thorleif. 1960. *Hebrew Thought Compared with Greek.* Trans. Jules L. Moreau. Philadelphia: Westminster.

Borochov, Dov Ber. 1905. "K voprosu o sione i territorii." *Evreiskaia zhizn* 7: 70 (in Russian).

1944. *Ketavim nivharim* [Selected writings]. Tel Aviv: Am Oved (in Hebrew).

1984. *Class Struggle and the Jewish Nation.* New Brunswick, NJ: Transaction.

Brenner, Yossef Haim. 1911. "Tzarat haleshonot [The quandary of languages]." http://www.benyehuda.org/brenner/baaretz_055.html.

1920. "Tel-Hai." At http://www.benyehuda.org/brenner/brenner207.html (in Hebrew).

1967. *Kol kitvei Y. H. Brenner.* [The collected writings of Y. H. Brenner]. Tel Aviv: Hakibbutz Hameuhad (in Hebrew).

Brinker, Menahem. 1994. "Nietzsche's Influence on Hebrew Writers of the Russian Empire." In *Nietzsche and Soviet Culture: Ally and Adversary*, ed. B. G. Rosenthal. Cambridge: Cambridge University Press.

Brosh, Tamar, ed. 1993. *Neum lekol et* [A speech for every occasion]. Tel Aviv: The Open University (in Hebrew).

Brunner, Jose. 2001. "Eichmann's Mind: Legal, Psychological and Philosophical Perspectives." *Theoretical Inquiries in Law* 1, no. 2, 1–35.

Buber, Martin 1973. *On Zion: The History of an Idea.* New York: Schocken Books.

1983. *A Land of Two Peoples: Martin Buber on Jews and Arabs.* Ed. Paul Mendes-Flohr. New York: Oxford University Press.

1984. *Teuda veyeud*, vol. 2. Jerusalem: World Zionist Organization Press.

Carlebach, Julius. 1978. *Karl Marx and the Radical Critique of Judaism.* London: Routledge.

Caygill, Howard. 1994. "Benjamin, Heidegger and the Destruction of Tradition." In *Walter Benjamin's Philosophy*, ed. A. Benjamin and P. Osborne. London: Routledge, pp. 1–32.

Celan, Paul. 1986. *Collected Prose.* Trans. Rosmarie Waldrop. Riverdale-on-Hudson, NY: The Sheep Meadow Press.

Central Bureau of Statistics. 2007. "Income Survey 2006." At http://www.cbs.gov.il/ hodaot2007n/15_07_150e.pdf (in Hebrew).

2009. "Objective & Subjective Indices of Poverty & Social Exclusion." At http://www.cbs.gov.il/ www/hodaot2009n/23_09_211b.doc (in Hebrew).

Chomsky, William. 1967. *Hebrew: The Eternal Language.* Jerusalem: Rubin Mass.

Chowers, Eyal. 1998. "Time in Zionism: The Life and Afterlife of a Temporal Revolution." *Political Theory* 26, no. 5: 652–85.

1999. "The Marriage of Time and Identity: Kant, Benjamin, and the Nation-State." *Philosophy and Social Criticism* 25, no. 3: 55–80.

2001. "Ahad Ha'am and the Jewish Volkgeist." In *Global Politics: Essays in Honour of David Vital*, ed. A. Ben-Zvi and A. Kleiman. London: Frank Cass, pp. 267–82.

2002a. "The Physiology of the Citizen: The Present-Centered Body and Its Political Exile." *Political Theory* 30: 649–76.

2002b. "The End of Building: Zionism and the Politics of the Concrete." *Review of Politics* 64, no. 4: 599–626.

2002c. "Gushing Time: Modernity and the Multiplicity of Temporal Homes." *Time and Society* 11, nos. 2/3: 235–49.

2004. *The Modern Self in the Labyrinth: Politics and the Entrapment Imagination*. Cambridge, MA: Harvard University Press.

2005. "Language and Democracy in the Thought of Hannah Arendt." In *Hannah Arendt: A Half-Century of Polemics*, ed. Idith Zertal and Moshe Zuckermann. Tel Aviv: Hakibbutz Hameuchad.

Cicero, Marcus Tullius. 2004. *De Inventione*. Trans. C. D. Yonge. Whitefish, MT: Kessinger.

Cohen, Ayelet. 2001. "Kochan shel Milim" [The power of words]. www.snunit.k12.il/seder/mabat/power2.html.

Cohen, Herman. 1971. *Reason and Hope: Selection from the Jewish Writings of Herman Cohen*. Trans. Eva Jospe. New York: Norton.

Cutter, William. 1990. "Ghostly Hebrew, Ghastly Speech: Scholem to Rosenzweig, 1926." *Prooftexts* 10: 413–33.

Dinaburg, Ben Zion. 1971–2. *Bemifne hadorot* [The changing of the generations]. Jerusalem: Mossad Bialik (in Hebrew).

1975. *Bema'avak hadorot shel am yisrael al artzo mihurban betar ad tekumat yisrael* [The struggle of the generations of Israel for its land]. Jerusalem: Mossad Bialik (in Hebrew).

Doron, Avraham. 2007. "Shaping Welfare Policy in Israel, 2000–2005." At http://www.taubcenter.org.il/files/H2007_Welfare_Policy_2000–2005.pdf (in Hebrew).

Dowty, Alan. 1998. *The Jewish State: A Century Later*. Berkeley: University of California Press.

Eco, Umberto. 1999. *Serendipities: Language and Lunacy*. New York: Orion.

Efrat, Zevi. 2000. "The Plan." *Theory and Criticism* 16: 203–10.

Ed. 2004. *The Israeli Project: Building and Architecture, 1948–1973*. Tel Aviv: Tel Aviv Museum of Art.

Elam, Yaeli. 2007. "Deciphering Political Canonical Texts: A Promise to Be Experienced." Master's thesis, Tel Aviv University.

Eliade, Mircea. 1959. *Cosmos and History: The Myth of the Eternal Return*. New York: Harper Torchbooks.

Eliot, Thomas Stearns. 1972. "Tradition and Individual Talent." In *Twentieth Century Literary Criticism: A Reader*. Ed. David Lodge. London: Longman.

Elon, Amos. 2004. *Requiem Germani* [The pity of it all: A history of the Jews in Germany *1743–1933*]. Tel Aviv: Kinneret, Zmora-Bitan, Dvir (in Hebrew).

Even-Zohar, Itamar. 1980. "The Emergence of a Native Hebrew Culture in Palestine, 1882–1948." *Cathedra* 16: 165–89 (in Hebrew).

Ezrahi, Yaron. 1997. *Rubber Bullets: Power and Conscience in Modern Israel*. Berkeley: University of California Press.

Falkenstein, Lorne. 1991. "Kant's Account of Intuition." *Canadian Journal of Philosophy* 21 (June): 164–93.

Fenves, Peter. 1991. *A Peculiar Fate: Metaphysics and World-History in Kant*. Ithaca, NY: Cornell University Press.

Fichte, Johann Gottlieb. [1808] 1922. *Addresses to the German Nation*. Trans. R. F. Jones and G. H. Turnbull. Chicago: The Open Court Publishing Company. At http://www.archive.org/stream/addressestothegeoofichuoft/ addressestothegeoofichuoft_djvu.txt.

Frankel, Jonathan. 1981. *Prophecy and Politics: Socialism, Nationalism, and the Russian Jews, 1862–1917*. Cambridge: Cambridge University Press.

Frankel, J., and S. Zipperstein, eds. 1992. *Assimilation and Community: The Jews in Nineteenth-Century Europe*. Cambridge: Cambridge University Press.

Freud, Sigmund. 1953–74. *The Standard Edition of the Complete Psychological Works of Sigmund Freud*. Ed. J. Strachey and A. Freud. London: Hogarth.

Funkenstein, Amos. 1993. *Perceptions of Jewish History*. Berkeley: University of California Press.

Gadamer, Hans-Georg. 2004. *Truth and Method*. New York: Continuum.

Gal, Allon. 1973. *Socialist-Zionism: Theory and Issues in Contemporary Jewish Nationalism*. Cambridge, MA: Schenkman.

Gans, Chaim. 2008. *A Just Zionism: On the Morality of the Jewish State*. New York: Oxford University Press.

Geiger, Abraham. 1985. *Judaism and Its History*. London: University Press of America.

Gilead, Amihud. 1985. "Teleological Time: A Variation on a Kantian Theme." *Review of Metaphysics* 38 (March) : 529–62.

Glinert, Lewis. 1987. "Hebrew." In *Contemporary Jewish Religious Thought*, ed. Arthur A. Cohen and Paul Mendes-Flohr. New York: Charles Scribner's Sons.

Gluzman, Michael, Hannan Hever, and Dan Meron. 2005. *Beir hahariga: bikur meuchar* [In the city of slaughter – A visit at twilight]. Tel Aviv: Resling (in Hebrew).

Goad, Harold. 1958. *Language in History*. Harmondsworth, UK: Penguin.

Goldberg, Leah. 2003. *The Modern Hebrew Poem Itself*. Ed. Stanley Burnshaw. Detroit: Wayne State University Press.

Golomb, Jacob. 1997. *Nietzsche and Jewish Culture*. London: Routledge.

Gordon, Aharon David. 1943. *Sefer A. D. Gordon: Mishnato udvaro*. Ed. Yehuda Iges. Tel Aviv: Ha'oved Hatzioni (in Hebrew).

Greenfeld, Liah. 1992. *Nationalism: Five Roads to Modernity*. Cambridge, MA.: Harvard University Press.

Grossman, David. 1987. *Hazeman hatsahov* [The yellow wind]. Tel Aviv: Hakibbutz Hameuhad.

Haakonssen, Knud. 1996. *Natural Law and Moral Philosophy*. Cambridge: Cambridge University Press.

Habermas, Jürgen. 1987. *The Philosophical Discourse of Modernity*. Cambridge, MA: MIT Press.

Har-Even, Shulamit. 2008. "The Limits of My Language, the Limits of My World." In *Hebrew Writers on Writing*, ed. Peter Cole. San Antonio, TX: Trinity University Press, pp. 189–203.

Harries, Karsten. 1998. *The Ethical Function of Architecture*. Cambridge, MA: MIT Press.

Harshav, Benjamin. 1993. *Language in Time of Revolution*. Berkeley: University of California Press.

Harvey, David. 1990. *The Condition of Postmodernity*. Cambridge, MA: Blackwell.

Hastings, Adrian. 1997. *The Construction of Nationhood: Ethnicity, Religion and Nationalism*. Cambridge: Cambridge University Press.

Hazony, Yoram. 2000. *The Jewish State: The Struggle for Israel's Soul*. New York: Basic Books.

Hegel, Georg. 1956. *The Philosophy of History*. New York: Dover.

Heidegger, Martin. 1962. *Being and Time*. Trans. J. Macquarrie and E. Robinson. New York: Harper and Row.

1977. *Basic Writings*. Ed. D. E. Krell. New York: Harper and Row.

Heilman, Samuel C. 1983. *The People of the Book*. Chicago: University of Chicago Press.

Heller, Agnes. 1995. "Where Are We at Home?" *Thesis Eleven* 41: 1–18.

1999. *A Theory of Modernity*. London: Oxford University Press.

Herder, Johann. 1800. *Outlines of a Philosophy of History of Man*. New York: Bergman.

1955. *Metakritik zur Kritik der Reinen Vernunft*. Berlin: Aufbau-Verlag (in German).

Hertzberg, Arthur, ed. 1971. *The Zionist Idea: A Historical Analysis and Reader*. New York: Atheneum.

Herzl, Theodor. [1896] 1946. *The Jewish State* [Medinat hayehudim]. Trans. Sylvie D'Avigdor. At http://www.jewishvirtuallibrary.org/jsource/Zionism/herzl2.html.

1897. "Haleumiut hayehudit shel Dr. Gidman [The national Judaism of Dr. Gidman]." At http://benyehuda.org/herzl/herzl_009.html (in Hebrew).

1902. *Altneuland*. At http://www.benyehuda.org/herzl/tel_aviv.html (in Hebrew).

1960. *The Complete Diaries of Theodor Herzl*. New York: Thomas Yoseloff.

1971. *Sipurim* [Stories]. Jerusalem: Zionist Library (in Hebrew).

1983. *Theodor Herzl Zionistisches Tagebücher II*. Berlin: Verlag Ullstein (in German).

Hirschfeld, Ariel. 2008. "He Had a Garden and He Still Has One." *Ha'aretz*, March 6.

2011. *The Tuned Harp: The Language of Emotions in H.N. Bialik's poetry*. Tel-Aviv: Am Oved (in Hebrew).

Hobsbawm, Eric. 1983. "Mass-Producing Traditions: Europe, 1870–1914." In *The Invention of Tradition*, ed. E. Hobsbawm and T. Ranger. Cambridge: Cambridge University Press.

    1990. *Nations and Nationalism since 1780: Program, Myth, Reality.* Cambridge: Cambridge University Press.

Holtzman, Avner. 1993. *Hakarat panim: massot al Micha Josef Berdyczewski.* Holon: Reshafim (in Hebrew).

Horowitz, Dan, and Moshe Lissak. 1986. *Miyishuv limedinah* [The origins of the Israeli polity]. Tel Aviv: Am Oved (in Hebrew).

Jabotinsky, Vladimir. 1947. *Ktavim.* Vol. 9. Jerusalem: Ari Jabotinsky Print.

    1972. *Olamo shel Jabotinsky* [The world of Jabotinsky: A selection of his works and the essentials of his teaching]. Ed. Moshe Bella. Tel Aviv: Dfusim (in Hebrew).

Jacobson, Eric 2003. *Metaphysics of the Profane: The Political Theology of Walter Benjamin and Gershom Scholem.* New York: Columbia University Press.

Jamal, Amal. 2011. *Arab Minority Nationalism in Israel.* London: Routledge.

Kalischer, Zvi Hirsch. [1862] 2002. *Drishat Zion* [Seeking Zion]. Reprint, Jerusalem: Rabbi Kook Institute (in Hebrew).

Kant, Immanuel. 1838. *Religion Within the Boundary of Pure Reason.* Trans. J. W. Semple. Edinburgh: Thomas Clark.

    1968. *The Critique of Pure Reason.* New York: Macmillan.

    1973. *The Critique of Judgment.* Trans. J. C. Meredith. Oxford: Oxford University Press.

    1983. *Perpetual Peace and Other Essays.* Indianapolis: Hackett.

    1992. *Theoretical Philosophy, 1755–1770.* Cambridge: Cambridge University Press.

    1996. *Critique of Practical Reason.* Trans. Mary J. Gregor. Cambridge: Cambridge University Press.

Kaplan, Danny. 2009. "The Songs of the Siren: Engineering National Time on Israeli Radio." *Cultural Anthropology* 24 (May): 313–45.

Kark, Ruth. 1992. "Land-God-Man: Concepts of Land Ownership in Traditional Cultures in Eretz-Israel." In *Ideology and Landscape in Historical Perspective*, ed. A. Baker and G. Biger. Cambridge: Cambridge University Press.

Karmi, Ram. 2001. *Lyric Architecture.* Tel Aviv: Ministry of Defense Publications.

Katznelson, Berl. 1941. "Introduction." In *Sefer hagvura* [The book of heroism], ed. Israel Heilperin. Tel Aviv: Am Oved (in Hebrew).

    1946. *Kitvei B. Katznelson* [The writings of Berl Katznelson]. Tel Aviv: Davar (in Hebrew).

Kedar, Nir. 2009. *Mamlakhtiyut.* Jerusalem: Yad Izhak Ben-Zvi.

Kedourie, Elie 1993. *Nationalism.* Oxford: Blackwell.

Keren, Michael. 1983. *Ben-Gurion and the Intellectuals: Power, Knowledge, and Charisma.* Dekalb: Northern Illinois University Press.

Kern, Stephen. 1983. *The Culture of Time and Space, 1880–1918.* Cambridge, MA: Harvard University Press.

Kimmerling, Baruch. 1983. *Zionism and Territory: The Socio-Territorial Dimensions of Zionist Politics.* Berkeley: University of California Institute of International Studies Press.

Klemperer, Victor. 2000. *The Language of the Third Reich.* New York: Continuum.

Kohn, Hans. 1993. *The Idea of Nationalism.* New York: Collier Books.

Koselleck, Reinhart. 1985. *Futures Past.* Cambridge, MA: MIT Press.

Krell, Detlef. 1992. "Das Unheimliche: Architectural Sections of Heidegger and Freud." *Research in Phenomenology* 22: 43–61.

Krochmal, Nachman. 1961. *Guide to the Perplexed of the Time.* Waltham, MA: Ararat.

Kuzar, Ron. 2001. *Hebrew and Zionism: A Discourse Analytic Cultural Study.* Berlin: Mouton.

Lahat, Golan. 2007. "Rethinking Progress: The Political Implications of Kant's Epistemology." Ph.D. diss., Tel Aviv University.

Lakoff, George, and Mark Johnson. 1980. *Metaphors We Live By.* Chicago: University of Chicago Press.

Laqueur, Walter. 1972. *A History of Zionism.* New York: Holt, Rinehart and Winston.

Lefebvre, Henri. 1991. *The Production of Space.* Trans. Donald Nicholson-Smith. Oxford: Blackwell.

Leibovitch, Yeshayahu. 1975. *Yahadut, am yehudi umedinat yisrael* [Judaism, the Jewish people, and the State of Israel]. Tel Aviv: Schocken (in Hebrew).

Levi, Shlomo, ed. 1952. *Bishnat hashloshim* [In the 1930s]. Tel Aviv: Davar (in Hebrew).

Levi, Zeev. 1989. "Kant and Jewish Ethics in Modernity." *Daat* 23 (Summer): 89–97.

Levin, Shmaryahu. 1949. *Bama'avak* [In the struggle]. Tel Aviv: Dvir (in Hebrew).

Liebman, Charles S. 1988. "Conceptions of the 'State of Israel' in Israeli Society." *Jerusalem Quarterly* 47 (Summer): 95–107.

Liebman, Charles S., and Eliezer Don-Yehiya. 1983. *Civil Religion in Israel: Traditional Judaism and Political Culture in Israel.* Berkeley: University of California Press.

Lilienblum, Moshe Leib. 1891. "Avanim lebinyan [Stones for the building]." At http://benyehuda.org/malal/mll102.html (in Hebrew).

Locke, John. 1980. *Second Treatise of Government.* Indianapolis: Hackett.

Lorberbaum, Menachem. 2002. *Medieval Jewish Thought.* Stanford, CA: Stanford University Press.

Lowy, Michael. 1992. *Redemption and Utopia: Jewish Libertarian Thought in Central Europe, A Study in Elective Affinity.* Trans. Hope Heaney. London: Athlone.

Lukács, Gyorgy. 1968. *History and Class Consciousness: Studies in Marxist Dialectics.* London: Merlin.

Luz, Ehud. 1985. *Parallels Meet: Religion and Nationalism in the Early Zionist Movement, 1882–1904.* New York: Jewish Publication Society.

Luz, Zvi, and Ziva Shamir, eds. 2001. *Al gilui vekisui balashon* [On the explicit and the allusive in Language: Studies on Bialik's essay]. Ramat Gan: Bar-Ilan University (in Hebrew).

Mack, Michael. 2003. *German Idealism and the Jew*. Chicago: University of Chicago Press.

Malpas, J. E. 1999. *Place and Experience: A Philosophical Topography*. Cambridge: Cambridge University Press.

Mandel-Levy, Naomi. 2009. "Ancient Language in a New Reality." Ph.D. diss., The Hebrew University.

Mapai. 1961. "Maza mapai laknesset hahamishit [Mapai's platform for the fifth Knesset elections]." At http://www.archavoda.org.il/AvodaArch/matza/ pdf/knesset5.pdf (in Hebrew).

Margalit, Avishai. 2009. *On Compromise and Rotten Compormises*. Princeton, NJ: Princeton University Press.

———. 2010. "Home and Homelessness: Isaiah Berlin's Zionism." *Dissent* 57 (Summer): 66–72.

Marx, Karl. 1971. *Karl Marx: Early Texts*. Ed. David McLennan. Oxford: Basil Blackwell.

———. 1975. *Karl Marx: Early Writings*. Trans. Rodney Livingstone and Gregor Benton. London: Penguin.

Mautner, Menachem, Avi Sagi, and Ronen Shamir. 1998. *Multiculturalism in a Democratic and Jewish State*. Tel Aviv: Tel Aviv University Press (in Hebrew).

Mayer, Michael. 1988. *Response to Modernity: A History of the Reform Movement in Judaism*. Oxford: Oxford University Press.

McMahon, Darrin M. 2006. *Happiness: A History*. New York: Atlantic Monthly Press.

Mendelssohn, Moshe. 1983. *Jerusalem, or on Religious Power and Judaism*. Trans. Allan Arkush. Hanover, NH: University Press of New England.

Mendes-Flohr, Paul. 1999. *German Jews: A Dual Identity*. New Haven, CT: Yale University Press.

Meron, Dan. 1986. *Taking Leave of the Impoverished Self: H. N. Bialik's Early Poetry*. Tel Aviv: Open University (in Hebrew).

Mintz, Alan. 1988. *Banished from Their Father's Table: Loss of Faith and Hebrew Autobiography*. Bloomington: Indiana University Press.

Mintz, Matityahu. 1988. *Zmanim hadashim, zmirot hadashot: Ber-Borochov 1914–1917* [New times, new tunes: Ber-Borochov 1914–1917]. Tel Aviv: Am Oved and Tel Aviv University (in Hebrew).

Morris, Benny. 1990. *1948 and After: Israel and the Palestinians*. Oxford: Clarendon.

———. 1996. "Letter from Jerusalem." *Journal of Palestine Studies* 25, no. 2: 77–87.

———. 2000. *Tikun ta'ut* [Correcting a mistake]. Tel Aviv: Am Oved (in Hebrew).

———. 2008. *1948: A History of the First Arab-Israeli War*. New Haven, CT: Yale University Press.

Morrison, Toni. 1987. *Beloved*. New York: Alfred A. Knopf.

Mosse, George. 1975. *The Nationalization of the Masses*. New York: American Library.

———. 1993. *Confronting the Nation: Jewish and Western Nationalism*. Boston: Brandeis University Press.

1997. *German Jews Beyond Judaism*. New York: Hebrew Union College Press.

Myers, David. 2003. *Resisting History: Historicism and Its Discontents in German-Jewish Thought*. Princeton, NJ: Princeton University Press.

Neumann, Boaz. 2009. *Teshukat hahalutzim* [Land and desire in early Zionism]. Tel Aviv: Am Oved (in Hebrew).

Nevo, Ruth. 2005. "Bialik: Caught in a World Whose God Is Dead." At http://israel.poetryinternationalweb.org.

Nietzsche, Friedrich. 1969. *Human, All Too Human*. Lincoln: University of Nebraska Press.

1985. *Untimely Meditations*. Trans. R. J. Hollingdale. Cambridge: Cambridge University Press.

1994. *On the Genealogy of Morals*. Cambridge: Cambridge University Press.

Nitzan-Shiftan, Alona. 2004. "Contested Zionism: Alternative Modernism: Erich Mendelsohn and the Tel-Aviv Chug in Mandate Palestine." In *Constructing a Sense of Place: Architecture and the Zionist Discourse*, ed Haim Yacobi. Hants, England: Ashgate.

Oakeshott, Michael. 1991. *Rationalism in Politics and Other Essays*. Indianapolis: Liberty Fund.

Ohana, David. 1995. "Zarathustra in Jerusalem." In *The Shaping of Israeli Identity: Myth, Memory, and Trauma*, ed. D. Ohana and R. Wistrich. London: Frank Cass (in Hebrew).

2008. *Lo cana'anim lo zalbanim* [Neither Canaanites nor crusaders]. Tel Aviv: Keter (in Hebrew).

O'Malley, Michael. 1990. *Keeping Watch: A History of American Time*. New York: Viking.

Ophir, Adi. 2000. *Lashon hara'a* [The order of evils: Toward an ontology of morals]. Tel Aviv: Am Oved (in Hebrew).

Oz, Amos. 1997. "To Renew the Jewish Settlement in Hebron." *Yediot Aharonot*, "24 Hours," January 16 (in Hebrew).

Pappe, Ilan. 1994. *The Making of the Arab-Israeli Conflict, 1947–1951*. London: I. B. Tauris.

Peri, Yoram, ed. 2000. *The Assassination of Yitzhak Rabin*. Stanford, CA: Stanford University Press.

Pick, Daniel. 1989. *Faces of Degeneration: A European Disorder, c. 1848–c. 1918*. Cambridge: Cambridge University Press.

Polybius. 1923. *The Histories*. Trans. W. R. Paton. New York: G. P. Putnam's.

Posener, Julius. 1937. "One-Family House in Palestine," *Habinyan* 2: 1–7.

Proust, Marcel. 1957. *Time Regained: In Search of Lost Time*. London: Chatto & Windus.

Rabinowitz, Isaac. 1985. "Pre-Modern Jewish Study of Rhetoric: An Introductory Bibliography." *Rhetorica* 3, no. 2: 137–43.

Ram, Uri. 1999. "The State of the Nation: Contemporary Challenges to Zionism in Israel." *Constellations* 6, no. 3: 325–38.

Ravitzky, Aviezer. 1977. *Haketz hameguleh umedinat hayehudim* [Messianism, Zionism, and Jewish religious radicalism]. Tel Aviv: Am Oved (in Hebrew).

Ribot, Théodule. 1891. *Heredity: A Psychological Study of Its Phenomena, Laws, Causes, and Consequences*. New York: Appleton.

Roemer, Nils. 2000. "Between Hope and Despair: Conceptions of Time and the German-Jewish Experience in the Nineteenth Century." *Jewish History* 14: 345–63.

Romein, Jan. 1978. *The Watershed of Two Eras: Europe in 1900*. Middletown, CT: Wesleyan University Press.

Rorty, Richard. 1989. *Contingency, Irony, and Solidarity*. Cambridge: Cambridge University Press.

Rose, Paul L. 1990. *Revolutionary Anti-Semitism in Germany, from Kant to Wagner*. Princeton, NJ: Princeton University Press.

Rosen, Chaim. 1955. *Ivrit shelanu* [Our Hebrew]. Tel Aviv: Am Oved (in Hebrew).

Roshwald, Aviel. 2006. *The Endurance of Nationalism: Ancients Roots and Modern Dilemmas*. Cambridge: Cambridge University Press.

Rotbard, Sharon. 2003. "Wall and Tower [Homa umigdal]." In *A Civilian Occupation*, ed. Rafi Segal and Eyal Weitzman. Tel Aviv: Verso.

Rotenstreich, Nathan. 1968. *Jewish Philosophy in Modern Times: From Mendelssohn to Rosenzweig*. New York: Holt, Rinehart and Winston.

Rozenthal, Robik. 2005. "Hisufim batzariah." *Ma'ariv*, October 3 (in Hebrew).

Sagiv, Assaf. 2008. "The Sabra's Lawless Legacy." *Azure* 33 (Spring). At http://www.azure.org.il/article.php?id=412.

Scholem, Gershom. 1971. *The Messianic Idea in Judaism*. New York: Schocken Books.

1972. "The Name of God and the Linguistic Theory of the Kabbala." *Diogenes* 80 (Winter): 164–94.

1975. *Devarim Bego* [Explications and implications]. Vol. 1. Tel Aviv: Am Oved (in Hebrew).

1987. *Od Davar: Pirkei morasha utechiya* [Explications and Implications] Vol. 2. Tel Aviv: Am Oved (in Hebrew).

Schwied, Eliezer. 1970. *Hayachid: olamo shel A. D. Gordon* [The individual: The world of A. D. Gordon]. Tel Aviv: Am Oved (in Hebrew).

Scott, James. 1998. *Seeing Like A State: How Certain Schemes to Improve the Human Condition Have Failed*. New Haven, CT: Yale University Press.

Scruton, Roger. 1979. *The Aesthetics of Architecture*. London: Methuen.

Shafir, Gershon. 1989. *Land, Labor, and the Origins of the Israeli-Palestinian Conflict, 1882–1914*. Cambridge: Cambridge University Press.

Shafir, Gershon, and Yoav Peled. 2002. *Being Israeli: The Dynamics of Multiple Citizenship*. Cambridge: Cambridge University Press.

Shapira, Anita. 1992. *Land and Power: The Zionist Resort to Force, 1881–1948*. New York: Oxford University Press.

1997. *New Jews, Old Jews*. Tel Aviv: Am Oved (in Hebrew).

2008. *Brenner*. Tel Aviv: Am Oved (in Hebrew).

Shimoni, Gideon. 1995. *The Zionist Ideology*. Hanover, NH: Brandeis University Press.

Simmel, Georg. 1971. *Georg Simmel: On Individuality and Social Forms*. Chicago: University of Chicago Press.

Skinner, Quentin. 1969. *Meaning and Understanding in the History of Ideas.* Middletown, CT: Wesleyan University Press.

Smith, Gary, ed. 1991. *On Walter Benjamin.* Cambridge, MA: MIT Press.

Smith, Steven. 2006. *Reading Leo Strauss.* Chicago: University of Chicago Press.

Sombart, Werner. 1913. *The Jew and Modern Capitalism.* Trans. M. Epstein. London: Fisher Unwin.

Steiner, George. 1969. *Language and Silence.* London: Penguin Books.

Stern, Paul. 1986. "The Problem of History and Temporality in Kantian Ethics." *Review of Metaphysics* 39 (March): 505–45.

Sternhell, Zeev. 1998. *The Founding Myths of Israel: Nationalism, Socialism, and the Making of the Jewish State.* Trans. David Maisel. Princeton, NJ: Princeton University Press.

Strauss, Leo. 1997. *Spinoza's Critique of Religion.* Chicago: University of Chicago Press.

Syrkin, Nachman. 1939. *Kitvei Nachman Syrkin* [The writings of Nachman Syrkin]. Tel Aviv: Davar (in Hebrew).

Tamir, Yael. 1993. *Liberal Nationalism.* Princeton, NJ: Princeton University Press.

Taylor, Charles. 2007. *A Secular Age.* Cambridge, MA: Harvard University Press.

Tchernichovsky, Shaul. 1950. *Shirim* [Poems]. Tel Aviv: Schocken (in Hebrew).

Terdiman, Richard. 1993. *Present Past: Modernity and the Memory Crisis.* Ithaca, NY: Cornell University Press.

Teveth, Shabtai. 1987. *Ben-Gurion: The Burning Ground, 1886–1948.* Boston: Houghton Mifflin.

Tisdall, Caroline, and Angelo Bozzolla. 1972. *Futurism.* London: Thames and Hudson.

Tocqueville, Alexis de. 1969. *Democracy in America.* Trans. G. Lawrence. New York: HarperPerennial.

Vazquez, Rolando. 2006. "Thinking the Event with Hannah Arendt." *European Journal of Social Theory* 9, no. 1: 43–57.

Vital, David. 1975. *The Origins of Zionism.* Oxford: Clarendon.

  2000. *A People Apart: The Jews in Europe, 1789–1939.* Oxford: Oxford University Press.

Volkov, Shlomit. 2002. *Bama'agal hamechushaf: yehudim, anti-shemim, vegermanim acherim* [The magic circle: Germans, Jews and Antisemites]. Tel Aviv: Am Oved (in Hebrew).

Wall, John. 2005. "Phronesis as Poetic: Moral Creativity in Contemporary Aristotelianism." *Review of Metaphysics* 59: 313–31.

Walzer, Michael, ed. 2006. *Law, Politics, and Morality in Judaism.* Princeton, NJ: Princeton University Press.

Walzer, Michael, Menachem Lorberbaum, Noam J. Zohar, and Yair Lorberbaum, eds. 2000. *The Jewish Political Tradition.* Vol. 1: *Authority.* New Haven, CT: Yale University Press.

Waxman, Wayne. 1993. "What Are Kant's Analogies About?" *Review of Metaphysics* 47 (September): 63–113.

Weber, Max. 1978. *Economy and Society*. Ed. G. Roth and C. Wittich. Berkeley: University of California Press.

———. 1994. *Weber: Political Writings*. Ed. P. Lassman and Ronald Speirs. Cambridge: Cambridge University Press.

Weizmann, Chaim. 1936. *Devarim* [Speeches]. Tel Aviv: Mitzpe (in Hebrew).

Whitford, Frank, ed. 1992. *The Bauhaus, Masters and Students by Themselves*. Woodstock, NY: Overlook.

Wistrich, Robert. 1982. *Socialism and the Jews: The Dilemmas of Assimilation in Germany and Austria-Hungary*. Rutherford, NJ: Fairleigh Dickinson University Press.

Wolin, Richard. 1982. *Walter Benjamin: An Aesthetic of Redemption*. New York: Columbia University Press.

Yerushalmi, Yosef Hayim. 2005. *Zakhor: Jewish History and Jewish Memory*. Seattle: University of Washington Press.

Yonah, Yossi. 1999. "Fifty Years Later: The Scope and Limits of Liberal Democracy in Israel." *Constellations* 6, no. 3: 411–28.

Yovel, Yirmiyahu. 1980. *Kant and the Philosophy of History*. Princeton, NJ: Princeton University Press.

———. 1998. *Dark Riddle: Hegel, Nietzsche, and the Jews*. University Park: Pennsylvania State University Press.

Zerubavel, Eviatar. 2003. *Time Maps: Collective Memory and the Social Shape of the Past*. Chicago: University of Chicago Press.

Zerubavel, Yael. 1995. *Recovered Roots: Collective Memory and the Making of Israeli National Tradition*. Chicago: University of Chicago Press.

Zipperstein, Steven. 1993. *Elusive Prophet: Ahad Ha'am and the Origins of Zionism*. Berkeley: University of California Press.

Zuckermann, Ghil'ad. 2007. "Israeli, daber israelit – muflaut hasafa haisraelit [Israeli, speak Israeli! – The marvels of the Israeli language]." *Iton 77*, no. 318: 16–21 (in Hebrew).

Index